CONTEMPORARY Black Biography

ISSN 1058-1316

CONTEMPORARY

$\mathscr{B}$lack

$\mathscr{B}$iography

Profiles from the International Black Community

Volume 22

Shirelle Phelps, Editor

GALE GROUP

Detroit
San Francisco
London
Boston
Woodbridge, CT

STAFF

Shirelle Phelps, *Editor*

Ashyia N. Henderson, David G. Oblender, Rebecca Parks, *Contributing Editors*

Linda S . Hubbard, *Managing Editor, Multicultural Department*

Maria Franklin, *Permissions Manager*
Shalice Shah-Caldwell, *Permissions Associate*

Dorothy Maki, *Manufacturing Manager*
Cindy Range, *Buyer*
Cynthia Baldwin, *Product Design Manager*
Gary Leach, *Graphic Artist*
Randy Bassett, *Image Database Supervisor*
Pamela A. Reed, *Imaging Coordinator*
Robert Duncan, Michael Logusz, *Imaging Specialists*

Victoria B. Cariappa, *Research Manager*
Barbara McNeil, Cheryl L. Warnock, *Research Specialists*
Patricia Tsune Ballard, Wendy K. Festerling, Tamara C. Nott, *Research Associates*
Andrew Spongberg, *Research Assistant*

ISBN 0-7876-2419-5
ISSN 1058-1316

10 9 8 7 6 5 4 3 2 1

Contemporary Black Biography
Advisory Board

Contents

Introduction

Contemporary Black Biography provides informative biographical profiles of the important and influential persons of African heritage who form the international black community: men and women who have changed today's world and are shaping tomorrow's.

Contemporary Black Biography covers persons of various nationalities in a wide variety of fields, including architecture, art, business, dance, education, fashion, film, industry, journalism, law, literature, medicine, music, politics and government, publishing, religion, science and technology, social issues, sports, television, theater, and others.

In addition to in-depth coverage of names found in today's headlines, *Contemporary Black Biography* provides coverage of selected individuals from earlier in this century whose influence continues to impact on contemporary life. *Contemporary Black Biography* also provides coverage of important and influential persons who are not yet household names and are therefore likely to be ignored by other biographical reference series. Each volume also includes listee updates on names previously appearing in CBB.

Designed for Quick Research and Interesting Reading

- **Attractive page design** incorporates textual subheads, making it easy to find the information you're looking for.

- **Easy-to-locate data sections** provide quick access to vital personal statistics, career information, major awards, and mailing addresses, when available.

- **Informative biographical essays** trace the subject's personal and professional life with the kind of in-depth analysis you need.

- **To further enhance your appreciation** of the subject, most entries include photographic portraits.

- **Sources for additional information** direct the user to selected books, magazines, and newspapers where more information on the individuals can be obtained.

Helpful Indexes Make It Easy to Find the Information You Need

Contemporary Black Biography includes cumulative Nationality, Occupation, Subject, and Name indexes that make it easy to locate entries in a variety of useful ways.

Available in Electronic Formats

Diskette/Magnetic Tape. *Contemporary Black Biography* is available for licensing on magnetic tape or diskette in a fielded format. Either the complete database or a custom selection of entries may be ordered. The database is available for internal data processing and nonpublishing purposes only. For more information, call (800) 877-GALE.

Online. *Contemporary Black Biography* is available online through Mead Data Central's NEXIS Service in the NEXIS, PEOPLE and SPORTS Libraries in the GALBIO file.

We Welcome Your Suggestions

The editors welcome your comments and suggestions for enhancing and improving *Contemporary Black Biography*. If you would like to suggest persons for inclusion in the series, please submit these names to the editors. Mail comments or suggestions to:

The Editor
Contemporary Black Biography
The Gale Group
27500 Drake Rd.
Farmington Hills, MI 48331-3535
Phone: (800) 347-4253

Photo Credits

PHOTOGRAPHS AND ILLUSTRATIONS APPEARING IN *CONTEMPORARY BLACK BIOGRAPHY*, VOLUME 22, WERE RECEIVED FROM THE FOLLOWING SOURCES:

All Reproduced by Permission: **Alexander, Margaret Walker,** photograph. AP/Wide World Photos. **Alexander, Sadie T. M.,** photograph. Corbis. **Allen, Tina,** photograph by Philip Ghee. **Anderson, Jamal,** photograph by Ric Feld. AP/Wide World Photos. **Andrews, Benny,** photograph by Nene Humphrey. **Ashford, Emmett L.,** photograph. AP/Wide World Photos. **Badu, Erykah,** photograph by David McNew. Reuters/Archive Photos. **Baker, Thurbert,** photograph by Ric Feld. AP/Wide World Photos. **Bell, Robert Mack,** photograph. Courtesy of Robert Mack Bell. **Benson, George,** photograph by Jack Vartoogian. Bolin, Jane M., photograph. Fisk University Library. **Brown, James,** photograph by Aaron Rapport. Fox Sports. **Bullock, Steve,** photograph. Courtesy of Steve Bullock. **Clark-Sheard, Karen,** photograph. Island Black Music. **Cook, Suzan D. Johnson,** photograph. Courtesy of Suzan D. Johnson. **Dutton, Charles,** photograph by Bob Galbraith. AP/Wide World Photos. **Edwards, Melvin,** photograph. Courtesy of Melvin Edwards. **Ellerbe, Brian,** photograph by Carlos Osorio. AP/Wide World Photos. **Evans, Faith,** photograph by Pacha. Corbis. **Fishburne, Laurence,** photograph by Peter Iovino/Saga. Archive Photos. **Gibson, Josh,** photograph. AP/Wide World Photos. **Hedgeman, Anna Arnold,** photograph. AP/Wide World Photos. **Hunter, Billy,** photograph by Stephen Chernin. AP/Wide World Photos. **Iverson, Jonathan Lee,** photograph. Courtesy of Jonathan Lee Iverson. **Jackson, Alexine Clement,** photograph. Courtesy of Alexine Clement Jackson. **Johnson, Hazel,** photograph. AP/Wide World Photos. **Jones, Roy, Jr.,** photograph. AP/Wide World Photos. **Kendricks, Eddie,** photograph. Corbis/Bettman. **King, Barbara,** photograph by Jane Holmes. **King, Regina,** photograph by Joel Levinson. Archive Photos. **Lee, Annie Frances,** photograph by Bill Miller Photography. Courtesy of Bill Scott. **Lee-Smith, Hughie,** photograph by Patricia Lee-Smith. **Levert, Gerald,** photograph by Lisa Peardon. Archive Photos Inc. **Lymon, Frankie,** photograph by Frank Driggs. Archive Photos, Inc. **McGruder, Robert,** phogograph. Courtesy of Robert McGruder. **McNair, Steve,** photograph. AP/Wide World Photos. **Mills, Florence,** photograph. UPI/Corbis-Bettmann. **Obasanjo, Olusegun,** drawing by Bill Bourne/Bourne Graphics. The Gale Group. **Pendergrass, Teddy,** photograph by Preston Neal. Corbis Images. **Peoples, Dottie,** photograph. Air Gospel. **Robinson, Sharon,** photograph by Alan Mothner. AP/Wide World Photos. **Robinson, Spottswood W. III,** photograph. AP/Wide World Photos. **Rock, Chris,** photograph by Kevork Djansezian. AP/Wide World Photos. **Strawberry, Darryl,** photograph by Ron Frehm. AP/Wide World Photos. **Swygert, H. Patrick,** photograph. Courtesy of H. Patrick Swygert. **Warner, Malcolm-Jamal,** photograph by Chris Pizzello. AP/Wide World Photos. **Washington, Dinah,** photograph. UPI/Corbis-Bettmann. **White, Jesse,** photograph by Seth Perlman. AP/Wide World Photos. **Williams, Doug,** photograph by Bill Haber. AP/Wide World Photos. **Wilson, William Julius,** photograph.

Margaret Walker Alexander

1915–1998

Writer

Though a younger generation of African American writers had long eclipsed the pioneering accomplishments of Margaret Walker Alexander by the time of her death at age 83 in 1998, the poet, novelist and academic had enjoyed friendships that spanned nearly a century of black literary achievement—from Langston Hughes to Alice Walker—and was well known and vividly remembered to many in the African American literary community. In 1942, Alexander became the first African American to win a leading literary competition, and one of just a handful of female African-American female poets ever. The sentiments expressed in her acclaimed 1942 volume, *For My People,* would later become inspirational, often-cited verse during the civil-rights era. Alexander was also the author other of what has been termed the first African-American historical novel, the 1966 work *Jubilee.* In an obituary penned for Alexander that was published in *The Nation,* Amiri Baraka called her "the living continuum of the great revolutionary democratic arts culture that has sustained and inspired the Afro-American people since the Middle Passage."

Alexander was born Margaret Abigail Walker in 1915 in Birmingham, Alabama, the daughter of a Jamaican-born Methodist minister with a deep love of classic literature and philosophy. A graduate of Northwestern University, Sigismund Walker had married music teacher Marion Dozier Walker; when their only child was still young, they relocated to New Orleans. Also present in the Walker household was grandmother Elvira "Vyry" Ware Dozier, who helped care for the little girl and told her fantastic bedtime stories about "slavery time."

Vestiges of Slave Era

The South in which Alexander grew up was still peopled by older African-Americans who had been born into slavery. Her great-grandmother—Vyry's mother—died just a month before Alexander's birth, but passed on the tales of a harsh life on the plantation to Vyry, who entertained her granddaughter with them. Though obvious changes had occurred in the intervening decades, discrimination and violence were still commonplace in 1920s New Orleans. One year, Alexander would recall, her father's job forced him to travel, and the women lived in tremendous fear when they were alone in the house. On another occasion, a drunken off-duty New Orleans police officer chased

Sigismund Walker home at gunpoint, enraged that an African American man had the audacity to carry a fountain pen in his pocket.

Growing up in a learned household, Alexander soon displayed both creativity and intelligence. She attended a private school, and earned her high school diploma by the age of fourteen. Both parents were instructors at New Orleans University (now Dillard University), and Alexander enrolled there as a teen. After two years, she decided to transfer to Northwestern University in the Chicago area in an attempt to escape the racism of the South. She was dismayed to find that prejudice and mistreatment plagued blacks who lived in sophisticated urban cities, too; she was even refused service once at a restaurant in Evanston, the quaint town that is home to the university.

Alexander and Richard Wright

In 1932, Alexander met the poet Langston Hughes. Raised in a home that boasted an impressive library of titles by African American writers, she was already a great fan of Hughes and his work, and well acquainted with the literary achievements of the Harlem Renaissance that he and others had launched the previous decade. Hughes encouraged the aspiring writer, and her first poem appeared in *Crisis*, W.E.B. DuBois's journal, in 1934. During her senior year, she began handing in assignments based on her grandmother's tales of life before and after slavery, but decided she needed more time to pursue it as a work of fiction. After graduation from Northwestern, Alexander was hired by the Works Progress Administration, the New Deal federal agency aimed at relieving the unemployment of the Great Depression and through building and improvement projects. Assigned to work with delinquent females, Alexander became deeply interested in one of Chicago's ethnic neighborhoods that was an unusual merging of Italian American and African American families, and began an uncompleted novel about it she tentatively entitled "Goose Island."

Later on staff at the WPA Federal Writer's Project, Alexander came to know Nelson Algren, Katherine Dunham, and Richard Wright, as well as several other unknown or up-and-coming personalities in the city. She and Wright shared many ideas and opinions, and developed a keen interest in each other's literary endeavors. Over the next three years they contributed to and encouraged each other's work: Wright helped Alexander fine-tune her verse, and wakened her interest in leftist political theory; in turn, she mailed him Chicago newspaper clippings about a young black man accused of rape. This story would form the basis for Wright's 1940 novel *Native Son.*

Alexander began to realize that her "Goose Island" manuscript was very similar to *Native Son*, and put it aside. The fruitful friendship between the pair ended on a visit by Alexander to New York City; Wright believed that she had gossiped about him to mutual friends, and cut her from his circle. Back in Chicago, Alexander suffered another setback when her WPA job was terminated by an act of Congress, so she decided to enroll in graduate school for an M.A. in English. After winning entry into the eminent University of Iowa Writers' Workshop, she earned her degree from the school in 1940. Again, she considered creating a thesis project centered on the oral history of her mother's family, but once again shelved the idea.

Heralded as Voice of Her Generation

A volume of poetry, *For My People,* was her Iowa thesis instead. The work was published by Yale University Press in 1942 after winning the university's Younger Poet's Award, a coveted literary prize. It made her the first African American to win a major literary competition, but even more remarkably, the publication of Alexander's volume marked the first book of poetry published by an African American woman since 1918. *For My People* was widely reviewed—somewhat of an accomplishment in itself at the time—though in some cases with subtly racist sentiment behind the praise. "Poetess Walker ... avoids the callow literary posturing that is the curse of most Negro versifiers," opined *Time* magazine. "The moral guileless-ness which may well rate as the most valuable gift of the Negro to American civilization is exemplified in almost every stanza in this slim twenty-four-poem book."

Through characters in *For My People* such as New Orleans sorceress Molly Means, and Poppa Chicken, an urban drug dealer and pimp, Alexander gave voice to a range of African American experiences during her era. But her title poem would endure: "For my people," she wrote, "For the cramped bewildered years we went to school to learn to know/the reasons why and the answers to and the people who and the/places where and the days when, in memory of the bitter hours/when we discovered we were black and poor and small and/different and nobody cared and nobody wondered and nobody/understood." Its final lines would serve as inspirational verse during the civil-rights struggles of the 1950s and `60s in the South. "Let a new earth rise," Alexander concluded in her 1940 poem. "Let another world be born. Let a bloody peace be written in the sky. Let a second generation full of courage issue forth; let a people loving freedom come to growth."

Began Both Family and Novel

After graduating from Iowa, Alexander realized, as her father once pointed out, "I would have to eat if I wanted to live, and writing poetry would not feed me," she recalled in *How I Wrote "Jubilee."* So following in the footsteps of two previous generations, she became a teacher at a small North Carolina college in 1941; the following year she taught at West Virginia State College. She wed Firnist James Alexander, a disabled war veteran, in June of 1943.

They began a family the following year that would number four children. In 1949 she became a professor of English at Jackson State College in Mississippi (now Jackson State University).

With the success of *For My People* behind her, Alexander began working in earnest on a historical novel based on her grandmother Vyry's tales of nineteenth-century black life. She fit in research on what would become *Jubilee* between her obligations as a working mother; for years she pored over historical documents across the South, read an immense amount of literature on the Civil War period, and cultivated helpful professional contacts with scholars and librarians in several states. She visited the towns where her great-grandparents had lived, and even tracked down her grandmother's sole remaining sibling. From 1955 to 1962, however, both she and her husband suffered from medical and financial setbacks, and the demands of a growing family forced Alexander to shelve her novel for seven years.

In 1962 Alexander, though mother of four children, took leave from her job and went back to the University of Iowa to earn a Ph.D. in English. Her manuscript became her dissertation, and she typed the last sentence of *Jubilee* in April of 1965, nearly three decades after beginning it as a Northwestern University student. Published in 1966, *Jubilee* recreates the life of Alexander's great-grandmother, here named Vyry, from her birth as a slave on a Georgia plantation. Divided into three sections—the antebellum years, the Civil War era, and the Reconstruction period—Vyry's tale stands in literary form as representative of untold thousands, based on Alexander's exhaustive amount of research into African American social and economic realities of the Old South. As a literary character, however, Vyry emerges as a woman who suffered immense hard-ship, yet rose above her circumstances to set an example for future generations, a woman guided by Christian principles and a deep sense of self-worth.

Her Great-Grandmother's Story

In *Jubilee,* Vyry is the last of over a dozen children born to a slave named Sis Hetta before she was thirty. Some were fathered by Hetta's slave husband, but others by the plantation owner, and Vyry is one of these biracial offspring. This last childbirth kills Hetta, and Vyry is raised by two adoptive mothers. One dies, and the second is sold away on the order of the plantation owner's wife, Salina. Vyry serves as a cook in family's mansion, and is terribly abused by this woman, who resents the fact that this slave child bears such a resemblance to her own daughter, Lillian.

As a young woman, Vyry falls in love with Randall Ware, who was born free, owns his own smithy, and can read and write. He urges her to run away with him and leave her young children behind, but she cannot, and when she attempts to flee with them, is captured and lashed. During the Civil War, all members of the plantation family perish except Lillian, who is traumatized by the war and its violence. Vyry—Lillian's only remaining "family"—remains with her, even after she is freed by the Emancipation Proclamation.

As *Jubilee* progresses, Vyry marries a former slave, Innis Brown, a kind man deeply committed to providing a stable, prosperous home for his family. The Reconstruction legislation provides men like Innis with a brief window of political and economic opportunity, but this progress is soon ended by a resurgence of white power in the South. Vyry and Innis move several times with their children, fleeing Ku Klux Klan posses, and she eventually becomes a respected local midwife and folk healer. Randall Ware returns, now a committed black activist, and though his boldness unsettles her, Vyry realizes there is justification for his beliefs, and allows him to take her son away for an education.

A Figure of Literary Eminence

Jubilee became a bestseller, and was translated into several European languages. Alexander continued to teach at Jackson State, and set up the school's black studies program in 1968. She published her second book of poetry, *Prophets for a New Day,* in 1970. Less political than *For My People,* its poems reveal a more spiritual direction. In one work, the civil-rights heroes of the 1960s are renamed as the prophets of the Bible: Martin Luther King is Amos, Medgar Evars is Micah, and the events in civil-rights era occur in religious metaphor. "At the Lincoln Monument in Washington August 28, 1963" compares the thousands of marchers with the enslaved Jews waiting for Moses to take them out of Egypt.

One day Alexander and another African American writer, Nikki Giovanni, read their poems at a conference, and the response was so enthusiastic that an editor invited them do a volume together. *A Poetic Equation: Conversations between Nikki Giovanni and Margaret Walker* was published in 1974 by Howard University Press, and reprinted nine years later with a new postscript. In 1977 Alexander filed a plagiarism suit against author Alex Haley for his bestseller *Roots,* claiming he had lifted several parts from directly from *Jubilee.* Haley said he had never read it, and the suit was later dismissed. Two years later she retired from Jackson State, but continued to tour as a popular lecturer.

Alexander wrote a literary biography, *Richard Wright: Daemonic Genius,* published in 1987. The 1972 pamphlet that chronicled the thirty-year process of writing her only novel was later reprinted in a 1990 volume of the same name, *How I Wrote "Jubilee,"* along with several other examples of her work. The Institute for the Study of the History, Life, and Culture of Black Peoples at Jackson State was later renamed in her honor, as was the street in the city on which she lived. Her last published work was the 1997 volume *On Being Female, Black, and Free: Essays by Margaret Walker, 1932-1992.* She died of cancer at the home of her daughter, Marion Colmon, in Chicago in November of 1998. A documentary film, *For My People: The Life and Writing of Margaret Walker,* appeared the following year, and contains interviews with Alexander and those who knew her.

Selected writings

Poetry

For My People, Yale University Press, 1942, with foreword by Stephen Vincent Benet, reprinted, Ayer Co., 1969.
The Ballad of the Free, Broadside Press, 1966.
Prophets for a New Day, Broadside Press, 1970.
October Journey, Broadside Press, 1973.
This Is My Century: New and Collected Poems, University of Georgia Press, 1989.

Prose

Jubilee (novel), Houghton, 1965, Bantam, 1981.
(Pamphlet) *How I Wrote "Jubilee,"* Third World Press, 1972, revised edition edited by Maryemma Graham, *How I Wrote Jubilee and Other Essays on Life and Literature,* Feminist Press, 1990.
(With Nikki Giovanni) *A Poetic Equation: Conversations between Nikki Giovanni and Margaret Walker,* Howard University Press, 1974, reprinted with new postscript, 1983.
For Farish Street, Green 1986.
Richard Wright: Daemonic Genius, Dodd, 1987.
(With Thea Bowman) *God Touched My Life: The Inspiring Autobiography of the Nun Who Brought Song, Celebration, and Soul to the World,* Harper & Row, 1992.
On Being Female, Black, and Free: Essays by Margaret Walker, 1932-1992, University of Tennessee Press, 1997.

Sources

Books

Dictionary of Literary Biography, Gale, Volume 76: *Afro-*

American Writers, 1940-1955, edited by Trudier Harris, 1988, Volume 152: *American Novelists Since World War II, Fourth Series,* edited James Giles and Wanda Giles, 1995.

Periodicals

Jet, December 14, 1998, p. 17.
Nation, January 4, 1999, pp. 32-33.
New York Times, December 4, 1998, p. 29.
Washington Post, April 28, 1977, p. A12; August 24, 1978, p. B6; January 10, 1999, p. X2.

—Carol Brennan

Sadie T.M. Alexander

1989–1989

Lawyer, civil rights advocate

Sadie Tanner Mossell Alexander was a tireless advocate for civil rights whose personal achievements only fueled her desire to evoke change for black people in the United States. A firm supporter of democracy, Alexander reasoned that the United States could only be a strong country if there were opportunities available for everyone. Coming from an upstanding Philadelphia family, Alexander was afforded many opportunities and she made good on them all. That she was the first black woman to receive a Ph.D in economics, the first black woman to graduate from the University of Pennsylvania Law School, and the first black woman to practice law in Pennsylvania are just some of the more significant of her many accomplishments.

Born January 2, 1898 in Philadelphia, Sadie Tanner Mossell was one of three children to Mary Tanner Mossell and Aaron Mossell, a lawyer and the first black graduate of the University of Pennsylvania Law School. Other notable relatives included her grandfather Benjamin Tucker Tanner, the founder of the African Methodist Episcopal (AME) Church Review, as well as uncles such as the painter Henry O. Tanner and Lewis Baxter Moore, a dean at Howard University. An aunt, Hallie Tanner Johnson, was a physician who founded the nurse's school and hospital at the Tuskegee Institute.

First Black Female Ph.D in Economics

At an early age Alexander's parents separated and she went to live with her mother in Washington, DC. Educated in the city's public schools, Alexander expected to stay in Washington to attend Howard University when she was informed by her mother that they would be returning to Philadelphia. Unbeknownst to her, Alexander's mother had enrolled her in the University of Pennsylvania.

High marks at Penn came easy and Alexander graduated with a degree in education in 1918. In addition to classes, Alexander founded the Penn chapter of the black sorority Delta Sigma Theta, which was based at Howard University, and became the group's first national president. She also earned her master's degree in economics in 1919 followed by her Ph.D in economics in 1921. She was the first black woman to get a doctorate in economics and would have been the first black woman to receive a Ph.D period, had it not been for Georgiana Simpson, who received her Ph.D from the University of Chicago a day earlier.

For her doctoral dissertation Alexander presented, "The Standard of Living Among One Hundred Negro Migrant Families in Philadelphia." It was, she wrote, "and attempt to arrive at conclusions concerning the migrants in Philadelphia, through an intensive analysis of the budgets of a small number of their group." The presentation of her Ph.D, regardless of Ms. Simpson's triumph 24-hours earlier, was a momentous occasion for Alexander. "I was embarrassed and thrilled at the same time," she's quoted as saying in her *Los Angeles Times* obituary. "Coming up the stairs to the platform, I heard a voice say, `Here she comes.' It was the president of Bryn Mawr. At that time Bryn Mawr didn't admit black students."

Followed Her Father

Although being the first black woman Ph.D in economics carried a great deal of weight in some quarters, it did little in helping its recipient find a job in early 1920s Philadelphia. Instead, Alexander went south to work as an assistant actuary at the black-owned North Carolina Mutual Life Insurance Company. She stayed there until 1923 when she returned to Philadelphia to marry Raymond Pace Alexander, a Harvard Law School graduate. With her new husband's encouragement Alexander enrolled in the University of Pennsylvania's Law School, becoming their first black woman graduate, echoing her father's achievement a generation earlier.

The couple went into practice together--she being the first black woman lawyer in Pennsylvania--and initiated legal battles designed to desegregate hotels, restaurants, movie theaters and other businesses in Philadelphia. Additionally, she served as assistant city solicitor for the city from 1928-1934. Both Alexanders helped found the National Bar Association, an organization for black lawyers and in 1948, Mrs. Alexander was appointed by President Harry Truman to his Committee on Civil Rights.

In a New York forum to discuss the committee's findings, Alexander identified the gap in America that existed due to the fear and hate between races and called for action. "We must act now," she's quoted as saying in the New York Times, "because the gap between what we believe as American ideals and what we practice is creating a moral dry rot within us. We are threatening the emotional and rational bases of our democracy. We must act because the mental health of America is threatened by this gap."

In addition to her law practice and various appointments, Alexander was active in many organizations designed to further the cause of racial equality and unify all Americans. She was secretary of the National Urban League for 25 years, a member of the National Advisory Council of the American Civil Liberties Union, and was also involved with Americans for Democratic Action. In the early 1960s she was appointed by President John Kennedy to the Lawyer's Committee on Civil Rights.

Slowed Down

The Alexanders also raised two daughters, both born in the mid-1930s. A strong advocate of women in the work place, Alexander was pioneering in her belief that a woman could have a challenging and rewarding career while raising children and maintaining a healthy family life. As she told Paula Giddings, author of *In Search of*

Sisterhood, "The satisfaction which comes to the woman in realizing that she is a producer makes for peace and happiness, the chief requisites in any home."

Upon the death of her husband in 1974 Alexander slowed her work schedule down considerably. While she continued her work with various organizations occasional law case, it was at a much less rigorous pace. She retired for good at the end of 1979 and was named by President Jimmy Carter as the chairperson of the White House Conference on Aging which took place in January of 1981. Two years later Alexander was diagnosed with Alzheimer's disease and moved to Cathedral Village, a Philadelphia retirement community. There she live quietly until 1989 when she died of pneumonia at the age of 91.

Her death marked the extinguishing of a flame that saw civil rights as a piece of a larger puzzle. According to Alexander, civil rights did necessarily mean just the advancement of black people; it meant the advancement of the country. As she told students at Spelman College in 1963, "In our struggle to secure equality of opportunity, personal security, respect for individual dignity, and rights of full citizenship we are making a heroic struggle not only for ourselves but, of greater importance, a struggle for the survival of the United States."

Sources

Books

Giddings, Paula, *In Search of Sisterhood: Delta Sigma Theta and the Challenge of the Black Sorority Movement,* Temple University Press, 1989.
Walker, Robbie Jean, *The Rhetoric of Struggle: Public Address by African American Women,* Garland, 1992.

Periodicals

American Economic Review, May 1991, p. 307.
Los Angeles Times, November 7, 1989, p. A-26.
New York Times, October 8, 1948, p. A-7; December 11, 1979, p. B-22; November 3, 1989, p. D-18.

—Brian Escamilla

Tina Allen

1955—

Sculptor

Sculptor and conceptual designer Tina Allen has created monumental memorial statues of distinguished Africans and African Americans. She has won commissions to sculpt the likenesses of Malcolm X and Nelson Mandela, among others. Allen also works in more abstract artistic venues that bring together ideas and objects from other countries in an attempt to create a less vicious, more loving world. "Essentially, I'm a conduit to express the unseen and to bring back and reposition the emphasis on the good and the great," Allen said in an interview with *Contemporary Black Biography*.

Born in New York in 1955, Allen was the daughter of Gordon "Specs" Powell, a studio percussionist for CBS Records. Her father was the first African American musician to play in the bands that provided live music for the popular Ed Sullivan and the Jackie Gleason television programs. Allen grew up in a household where well-known musicians often visited and creative expression was greatly encouraged.

Allen's parents divorced when she was a child, and she then moved with her mother to Grenada. She spent the next four years there, and was deeply influenced by the radically pleasant society she found on the island. Grenadine native arts—calypso music, the figurative arts, and its indigenous religion—all left a tremendous impression on Allen.

Discovered Talent for Sculpting

Allen had been painting since the age of five, but her budding artistic talent took a new direction when she met Lithuanian-born sculptor William Zorach on a Grenada beach one day when she was ten years old. She came upon the New York City artist while he was vacationing on the island. Allen showed him her work and he had an opportunity to meet her family. A few years later, after Allen and her family returned to New York City, Zorach became her mentor and allowed her to visit his Brooklyn studio. At the time, she was also enrolled in a museum-sponsored art program for artistically gifted youths.

Allen created her first three-dimensional work when she was given an assignment in a high school art class to make an ashtray from clay. She was reading Aristotle for another class and, when she arrived home, decided to make a bust of the Greek philosopher instead. Allen

At a Glance . . .

Born December 9, 1955, in Hempstead, NY; daughter of Gordon "Specs" (a percussionist) and Rosecleer Powell; married Roger Allen; children: Koryan, Josephine, Tara. *Education:* University of South Alabama, B.F.A., 1978; also studied at the New York School of Visual Arts, the Pratt Institute, and the University of Venice.

Career: Artist. Taught art in Alabama, early 1980s, and hosted a local television show in Mobile.

Member: Art 200; board member, International Center for African-American-Asian Relations; board member, Los Angeles Support Committee for the African National Congress.

Awards: Fannie Lou Hamer Award; Urban League Award, 1988.

Addresses: *Gallery*— M. Hanks Gallery, P.O. Box 5386, Santa Monica, CA 90406.

recalled in the interview with *CBB* that when she presented the bust to her class, the teacher's first reaction was, "Where did you get this?" She soon began winning competitions and awards, and as Allen told *CBB*, though she had originally intended to paint, "sculpture was more natural for me than painting. I loved to paint, but I had more of a feeling for three dimensions, and I could move very quickly... even after all these years of study, I'm only about ten or fifteen percent better that the first time I started. Because when I started to sculpt, I could do hands, I could do feet, I could do eyes, I could just do it."

Years of Struggle

Allen studied art at the University of South Alabama, and lived in Mobile for a time. She was a VISTA volunteer and, for nearly a decade, hosted a local television show on the arts. She eventually moved to New York City, where she attended the Pratt Institute and the New York School of Visual Arts. Allen struggled to win small commissions that would keep her afloat financially and eventually realized that she needed to set her sights higher. In 1986, she entered a competition in Boston for a commission to create a memorial statue of African American labor activist A. Philip Randolph, who founded a union for train

porters in 1925. To her surprise and delight, Allen won the $85,000 commission and her career began in earnest.

After completing the statue of Randolph, Allen created statues of other African American leaders. In a profile of Allen on the University of Texas at Austin web site, she describes her body of work as "writing our history in bronze" and her creations as "totems that tell the children this, `this kind of behavior, this kind of person is worthy of attention." Her work also attracted the attention of South African leader Nelson Mandela, whom she met when he visited Los Angeles in the summer of 1990. At the meeting, Allen presented Mandela with one of her works, *Icon I: Tribute to the African-American Man.*

Work Commemorated Humanitarian Achievements

Eventually, the South African government selected Allen to erect a statue on the island where Mandela was once imprisoned. The work, which is modeled on the Statue of Liberty, is five stories in height. Allen has also created a 13-foot statue of the late author Alex Haley for a public square in Knoxville, Tennessee. The statue depicts Haley looking in the direction of his beloved Great Smoky Mountains and holding a copy of his groundbreaking novel, *Roots.* In addition to her statue of Haley, Allen has created likenesses of Sojourner Truth, Marcus Garvey, and Malcolm X.

Allen's art extends beyond standard figurative sculpture. She has also created a four-story pictorial relief wall for the King/Drew Medical Magnet High School in Los Angeles. The pictorial wall features events from the lives of Dr. Martin Luther King. Jr. and blood preservation pioneer Dr. Charles Drew. She makes much smaller abstract sculptures as well, and collectors of her art include Hilary Rodham Clinton, Muhammad Ali, Denzel Washington, and Robert DeNiro.

Merged Aesthetics with Practicality

Allen also executes conceptual projects as well. For a Children's Peace Park in South Africa, she is "commissioning" small works in bronze from children around the world to be placed at the memorial site. "Even though I'm sculptor, I also don't always feel that I need to express mypersonal ego as much as I need to use art as a way to heal and communicate," Allen told *CBB.* The sculptures from Japanese, Mexican, and American children commemorate the many children who died during South Africa's violent struggle for racial equality. During her travels throughout various parts of Africa, Allen was moved by the differing standards of physical beauty within African culture. She has infused her work, which is often praised for its emphasis on the more "African" facial features of her subjects, with an added dimension. "For an African," Allen told *CBB*, "the emotional nature of a person is part of their beauty, not just the bones and the skeleton... I'm trying to lift up the idea that human strength and courage are beautiful, and we have to redefine what beauty is about."

Allen travels extensively, both for her work and personal enrichment, and spends her free time reading books on religion and mythology. She is still inspired by the ideas of the Greek philosophers. "We need to go back to Plato and Socrates...for their pharmacies, to dig up some medicine to help us in a universe where the center of it is love and service," Allen told *CBB*. She also serves on the board of directors of the International Center for African American Asian Relations, which aims to improve cross-cultural ties. Allen sees her work as part of a global mission to create the kind of warm, harmonious community that she experienced as a child in Grenada. "If a human being is no longer tender and loving, they can't raise their children so that they want to live, the game is over. The minute you no longer are able to raise a generation willing to carry the future on their backs, the game is over," Allen told *CBB*.

Sources

Periodicals

Essence, January, 1995.

Other

Additional information for this profile was obtained from an interview with Tina Allen on May 19, 1999 and from a profile of Allen on the University of Texas at Austin web site in conjunction with its proposed memorial sculpture of Dr. Martin Luther King Jr. at http://www.utexas.edu/general/mlksculpture/Maintext.html.

—Carol Brennan

Jamal Anderson

1972—

Professional football player

As the steamroller running back for the Atlanta Falcons, Jamal Anderson is fast becoming a National Football League superstar. Finally hitting his full professional stride in the 1998 season, Anderson was a pivotal force in that historically hapless team's most successful year ever. His 1,846 rushing yards was the seventh-best all-time tally, and he scored an NFL record with 410 carries. If he maintains such a level of achievement and stays healthy, Anderson easily could become one of the greatest runners in NFL history.

Anderson is nearly as well known for his personality as for his rushing power. Having grown up surrounded by many of the world's most high-powered African American celebrities—including Muhammad Ali, Richard Pryor, Mike Tyson, and Michael Jackson—he takes to the limelight like a natural entertainer. Supremely confident, talkative, friendly, cocky, and witty, Anderson is a journalist's dream come true. Fortunately, he delivers his bluster with a pinch of self-parody, enough so he always remains likeable. As one of his teammates has said, the braggadocio is just Anderson's "shtick."'

Anderson has gained notoriety for creating and populariz-ing (with some high-profile help from tight end O.J. Santiago) the Falcons' 'Dirty Bird' celebration dance. Like many other NFL franchises, the Falcons now have a unique inspirational end zone move—which resembles a 1960's Funky Chicken wearing shoulder pads and some 1990's attitude.

But the star back has different facets. For example, Anderson was touched by the story of Daniel Huffington—the high school football player who donated a kidney to save his grandmother's life, and thereby terminated his football prospects. So Anderson flew Daniel into Atlanta and showed the young man around for an entire weekend to experience an NFL game from the inside. He also readily agreed to appear at Daniel's high school gradua-tion, delighting the students with his down-to-earth yet serious speech there. 'Dirty Bird' or not, this player clearly has heart—as a relentless athlete and as a human being.

While Anderson does not possess breakaway speed, his low center of gravity and tremendous power—he can squat 670 pounds, and bench 465—makes him exceed-ingly tough, and damaging, to tackle. He has a brutally effective stiff-arm technique that can sledgehammer a defender or two in an instant. Moreover, he has surpris-

At a Glance . . .

Born Jamal Anderson September 30, 1972, in Orange, New Jersey. Son of James and Zenobia Anderson, who had eight children. James, a former Newark police officer, became premier security consultant for the African American and Muslim communities, specializing in sports and entertainment figures. *Education:* Attended Moorpark (CA) Coll.,two years, then the Univ. of Utah (Salt Lake City) for his final two years of college.

Career: Captain of the football team at El Camino Real High School. As senior, was All-State, All-League, All-Region, All-Valley, *LA Times* All-Star choice, and Most Valuable Player. At Utah, was an All-WAC conference pick in 1993, averaging 5.7 yards per carry and gaining 242 yards on 35 pass receptions. Drafted in 1994 by the Atlanta Falcons in the seventh round. Became a starter in the 1996 season, and immediately proved to be one of the NFL's dominant backs, running for over 1,000 yards that season and again in 1997—only the third Falcon running back to pass 1,000 in successive years. In 1998, rushed for 1,846 yards, caught for another 319, and was All-Pro for first time. Rushing yardage was second only to Denver's Terrell Davis, who broke 2,000. Established a new NFL record with his 410 carries. Seen by most as the central force in garnering the Falcons' first division title in 18 years.

Awards: Picked as NFC Offensive Player of the Week in 1996. Named offensive MVP by coaches three times in 1997 season.

Addresses: Atlanta Falcons, One Falcon Place, Suwanee, GA 30024.

has with the quickness, well, there's not many people that size who can make people miss. And when he does get tackled, he's hard to bring down.'' As Reeves put it in the *Atlanta Journal and Constitution,* ``he doesn't give you much of a target to hit. All you see is helmet, shoulder pads, and knees, and those things are no fun to hit.''

Obviously Anderson is a physical player—one who enjoys getting down and dirty and ending the game with some blood on his uniform. But when he wants to cut and evade, he can do that too. Anderson described his style in *The Sporting News:* "I pride myself on being able to run you over, [or] run around you and make you miss. Every time you face me, you don't know what you're going to get. You may get a shoulder in the mouth, you may get a stiff-arm, you may get shook.'' In a *CNN Sports Illustrated* piece, Anderson gleefully related the impact his stiff-arm has on opponents: "It's very embarrassing for a defender. Imagine just walking into a jab. BAM! And then they're thinking about it the rest of the game, every time they come over to you. It's great.''

St. Louis Rams linebacker Roman Phifer told a *Sports Illustrated* reporter, "He's got great feet. If he has room, he'll make a move, but when it's tight he puts his head down. With his power, he also goes forward.'' In the same article, New Orleans Saints linebacker Mark Fields said, "He's a tough, smart runner. You think you've got him tackled, and he'll stick a hand down, catch himself and crawl and scratch for a few more yards.'' As quoted on the Falcons' Website, Dallas defender George Teague said getting hit by Anderson "was like being run over by an entire convoy of trucks.''

As if this is not enough, Anderson also seems to gain strength in the second half. Just as the defense starts to flag from exhaustion, Anderson picks up steam. His hard-hitting style keeps the ball in Atlanta's hands, eating up the clock, as he helps propel the team toward the end zone. As Anderson said in the *Atlanta Journal and Constitution,* "In the first half of any game, I don't even try to avoid people. You keep beating on folks like that for 30 minutes, and sooner or later they start that sashay-tackling, you know?'' In another article in that paper, Detroit Lions defensive tackle Luther Elliss has this to say about Anderson after the Falcon runner blasted 147 yards of rushing one game: "There were numerous times when we were in a position to make a tackle in the backfield, and we weren't able to wrap him up. [Anderson's] a good enough back that he's going to break a lot of those tackles. Plus, it's late in the game, you're tired and he's a load.'' In one game, Anderson carried the ball 11 times in the last six and

ingly quick moves for a 5'11", 234-pound juggernaut. And Anderson is a superb receiver. He is the type of runner who strikes fear in the souls of defenses.

As Atlanta head coach Dan Reeves—another major factor in the team's miraculous turnaround from '96 to '98—told The *Sporting News,* ``He's an extremely powerful runner and he's got great hands. He's also got unbelievable confidence in himself.'' Quoted in *CNN Sports Illustrated,* Reeves also said, ``To combine the power he a half minutes of the game to run out the clock on a 76-yard drive.

A Family Accustomed to Greatness

Jamal's father, James Anderson, met Muhammad Ali in 1973 at a national Muslim convention in Chicago, where he had been assigned to provide security for the boxing great. Once Ali and Anderson—a former Newark police officer and a lieutenant at Mosque 25—bonded, Anderson began his illustrious career as security man to African American sports luminaries and entertainers. The family moved from New Jersey to Woodland Hills, California, in 1979, and James Anderson's roster of clients over the years has included Sugar Ray Leonard, Donna Summer, Pryor, Jackson, Boyz II Men, and Tyson, among many others.

Growing up in such an environment was something of a modern fairy tale. 'Uncle Muhammad' would entertain Jamal and his seven siblings with magic tricks when he would visit. Donna Summer read him bedtime stories. Sugar Ray allowed him into the locker room after world championship bouts and sang at Jamal's birthday parties. Jim Brown—Jamal's greatest sports hero, to whom he paid permanent tribute by switching to jersey number 32 when he was ten years old—would show up at Jamal's Pop Warner games. Byron Scott, the former Lakers guard, came by the house to cut his hair. Pryor let Jamal roller-skate on his tennis courts. Anderson's was obviously not a typical childhood.

Having all these international superstars in his extended family had several effects on Anderson. Most important, perhaps, it instilled a belief that he himself was destined for greatness. In addition, Anderson developed ease with celebrity and the media, as well as a hunger. The Andersons have always interacted with their superstar clients and friends on a natural, down-to-earth level. Despite Anderson's public display of ego, his family keeps him honest. His whole life he has known the truth about celebrities: they are just like everyone else.

In January 1999, a *CNN Sports Illustrated* reporter asked Anderson whether he was nervous during the countdown week for the Super Bowl. "I guess it really, really helps when you've been around the people I've been around,'' he responded. "I've been around the fanfare, I've seen around the ups and downs. All along, I've known these people on a personal level, and they've always remained the same people.'' In *USA Today* Anderson said, "I grew up around a lot of people who were called the greatest, but my family always treated them like anybody else. People tell me, 'You saw those superstars when they were being

real.' But I prefer to say I saw them when they were just genuine people.''

While Anderson's home life instilled a sense of humility in him, it also fostered the drive to aim as high as possible, to shoot for supremacy. With such extreme standards of achievement all around them, Jamal and his siblings were fiercely competitive. Second best was not a respected outcome. In the *Atlanta Journal and Constitution,* Anderson said, "From watching all those [football] films and being around all those celebrities, I learned that if you're going to play, you've got to be the best. Always be No. 1—win, win, win. And the competition among my [four] brothers and [three] sisters was fierce.''

There were plenty of other people around to reinforce that notion. As the *USA Today* piece described, Anderson received a call from 'Iron Mike'—who has been a big brother figure to Jamal—in the middle of the 1998 season: ```You're doing good, but you need to be No. 1!' Tyson bellowed. 'You've got to gain 2,000 yards this season! You've got to be the best!''`

Obsession with Sports Started Early

Anderson was obsessed with NFL films when other kids were getting off on Rocky and Bullwinkle. From the get-go, he knew that football was going to be his Big Thing. His first hero—and still the greatest—was Jim Brown. Anderson played in the Pop Warner league, and then went on play hard at El Camino Real High School, where he was an All-League, All-Region, and All-Valley selection. As a senior, he was team captain, an All-State and *LA Times* All-Star choice, and Most Valuable Player. But he played in other ways too, completely neglecting the academic side of things. After spending a couple of years at Moorpark College (CA), Anderson was recruited by many of the big schools: USC, UCLA, and Arizona. But he chose the University of Utah, because he liked the fact that the school stressed academics as much as athletics for its players.

His senior season was very strong; he rushed for 1,030 yards, averaging 5.7 a carry, and was picked for all-WAC conference. In the Freedom Bowl against Southern Cal Anderson turned in a fine performance, with 133 total yards.

Anderson expected to be plucked up in the first two or at most three rounds of the 1994 draft. His family organized a big celebration for the first draft day. But recruiters *seriously* mis-evaluated the running back, seeing him as a little too small and average as a blocker to play fullback, and not fleet enough to qualify as feature back. By the time he was nabbed in the seventh round, 200 players had been chosen ahead of him. The experience was a painful blow for Anderson, and not something he will soon forget.

As Anderson pronounced in *Sports Illustrated,* "That isn't something you get over in a year or two. This is careerlong." No doubt his opponents will continue to pay for this slight. Meanwhile, Terrell Davis, the phenomenal Denver Bronco back that led the NFL in yardage in 1998, with 2,008, had been drafted 196th. Recruiters will admit that theirs is an inexact science, but many of them must feel downright foolish for passing up these two—arguably, the best backs in the game.

Started Breaking Records in 1996

With Craig "Ironhead" Heyward playing Pro Bowl-quality ball for the Falcons, Anderson had to bide his time before he got to show what he could do. His rookie season he ran the ball all of two times, for a net one yard loss. In 1995, Anderson got to play in all the games, though not as the starter, and he rushed 39 times for a total of 161 yards— a 4.1 average. Plus another 42 yards from four pass receptions. However, he made a serious impression as a kickoff returner, with 24 runs totaling 541 yards—an impressive 22.5 average.

In 1996, Anderson got his chance at last to demonstrate what he knew he could do. He ended the season with 1,055 yards—only the seventh Falcon player to pop the 1,000-yard barrier and the eleventh best in the league. But he ran up some impressive comparative stats that season: his 4.55 yards per carry ranked second in the NFL; he was third for receptions by a running back, with 49; seventh in total yards from scrimmage, with 1,528; fourth in rushes of over 10 yards, with 30, and so on. He rushed over 100 yards in three games, and totaled over 100 yards all-purpose in seven. Jamal Anderson had arrived.

Unfortunately, the Falcons had not. The team finished the season with a miserable 3-13 record. But in 1997, the team started to gel, with Coach Dan Reeves moving away from the run-and-shoot strategy to a more run-based game. Chris Chandler, the veteran journeyman quarterback, had an excellent season. Blocking improved for Anderson, thanks largely to the efforts of Bob Christian. Despite a nasty ankle sprain, which squelched Anderson's production in the first half of the season, he finished with another 1,000 yards plus season—only the third Falcon to achieve that feat.

Coach Reeves deserves a lot of the credit for turning the team around. Anderson's talent has been an immeasurable weapon, but without the right strategist, talent itself rarely is enough. It took Reeves a little while to get the Falcons cruising: they lost the seven out of the first eight he coached. But then came an incredible 11-game winning streak. At the time of Superbowl XXXIII, they had won 22 of their last 26 games.

But the 1998 season was the true turning point. Anderson turned in one stunning game after another, excelling in the rush, at receiving, and as a blocker. Chandler threw better than he ever had in his long career, and Falcons receptions was superb. Atlanta astonished the league by turning in a 14-2 final record. They trounced the Dolphins 38-16 and then defeated the Vikings, who succeeded in shutting Anderson down but not Atlanta. Meanwhile, Anderson launched a good-natured but very public campaign to be elected NFL MVP.

Denver prevailed in the Super Bowl, snagging the coveted distinction of back-to-back championships. Anderson rushed for nearly 100 yards, close to Terrell Davis' total. But Atlanta made costly mistakes, and the Denver offense, driven by the elite veteran quarterback John Elway, was magnificent.

But the Falcons have become a formidable force, and another Super Bowl appearance is far from impossible. Anderson likely has many years of pro ball ahead of him, and at the rate he is going he will soon fit right in among his father's clientele of world conquerors.

Sources

Periodicals

Atlanta Journal and Constitution, August 25, 1994; November 6, 1998, p. E01.
Sports Illustrated, December 28, 1998, p. 50.
The Sporting News, November 30, 1998, p. 26.
USA Today, November 13, 1998, p. 3C.

Other

CNN Sports Illustrated (online), November 4, 1998; January 12, 1999; January 23, 1999.
The Atlanta Falcons' website: http://www.nfl.com/Falcons.

—Mark Baven

Benny Andrews

1930—

Artist, activist

Benny Andrews, a painter and collage artist, has spent his entire career working outside the mainstream of American art. During the 1950s and 1960s, when the art world was dominated by abstract painting, Andrews insisted on pursuing his primary interest: capturing ordinary people on canvas. He continues to create representational artwork today. "There are not many artists in the twentieth century who have had that kind of concern for simple people, for the dignity of people no matter where they come from, and who manage to communicate that spiritual dignity in a very physical way," Michael Brenson, art critic and curator, said in the documentary video *Benny Andrews: The Visible Man.*

Although originally dismissed as a "regional" artist, Andrews, who was born and raised in Georgia, eventually managed to find a place for himself in the art world. In addition to his success as a painter, Andrews earned a reputation as a political activist, fighting for recognition of African American artists and culture.

"Andrews's themes and techniques identify him as a great Southern African American artist," Grady T. Turner wrote in a review that appeared in *Art in America.* "But in a

broader sense, his works convey a humanist sensibility that largely skipped the art mainstream of his generation. His social concerns made him hard to place in an era dominated by formal concerns, but today he can be seen as a spiritual predecessor of many contemporary artists."

Encouraged by Artist Father

Benny Andrews was born on November 13, 1930, in Madison, Georgia; he was the second of a family of ten children. His parents, George and Viola (formerly Perryman) Andrews, were sharecroppers, "the lowest form of human work one could ever imagine," Andrews was quoted as saying in *World Artists.*

Benny was only allowed to attend high school during the winter months, when he was not needed to pick or plant cotton. "My parents...always read and subscribed to newspapers and magazines, and we had a radio, which was rather unusual," Andrews stated in *Benny Andrews: The Visible Man.* "We also went to the movies a lot, and those were the kind of things that supplemented a very poor education."

While in many ways he had a typical Southern upbringing, the Andrews family placed an atypically high value on creative pursuits. George Andrews was a prolific, self-taught artist—years later, George's and Benny's work appeared together in an exhibit that traveled to several museums—and both parents encouraged the children to draw and paint. "They complimented us on what we did. They encouraged us to do things," Andrews commented in *Benny Andrews: The Visible Man.* "It was not geared to any career or anything, it was just more or less to express yourself." The encouragement worked; while Benny became a successful visual artist, another brother, Raymond, wrote several acclaimed novels.

After graduating from Burney Street High School in 1948, Andrews received a college scholarship for his work in the local 4-H organization. He spent a summer in Atlanta painting murals, then enrolled in Georgia's Fort Valley State College. Two years later, when the scholarship ended, he enlisted in the Air Force. Andrews trained in

Texas, then served in Korea until 1954, attaining the rank of staff sergeant.

Returning to civilian life, Andrews enrolled at the prestigious School of the Art Institute of Chicago. Ironically, the South's segregated school system helped to make this advancement possible: rather than admit black students to all-white institutions, Georgia paid partial tuition for them to attend college out of state.

The Art Institute opened his eyes to a world that Andrews had never before experienced. "The first museum I went to was when I went to school at the Art Institute. I was 24-years old," he said in *Benny Andrews: The Visible Man.* During this period, Andrews began experimenting with collage, a medium that he explored throughout his career. "I started working in collage because I found...I didn't want to lose my sense of rawness," Andrews stated in *Folk: The Art of Benny and George Andrews.* "I didn't realize it at first but in a sense, I'm really constructing, not painting my work...I needed something both tactile and tangible."

In the 1950s, abstract expressionist painting dominated the art world, and the Art Institute was no exception. Andrews, who insisted on pursuing representational painting with a political sensibility, found little support for his work. "Needless to say, in the eyes of the school, I was a total failure, and I found that very easy to live with—in fact I gained a certain amount of strength from the academics' utter dislike of what I chose to do," Andrews said in *World Artists.*

During his years at art school, Andrews earned money as an illustrator for record companies, creating covers for Duke Ellington and other top musicians. Blue Note, which gained recognition for its innovative cover designs, bought his work regularly. Andrews also drew advertising illustrations for various theater companies in Chicago.

Andrews married Mary Ellen Smith, a photographer, in 1957 (one source says 1959), and earned his BFA in 1958. Soon after graduating, the couple moved to New York, settling on the Lower East Side. During the next seven years, they had two sons, Christopher and Thomas, and a daughter, Julia. His wife took an office job to support the family, while Andrews stayed at home, took care of the children, and painted.

In New York, as in Chicago, Andrews found that most galleries and museums focused on abstract work rather than representational art. As a result, critical acceptance and gallery exhibitions were slow in coming. "He developed a powerful figurative art which was overlooked for some years as regionalist or retrograde," Patricia P.

Bladon wrote in *Folk: The Art of Benny and George Andrews*. "His work was also neglected by galleries and critics, even in the free-spirited sixties."

Fought for Recognition of Black Artists

After years of struggling, Andrews slowly began to achieve some recognition for his art. Between 1960 and 1970, he had eleven solo shows at the Paul Kessler Gallery in Provincetown, Massachusetts, and three at the Forum Gallery in New York City. In 1965, Andrews received a John Hay Whitney Fellowship, which was renewed the following year.

In spite of his personal success, Andrews felt increasingly bitter about the art world's lack of recognition for African American artists and culture. In the late 1960s Andrews organized a group called the Black Emergency Culture Coalition, which included over 150 black artists. In 1969 the group held a demonstration against the exhibit "Harlem on My Mind" at New York's Metropolitan Museum of Art. No black scholars or historians had participated in organizing the show, which Andrews saw as "a continuation of the paternalistic approach" to understanding African American culture (quoted as saying in *World Artists)*. "Though I never enjoyed picketing or being vocal in public forums about obvious racism in cultural institutions, I never had second thoughts about my responsibility to protest," Andrews wrote in the essay "Roads," printed in *Folk: The Art of Benny and George Andrews*.

The coalition's next target was the Whitney Museum of American Art, also based in New York City. The museum's permanent collection contained only ten works by black artists, and its biennial exhibitions rarely included works by African Americans or women. In 1969 the museum's curators agreed to hold an exhibition titled "Contemporary Black Artists in America," but the coalition objected to the way it was handled and decided to boycott the show. Of the 75 artists scheduled to participate in the exhibition, 15 withdrew in sympathy with the boycott.

In 1971, 50 black artists participated in the show "Rebuttal to the Whitney Museum Exhibition" at the Acts of Art Galleries in New York. Two years later, Andrews curated an exhibition of work by black artists, titled "Blacks: USA: 1973" at the New York Cultural Center. The show was what should have been mounted at the Whitney, Andrews asserted.

In addition to his painting and political activism, Andrews taught art classes in prisons, and headed a volunteer program for the Society of the Prevention of Cruelty to Children. Beginning in 1969, Andrews worked as an art instructor at Queens College in New York. The following year, Andrews wrote an essay titled "On Understanding Black Art," which appeared in the *New York Times*. Since then, Andrews has contributed numerous articles to arts publications, including *Artworld, Art Papers*, and *American Visions*.

From 1982 to 1984, Andrews held the position of visual arts director at the National Endowment for the Arts. During his tenure, he established many outreach programs throughout the country. "He's just had an incredible leadership role with different groups...," Jane Farver, director of exhibitions at Queens Museum, was quoted as saying in *Benny Andrews: The Visible Man*. "What he did to open doors for other people can't be overestimated— it's enormous, what he's done."

Continued to Pursue Representational Art

Andrews has received numerous prestigious awards for his art, including fellowships from the New York Council on the Arts and National Endowment for the Arts. His work appears in the collections of more than 20 museums nationwide. These include the Detroit Institute of Art; the High Museum of Art in Atlanta, Georgia; the Metropolitan Museum of Art in New York; the Museum of Modern Art, New York; and the Philadelphia Academy of Art. In 1986, Andrews married artist Nene Humphrey, having divorced his first wife ten years earlier.

In 1990, the Memphis Brooks Museum of Art in Memphis, Tennessee, staged the exhibition, "Folk: The Art of Benny and George Andrews." The exhibition, which demonstrated the influence of the folk artist George on the trained artist Benny, later traveled to six other museums. "Both are inexplicably unique; yet, somehow each amplifies and crystallizes the other's voice and vision," wrote Judd Tully in the catalog for the exhibition.

Some critics have claimed that Andrews' interest in collage refers back to his childhood, when art materials were scarce but the desire to create was too strong to ignore. "Collage is at the heart of his art...," J. Richard Gruber, deputy director of the Morris Museum of Art, said in *Benny Andrews: The Visible Man*. "He grew up using anything he could, as did his father as an artist, as did his family....And to the present day he uses what is at hand— fabric, scraps—and reuses works until they've found their proper home."

In his drawings, paintings, and collages, Andrews continues to pursue representational art, which has been his focus throughout his long career. "Benny Andrews is a remarkable draftsman whose work is characterized by great economy of means," Patricia P. Bladon wrote in *Folk: The Art of Benny and George Andrews*. "He infuses his drawings with the same integrity and passion which characterize his large-scale paintings."

"Given the seismic shifts in the art world since the late 1950s, Andrews's career is striking in its continuity," Grady T. Turner wrote in a review that appeared in *Art in America*. "As an art student, he found an expressionistic figurative style that he continues to develop to this day, when it seems fresher and more relevant than ever."

While Andrews struggled for recognition—for himself as an artist, for other African American artists, and for African American culture in general—fame has never been his primary goal. "Do something you like to do," was the advice he gave in the video *Benny Andrews: The Visible Man*. "If you like to write, if you like to sing, if you like to dance, do it for the pleasure of doing it....If you develop your imagination, you can almost do anything."

Sources

Art in America, February 1998, p. 105.
Benny Andrews: The Visible Man (documentary video), by Linda Freeman and David Irving, L & S Video, 1996.
Folk: The Art of Benny and George Andrews (exhibition catalog), by Patricia P. Bladon and Judd Tully, Memphis Brooks Museum of Art, 1990.
St. James Guide to Black Artists. St. James Press, 1997.
World Artists, 1950-1980. H.W. Wilson, 1984.

—Carrie Golus

Emmett Ashford

1914—1980

Major League Baseball Umpire

Most people can easily name Jackie Robinson as the player who broke the color barrier in professional baseball. A lesser number, but still sizable, may also be able to correctly identify Frank Robinson as major league baseball's first black manager. But chances are, the number of correct responses would drop dramatically when asked for the name of the man who became the first black umpire in professional baseball. His name was Emmett Ashford. In 1966, after more than 15 years of working college games, fly-by-night leagues, and the minors, the then 51-year old Ashford was called up by the American League and broke yet another racial barrier in professional sports. With a flamboyant showmanship and animated style of calling the game, Ashford delighted crowds and created the unlikely event of an umpire--often the most hated man on a baseball diamond--being asked for his autograph. Although he only worked in the majors for five years before retiring, Ashford's life was a model of perseverance and refusing to give up on a dream despite the odds.

Emmett Littleton Ashford was born November 23, 1914 in Los Angeles, California. His father left when Ashford was a year old leaving his mother to raise Emmett and his newborn baby brother on her own. Ashford credit's his mother for his tenacity. "My mother was a secretary for a black newspaper, The California Eagle, for many years," he reminisced to Larry R. Gerlach, author of The Men in Blue: Conversations with Umpires. "She was quite an active person, and I know I got my ambitious traits from her."

With his father gone and being the oldest boy, Ashford took it upon himself to work after school. First by selling magazines and shining shoes, then working as stockboy and cashier at a local supermarket. Still, he managed to keep his grades up and also participated in school activities. By the time he was at Jefferson High School he was the first black student body president, the editor of the school newspaper and a member of the Scholarship Society. He even had enough energy to join the track team.

The First Time

After a brief stint at Los Angeles Community College, Ashford enrolled at nearby Chapman College. Since he was not fast enough for the Chapman track team, he played baseball for Chapman and then for a semipro team

At a Glance . . .

Born Emmett Ashford on November 23, 1914 in Los Angeles, California. Married Virginia. *Education:* B.S., Chapman College. *Military:* U.S. Navy, 1943-1946.

Career: Umpire in Southwest International League, July 1951-July 1952; Arizona-Texas League, August-September 1952; Western International League, 1953: Pacific Coast League, 1954-1965; American League, 1966-1970; All-Star Game, 1967; World Series, 1970.

Awards: Emmett Ashford Memorial Baseball Field, Los Angeles, California, 1982.

called the Mystery Nine, where he was the team's worst player who spent most games on the bench. One Sunday, however, the regular empire didn't show up so the teams recruited Ashford to take his place, since he was not going to play anyway. Begrudgingly, Ashford took the umpire's spot. "But a strange thing happened," Ashford recalled to Gerlach. "By the seventh inning they loved my umpiring. They would take up collections during those games, and the collection that Sunday was extremely heavy. Thenceforth the team decreed that I should umpire."

Ashford found that he loved to umpire. Now working at a branch of the U.S. Post Office, he would spend his free time umpiring whenever he could. For a while, during World War II, he took a break from both after joining the Navy. But his last post at the Naval Air Station in Corpus Christi, Texas found him working as a postal clerk and running the baseball team on the base. That was also where he heard that Jackie Robinson had been signed to the Brooklyn Dodgers to become the first black man to play professional baseball. Lying on his cot after hearing the radio announcement, Emmett Ashford told himself he was going to be the first black umpire.

After the Navy, Ashford returned to Los Angeles, his job at the post office and a more focused pursuit of umpiring. Soon he was umpiring high school games, then junior college games, then the college circuit with big universities like UCLA and USC. Soon he had a four-game tryout with the Class C Southwest International League. To avoid any potential trouble of having a black umpire they decided to have the tryout in Mexicali, Mexico where the local team was playing the club from Tucson, Arizona. When Ashford arrived the other two white umpires refused to work with him and the first game was delayed by a half

hour while they searched for another umpire to work the bases while Ashford worked the plate. When they did, Ashford umpired the rest of the games without incident and knew for sure he wanted to be an umpire.

The following week, while at his job at the post office, the president of the league called Ashford to see if he wanted to finish the season. As soon as he hung up the phone, he marched into the postmaster's office and got a leave of absence for three months. Although he was umpiring, it was hardly the realization of Ashford's dream. The white umpires shunned him and he could rarely stay in the same hotels and eat in the same restaurants. Ashford simply made it part of his routine to get to a location early and scout out a place to stay and places to eat.

Followed His Dream

The next season the league offered Ashford a contract to work the whole year. "The postmaster was under political fire at the time, and I couldn't get that leave of absence again," he reminisced to Gerlach. "So I had to make the decision which everybody has to make in his life sometime. How many men go to their graves without ever doing what's in their hearts?" Ashford stunned just about everyone he knew by resigning from the post office in 1951, giving up a steady paycheck and 15 years seniority to umpire in a Class C baseball league. Midway through the season, the league folded.

Because there were so many leagues, however, Ashford was only out of work for a short time after knocking around the Class C league for a while made it to the Class A Western International League in 1953. The next year he got called up to the Pacific Coast League, a Triple-A league one stop away from the majors, although Ashford was realistic. "Just let nature take its course," he told Laurence Davies of the *New York Times* in 1954. Right now I'm learning and I hope to graduate to the majors on my ability--that and nothing else." When asked if he anticipated trouble from players, Ashford replied, "Ball players are a peculiar lot. The game is their bread and butter. If you call 'em right--the strikes and balls and the base decisions--that's all they want. They don't care whether you're white or black, Eskimo or Indian."

Ashford went along with the Pacific Coast League hoping his day would come when he get the call to move up to the major leagues. Meanwhile, white umpires he trained were passing over him to work in the big stadiums of the National and American Leagues. By the end of the 1965 season, Ashford was 50-years old and ready to call it quits. Then he got the call he'd been waiting to get for 15 years. He was now an umpire for the American Leagues; the first black umpire in professional baseball.

The First Game

His first game would be the Cleveland Indians at the Washington Senators on April 11, 1966. Vice President Hubert Humphrey was slated to throw out the first ball and because of the Secret Service, Ashford and his wife were almost not let into the stadium when he told them he was an umpire, even though it had been in all the papers. Eventually, he was let in and although he only had one call the whole game while working third base, he had made it. "The players came up and shook my hand and I received an armload of telegrams from nice people," he told *Ebony* after the game. "Of course, I was a little nervous at first, but wild horses couldn't have kept me out of there. I waited 15 years for this and now I'm finally there."

Some criticized Ashford for dancing around and being a showboat, words which rolled right off him. "I'm an individual," he explained to *Ebony*. The league president has told me to be myself. I'm different, of that there's no doubt. But as long as I am competent, what does it matter? Everyone should keep some boyish enthusiasm in their hearts and use it in their work." For his five years in the major leagues, Ashford was a fan favorite who'd receive cheers with his animated calls even if they were against the home team.

In 1967 Ashford was chosen to work the All-Star game but his crowning achievement was working the 1970 World Series between Baltimore and Cincinnati. Ashford did not get to work home plate during the series, however, as it only went five games and he was slated to be behind the plate on the sixth game. Still, it was the culmination of his life's dream and he retired at the end of the season. "Trying to top the exceptionally good year and the thrilling events of the 1970 World Series would be superfluous and anticlimactic," he told Joe Durso of the *New York Times*. "Hence the decision to depart on top."

After retiring Ashford kept his hand in baseball, first by umpiring an amateur summer league in Alaska, as well as working for then-baseball commissioner Bowie Kuhn as his West Coast representative. In that role, Ashford took his exuberance around the world as a goodwill ambassador for baseball, which he did until illness prevented it and then his death in 1980. Few knew better than Emmett Ashford the importance of stepping up to the plate one more time when the game seemed hopeless. As he confessed to Gerlach, "I feel proud having been an umpire in the big leagues not because I was the first black man, but because the major league umpires are a very select group of men. But the greatest satisfaction I've gotten is the feeling of accomplishment in doing what I set out to do in the first place when they said it couldn't be done."

Sources

Books

Gerlach, Larry R., *The Men in Blue: Conversations with Umpires,* University of Nebraska Press, 1980.

Light, Jonathon Fraser, *The Cultural Encyclopedia of Baseball,* McFarland & Company, Inc., 1997.

Rust, Art, Jr., *Get That Nigger Off The Field: An Oral History of Black Ballplayers from the Negro Leagues to the Present,* Shadow Lawn Press, 1992.

Periodicals

Ebony, June 1966, p. 65.

Jet, March 20, 1980, p. 53; June 26, 1980, p. 51; April 12, 1982, p. 45.

New York Times, September 16, 1965, p. 62; December 4, 1970, p. 65.

New York Times Magazine, June 13, 1954, p.59.

—Brian Escamilla

Erykah Badu

1971(?)—

Vocalist

Her trademark African head wraps helped inspire a vogue for African clothing in the late 1990s, and her music seemed to carry layers of African American experience, wrapped up and elegantly presented with the latest hip-hop beats. Erykah Badu was a breakout star of 1997, selling over two million copies of her debut album, *Baduizm*. An original artist, she composed and performed a fusion of soul, hip-hop, and jazz. Both romantic and a bit intellectual, Badu is steeped in African American spirituality, and exudes it in her personal presence. "Sometimes," she told *People* when the magazine named her one of 1998's "50 Most Beautiful People" of the year, "I do feel quite Queen Nefertiti-ish."

Born around 1971 in Dallas, Badu was the oldest of three children. She was raised by her mother Kolleen Wright and her grandmother on the city's rough south side. Badu told *USA Today* that she fell in love with the music of Stevie Wonder "at maybe age two." Her given name, which she has called her "slave" name," was Erica Wright. Badu respelled her first name in high school, and in college took the name Badu, which means "giver of truth and light" in Arabic.

Artistic Activities in Youth

Badu's unusual creativity was evident at a young age. She made her own clothes while in grade school, and her mother encouraged the drawings, poems, letters, and writings that filled her daughter's school notebooks. Badu performed in community theater in Dallas during her school years and majored in theater at Louisiana's Grambling State University before dropping out to pursue music. She has also had formal training as a dancer.

Badu and her cousin, Robert "Free" Bradford, formed a duo called Erykah Free and performed at progressive nightspots around Dallas. Initially, they struggled to find success in the music business and Badu had to take work as a waitress and as a hostess at Dallas's Steve Harvey comedy club. She remained determined and, by the early 1990s, Erykah Free was the opening act for some of the big hip-hop acts of the day, such as Wu-Tang Clan, A Tribe Called Quest, and Mobb Deep. Mixing abundant creativity and an astute understanding of the music business, "I learned that in order to be a successful entertainer, you

At a Glance . . .

Born Erica Wright in Dallas, Texas, ca. 1971; daughter of Kolleen Wright; changed first name to Erykah in high school; changed last name to Badu in college. *Education:* Attended Grambling State University in Louisiana; studied theater.

Career: Hip-hop/soul/jazz vocalist, songwriter, producer, and video director. Performed with cousin Robert "Free" Bradford in duo Erykah Free, early 1990s; Erykah Free opened for touring rap acts, early 1990s; signed to Kedar Entertainment label, 1995; released *Baduizm,* debut CD, 1997; released *Live!* CD, 1997; appeared on soundtrack of film "Eve's Bayou," 1998.

Awards: Two Grammy awards, four Soul Train Awards, two NAACP Image Awards, and one American Music Award in 1998, for *Baduizm.*

Addresses: *Label*–Kedar Entertainment, 1755 Broadway, 7th floor, New York, NY 10019; *Booking agent*–William Morris Agency, 1325 Avenue of the Americas, New York, NY 10019.

ed jazz listeners of the tragic vocalist Billie Holiday, not only because of a strong surface resemblance but also in the way Badu seemed deadly serious and mature beyond her years. The album's production used bass-heavy hip-hop beats in a way that, in 1997, was startling and new. These beats were brought down to a quiet level and provided subtle texture for the jazz instrument work (including a contribution from jazz bassist Ron Carter) and the varied poetic structures above them. Badu sang rather than rapped, but the hip-hop flavor of the music was unmistakable. The long opposition between R&B and hip-hop was beginning to dissolve, and Badu was out in front of the trend. She had followed rap since its inception and, as she told *USA Today,* "my music kind of fused into a soul/hip-hop understanding." The varied subjects of Badu's songwriting, which touched on relationships, spirituality, and social themes, helped her appeal to different audiences.

Badu's debut album shot to the top of the *Billboard* R&B chart, and eventually made it all the way to Number Two on the pop chart, benefitting from the surprising crossover success of the lyrically complex and oblique "On and On." *Baduizm* was reported to have sold 1.7 million copies in a span of three months. During the summer of 1997, Badu was in high demand as a concert performer. At her concerts, she burned sandalwood incense and discussed numerology with her audiences. "I like to take a salt bath before I appear in public, to create my own sense of calm," Badu told *People.* She released her *Live!* album in late 1997, which was recorded before an invited audience at a New York studio. *Live!* went platinum and nearly matched the stellar performance of her debut album.

have to be a really good businesswoman," she told *Ebony.*

Badu's big break occurred when R&B executive Kedar Massenburg, who also launched the career of D'Angelo, met Badu and noted the strength of her personality. "It wasn't so much the music, but more her presence and the way she commanded the audiences. They looked as though they were hypnotized," Massenburg told *Essence* magazine. Massenburg signed Badu, as a solo act, to his Kedar Entertainment label in 1995.

Single Distributed at Awards Program

Massenburg's next step was to pass out 1,000 copies of Badu's debut single, "On and On," at the 1996 Soul Train Music Awards. "And man, when I heard it banging out of somebody's car going down the street that same night, I knew I had something," he later told the *Atlanta Constitution.* Industry excitement over the innovative young newcomer grew, fueled by a video for "On and On" and the release of her *Baduizm* album in early 1997.

Baduizm was a sensation. Badu's virtuoso vocals remind-

Directed Music Videos

During 1998, Badu was a major presence at music awards programs. She took home two Grammy awards (one for Best Female Vocal for "On and On"), four Soul Train Awards, and an American Music Award. She continued to dazzle the music world with her many talents and directed the videos for her songs "Next Lifetime" and "Otherside of the Game." *Live!* also contained a hit single, "Tyrone," that was described by *Ebony* as "the Black women's anthem for dissing and dismissing do-wrong brothers." Badu sang on the soundtrack of the film "Eve's Bayou," and made a guest appearance on an album by the progressive hip-hop group the Roots.

Badu gave birth to a son, Seven Sirius, on November 18, 1997. The father was Andre (Dre) Benjamin of the rap group OutKast, with whom Badu had a long-distance relationship. She chose her son's name because it combined a divine number that could not be divided with the name of the brightest star in the firmament. Badu also announced plans to have six more children. "That's right, six more babies in five years," she told *Ebony*. "Time passes so fast. I just follow and have faith. I know that I make the right decisions." In 1999, *Rolling Stone* magazine selected *Baduizm* as one of the fifty greatest albums of the 1990s.

Selected discography

Baduizm, Kedar/Universal, 1997.
Live!, Universal, 1998.

Sources

Books

Graff, Gary, Josh Freedom du Lac, and Jim McFarlin, *MusicHound R&B,* Visible Ink, 1998.
Larkin, Colin, ed., *The Guinness Encyclopedia of Popular Music,* Muze U.K., 1998.

Periodicals

Atlanta Constitution, May 21, 1997, p. D9.
Ebony, July 1998, p. 68.
Essence, August 1997, p. 90.
Jet, February 16, 1998, p. 60.
Los Angeles Times, February 22, 1998, p. CAL 4.
New York Times, July 8, 1997, p. C9.
People, May 11, 1998,, p. 80.
Rolling Stone, May 13, 1999, p. 76.
USA Today, June 30, 1997, p. D6; March 2, 1998, p. D3.

—James M. Manheim

Thurbert Baker

1952—

Attorney General of Georgia

As the first African American attorney general of Georgia, Thurbert Baker had come a long way from a boyhood spent on a rural North Carolina farm. After building a successful legal career in Georgia, Baker was elected to Georgia's state legislature and loyally worked his way up thorough the Democratic ranks in the state's House of Representatives. Representing a new breed of black Southern politician, Baker built upon his solid professional credentials to forge biracial coalitions. He was on the radar screens of many political pundits as they tried to forecast which state officeholders would emerge as the leaders of the early twenty-first century.

Baker was born in Rocky Mount, North Carolina, on December 16, 1952. He grew up on a farm and was raised by a single mother. The family suffered severe financial hardships and, at the age of eleven, Baker was sent to pick cotton and tobacco in nearby fields. His meager earnings of $1.50 a day were used to help support the family. "It [picking cotton] taught me the value of family [and] hard work, and motivated me to get an education so that one day I might do better," he told the *Florida Times Union*.

Law Career in Georgia

Despite his financial difficulties, Baker was able to earn a bachelor's degree in political science from the University of North Carolina at Chapel Hill in 1975. He soon enrolled at Atlanta's prestigious Emory University Law School, and received his law degree in 1979. In the early 1980s Baker worked as a lawyer in and around Atlanta, litigating cases both at the federal level and in Georgia's criminal and civil court systems. Along with his wife Catherine and their two daughters, he settled in suburban Atlanta's DeKalb County.

In 1988, Baker entered the race for the 70th House District seat in the Georgia House of Representatives. Running as a Democrat, he captured the seat by defeating the white incumbent. This triumph was especially impressive because the district at that time had a white majority. In 1990, Baker became active in the gubernatorial campaign of progressive Democrat Zell Miller. When Miller emerged victorious, Baker was rewarded with the post of assistant House floor leader. Two years later, he rose to the position of floor leader. As the chief point man for the governor's legislative initiatives, Baker was in charge of bringing bills to the floor, twisting the arms of reluctant legislators, and generally bending the legislative machinery to the state administration's will.

Helped Pass "Two-Strikes" Law

During his career in the state House, Baker played a key role in the passage of numerous pieces of legislation. This legislation included anti–drunk driving bills, a measure that reduced the lengthy series of appeals available to Death Row inmates, and a package of welfare reform measures. Baker's leadership skills were evident during a vigorous fight to pass Miller's proposal mandating a sentence of life in prison without parole for habitual criminals—the so-called "two strikes law." During his campaign for attorney general, Baker told the *Florida Times-Union,* "We would not have 'two strikes' legislation in this state but for the blood and guts I left on the House floor."

With this substantial record of accomplishment behind

him, Baker emerged in 1997 as a leading candidate to succeed Georgia Attorney General Michael Bowers, who was stepping down to pursue the governorship. Although several prominent state Democrats were interested in the position, Governor Miller selected Baker for attorney general. "It proves what my mother told me at an early age," Baker told the *Times-Union.* "This country is full of opportunity for those who prepare themselves, are willing to work hard and be part of the solution, not the problem."

Promoted Domestic-Violence Measure

Upon taking office, Baker listed crackdowns on domestic violence, Medicaid fraud, and consumer fraud as his top three priorities as attorney general. He also gained recognition for bringing Georgia into line with other states who were suing the tobacco industry for alleged damages to public health. Under Baker's predecessor, Georgia was one of the few states that had declined to take action. He initiated prosecution of fraudulent telemarketers operating in Georgia and, in early 1998, asked state lawmakers to impose minimum mandatory terms for beating a family member, with added penalties if the victim was age 65 or older.

This issue became a central point of contention during Baker's election campaign in 1998 against Republican David Ralston. Although some political observers noted Baker's long commitment to domestic-violence issues, they also pointed out that Baker displayed uncanny political instincts by choosing an issue that would resonate with Georgia's white female voters, who were often a swing voting bloc within the state. Baker also raised eyebrows when he proposed denying parole for certain violent criminals, a controversial idea that was criticized by the state parole board. Baker went on to win the election by a narrow margin and became the first African American to be elected to statewide political office in Georgia. As of 1998, he was the only African American attorney general in the United States.

Sources

Periodicals

Atlanta Journal-Constitution, October 21, 1998, p. A14; October 30, 1998, p. C3; November 4, 1998, p. D3.
Florida Times-Union, May 3, 1997, p. A1; November 11, 1997, p. B1; January 12, 1998, p. A5; May 7, 1998, p. B1.
Jet, June 2, 1997, p. 8.

Other

Additional information for this profile was obtained from

the Georgia state government web page at www.ganet.org/ago/gaagintro.html.

—James M. Manheim

Robert Mack Bell

1943—

Judge

Robert Mack Bell is the first African American to head Maryland's highest court, the Court of Appeals. Bell also is one of Maryland's most experienced judges. At the age of 31, he was the youngest judge in the state. He has served for several years as a sitting judge on the seven-member Court of Appeals.

Conservatives considered Bell a liberal and a leading dissenter in decisions ratifying the death penalty. When Maryland governor Parris N. Glendening appointed Bell as a judge in 1996, political controversy ensued. While Bell's appointment to the post pleased Maryland's African American constituency, conservatives voiced their displeasure with his judicial decisions. Since becoming a member of the court in 1991, Bell had consistently voted to reverse death sentences. "In death penalty and criminal procedure cases...he [Bell] comes down in favor of applying a rule in the defendant's favor, though not advocating any wholesale...change in the law," Edward A. Tomlinson, a professor at the University of Maryland, commented to Abramowitz and Torry of *The Washington Post*. University of Maryland law professor William L. Reynolds, described in the *Post* as a longtime court observer, remarked that, "Bell writes excellent opinions...thoughtful, extremely well researched and non-ideological....Bell does not have an ax to grind." One conservative argued that Bell was too permissive. "He has the reputation of being a bleeding heart liberal," former gubernatorial hopeful Ellen Sauerbrey, a Republican, stated in the *The Sun*. "Judge Bell is frequently the lone dissenter who votes to return violent criminals to their communities."

Bell strongly disagreed with the claims of conservatives that he was a "bleeding heart liberal." "I do dissent in death penalty cases," he stated in an interview with *CBB*. "The reason for it is because I believe you ought to cross the t's and dot the i's in cases where the punishment is so final. I try to call them the way I see them, based upon the record that's before me. I'm not a judicial activist as the word liberal tends to suggest." He also defended his serious, strict approach to sentencing in death penalty cases. Bell also remarked to *CBB* that sending someone to jail should not be easy and that each defendant should be given the benefit of the doubt.

During the mid-1970s, Bell was appointed to the District Court of Maryland in Baltimore by then governor Marvin Mandel. Before this appointment, he worked from 1969 to

At a Glance . . .

Born Robert Mack Bell, July 6, 1943, in Rocky Mount, NC; raised in Baltimore, MD; son of Thomas (a laborer) and Rosa Lee (a house cleaner) Bell. *Education:* Morgan State College, AB, 1966; Harvard University Law School, JD, 1969.

Career: Associate, Piper & Marbury, 1969-74; judge, Maryland District Court District One, Baltimore City, 1975-80; associate judge, Baltimore City Circuit Court, Eighth Judicial Circuit, 1980-84; judge, Court of Special Appeals, Sixth Appellate Circuit in Annapolis, MD, 1984-91; associate judge, Maryland Court of Appeals, Baltimore, 1991-96, chief judge, 1996–.

Awards: Distinguished Performance and Accomplishment Award Morgan Alumni, 1975; Distinctive Achievement Award Phi Alpha Theta, 1976; Community Service Award Hiram Grand Lodge AF and AM, 1976.

Member: Maryland State Bar Association, 1987–; Sentencing Guidelines Board; Judicial Compensation Committee, 1993–; board of directors, The African American Community Foundation, 1994–; University of Maryland Law School Board of Visitors, 1994–; board of trustees, Chesapeake Center for Youth Development, Inc., 1994–.

Addresses: *Office*—634 Courthouse East, 111 North Calvert Street, Baltimore, MD 21202.

1974 as an associate at the corporate law firm of Piper & Marbury. From 1980 to 1984, he served as an associate judge on the Baltimore City Circuit Court. In 1984, Bell was named as a judge on the Court of Special Appeals in Annapolis and remained there until 1991. In 1988, he actively supported the practice of having circuit judges run for re-election, contending that elections would ensure that minorities and women were represented on state benches. Throughout his career, Bell has served as a mentor to young African American lawyers.

During his inaugural address to Maryland's judiciary in 1997, Bell called for the creation of six new judgeships and legislative consent for $9,000 in pay raises for judges. By 1999, 15 new judgeships had been created and $11,000 allocated for judicial pay raises. Bell also pledged to restore people's confidence in the judicial system. "My

intention and vision is for the Maryland judiciary to increase its focus on public outreach, to inform the public better as to how best they can negotiate what is to some a mysterious and sometimes tricky path to justice," he asserted in *The Sun*. "Through both written and electronic judiciary outreach programs, we intend to make our courts, and especially their procedures, more understandable and user-friendly."

Bell was born in Rocky Mount, North Carolina, on July 6, 1943. His father, Thomas, a laborer, and his mother, Rosa Lee Bell, a house cleaner, separated when Bell was very young. His mother raised all three of her sons as a single parent. "I don't remember ever having lived with him," Bell said of his father to *CBB*. Bell grew up in a tough, impoverished African American neighborhood in eastBaltimore. "I fought a good bit when I was growing up, going to and from school," he commented to *CBB*. "And of course I was stopped by the police from time to time. My mother was concerned that I got in at a decent hour and didn't run in the streets too much." During his elementary school years, Bell read Perry Mason detective and mystery stories and began to think about becoming a lawyer.

At the age of 16, Bell found himself on the wrong side of the law. While he was president of the student body at Dunbar, a then-segregated high school, Bell helped orchestrate a sit-in at Hooper's cafeteria, which also was segregated. He and the other demonstrators were arrested and eventually convicted of trespassing. The group appealed the conviction and brought their case before the Court of Appeals, where it was refused legal recognition. Aided by lawyer Juanita Jackson Mitchell and Thurgood Marshall, chief counsel of the NAACP, the group took its case to the U.S. Supreme Court. The case was again rejected. In 1963, following the passage of anti-segregation laws by Maryland's general assembly, the Court of Appeals considered the case again and overturned the convictions.

Bell's experience with the court system had inspired him to pursue a legal career and follow in the footsteps of his hero, Thurgood Marshall. While majoring in history at Morgan State College, Bell sat on the disciplinary committee. He also became chief justice of his dormitory court. After receiving his bachelor's degree in 1966, Bell was accepted into Harvard University Law School. He enjoyed his classes at Harvard, especially a criminal law course taught by appellate lawyer, Alan Dershowitz. Bell graduated from Harvard University Law School in 1969.

When Bell was appointed to Maryland's District Court in the mid-1970s, many of his decisions were controversial. In 1975, he infuriated politicians and city police officers by dismissing several prostitution cases because of inadequate evidence. The following year, his decision to release a man from custody due to lack of evidence backfired when the man killed his wife. In 1980, Bell was nominated for the Supreme Bench (now the Circuit Court) and was elected from a field of ten candidates.

During the 1980s and 1990s, Bell climbed the judicial ladder. After Governor Glendening appointed Bell as chief judge of the Court of Appeals in 1996, he presided over a court that handled nearly 200 cases per year. In addition to his customary tasks on the bench, he has managed more than 3,000 employees and controlled a yearly budget of over $2 million. In 1999, he gave the commencement address at Baltimore University's law school. He commented to *CBB* that he told the school's graduates, "One ought tostand up for one's principles. Don't run away from a sensitive issue because you think it's going to affect your career. It may very well affect your career but it need not be a negative affect."

Sources

Books

The American Bench, 1997-98, p. 1162.
Leadership Directories, the Leadership Library, http://1di.bvdep.com/1diintra.dll?

Who's Who Among African Americans, Gale, 1996-97, p. 100.
Who's Who in American Law, Marquis Who's Who, 1998-99, p. 48.
Who's Who in the East, Marquis Who's Who, 1999-00, p. 63.

Periodicals

Baltimore, March 1997, pp. 47-49; pp. 100-101.
Baltimore Sun, January 30, 1997, p. B.
Capital, February 15, 1999, p. A6.
Ebony, October 1997, p. 122+.
National Law Journal, November 4, 1996, pp. A1, A.5.
Washington Post, October 23, 1996, Sec. B, pp. 1, 5; October 24, 1996, Sec. B, pp. 1, 7; April 3, 1997, Sec. D, p. 5; October 23, 1998, Sec. C, p. 6.

Other

Additional material for this profile was obtained through an interview with Robert Mack Bell, and through his resume on the internet at http://www.mdarchives.state.md.us/msa/mdmanual/29ap/html/msa11654.html.

—Alison Carb Sussman

George Benson

1943—

Jazz guitarist and vocalist

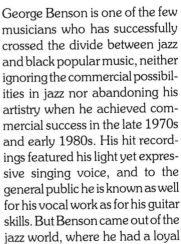

George Benson is one of the few musicians who has successfully crossed the divide between jazz and black popular music, neither ignoring the commercial possibilities in jazz nor abandoning his artistry when he achieved commercial success in the late 1970s and early 1980s. His hit recordings featured his light yet expressive singing voice, and to the general public he is known as well for his vocal work as for his guitar skills. But Benson came out of the jazz world, where he had a loyal cadre of fans, and returned to jazz when his connections with that world threatened to become stretched too thin. He is one of the figures most responsible for the presence of sophisticated jazz musicianship in the world of black popular music generally.

Born on March 22, 1943 in Pittsburgh, Pennsylvania, Benson showed prodigious talent from an early age, winning a singing contest when he was only four years old and enjoying a short career as a child radio performer under the name of "Little Georgie Benson." He started playing the guitar when he was eight, but it was as a vocalist that he spent much of his vast musical energy as a teenager, organizing and performing with a succession of rhythm-and-blues and rock bands around Pittsburgh. He made recordings for RCA Victor's X Records subsidiary in the middle 1950s. But Benson's stepfather encouraged his instrumental efforts by constructing a guitar for him, and in his late teens he began to concentrate exclusively on guitar. Seeking out the music of modern jazz's golden age, he became more and more interested in jazz, and was particularly inspired by recordings of saxophonist Charlie Parker and guitarists Charlie Christian and Grant Green.

Discovered by John Hammond

In 1961 Benson jumped to the national stage when he joined the group backing jazz organist Jack McDuff. He played and recorded with McDuff for four years. Then he struck out on his own: he moved to New York City, then the capital of the jazz universe, and formed his own band. There Benson made two acquaintances who proved crucial in setting him on the path to jazz stardom: guitarist Wes Montgomery, whose soft tone and graceful octave playing provided Benson with his most important stylistic inspiration, and Columbia Records producer and executive John Hammond, whose unerring eye for talent brought

At a Glance . . .

Born March 22, 1943, in Pittsburgh, PA; wife's name Johnnie; seven children, three deceased.

Career: Guitarist, vocalist, and composer. Played electric guitar in quartet of jazz musician Jack McDuff, 1962–65; worked as sideman and led own quartets as guitarist and vocalist, 1965–; signed recording contract with Columbia label, 1965; worked with producer Creed Taylor, first at A&M Records, then at CTI, 1968–74; signed with Warner Brothers label, 1976; released *Breezin'*, one of the top-selling jazz albums of all time, 1976; moved to GRP label, 1995; released *Standing Together*, 1998.

Awards: Many Grammy awards, including Record of the Year 1977; Best Instrumental Performance, 1977; Best R&B Male Vocal Performance, 1980; Best Jazz Vocal Performance, 1980; and Best Pop Instrumental, 1983. Platinum and gold record certifications for numerous albums.

Addresses: *Personal Management*–Turner Management Group, 3500 W. Olive Ave., Suite 680, Burbank, CA 91505.

such seminal musicians as Bob Dylan and Bruce Springsteen to the label. Impressed by Benson's growing list of sideman credits, which included work with such luminaries as Herbie Hancock, Freddie Hubbard and later Miles Davis, Hammond signed Benson to Columbia in 1965.

Benson's first two Columbia albums were *It's Uptown* and *Benson* Burner. His 1960s LPs, two of which were produced by Hammond himself, were in the main bop-influenced vein of the jazz of the time, and they garnered the guitarist, who was still in his early twenties, plenty of positive attention in the jazz community. Searching for wider public recognition, Benson switched labels several times, landing first with Verve (1967), and then with A&M (1968) and CTI (1970–71). He came under the influence of jazz producer Creed Taylor, who had also worked with Montgomery, and who encouraged Benson's natural versatility, backing him with various ensembles and cutting vocal tracks with him that reawakened Benson's interest in singing.

Success with Pop Vocal Track

It was another label move that paved the way for Benson's breakthrough to mass success. Signing with Warner Brothers in late 1975, he released the album *Breezin'* the following year. While much of the album reprised the light guitar-and-strings sound that was common in Benson's CTI work, he took two great and accessible steps forward. First, Benson included on the album a frankly pop-oriented vocal, the Leon Russell composition "This Masquerade." The song reached the Number One position on jazz and R&B charts and drove the album to the same position on the pop charts. Benson's second innovation on *Breezin'* was the introduction of what would become his trademark: scat singing along with his guitar, doubling it at the interval of an octave.

The combination was irresistible, and by some accounts *Breezin'*, which won three Grammy awards, became the best selling jazz album of all time. Benson's pop vocals were self-assured and pleasant; he was in front of the curve which would lead to the highly successful, jazz-inflected "Quiet Storm" formats in black radio of the 1980s. The scat singing seemed to connote a satisfying kind of oneness between Benson and his guitar. "When I pick up the guitar, it's an extension of what I am," Benson told *Guitar Player* magazine. A series of commercially successful albums followed, most of which emphasized Benson's singing. All six of Benson's Warner Brothers albums of the late 1970s and early 1980s were certified gold (sales of 500,000 copies), and four of them went platinum (sales of 1,000,000 copies). Benson credited his success in part to his conversion to the faith of the Jehovah's Witnesses.

Like other jazz players who have followed commercially oriented paths, Benson has taken criticism from jazz purists who felt that he had abandoned his early artistry. Writing about 1978's *In Your Eyes,* for example, Richard S. Ginell observed in the *All Music Guide to Jazz* that "[f]or jazz fans, Benson's albums at this point become a search for buried treasure, for his guitar time is extremely limited." Benson apparently took the criticism to heart, for in 1989 he made a full-blast return to jazz, recording *Tenderly,* an album of standards, with the legendary jazz pianist McCoy Tyner, and touring with Tyner's trio that year. In 1990 he recorded the album *Big Boss Band* with Count Basie's orchestra.

Moved Between Jazz and Pop

The music he made when he returned to jazz showcased part of what was best about Benson's music: his versatil ity. He was equally at home with small ensembles, with a big band, with a string section, with hard bop, with Latin-inflected selections, with popular stylings. Through the 1990s Benson, his popularity assured, appeared in a wide variety of concert situations, and continued to manage well the balance he had achieved between the worlds of jazz and pop. He moved to the jazz-oriented GRP label in 1996, releasing the album *That's Right,* a quiet-storm-styled work, and following it up 1998's *Standing Together* in the same smooth-jazz vein.

For all his success, Benson's life has been shadowed by personal tragedy. He has lost three of his seven sons, one to kidney failure, one to crib death, and one to gunshot injuries stemming from a bar fight. His losses led to an unusual commission in 1998: he was asked by father Mohammed Al Fayed to write s song in commemoration of Dodi Al Fayed, who died along with his friend Princess Diana of England in a 1997 automobile crash in Paris. "During the writing, I asked my wife to come listen to what I had written," Benson was quoted as saying in *Jet.* "But when I got to certain parts, it became too difficult. My lips were trembling. I was thinking about my own losses and couldn't get past it. It stopped me cold."

Selected discography

George Benson/Jack McDuff, Prestige, 1965.
It's Uptown, Columbia, 1965.
Benson Burner, Columbia, 1966.
The George Benson Cookbook, Columbia, 1966.
Giblet Gravy, Verve, 1967.
The Shape of Things to Come, A&M, 1968.
The Other Side of Abbey Road, A&M, 1969.

Beyond the Blue Horizon, CTI, 1971.
White Rabbit, CTI, 1972.
Bad Benson, CTI, 1974.
Breezin', Warner Bros., 1976.
In Flight, Warner Bros., 1977.
Weekend in L.A., Warner Bros., 1978.
Livin' Inside Your Love, Warner Bros., 1979.
Give Me the Night, Warner Bros., 1980.
In Your Eyes, Warner Bros., 1983.
20-20, Warner Bros., 1984.
Twice the Love, Warner Bros., 1988.
Tenderly, Warner Bros., 1989.
Big Boss Band (with the Count Basie Orchestra), Warner Bros., 1990.
Love Remembers, Warner Bros., 1993.
That's Right, GRP, 1996.
Standing Together, GRP, 1998.

Sources

Books

Contemporary Musicians, volume 9, Gale, 1993.
Erlewine, Michael, *et. al, The All Music Guide to Jazz,* Miller Freeman, 1998.
Kernfeld, Barry, ed., *The New Grove Dictionary of Jazz,* St. Martin's, 1995.
Romanowski, Patricia, and Holly George-Warren, *The New Rolling Stone Encyclopedia of Rock & Roll,* Fireside, 1995.

Periodicals

Down Beat, October 1991.
Guitar Player, June 1999, p. 135.
Jet, September 7, 1998, p. 55.

—James M. Manheim

Billy Blanks

1955 (?)—

Martial arts champion, inventor of Tae-bo

Billy Blanks first earned a name for himself in the 1970s and 1980s, when he won a series of martial arts competitions. A seven-time world karate champion, he was captain of the U.S. Karate team, and won 36 gold medals in international competition. In 1980, he was captain of the U.S. Olympic Karate team. Later, Blanks worked in the Hollywood film industry, appearing in more than 20 films, including *Blood Fist* (1989), *Balance of Power* (1996), and *Kiss the Girls* (1997).

But Blanks is most famous as the originator of Tae-Bo, a unique fitness program that combines martial arts, boxing, and aerobics. For more than a decade, Blanks and his system were known only to a small circle of fans who worked out at his fitness center in Sherman Oaks, California. Blanks first became a household name in the late 1990s, when he launched his Tae-Bo exercise tapes through a series of nationally-broadcast "infomercials"—commercials that are similar to, and last as long as, regular television programs.

"Do you know Tae-Bo? If you watch television, it's a good bet you do," James A. Fussell wrote in the *Chicago Tribune*. "The fist-pumping, high-flying hybrid of kick boxing and aerobics created by actor and former karate champion Billy Blanks is all over the tube via infomercials." While the vast majority of infomercials fail, Blanks' Tae-Bo system became a hot fitness trend in late 1998, selling nearly a million videotapes in just six months.

According to the biography of Blanks available on the Tae-Bo website, he was able to accomplish all this "despite dyslexia which would impede his learning, poverty, an anomaly in his hip joints which would impair his movement, [and] a clumsiness which would earn him the taunts of his siblings and cause his coaches to think he would never amount to much."

Won Martial Arts Championships

Blanks was born the fourth of fifteen children, and raised in a poor, crime-ridden neighborhood in Erie, Pennsylvania. "All we heard was sirens," Blanks told Dan Jewel of *People Weekly*. His strict, hard-working parents—Isaac, a factory worker, and Mabeline, a homemaker—made sure that the children stayed out of trouble, though. "My father taught me that to get something out of life, you have to work for it," Blanks was quoted as saying in *People Weekly*.

Blanks had a difficult time at school; many years later, he was diagnosed as dyslexic. But his life changed when, at age 12, he saw Bruce Lee perform as Kato on the TV show "The Green Hornet." Blanks was captivated, and immediately signed up for karate lessons, which he paid for himself by working part-time as a garbage collector. "I was supposed to be the black sheep," he told Dan Jewel of *People Weekly*. "Karate gave me confidence." Blanks became a seventh degree black belt in Tae Kwon Do, the Korean form of karate; he also holds black belts in five other forms of martial arts.

By the time he was 20 years old, Blanks had married his high-school sweetheart, Gayle Godfrey. Godfrey was just 17, and had a two-year-old daughter, Shellie, from a previous relationship. The couple later had a son, Billy Jr. Blanks supported the family by working as a janitor, and later as an employee in a chemical plant. "It's an astonishing thing," Gayle told *People Weekly*. "A lot of men don't take care of their own children, let alone someone else's."

Meanwhile, he was a rising star in the martial arts community, winning state, national, and international championships. In 1975, he became the first Amateur Athletic Union Champion, a title he would win five times. A seven-time world karate champion, he was captain of the U.S. Karate team and won 36 gold medals in international competition. In 1980, he was captain of the U.S. Olympic Karate team. Two years later, he was inducted into the Karate Hall of Fame. Blanks also excelled as a boxer; in 1984, he became Massachusetts Golden Gloves

champion in the light-heavyweight class, and the Tri-State Golden Gloves Champion of Champions.

"I think of karate as a way of life—a way to learn self-discipline, self-control, and things like that—instead of as a way to beat up dozens of people," Blanks told D. C. Denison of the *Boston Globe* in 1986. As karate champion, however, Blanks has been challenged by people who expect Hollywood-style fighting. "Once 11 guys wanted to fight me at one time," he told the *Boston Globe*. "... I kicked the first guy in the chest, pretty hard, and the rest of them got scared and stopped."

Developed Tae-Bo Fitness Program

In 1988, Blanks moved his family to Los Angeles, determined to break into movies as martial-arts champion Bruce Lee had. Initially, Blanks worked as a bodyguard to actress Catherine Bach. Soon afterward, he landed a role in the 1989 film *Bloodfist*. Since then, he has appeared in more than 20 movies, including *Driving Force* (1989), *Lionheart* (1990), *The Last Boy Scout* (1991), *Balance of Power* (1996), and *Kiss the Girls* (1997). Blanks has also made several television appearances, including *S.O.F. Special Ops Force* (1997) and *The Parent 'Hood* (1997).

Meanwhile, in 1989, Blanks opened a small gym in Sherman Oaks, California, and began to develop his unique Tae-Bo system. His goal was to develop a fitness program that was as strenuous and enjoyable as martial arts, without the more traditional aspects that kept many women from participating. Blanks replaced bowing and uniforms with music and dance, and designed a fitness routine that combined stretching, boxing, weights, and karate.

In 1991 Blanks retired from martial arts competitions, deciding to concentrate on working in films and developing his fitness center. In 1995, the studio moved to a larger location, also in Sherman Oaks. "I've been teaching Tae-Bo for 11 years, and I've seen my studio go from 16 people to 16,000 people," Blanks told James A. Fussell of the *Chicago Tribune* in 1999. Tae-Bo remains a family business: Blanks' wife Gayle is his business manager, while daughter Shellie works as a trainer at the gym.

By 1997, Blanks had become one of the most sought-after fitness trainers in Hollywood. "Blanks is so in demand these days that celebs even deign to mix with the masses to punch-and-kick at the no-frills Billy Blanks World Training Center in Sherman Oaks, CA," Dan Jewel wrote in *People Weekly*. Despite Blanks' rising stardom, he still made time to teach eight classes a week at his center, Jewel wrote. At $9 each, the classes were so crowded that the fire department had to limit the number of participants, for safety reasons.

"He's like a teacher that you hate—but you love when you get an 'A,'" actress Lela Rochon, whom Blanks trained for her role in the action film *Knock Off*, was quoted as saying in *People Weekly*. "I revolve my life around it," actress Carmen Electra was quoted as saying in *People Weekly*. "... you never know who you're going to see. One day, LL Cool J was here, Queen Latifah was in a corner, and Alicia Silverstone was in class."

Launched Tae-Bo Videotapes

After more than ten years of teaching Tae-Bo at his fitness center in California, Blanks decided to launch the system nationally, using videotapes promoted through infomercials—a strategy known as "direct-response" in the marketing industry. The infomercials were an unqualified success: nearly a million videotapes were sold in just six months.

Later, Blanks made the unusual decision to promote the videos through both infomercials and a more traditional distribution channel—retail stores. "In most cases, direct-response campaigns and retail promotions never run simultaneously," Eileen Fitzpatrick wrote in *Billboard* magazine.

Blanks also promoted Tae-Bo through appearances on top television shows. In February of 1999, Blanks appeared on *ER*. "There was the brawny Billy Blanks, celebrity fitness dictator, playing himself and turning the emergency room into a high-kicking, heart-palpitating aerobathon," Ellen Warren and Teresa Wiltz wrote in the *Chicago Tribune*. Also in February, Blanks had a week-long stint on *the Oprah Winfrey show*. "If anyone hasn't yet heard of Billy Blanks or Tae-Bo, they will by the end of the month," Eileen Fitzpatrick wrote in *Billboard*. "... if Blanks' video series performs anything like some of the fiction titles featured on Winfrey's book club, it's sure to shoot to the top of the sales charts."

"We expect the Oprah show to double reorders for the titles," Larry Hayes, head of Ventura Distribution, was quoted as saying in *Billboard*. "The Tae-Bo people took an amazing risk by rolling out this product to retail before its direct-response campaign had peaked. But they felt there was no reason to hold it back. It's still the biggest seller in direct response and is driving retail sales."

"Blanks has single-handedly reignited the fitness category at retail," Eileen Fitzpatrick wrote in *Billboard* magazine. "Without a new star to drive sales, the genre has been rotting on the shelf. Blanks ... looks like he's the guy who can bring it back from the dead."

Blanks has denied the suggestion that Tae-Bo is just a fitness fad, soon to be replaced by the next big thing. "No way in the world," he told James A. Fussell of the *Chicago Tribune*. "Tae-Bo's been successful because I waited a long time before I introduced it to the public. Since I put this infomercial out, people think this is a new exercise. But it's not a new exercise."

While Tae-Bo has been a huge economic success, Blanks is "not just a guy who wants to make money," he told Dan Jewel of *People Weekly*. Instead, he sees his work as a crusade: "I tell [clients], 'If you want to sweat, go sit in a whirlpool. I want you to get some power, I want you to feel like you can overcome everything.' I tell them, 'Be a conqueror!'"

Sources

Periodicals

Billboard, Feb. 27, 1999, p. 62.
Boston Globe Magazine, June 8, 1986, p. 2.
Chicago Tribune, Feb. 23, 1999, p. 7; Feb. 15, 1999, p. 2.
People Weekly, Dec. 15, 1997, p. 79.

Other

Tae-Bo website, http://www.taebo.com/billy.html

—Carrie Golus

Jane Bolin

1908—

Judge

Although she never cared to think in these terms, Jane Bolin would often have her name followed with the descriptive, "first black woman to..." In her mind, she was simply following her life's path, pursuing goals in a profession she cared for deeply, not unlike any other man or woman, black or white. Still, the facts are undeniable that part of Bolin's life path involved opening doors which had been, until her arrival, closed to black women and so the description, while not necessarily welcome, is accurate. Jane Bolin was the first black woman to be graduate from Yale Law School, the first black woman to work as corporate counsel for the city of New York, the first black woman to be admitted to the Bar Association of the City of New York and most significantly, the first black woman judge in the United States. "Everyone else makes a fuss about it, but I didn't think about it, and I still don't," she told David Margolick of the *New York Times* in 1993. "I wasn't concerned about first, second or last. My work was my primary concern."

Born Jane Matilda Bolin on April 11, 1908 in Poughkeepsie, New Yorkshe was the youngest of four children born to Gaius C. Bolin, a lawyer and first black graduate of Williams College, and Matilda Ingram Bolin, a white

Englishwoman. Her mother had become ill when Bolin was young and died when she was eight years old. As a single parent her father devoted a great deal of time and energy to his children while simultaneously running his own small law practice in Poughkeepsie. It was in her father's office with the rows and rows of law books, that Bolin, an avid reader and excellent student, first thought of becoming a lawyer.

First Black Woman Graduate of Yale Law School

After high school in Poughkeepsie Bolin began attending Wellesley College in 1924, one of two black women to enter that year. She later recalled her life at Wellesley as a lonely time where she was ignored socially and received little encouragement from the faculty. As a senior, when she told her adviser about her plans to become a lawyer, she was sternly instructed to think of something else. There was no future for a black woman as a lawyer, she was told. Upon graduating in 1928 Bolin was named a "Wellesley Scholar" a distinction given to the top 20 women in their class.

In sharp contrast to her adviser at Wellesley, Bolin's father knew his daughter could become a lawyer—he just did not want her to. "He was very opposed to the idea at first," Bolin recalled to Judy Klemesrud of the *New York Times.* "He assumed I'd be a schoolteacher. He didn't think that women should hear the unpleasant things that lawyers have to hear." Bolin so feared her father's disapproval that she did not tell him her plans until she had already interviewed and was accepted by Yale Law School. With her father's reluctant blessing, Bolin went through the school and graduated in 1931, the first black woman to do so.

With law degree in hand Bolin affixed her name to the

front door of her father's Poughkeepsie practice until 1933 when her marriage to fellow lawyer, Ralph E. Mizelle took her to New York. The couple practiced law together until 1937 when Bolin applied for a position in the Office of the Corporation Counsel of the City of New York, the city's law office. Although initially dismissed during her interview for the position by an assistant, Corporation Counsel Paul Windell walked in the office and hired her on the spot, giving Bolin the distinction as the first black woman to become an Assistant Corporation Counsel. In this role Bolin was assigned to the Domestic Relations Court where she represented petitioners who could not afford their own lawyer.

First Black Woman Judge in the United States

Bolin had held the position of Assistant Corporation Counsel for two years when she was summoned by the office of New York's mayor, Fiorello LaGuardia, to meet the mayor at the New York City building of the World's Fair which had just opened. Concerned that someone had complained about her performance in the Corporation Counsel's office and the mayor was going to reprimand her, Bolin persuaded her husband to accompany her to the meeting. Her concern turned to surprise which then turned to numbness when she learned Mayor LaGuardia's intent was swear her in as a judge. The first black woman judge in the United States. The swearing in took place on a Saturday and Bolin took her place on the bench the following Monday. It would be a position she would hold for the next 40 years.

Bolin was assigned to the Domestic Relations Court, which in 1962 became known as the Family Court of the State of New York. This position gave Bolin a front row seat to virtually every aspect of legal trouble that could engage a New York family. From battered spouses and neglected children to paternity suits and, increasingly over her 40-year career, homicides committed by juveniles. "We always had homicides, but not in the numbers we have today," Bolin told Klemesrud of the *New York Times* at the time of her retirement. "I've never seen anything like this, the extent of this violence, never." Adding, "Sometimes, from the bench, I ask the children, `Why, why, why?,' and I never get a satisfactory answer. They look at you, they stare at you, and they don't say anything."

A Reluctant Retiree

While a justice Bolin also sought to bring about changes to the way things were handled in the New York legal bureaucracy. One change was the assignment of probation officers to cases without to race or religion. "When I came in, the one or two black probation officers handled only black families," she recalled to Klemesrud. "I had that changed." A second change was ensuring private child care agencies that received public funding would accept children regardless of ethnic background. "They used to put a big N or PR on the front of every petition, to indicate if the family was black or Puerto Rican," she told Klemesrud. Bolin had that changed as well.

In her own family life Bolin had a son, Yorke Bolin Mizelle, in 1941. In 1943 her husband died and she remained widowed until 1950 when she remarried Walter P. Offutt, Jr., a clergyman. He passed away in 1974 from lymphoma. Four years later, in 1978, Bolin reached the mandatory retirement age of 70 and was forced to step down from the bench, although she was very much opposed to the idea. She then became a member of the Regents Review Committee of for the New York State Board of Regents where she reviewed disciplinary cases.

In addition to her work on the bench Bolin served on the board of many agencies and organizations including the Child Welfare League, the National Board of the NAACP, the New York Urban League, the Dalton School, and Wiltwyck School for Boys, which she helped found with Eleanor Roosevelt and others. All activities that paralleled a lifetime of professional work designed to help people. "I've always done the kind of work I like," she admitted to Klemesrud. "I don't want to sound trite, but families and children are so important to our society, and to dedicate your life to trying to improve their lives is completely satisfying."

Sources

Periodicals

Jet, July 28, 1997, p. 19; July 27, 1998, p. 19.
New York Times, April 8, 1937, p. A-3; July 23, 1939, p. A-7; April 14, 1943, p. A-24; December 8, 1978, p. A-22; May 14, 1993, p. B-8.

Other

Additional information for this profile was obtained from the Rare Books and Manuscripts division of the Schomburg Center for Research in Black Culture.

—Brian Escamilla

James Brown

1951—

Television sports commentator and host

James Brown, known as "JB," is among the country's best television sports show hosts. As co-anchor of *FOX NFL Sunday,* along with numerous other shows and events, Brown has covered an unusually wide range of sports. He has moved beyond the realm of sports and hosted America's Black Forum and the prime-time home video showcase, "The World's Funniest!" Brown has the experience and talent to achieve success in whatever he pursues.

he could not compete directly with the name recognition or expertise of a Doctor J or Magic Johnson. Instead, he chose to pursue a career as a play-by-play commentator, anchor, and host. Most of these positions, however, were traditionally held by white men. In an article in *USA Today,* Brown remarked, "I don't have the marquee value ex-NBA players and coaches have, and I'm black. I've had to overcome both hurdles."

A former athlete whose professional career was cut short, Brown is respected for his excellent rapport with sports figures, poise, insight about the games and players, quick-wittedness, and adaptive ability to master virtually any sport. Brown approaches new assignments by reading as much as possible about his subject and consulting experts in the field. This type of extensive preparation has earned Brown the reputation as one of the hardest working and knowledgeable sports commentators in the business.

Although he is not the first African American to achieve stardom as a sportscaster, Brown is still something of a pioneer. Historically, almost all of the African Americans who worked in sports broadcasting were famous athletes or coaches within their particular sport. Brown realized that

Brown has tackled some sports that are considered foreign to African Americans, such as professional hockey. He has served for several years as the host of FOX's hockey pre-game and halftime shows. With his rigorous work ethic and sharp mind, he consistently excels. Describing his approach in *USA Today,* Brown said, "If you do your homework and become fundamentally conversant with the sport, you can understand what's happening on the ice and ask intelligent questions."

Inspired to Achieve

Born in Washington, D.C., in 1951, Brown's father died when he was very young. His mother, Mary Ann, raised

At a Glance . . .

Born James Brown February 25, 1951, in Washington, D.C. to John and Mary Ann Brown. *Education:* Harvard Univ., BA in American government, 1973.

Career: Drafted in fourth round by NBA's Atlanta Hawks, but cut from the team during his first season; worked in sales at Xerox for seven years, followed by one and a half years at Eastman Kodak; joined CBS as a college basketball analyst and NFL play-by-play announcer, 1984-94; joined the FOX network, 1994--; worked on boxing matches for HBO Sports, contributes to HBO's Real Sports with Bryant Gumbel, hosts World's Funniest! (home videos), and hosts nationally syndicated America's Black Forum.

Awards: Emmy Award for "Let Me Be Brave--A Special Climb of Kilimanjaro," National Academy of Television and Sciences (NATAS), 1992; inducted into the Harvard Hall of Fame, 1996; Sportscaster of the Year Award, Quarterback Club of Washington, 1996; Emmy Award as Outstanding Host of FOX NFL Sunday, 1999.

Addresses: *Office*—FOX Sports; 10201 West Pico Blvd., Los Angeles, CA 90035.

him and his four siblings--three older brothers and a sister--as a single parent. Brown considers his mother to be his primary influence and inspiration. By all accounts a strong parent, she required her children to focus on academic achievement. Athletic pursuits and social activities were considered secondary to academics, and homework was given top priority. Brown recounted an example of this to *USA Today,* "One time in high school we were practicing late at DeMatha, and my mother—we still call her `Sarge'—called coach Wooten. She called him off the court and told him he promised I'd be home by 7 p.m. to study. And he said, `You're right. James will be home soon.'"

Brown attended DeMatha Catholic High School, which is renowned for combining an excellent sports program with strong college-preparatory academics. He excelled in both areas. Under the guidance of Coach Morgan Wooten--an illustrious high-school coach who was nominated for the Basketball Hall of Fame--Brown became an All-Metropolitan and All-American basketball player. In addition to his mother, Wooten became an important mentor and influ-

ence for Brown and helped him to develop a strong work ethic.

Brown excelled in the classroom as well. In addition to being naturally intelligent, he was an avid reader who applied himself to his scholastic endeavors. Although he was recruited by many of the nation's top college basketball programs, Brown accepted an academic scholarship from Harvard University because of its traditions and its stimulating intellectual atmosphere. Brown's decision to attend Harvard was heavily influenced by his mother. As he remarked to *USA Today,* "When I got scholarship offers from everywhere, I thought about going to UCLA. But [Mary Ann] said, `No. It's Harvard, because to have long-term success, you've got to have the best education.'" Brown heeded his mother's advice and, many years later, he told *USA Today* that "I'd make the same decision again." He was a star athlete at Harvard, earning All-Ivy League honors every year after his freshman season. In 1973, Brown earned a bachelor of arts degree in American government.

Strengthened by Adversity

Drafted in the fourth round by the Atlanta Hawks, Brown was dealt a devastating blow when he was cut from the team early in his first season. "When I was cut from the Hawks, I cried like a baby," Brown told *USA Today.* "I cried for days. I couldn't believe it." Although his dream of becoming a professional athlete had been derailed, Brown refused to give up. As he told *USA Today,* "Even though I thought I should have made the team, something taught to me by my high school coach, Morgan Wooten, stuck with me. He always said, `The person who works the hardest usually succeeds the best.' And from that time on, I decided no one would outwork me." When Brown asked the coach of the Hawks, Cotton Fitzsimmons, why he had been cut from the team "He told me that I have a quality education to fall back on that the other guy doesn't have," he related to *USA Today.* "So I vowed never to let an opportunity go by that I wasn't prepared for."

For several years, Brown worked in sales at Xerox and Eastman Kodak. To maintain his interest in sports, he began doing some work for a local television station. As Brown remarked in the *Washington Post,* "I thought it would be nothing more than an avocation—just a way to wash ball out of my system. But the media bug kind of bit me." He started working as a play-by-play announcer for college and pro basketball games for local ABC and NBC affiliates. "The guy who helped me the most early was Rich Hussey at NBC," Brown told *USA Today.* In an interview with *Contemporary Black Biography,* he remarked that Hussey "wasn't afraid of offending me when he helped make me aware of some regional pronunciations. I was very grateful for his candor."

From 1984 until 1994, Brown worked for CBS as an NFL play-by-play announcer and basketball analyst. He also had the opportunity to work with esteemed sportscaster Frank Glieber on college and NBA basketball telecasts. Glieber talked about Brown in an interview with *USA Today,* "James has got a great deal of promise. He's extremely intelligent, with a strong knowledge of the game. His biggest drawback is his credentials in the eyes of the fans. When I say I'm working with James Brown, people say 'the singer?' At first they ask, 'who is this guy?' Then when they hear what he has to say, they really ask 'who is this guy?' All James needs to do now is to loosen up and let his personality take over more."

Attained Stardom at CBS

At CBS, Brown became a media star who was unafraid to take onchallenging assignments. He co-hosted the NCAA basketball championships, hosted freestyle skiing telecasts from the 1994 Winter Olympics, and narrated the Emmy Award-winning show "Let Me Be Brave—A Special Climb of Kilimanjaro." While working for CBS, Brown came to the realization that his talents were best suited for hosting and play-by-play announcing. In 1987, he became a play-by-play announcer for NFL telecasts. CBS Sports executive producer Ted Shaker told the *Washington Post,* "He's worked his tail off. It just didn't drop out of the sky into his lap. He's willing to make whatever sacrifices to get better. There's still a ways to go. He has tremendous capability. I just like him on the air. I trust him."

By the late 1980s, Brown had become only the second African American sportscaster—after Bryant Gumbel—to attain premier status on a national network. Speaking to the *Washington Post* in 1989, NBC football analyst Reggie Rucker said, "Right now, James is the flagship of the fleet. He makes all of us in the business very proud." Brown was well aware that few African Americans were given the opportunity to work as play-by-play announcers or studio anchors, and hoped to be an agent for change. As Brown remarked to the *Washington Post* in the early 1990s, "To my understanding it's been that way for a long time. I've continued to talk about it because maybe it will help sensitize people to the fact there are so few of us. By talking about it, and with the modest degree of success I'm having, I'm hoping it's going to change. In conversations I've had, I continue to hear the same old thing abouthow there's not a big enough pool [of minority broadcasters] to draw from. I think it's there and it depends on how aggressively you go after that pool. Also, there being so

few in the ranks, those of us who are here are very closely scrutinized. You have to understand that comes with the territory and accept it."

Switched to FOX

In 1994, the FOX network hired Brown as the co-host of *FOX NFL Sunday* with Terry Bradshaw, a retired Hall of Fame quarterback. In addition to Bradshaw, Brown was teamed with former Raiders All-Pro Howie Long and former Cowboys coach Jimmy Johnson, who was later replaced by Cris Collinsworth. Brown's role on the show is perhaps the most difficult because he must serve as an "air traffic controller." In other words, he must combine all elements of the show and do so in such a way that it appears effortless. The show proved to be a tremendously popular lead-in to Sunday afternoon football games on FOX.

In addition to his work on *FOX NFL Sunday,* Brown assumed the duties of the network's NHL hockey show in 1995. An avid boxing fan, he has also hosted boxing events on HBO. Brown has hosted "The World's Funniest!" home video show and America's Black Forum, contributed to Real Sports with Bryant Gumbel, and emceed a special show with figure skaters Nancy Kerrigan and Tonya Harding. On the show, Harding admitted to her role in a plot to injure Kerrigan so thatshe would be unable to compete in the 1994 Winter Olympics. Brown commented about the show in an interview with *USA Today,* "I still find it hard to believe she [Harding] didn't become aware of some snippet of information or some hint early on [of the conspiracy], although she was afraid and in an abusive relationship. What I do believe is how remorseful she is and how much she asks for forgiveness. She feels her life has been ruined....She says she has new people around her and has found religion, God. She says she's truly made peace with the whole issue and wants to go beyond it."

Brown is a deeply religious man who has been involved in a number of charitable organizations, including the Special Olympics, Big Brothers, Fellowship of Christian Athletes, Youth Life Foundation, All Stars Helping Kids, the Neimann-Pick Disease Foundation, and The Marrow Foundation. He has also received numerous awards and distinctions, including the 1996 Sportscaster of the Year Award from the Quarterback Club of Washington. In 1999, Brown won a Sports Emmy Award for his work on *FOX NFL Sunday.*

Through hard work and talent, Brown has achieved much in his life. As FOX executive producer Ed Goren remarked in the *Atlanta Journal and Constitution,* "He has become the voice and face of not just FOX sports, but FOX. When you think CBS, it's not just Jim Nantz but Dan Rather. At FOX, there is no nightly news, so J.B. really becomes a spokesman for the entire network." In the same article, Brown attributed his success to advice he had received early in his career, "I go back to some advice I got many years ago from Petey Green, who used to host a public affairs show in Washington, D.C. He told me if you come into this business, stay versatile. It'll keep you working long after others who concentrated on just one thing."

Sources

Periodicals

Atlanta Journal and Constitution, September 20, 1997, p.

H2.

USA Today, April 26, 1985, p. 3C; May 11, 1995, p. 3C; January 22, 1997, p. 2C; February 4, 1998, p. 2C.

Washington Post, June 22, 1989 p. B11; November 8, 1991, p. C2.

Other

Additional information for this profile was obtained from an interview with *Contemporary Black Biography* on June 23, 1999.

—Mark Baven

Steve Bullock

1936—

Non-profit organization executive

Steve Bullock's life epitomizes the incredible accomplishments of African Americans who surmount family hardships. The youngest of 22 children, Bullock overcame the burdens of history and poverty to rise into the upper echelons of the American Red Cross. In fact, when Elizabeth Dole stepped down as head of the national organization to pursue her own political aspirations in January of 1999, she selected Bullock to serve as acting president.

Bullock's father, William Henry Bullock, was born in North Carolina in 1865, the beginning of the Reconstruction era. Word of the emancipation of the slaves was slow to spread throughout the countryside, and Bullock's father was technically born into slavery. William Bullock eventually worked as a sharecropper in North Carolina. He was 72 years old when his youngest son, Steve, was born in July of 1936 in Enfield, NC, the youngest of 14 children born to William's third wife, Ida Mayo Bullock. Ida gave her youngest child the middle name of Delano in the hope that it would encourage him to emulate President Franklin Delano Roosevelt's commitment to the disadvantaged. It proved to be a name that Bullock would honor throughout his life.

At approximately the same time that Steve was born, his father was severely injured in a farming accident. Therefore, his mother became the sole financial and emotional support system for Bullock and his older siblings. Not surprisingly, Bullock's mother proved to be one of his greatest sources of inspiration. "Just seeing her make something out of nothing made me determined to go out and do something for myself and others," Bullock commented in *Reflections Magazine*. "She was really a driver," he added in an interview with Pat Jenkins in *Kaleidoscope Magazine*. Bullock recalled his mother's response when she learned that he had graduated fifth in his high school class of 42: "Well," she declared, "that's what happens when you just do enough to get by."

Dedicated Career to Public Service

Like many people of his generation, Bullock was greatly influenced not only by his mother's incredible work ethic, but also by racism. Having picked cotton and peanuts, Bullock was determined to attend college in order to escape the sharecropper's lifestyle. He attended Virginia Union University and focused on a life of public service. "My calling," Bullock explained to Courtland Milloy of the

At a Glance . . .

Born Steve Bullock in July 1936, in Enfield, NC; son of Ida Mayo Bullock and William Henry Bullock; married to Doris Kelly Bullock ; children: Eric, Brian, Kelly. *Education:* Virginia Union University, BA; University of St. Thomas, St. Paul, MN, MBA; Georgia State University, graduate work in urban administration.

Career: American Red Cross, 1962-, including assistant manager, Washington, D.C. chapter, 1973; executive director, St. Paul Area chapter, manager, Minnesota-Wisconsin Division, 1976-82; chief executive officer, Greater Cleveland Chapter, 1982-98; acting president, 1998-.

Selected memberships: Association of MBA Executives; American Society for Training and Development; NAACP; Urban League; Alpha Phi Alpha Fraternity.

Awards: President's Award for Employee Excellence in Management, American Red Cross, 1997; Black Professional of the Year, Black Professional Association, Cleveland, 1997.

Addresses: *Offices*–American Red Cross, Greater Cleveland Chapter, 3747 Euclid Avenue, Cleveland, OH 44115-2596; American Red Cross, National Headquarters, 1621 N. Kent Street, Arlington, VA 22209-2106.

Washington Post, "came out of seeing so much suffering in my life, and I became determined to spend my life trying to relieve that suffering wherever I found it and whatever the cause may be."

After graduating from Virginia Union with degrees in history and sociology, Bullock was drafted. During his tour of duty, he spent most of his time in Niagara Falls, New York and also served in Vietnam. Following his discharge from the Army, he joined the American Red Cross as a case worker on military installations in Europe and Southeast Asia. Bullock suddenly found himself doing exactly what he envisioned, traveling internationally and helping others.

Joined the American Red Cross

Throughout his career with the Red Cross, Bullock gained a reputation as a caring man who helped to build bridges between people. As Dr. Marvin A. McMickle, his pastor and friend from the Antioch Baptist Church in Cleveland, explained in a discussion with Tom Pope and Paul Clolery of the *NonProfit Times,* "He has an interactive ability to bring people together." Bullock used his talents to direct special Red Cross international projects and, in 1968, visited American prisoners of war in Southeast Asia as a member of a Red Cross team.

From 1976 to 1982, Bullock served as executive director and manager of the Minnesota-Wisconsin division. He then became chief executive officer of the Greater Cleveland Chapter in 1982. Under Bullock's guidance, the Cleveland chapter evolved from an agency which offered only CPR training and disaster relief to one that provided smoke detectors for low-income residents, developed emergency evacuation plans, and trained disadvantaged people for careers in medicine. He successfully drew the American Red Cross national convention to Cleveland and, in 1998, brought in Elizabeth Dole for a fund-raising event.

Bullock was an active member of several local organizations, including the Mayor's Black on Black Crime Commission and Leadership Cleveland. During his tenure as executive director of the Greater Cleveland Chapter, Bullock tripled the organization's funding, built a new headquarters, and significantly increased the amount of donations received from the African American community. He also cultivated relationships with the national leadership team and worked closely with them on strategic organizational issues. In 1988, Bullock served as chairman of the President's Advisory Council for the Red Cross, a group of senior Red Cross field executives which counsels management on issues facing the organization. In 1995 Elizabeth Dole, the national head of the Red Cross, appointed Bullock to lead the 1996 National American Red Cross Marketing and Fund-raising Campaign. The American Red Cross honored Bullock with the President's Award for Employee Excellence in Management in 1997.

Bullock's professional success can be attributed to several factors. Colleagues note his effectiveness in hiring qualified people to manage the day-to-day operations of his organization and empowering them to lead, thereby freeing himself to raise public awareness of the Red Cross and its goals. His belief in a Supreme Being and his willingness to accept the consequences of his own actions are also cited as important factors. When he's not working with the Red Cross, Bullock enjoys playing golf and listening to jazz.

Sources

Periodicals

Clevelandlife, March 1991.
Cleveland Live.
Cleveland Plain Dealer, January 24, 1999, p. B1, 3.

Kaleidoscope, August/September, 1996.
NonProfit Times, February 1999.
Reflections Magazine.
Sun Press, January 28, 1999.
Washington Post, March 24, 1999, p. B1, 4.

Other

Additional information for this profile was obtained from American Red Cross press releases.

—Lisa S. Weitzman

Karen Clark-Sheard

19(?)(?)—

Gospel vocalist

Gospel singer Karen Clark-Sheard has performed with her older sisters since she was six years old. The Clark sisters, Jacky, Denise, Elbernita (Twinkie), Dorinda, and Karen, grew up in Detroit and learned to sing from their mother, the legendary gospel performer Mattie Moss-Clark. As a performing group, the Clark Sisters have won two Dove Awards, two Gospel Music Workshop of America Excellence Awards, a Stellar Award, and a National Association for the Advancement of Colored People Award. They have also been nominated for three Grammy Awards and five Stellar Awards.

In 1998, Clark-Sheard released her first solo album, *Finally Karen . . . Live!* On this album, she sang "The Safest Place" with her daughter Kierra and also performed a duet with Faith Evans on the song "Nothing Without You." The album included a new version of the traditional gospel song "Balm in Gilead" and "Just For Me," a ballad contributed by Boyz II Men, Clark-Sheard's sisters also performed an arrangement of "Jesus Is A Love Song." The *Cleveland Call and Post* remarked that *Finally Karen* was," a blessing to the Body of Christ which spans the bridge between secular and sacred with faithful love in equal parts for gospel, pop and R & B fans alike."

In 1996, Clark-Sheard performed with Kirk Franklin, Hezekiah Walker, and Donald Lawrence on the song "Don't Give Up," a recording first released on the *Don't Be A Menace* movie soundtrack. Proceeds from the song were donated to the effort to rebuild African American churches throughout the United States that had been destroyed by arson fires. Clark-Sheard's performance on "Don't Give Up" attracted the interest of Hiram Hicks, president of Island Black Records, and he offered her a recording contract. Embarking upon a solo career was a difficult decision for Clark-Sheard. She consulted with her sisters and her husband, Reverend John Drew Sheard, before making her decision. In 1997, Clark-Sheard signed a contract with Island Black Records.

Proponents of traditional gospel music have criticized Clark-Sheard's unique style, while others have praised the contemporary flavor of her music and the beauty of her singing. The *Portland Skanner* used the words "angelic" and "anointed" to describe Clark-Sheard's vocal skills. In *Billboard,* her voice was likened to "a thing unleashed." The *Detroit Free Press* called Clark-Sheard's vocal stylings "velvety" and "soul-stirring."

In 1998, *Finally Karen* won a Soul Train Lady of Soul Award for best gospel album. It also received a Grammy nomination. That same year, Clark-Sheard performed with other notable gospel artists at the six-day Gospel Music Workshop of America gathering in Philadelphia. At the 1999 Stellar Awards, she won awards for Female Vocalist of the Year, Contemporary Female Vocalist of the Year, and Music Video of the Year. Her daughter also captured a Stellar Award for Children's Performance of the Year. In 1999, Clark-Sheard participated in a one-hour program, "Verity Records' Women Of Worship Gospel 1999," which celebrated African American history through gospel music and inspirational readings. She also performed in a Broadway play, *Mr. Right Now!*

Selected discography

Finally Karen . . . Live!, Island Black Records, 1998.

Sources

Periodicals

Billboard, August 2, 1997, p. 45; October 25, 1997, p. 56; August 29, 1998, p. 61; September 19, 1998; February 6, 1999, p. 27.
Cleveland Call and Post, May 7, 1998, p. 1C.
Detroit Free Press, June 19, 1998.
Ebony, April 1998; August 1998, pp. 74-76.
Rhythm and Blues Entertainment News, November 8, 1997.
The Skanner (Portland, OR), November 19, 1997, p. 8.
Tri-State Defender, November 12, 1997, p. 5.

Other

Additional information for this profile was obtained from Island Black Records and from the *Charisma* Website at http://www.strang.com/cm/stories/cu297220.htm; the *LA Gospel Festival* Website at http://www.lagospel.com/karenc.htm; and *Plugged Music* Website at http://www.pluggedmusic.com/karenc.htm.

—Eileen Daily

Suzan D. Johnson Cook

1957—

Cleric

From the time she was 13-years-old, Dr. Suzan Johnson Cook knew that she wanted to be a minister. Born on January 28, 1957 in the Bronx, Johnson initially pursued a career in television before entering the ministry. Having revitalized the Mariners' Temple in lower Manhattan, she then founded the Bronx Christian Fellowship, one of the Bronx's fastest growing new churches.

Johnson Cook's strength seems rooted, at least in part, in her strong family background. As she described to Chrisena Coleman of *Belle,* her family was highly focused and goal-oriented. "I came from a family with southern roots and hard-working parents who provided the best they could, and my brother and I built on that foundation. In our upbringing, you show your appreciation by doing well and that's what is important. It was the strong foundation that really made a difference...I am the product of an entire village that encouraged me to be the best I could be without comparing myself to others. I received a lot of nurturing in my formative years and adult life. When you are surrounded by achievement, you tend to achieve. When you are surrounded by love, you are loving. I am the totality of many people." As she further detailed in an interview with Louisa Kamps of the *New York Post,*

"The ethic around me was always, 'It may be against all odds, but if the moment's right, you can do it—no one can shake you.'"

A cornerstone of Cook's foundation was the Church. During her years at Boston's Emerson College in the early 1970s, she was greatly influenced by Katie Cannon, a minister who taught at Temple University. Through Cannon's example, Cook decided to pursue a career in the ministry. While at Emerson College, she focused on studying communications and graduated with a bachelor's degree in speech in 1976. Drawing on her educational training, Cook worked from 1977 until 1980 as a television producer and on-air host in Boston, Miami, and Washington, DC. She also toured with an African American theatrical group and worked in public relations. It was not until she was a communications consultant with Operations Crossroads Africa in the late 1970s that Cook seriously considered the ministry.

Entered the Baptist Ministry

In 1981, Cook began to become more active in church activities. From 1981 until 1983, she assisted the executive

At a Glance . . .

Born Suzan D. Johnson on January 28, 1957 in New York City. Married to Ronald Cook; children: Samuel David and Christopher Daniel. *Education:* Emerson College, Boston, MA, BS, Speech, Cum Laude, 1976; Columbia University Teachers College, New York, MA, 1978; Union Theological Seminary, New York, M.Div., 1983; United Theological Seminary, Dayton, OH, D.Min., 1990.

Career: Television producer, on-air host, WBZ-Boston, WPLG-Miami, WJLA-Washington, DC, 1977-80; public relations officer, Bronx-Lebanon Hospital Center, Bronx, NY, 1980-81; adjunct professor, New York Theological Seminary, 1988-; domestic policy analyst, The White House, 1993-94; senior pastor, Mariners' Temple Baptist Church, New York, 1983-96; executive director, Multi-Ethnic Center, New York, 1985-; senior pastor/CEO, Bronx Christian Fellowship, Bronx, NY, 1996-.

Memberships: First vice president, New York Coalition of 100 Black Women, 1996-97; advisory board member, President's Initiative On Race & Reconciliation, 1997-98.

Selected awards: Woman of Conscience Award, National Council of Women, United Nations, 1989; Martin Luther King Award, CBS TV, 1995; One of top 15 Women in Ministry, *Ebony*, November 1997; Visionary Leaders Award, SOBRO, 1997.

Addresses: Executive Towers, 1020 Grand Concourse, Suite 6-F, Bronx, NY 10451.

minister of the American Baptist Churches of Metropolitan New York with various projects involving media coverage and development for area churches. She also completed a masters of divinity degree at the Union Theological Seminary in New York. In October of 1983, Cook assumed the senior pastorate at Mariners' Temple Baptist Church in Manhattan. She also became the first African American woman to be elected to a senior pastorate in the American Baptist Churches in its 200-year history.

At the time Cook inherited the congregation, the church building was dilapidated and membership had dwindled to only 15 people. Most of these people, according to Mark Lowery of *Newsday Magazine*, were "authentic 'have-nots' in one of the world's richest cities." As Cook recalled to Ralph Gardner in *Cosmopolitan*, "I started out with a heavy evangelical campaign, climbing stairs, knocking on doors." Within six months, membership in the congregation had reached 250 members. By 1994, membership at Mariners' Temple had blossomed to 1,000 parishioners in what had become one of Manhattan's fastest growing churches. Cook not only conducted services on Sunday, but also held lunch-hour services each Wednesday for the City Hall-Chinatown business community. These services became known as the "lunch hour of power."

One of Cook's principal objectives was to give members of her congregation a sense of hope. She believed that education and literacy were the keys to success that would allow her parishioners to control and change their lives. Towards this end, Cook sought to provide her congregation with what Gardner termed a "survival support system," to which they could turn for everything from tutoring to an after-school snack. She established a home for the mentally disabled and reached out to Manhattan's politically powerful Chinese community. She also directed Black Women in the Ministry, a program sponsored by the New York City Mission Society that was designed to encourage other African American women to pursue the ministry.

Cook's energy and charisma served as a strong motivational force and attracted many new followers to her parish. Carl Flemister, noted in a discussion with *Cosmopolitan* that, "She allows herself to be a conduit through which the mysterious power of God passes on to other people." Using a touch of stagecraft to enliven her sermons and blessed with a contagious sense of power, Cook was able to relate well with members of her congregation. As she explained to the *New York Post*, "Preaching to economic groups that tend to have low-esteem issues, I try to stir up the gifts that are in them. I like to do creative, non-traditional things…I have felt empowered and have empowered other people." As a fellow minister remarked in *Ebony*, "She is better than anyone I know in relating the Gospel to the present-day needs of people."

Founded Bronx Christian Fellowship

In 1996, after 13 years as pastor, Cook left her ministry at Mariners' Temple and decided to start a new congregation in the Bronx. As she explained to David Gonzalez of the *New York Times*, "I wanted to embrace the community which had produced and nurtured me." While waiting for a new church building to be constructed, Cook conducted services on Tuesday nights at the Bronx Museum of the Arts and on Thursdays at the Epworth United Methodist Church. Her new congregation, the Bronx Christian Fellowship, dedicated its new church building on March 23, 1997. In addition to its Sunday worship services, the Bronx Christian Fellowship sponsored various inter-generational programs including a lunch-hour bible study, a children's play date, Sunday school, a men's fellowship ministry, and an extensive music ministry. "Our ministry," Cook affirmed in *Community News,* "reaffirms that God is at the center of our lives and we acknowledge that there is more than an emotional response to faith. When we are strong then our communities can be strong. Bronx Christian Fellowship serves as a catalyst for growth on all levels, spiritual, intellectual, emotional, and social. Faith is best experienced when our mind, bodies, and souls are all spiritually fed."

As Cook's return to the Bronx indicated, a belief in a strong community is one of the driving forces in her life. Her Bronx community sustained and nourished her as a child. "I remember the energy of our community," Cook related to Michael Allen of the *Daily News,* "as if we were all moving as one wave, not waves clashing against each other. We had a common purpose, a common cause, and we worked toward making it happen...It was a spiritual movement." Cook noted in a discussion with Lowery in *Newsday Magazine* that, from the time of slavery "The black preacher has always had the nod to be a public spokesman....[T]hey must constantly decide whether to act in the best interests of their communities or sell out. If you decide to represent your community, that means everywhere – in the White House, the courthouse and the jailhouse."

On many levels, Cook's life has exemplified a commitment to building strong communities. In the fall of 1985, she founded the Multi-Ethnic Center. This after-school program for community youth and their families promotes excellence in education, self-esteem, career/life skills preparation, and the building of neighborhood partnerships. By funneling the boundless energy of children into creative activities like drama and dance, the center has promoted inter-ethnic dialogue within the surrounding community and helped to introduce performing arts into a culturally-deprived area.

Assumed Local and National Responsibilities

In 1990, Mayor David Dinkins appointed Cook as the first female chaplain of the New York City Police Department. As chaplain of the police force, she provided spiritual counseling to all members of the department and their families. Cook was often summoned to the scene of police incidents and was on call for emergencies at all times. She also performed the invocations and benedictions at police department ceremonies and was frequently invited to attend the personal events of department employees and their families. As Cook reflected in a conversation with R.A. Cheryl Acosta of *Civilians,* serving as a police chaplain drew upon her faith in ways that were different from her traditional ministry. "I find it a real challenge," she noted, "to translate a spiritual message into a practical one."

In 1993, Cook was selected to serve as a Fellow on the White House Domestic Policy Council. While in Washington, she worked with an assistant to President Bill Clinton on issues such as violence, homelessness, and community empowerment and also assisted with conference planning and speech writing for the President. She also served with the Department of Housing and Urban Development Secretary on Faith Initiatives from 1994 until 1997.

Cook was appointed to a one-year term on President Clinton's National Advisory Board on Race in 1997. As envisioned by Clinton, the panel would propose policy solutions to heal racial tensions as a necessary step in preparing the country adequately for the twenty-first century. As with many African Americans, Cook was no stranger to racism. When her parents moved to their Bronx neighborhood, they integrated the predominantly Italian and Jewish area. Cook vividly recalled a childhood experience. "I was excited about my first day of school," she reminisced with William Douglas of *Newsday,* "and I invited another young lady to sit next to me on the school bus, and she said, 'I can't sit next to you.' I said why? 'Because you're black...my mother said I can't sit next to one of you.'" This moment, she concluded, "was the beginning of what the rest of my life was going to present...The seeds of racism were already planted." As she remarked to Gonzalez in the *New York Times,* "In the life of every African-American there is a turning point when you recognize there is a difference."

Cook ultimately agreed to serve on the President's race board because she fervently believed that race relations was the most critical issue facing America. While she readily admitted that she did not think the panel would be capable of erasing centuries of fear and distrust, she did believe that its formation would be, according to Gonzalez, "a sign that the time has come to begin talking about issues glossed over by others who feel that civil rights is just a lesson in a history class and that affirmative action has run its course." As Cook explained to Douglas in *Newsday,* she hoped that "a healing process will happen out of our pain and growth." Moreover, she firmly believed that the clergy needed to play a critical role in this transformation.

"If the faith community is going to ever be a transforming agent in this society," Cook was quoted as saying in the Boston Globe, "we've got to get beyond that 11 o'clock service and the church's four walls and go places that aren't comfortable." As the board concluded its work, Cook pushed for a permanent race council. Such a body, she stressed to Ann Scales of the *Boston Globe,* "would bring sustaining power to race matters and make it harder for future presidents to disband the panel without being accused of abandoning the goal of racial harmony."

Expanded into Video and Print Ministry

Cook founded Sujay Ministries, an audio and video ministry designed to meet the needs of urban professionals and the youth. In 1994 she also established JONCO Productions, which is designed to promote Cook's oral, video, and written motivational works and concepts. Cook has also published five books in her efforts to reach a larger audience. Realizing that her female parishioners had needs that were often not specifically addressed in her general sermons, Cook compiled *Sister to Sister: Devotions for and from African-American Women,* a varied collection of real-life tales, in 1995. "There's always been the tradition of African-American oral storytelling," Cook told Kamps, "and my hope is that women can see themselves in the other women's stories and find strength from that."

Cook further expanded upon this theme in *Sister Strength,* which was released in 1998. This collection addressed relevant issues confronting women, including spousal abuse, aging, self-esteem, survival in corporate America, marriage and parenting, grief, stress, spiritual renewal, positive thinking, and self-reliance. As the trade review mentioned, "Connecting faith to real-life issues, *Sister Strength* celebrates the human spirit and a woman's ability to find joy in spite of pain, faith in the midst of uncertainty, and hope that overcomes despair. A devotional for and from African-American women that will encourage all women to fulfill their God-given calling in life." Not content to rest on her laurels, Cook declared to Yvonne Delaney of the *Amsterdam News* that "[m]y goal is to continue using my God-given gift to motivate women to believe that they are queens and that they can do and have anything by putting their talents and resources to good use. I want to raise the level of women's consciousness and take them to a higher level in the next millennium."

Cook is a strong, committed woman who is devoted to issues of race, religion, and community. Motivation and empowerment are the common themes that cohesively bind her efforts together. She is perceived as a leader both within the lay and religious communities, and some believe that she may eventually run for elected office. As she related in *Belle,* "I am a confident, courageous and capable woman. I have committed my life to a mission of seeking justice for people. I am seeking to bring out the best in people so they will soar to their highest. I am a pastor, urban practitioner, civil rights activist, wife, mother, daughter, author and public speaker. I am one who believes I've been blessed by God in order to be a blessing to others. I seek to use my gift in places that will honor and affirm God and other people. I am constantly growing, achieving and evaluating my life." Cook will certainly continue to inspire all those whom she touches to do the same.

Selected writings

Wise Women Bearing Gifts: Joys & Struggles of their Faith, Judson, 1988.

Preaching in Two Voices: Sermons On the Women in Jesus' Life, Judson, 1992.

Sister to Sister: Devotions for and from African-American Women, Judson, 1995.

Too Blessed To Be Stressed: Words of Wisdom for Women on the Move, Nelson, 1998.

Sister Strength: A Collection of Devotions for and from African-American Women, Nelson, 1998.

Sources

Periodicals

Amsterdam News, December 24-30, 1998.
Belle, Winter 1998, pp. 63, 72.
Boston Globe, May 21, 1998. p. A9; June 19, 1998, p. A3.
Carillon, November/December 1998.
Civilians, Vol. 61, Issue 5, 1998, p. 10.
Community News, March 24-April 6, 1997.
Cosmopolitan, December 1987, p. 243.
Courier-Journal, June 2, 1998, pp. B1, 5.
Daily News, June 29, 1996, p. 16; July 13, 1997; April 5, 1998, p. 11.
Ebony, March 1996; November 1997, pp. 102-9; May 1998.
Essence, July 1994, p. 44.
Heart and Soul, July/August 1998, p. 70.
Jet, June 30, 1997, p. 38.
Newsday, November 18, 1990; July 13, 1997, p. A8.
New Voice of New York, January 21-27, 1999.
New York Post, February 6, 1996, p. 33.
New York Times, June 21, 1997, p. A23.
Upscale, December/January 1999.

Other

Additional information for this profile was obtained from the Between Sisters Web Site, JONCO Productions Press

Releases, the United States Information Agency Web Site, and the White House Web Site.

—Lisa S. Weitzman

Charles S. Dutton

1951—

Actor

Charles S. Dutton liked to joke that he went "from jail to Yale." He is certainly the only star of a television series who ever did hard time in a state penitentiary, the only artist to leapfrog from the meanest streets in Baltimore to a prestigious Ivy League drama school, and from there to stardom on stage and screen. Dutton is best known as the character Roc on the FOX Network television show of the same name. He has also received some of the best roles available to African American actors in stage plays by the Pulitzer Prize-winning author August Wilson. As John Stanley noted in the *San Francisco Chronicle,* Dutton "has come to symbolize how the American dream can be ripped in half--but then pasted back together."

"By all odds, Charles Dutton should be dead," wrote Kenneth R. Clark in the *Chicago Tribune.* "The life he was born to lead afforded hundreds of opportunities for an early demise, and he took advantage of most of them." Dutton has conceded that he has spent a dozen years of his life behind bars, if he includes his years in reform school. "At one time, prison was all I knew," the actor admitted in the *San Francisco Chronicle.* "I was a hell raiser, and I'd come to enjoy it. The other prisoners would

have scowls on their faces each morning, but I always had a smile. I was the kind who'd never start a fight, but I'd always finish it. There came the time when I envisioned myself doing something with the rest of my life. Something inside me told me that I wasn't going to be a hell raiser forever."

On *Roc,* Dutton portrayed a law-abiding, hard-working citizen with a blue collar job, modest ambitions, and an intolerance for criminals. The show tackled tough issues such as urban crime and its effect on city residents, and Dutton helped to craft the scripts from his own firsthand experiences. "*[Roc]* had to be grounded in a foundation of reality," he asserted in the *San Francisco Examiner.* "I'm not one to criticize comedy shows. But I was determined that this show would not be like any show before it. The emotions are real. The violence is real. The danger has to be real. Let's not play at it."

Dutton was born the second of three children on January 30, 1951, in Baltimore, Maryland. He and his family lived in a public housing project just south of the Maryland Penitentiary, one of the toughest prisons in the nation. "I could see it from my bedroom," Dutton recalled in *USA*

At a Glance . . .

Born January 30, 1951, in Baltimore, MD; son of a laborer; married Debbi Morgan (an actress), 1989, divorced 1994. *Education:* Hagerstown Junior College, A.A., 1976; Towson State University, B.A., 1978; Yale University, M.A., 1983.

Career: Actor, 1978–. Principal stage appearances include roles in *Ma Rainey's Black Bottom,* 1984; *Joe Turner's Come and Gone,* 1988; and *The Piano Lesson,* 1990. Principal motion picture appearances include roles in *Crocodile Dundee II,* 1988; *Alien 3,* 1992; *The Distinguished Gentleman,* 1992; *Menace II Society,* 1993; *Rudy,* 1993; *Surviving the Game,* 1994; *A Low Down Dirty Shame,* 1995; *Get On the Bus,* 1996; *A Time to Kill,* 1996; *Mimic,* 1998; *Blind Faith,* 1998; *Black Dog,* 1998; *Cookie's Fortune,* 1999; and *Random Hearts,* 1999. Principal television appearances include the title role in *Roc,* broadcast on FOX, 1991-95; *Homicide: Life on the Street,* 1996; *Full Time Felon,* 1997; *True Women* (miniseries), 1997; and *The '60s* (miniseries), 1999. Made debut as a television director on *Full Time Felon,* 1997.

Awards: Drama Desk Award, Theater World Award, and Tony Award nomination, all 1985, all for *Ma Rainey's Black Bottom;* Tony Award nomination, 1991, for *The Piano Lesson.*

Addresses: c/o Twentieth Century-Fox Television, 5746 Sunset Blvd., Los Angeles, CA 90028.

Today. "In my neighborhood, more guys went to prison than school." The product of a broken home, Dutton grew up strong and aggressive. Even his nickname bore evidence of the trouble to come. "When I was a kid, we had rock fights," he explained in the *Chicago Tribune.* "My gang would line up on one side of the street and another gang would line up on the other side, and we'd let fly. I was always out front, leading the charge, and ... get my head busted about twice a month. As a result, the guys started calling me 'Rockhead.' Somewhere along the line, the 'k' and the 'head' got dropped and it's been Roc ever since."

Dutton had a nickname that would follow him to stardom, but several years would pass before he ever appeared on stage. Even though his family eventually moved out of the projects, he still got into trouble regularly and was in and out of reform school from the age of twelve. "I quit school in the seventh grade, not because I couldn't make it academically, but because I thought there was more happening on the street corner," he declared in the *Detroit Free Press.* "In my generation, you were expected to go to jail. All my buddies went, and all the guys we looked up to went."

At the age of 17, "Roc" Dutton fulfilled that expectation. "A guy came at me in a fight and stabbed me eight times and I killed him," he stated matter-of-factly in *USA Today.* Convicted of manslaughter, he was sent to the penitentiary in 1967 but released on parole in less than two years. In 1969 he was sent back to jail for possession of deadly weapons. A three-year sentence became an eleven-year sentence when he was convicted for assaulting a prison guard. By the mid-1970s, Dutton found himself looking at a long stretch in a violent, overcrowded urban prison.

"Prison Saved My Life"

Dutton does not shrink from his memories of those desperate years in jail. "I'm neither proud nor am I ashamed," he disclosed in the *San Francisco Chronicle.* "As I see it now, prison saved my life." Dutton took his penchant for trouble making with him to jail, joined the Black Panthers and leftist movements, and quarreled with guards and other inmates. On one occasion, he refused to work and was sent into solitary confinement. The *Chicago Tribune's* Clark described the conditions: "Solitary confinement meant a 5-by-7-foot cell with a sink, but no bed and no commode. The latter consisted of a hole in the floor [that] vindictive guards could back up at will, flooding the cell ankle-deep in sewage. Prisoners locked naked therein were fed once every three days and were allowed 'one piece of reading material,' though the only light by which to read was that which seeped under the door."

Dutton had grabbed a book from his cell on the way to solitary. It was a collection of short plays by African American playwrights that had been sent to him by a girlfriend. Dutton had never read a play and had never seen one performed. The book was his only companion for three days, however, so he read all of the plays. The one that affected him most deeply was *Day of Absence* by Douglas Turner Ward. "It's about the day all the blacks in a small Southern town decided not to come to work and the whites realized they couldn't live without them," Dutton described in the *Chicago Tribune.* "It's played by a black cast in white-face and it's hilarious. I read it over and over and told myself, 'When I get out of here, I'm going to stage this.'" Dutton added, "I found my humanity in that cell and I was a changed man when I got out. The prison officials all thought I'd gone crazy, but they let me put on the play."

Dutton formed a theater group in the prison and prepared the play for presentation at a talent show. "Doing the play before a sea of very hard men, I felt this eerie kind of power," the actor observed in the *San Francisco Examiner*. "I could make them quiet, I could make them think. It was the only thing positive I had at that time in my life, the only immediate remedy for prison life. I suddenly knew what I was born to do."

Danger still threatened, however. Some weeks after Dutton had established a regular theater workshop in the prison, he was stabbed by a fellow inmate. The wound was severe, puncturing Dutton's lung. He was hospitalized for two months and underwent several operations. Dutton recalled in the *Los Angeles Times* that the long recuperation period gave him time to think. Although the unspoken code of the prison called for Dutton to exact revenge, he decided that he was finished with violence. Dutton maintained, "I told myself: 'If I live through this, I'm retiring from this world of stupidity.'"

Earned Degree in Theater

When he recovered, Dutton was sent to another penitentiary, this one in western Maryland. There he was a model prisoner, earning his high school equivalency diploma with good grades. He persuaded the warden to allow him to take courses at the nearest junior college, and in 1976—the same year he was paroled for the last time—he received an Associate of Arts degree. He returned to Baltimore and finished his college education at Towson State University, majoring in theater.

A professor at Towson State persuaded Dutton to apply to the prestigious Yale Drama School in New Haven, Connecticut. Dutton was skeptical, but he paid the application fee and took the train north for an audition. He was baffled when he found out he had been accepted. "I was afraid to leave my apartment for fear that something would prevent me from getting to Yale. That some twist of irony would destroy me at the very moment that life was turning toward the better," Dutton recounted in the *San Francisco Chronicle*.

Though irony did not intervene, Lloyd Richards and August Wilson did. As a student at Yale, Dutton worked closely with Richards, the longtime dean of the drama school. Dutton also met playwright Wilson, who began to create characters for him in works-in-progress. One such

work was *Ma Rainey's Black Bottom,* the story of several jazz musicians in the 1920s. Dutton took a role in the play during repertory performances at Yale, then went with the show when it opened on Broadway. Dutton's work in that drama earned him his first Tony Award nomination. More importantly, it paved the way for parts in other August Wilson works, including *Joe Turner's Come and Gone* and *The Piano Lesson.*

By the time *The Piano Lesson* had its Broadway debut in 1990, Charles Dutton was a stage star. He had also worked sporadically in television, appearing on *Miami Vice* and *Cagney & Lacey,* and had taken some supporting roles in films. Still, he preferred live theater with its energy and audience response. "I never imagined myself working in television or doing a sitcom," Dutton noted in the *San Francisco Examiner.* "I was reluctant because I didn't want to come to Los Angeles as another hired hand on a television show." In the New Orleans *Times-Picayune* he pointed out, "When you go to Yale Drama School and you're trained in the classics, you think you just want to do *King Lear* and *Othello* your entire life. Until you have to pay your rent."

From the Stage to the Big and Small Screens

Television producer Stan Daniels caught Dutton's acclaimed performance in *The Piano Lesson* and offered the actor an attractive proposition. Daniels thought Dutton would prove a strong presence on the television screen, so they worked together to create a situation comedy about a working-class Baltimore family. Dutton even used his nickname for the central character, and he insisted that the other roles be filled with fellow stage actors. "I think the ground-breaking aspect of this show is ... the acting," Dutton emphasized in the *Times-Picayune* when *Roc* debuted on the Fox network in 1991. "These actors and these directors and these writers will find material that we can do something a little different with for situation comedy." Dutton himself contributed significant images and situations from his memories of Baltimore. "Originally, I wanted to do the black man's version of [legendary actor-comedian] Jackie Gleason's *The Honeymooners,*" he informed a *San Francisco Chronicle* correspondent. "Ralph Kramden was always struggling for something better and I wanted to recapture that quality of the common man, show that the black man struggles just as hard. The 'Honeymooner' part of it was changed around a lot, but we still tried to keep that Gleasonesque quality."

In addition to working on *Roc,* Dutton developed a career as a movie actor. He appeared in films such as *Alien* 3

(1992), *The Distinguished Gentleman* (1993), *Menace II Society* (1993), *Rudy* (1993), *Surviving the Game* (1994), and *A Low Down Dirty Shame* (1995). Following the cancellation of *Roc* in 1995, Dutton continued to work in television and appeared in two episodes of the NBC drama *Homicide: Life on the Street* in 1996. That same year, he was cast as George in the Spike Lee film *Get On the Bus,* which told the fictional story of a group of African American men who were riding on a bus to the Million Man March in Washington, D.C. He also appeared as Sheriff Ozzie Walls in the film *A Time to Kill.*

Dutton directed his first television show, *Full Time Felon,* for the HBO cable network in 1997. He also appeared as Josiah on the show *True Women.* In 1998, Dutton starred with Mira Sorvino in the science fiction thriller *Mimic,* and in the critically acclaimed film *Blind Faith,* which aired on Showtime. He also appeared with Patrick Swayze in the action adventure film *Black Dog.* In 1999, Dutton played the role of Willis Richland in the film *Cookie's Fortune* starring Glenn Close and Julianne Moore. The film, directed by Robert Altmann, told the story of a murder mystery that occurred in a small Mississippi town. That same year, Dutton also appeared in the television miniseries *The '60s* and the Sydney Pollack film *Random Hearts.*

Sources

Books

Contemporary Theatre, Film and Television, Gale, 1997.
Who's Who Among African Americans, 11th edition, Gale, 1998.

Periodicals

Chicago Tribune, August 25, 1991.
Detroit Free Press, November 17, 1991.
Emerge, August 1992.
Los Angeles Times, January 20, 1990; August 25, 1991.
Orlando Sentinel, May 20, 1990.
Press (Atlantic City, NJ), June 1, 1992.
San Francisco Chronicle, October 20, 1991.
San Francisco Examiner, August 24, 1991; February 24, 1992.
Times-Picayune (New Orleans, LA), September 13, 1991.
USA Today, April 17, 1990.
USA Weekend, February 28, 1992.

Other

Additional information for this profile was obtained from the National Black Arts Festival website; the E! Online web site; and the bigstar.com web site.

—Mark Kram and David Oblender

Melvin Edwards

1937—

Sculptor

Whether the piece is a small mask hung strategically on a wall or a large, standing sculpture in the middle of a courtyard, the metalworks of Melvin Edwards command power, intensity, and attention. Originally a painter, Edwards discovered the craft of welding metal, and it is within this medium that he has found a prominent voice in the world of art. He was born on May 4, 1937 in Houston, TX. His family loved reading and were all artistically gifted. Reading broadened young Melvin's horizons, and he devoured books ranging from do-it-yourself manuals to histories, adventure novels and *National Geographic Magazines,* which first exposed him to the wonders of Africa. His parents, moreover, ensured his exposure to the world of the arts. His father, Melvin, Sr., who worked during the day as a corporate waiter, spent evenings working in Houston's nightclubs as a photographer, while his mother, Thelmarie, was a talented seamstress.

From an early age Edwards displayed a strong creative bent, an interest which was recognized and encouraged by both his family and his school teachers.   A diligent draftsman, he participated in his high school's elective art program. As a junior, he was one of six students chosen to attend classes at Houston's Museum of Fine Arts. This experience greatly influenced Edwards. As he told Gail Gregg of *ARTNews,* "Being able to see work in a museum was very special, very important." He saw works by Michelangelo and Leonardo da Vinci for the first time, which also sparked his lifelong interest in human anatomy.

Art was not Edwards' only interest as a high school student. He was also a talented athlete. Edwards was a member of the swimming and baseball teams and he played football well enough to earn a football scholarship to the University of Southern California. Before enrolling at USC, however, Edwards began his college education in art and art history at Los Angeles City College. He then transferred to USC in 1957 and spent a year at the Los Angeles County Art Institute. While attending the art institute, Edwards was profoundly influenced by his fellow students because their primary focus was perfecting their artistic talents. The following year, Edwards returned to USC.

During his college career, Edwards' primary artistic focus was painting. Just prior to graduation, he took a course in welding, a course which would transform his art forever. Although drawing would always prove to be an aid in his structural process, welding transformed Edwards from a painter into a sculptor. As he later reflected in an interview with Brooke Kamin Rapaport of *Sculpture,* "I've never romanticized the power in working with metal, but I have always liked the stronger, more expressive side of art ... Art makes you look at your world, and you see other things about your world that give you ways of extending your own vision. Welding opened up sculpture for me."

Following graduation, Edwards continued to audit night classes at the university until he was able to afford his own studio and equipment. His career took off after a show at the Santa Barbara Museum of Art in 1965, only two years

At a Glance . . .

Born Melvin Edwards May 4, 1937 in Houston, TX; mother Thelmarie Edwards (seamstress), father Melvin Edwards Sr. (corporate waiter, photographer); Married to Jayne Cortez; three daughters. *Education:* University of Southern California, BFA, Los Angeles; studied at Chouinard Art Institute, Los Angeles.

Career: Taught at San Bernardino Valley College, 1964-65; California Institute of the Arts, 1965-67; Orange County Community College, 1967-69; assistant professor, University of Connecticut, 1970-72; Rutgers University, 1972-; Livingston College; Mason Gross School of the Art, Visual Art Department.

Awards: Long Beach Museum of Art Award, 1967; Santa Barbara Art Association Award, 1969; National Endowment for the Arts & Humanities, 1970; Los Angeles County Museum Grant; John Hay Whitney Fellowship; Los Angeles County Art Institute Fellowship; NJ State Arts Council/National Endowment for the Arts Fellowship, 1984; Fulbright Fellowship to Zimbabwe, 1988-89.

after he began work on what would prove to be his most momentous collection of pieces, "Lynch Fragments." He moved to New York in 1967, and solo shows followed at such institutions as the Walker Art Center in Minneapolis (1968), the Whitney Museum of American Art (1970), and the Studio Museum in Harlem (1978).

Edwards came of age both personally and professionally during the turbulent civil rights era of the 1960s. Politics, violence against African Americans, and the cultural legacy of Africa constitute his primary subjects. Involved in the community activism of his colleagues, Edwards sought through his art to deal with African American history and culture. As he began to explore the themes of racism and injustice, he told *ARTNews,* "It seemed logical that in some way I should be able to participate through my work."

Politics, according to Nancy Princenthal of *Art in America,* has always been an implicit theme in Edwards' work. His titles, metaphors, allusion to tribal artifacts and rituals, and the "sustained formal tension" of his work all embody the spirit of his activism and his attitude towards the plight of his people. Edwards drew upon the rich and varied aspects of his life and welded them into sculpture that, as Gregg noted in *ARTNews,* "not only confronts struggle but also celebrates it." Welding together hooks, knife blades, hammers, chains, handcuffs, saws, farming implements, and railroad spikes, Edwards transformed these relics of his childhood in the segregated South to create compositions that suggest tension, repression, and violence. Interestingly, despite the messages implicit in the implements themselves, under Edwards' creative powers they ultimately seem inconsequential and almost weightless in comparison with the strength of a piece as a whole. As Vivien Raynor of the *New York Times* astutely commented, "Since [Edwards] does little to change the appearance of his ingredients, one can only conclude that they are transformed because he has chosen them." Through his artistic talents, Edwards has been able not only to convey the African American struggle but to give it universal meaning to a broad-based audience, constructing an uplifting, hopeful whole from both the pleasant and the painful fragments.

While the political overtones in Edwards' work are clearly discernible, he has always chosen an abstract approach to address these issues. As Gregg explained in *ARTNews,* "the exploration of abstraction has remained as critical to the soul of his sculpture as its narrative content." In the catalogue to Edwards' show at the Neuberger Museum in Purchase, NY in 1993, art critic Lowery Stokes Sims continued this analysis, noting that one sees in Edwards' art "the vindication of a steadfast commitment ... to an abstract vocabulary that encapsulates the essence of American modernism, and at the same time expresses an often neglected aspect of the African esthetic essence."

The energy and drama of the American political scene affected not only Edwards' artistic output, but also his passion for African art and traditional crafts. Beginning in 1970 Edwards traveled extensively throughout Africa and even earned a Fulbright Fellowship to Zimbabwe in 1988. During his travels, he sought out village blacksmiths and bronze casters in order to study their centuries-old techniques. During his first trip, he met Nana Osel Bonsu, an Asante and a master woodcarver. In 1971 he met Omoregbe Inneh, the chief of the Benin bronze casters. These esteemed men, both of whom were university teachers as well as practitioners of African sculptural traditions, provided ample inspiration for Edwards.

The series of reliefs in "Lynch Fragments" best epitomize Edwards' style and form. Begun in 1963, Edwards worked on this series for many years. By 1993 there were approximately 200 "Fragments," made in three periods: 1963 to 1967, 1973, and 1978 to the present. While few of the pieces overtly address lynching, Edwards explained to Rapaport in *Sculpture* that he intended the "titular continuity to bring that scale of intensity and that kind of power to all the works … [The lynching theme, moreover,] has allowed him to wrestle or grapple with a particular social phenomenon and what it means metaphorically or symbolically." Like Edwards' other sculptures, the "Fragments" incorporate chains, bolts, scissors, padlocks, nails, gears, axes, hammers, and other tools, all welded together into sculptures of incredible energy and intensity. Together, they explore the cruelty which humans inflict upon each other. With no one sculpture standing more than 12 inches, they are each hung on the wall at eye level, thereby increasing the sense of confrontation between the object and the viewer. This display also helps to accentuate the impression that these sculptures, and particularly the earlier ones, are actually masks in the African tradition. Expressing not only fear, violence, vigilance, sexuality, and play, these "fragments" welded together as mask-like compositions also seem to be faces, looking, pointing, warning, no matter, as critic Michael Brenson of the *New York Times* noticed, "how much them seem to be impaled, wedged in, enslaved."

While the earlier pieces tend to be rather small and dense, the later additions to "Lynch Fragments" are more linear and varied. Some even contain a striking bolt of color created by polished steel and the raw seams of the dark residue produced from the forging process. The later pieces often bear no relation to heads or masks, and while at times surrealistic, they have a hard physical weight which surrealism never had. At the same time, according to art critic Judith Wilson in *Art in America,* they seem more active, more inventive in terms of direction and space. "It is as if the artist has returned from the contemplation of a blood-soaked history to announce a new promise of freedom." In the last phase of the series, the sculptures are also physically larger, a tendency which Edwards attributed to his having worked outdoors during his Fulbright fellowship in Zimbabwe.

The implicit meaning as well as the techniques which lie behind "Lynch Fragments" are symbolic of Edwards' entire body of work. The series, in essence, compressed the continuum of the African American experience and the historic oppression of African Americans into tightly-constructed, highly-emotional forms. While the forms themselves may be abstract, their jagged edges and cold, black steel surfaces communicate pain and fury. And yet, through Edwards' craftsmanship and touch, they also instill the viewer with thoughts of remembering and overcoming. Thus they are celebratory as well as angry. As Catherine Fox of the *Atlanta Journal and Constitution* explained, "Just as the reference to African masks symbolizes a rich artistic heritage, the use of forging pays homage to the ancient craft of blacksmithing practiced in Africa. And while the inclusion of axe and shovel blades might

suggest slave labor, it also represents hard work." Even chains can suggest kinship, cooperation, and links – to the past, to the people—as well as memories of imprisonment and hurt. As Brenson remarked in the *New York Times,* "the ease with which the artist manipulates seemingly unbendable steel bars is essential to a body of work that is very much about the fullest possible understanding of freedom. No matter how aggressive the solid shapes, attention is inevitably drawn to the voids."

While the pieces of "Lynch Fragments" certainly comprise a large portion of Edwards' portfolio, he has not restricted his art simply to this one series or even just to smaller-sized sculpture. In fact, he has also made a significant impact on the art world through his large public sculptures, a medium with which he first experimented in 1969. Unlike in his smaller pieces, these larger pieces have a lighter spirit and a different feel, leaving an initial impression of memory and hope. Most importantly, his larger, outdoor pieces tend to be constructed from stainless steel as opposed to steel, as Edwards capitalized on the play of light off his pieces. Similar to his smaller works, though, Edwards utilized each sculpture to further his exploration of the African American culture. As Brenson suggested in the *New York Times,* in large-scale works such as "Tomorrow's Wind," Edwards was "clearly less interested in originality than he [was] in making an intense and full human statement." As Edwards himself told Michael Kimmelman of the *New York Times,* public art makes life "better for living." Ultimately, while his smaller pieces chronicle an inward journey to personal and racial memory, the larger pieces, Brenson concluded, "look outward and roll ahead."

Edwards' talent and his unusual work have earned him a respected place in the art world and as a regular exhibitor at museums. However, the charged content of his work historically seemed to distance private dealers and collectors from his work. In fact, it was not until 1990 that Edwards had his first solo show at a commercial gallery, the CDS Gallery in New York. As Edwards himself admitted to Rapaport in *Sculpture,* he "became an adult in a very confrontational period in relation to African people in the world," a fact which he believes impacted the public recognition of his work. He has, however, begun to benefit from the general trend in American culture which seeks to embrace multiculturalism and pluralism. Since 1972, Edwards has maintained a professorship at Rutgers University in New Jersey, where he has taught drawing, sculpture, and art history.

Taken as a whole, Edwards' work, in its constancy of tone and its independence from artistic trends, has paid homage not only to the creativity of humans but also to African American history, which he has illuminated so expressively. This history, according to Edwards, is his, and the struggle is not over. His continued fight is manifested in his enduring body of work, and, as Susan Wadsworth of *Art New England,* suggested, "once his work is seen, it cannot be dismissed nor forgotten."

Selected works

"My Bell and One Thing," 1966 (steel).
"Untitled steel," 1967.
"Pyramid Up & Down Pyramid."
"The Yellow Way."
"Hard Times."
"Benny Andrews."
"Lynch Fragments."
"B Wire-corner."
"B Wire-pyramids."
"B Wire-womb."
"B Wire-chain Curtain."
"Rockers."
"Wachung."
"Asafokra."
"Felton."
"Thelmarie."
"Tambo."
"For Richard Wright."
"Asafo Kra No."
"To Listen."

"Tomorrow's Wind," 1991.
"Confirmation."
"Unruly."
"Conversation with Igun."
"Sekuro Knows," 1988.
"Some Bright Morning," 1963.
"Afro Phoenix No. 2," 1963.

Sources

Periodicals

Art in America, October 1980, pp. 136-137; September 1990, pp. 190-191; March 1993, pp. 60-65; January 1997, pp. 96-97.
Art New England, February/March 1995.
ARTNews, September 1990, p. 157; February 1995, pp. 104-107; October 1996, p. 135.
Atlantic Journal and Constitution, February 1, 1991, p. D2.
New York Times, December 23, 1988, p. C36; March 30, 1990, p.C28; March 8, 1991, p. C30; July 26, 1991, p. C28; May 23, 1993, p. 2, 35; March 31, 1996, p. NJ15.
Scholastic Art, April-May 1996, pp. 2-3; March 1998, pp. 12-13.
Sculpture, October 1996, pp. 24-27; October 1998.
Time, March 31, 1980, p. 72.

—Lisa S. Weitzman

Brian Ellerbe

1963—

College basketball coach

Brian Ellerbe's coaching career is a testimony to the value of hard work and of being in the right place at the right time. After a decade of traveling around the country from one college basketball coaching job to another, Ellerbe suddenly found himself with the opportunity of a lifetime when he was named basketball coach at the University of Michigan. Assuming the job on an interim basis, he lead the team to a conference tournament championship and the second round of the NCAA Tournament. The following season, he was officially named as head coach.

Ellerbe was born September 1, 1963 in Capitol Heights, Maryland, the youngest of nine children. He attended Bowie High School in Bowie, Maryland, and was the leading scorer in Washington, D.C. area high school basketball during his junior and senior seasons. He earned first-team All-Washington Metro honors and played in the 1981 Capital Classic All-Star Game along with Michael Jordan and Patrick Ewing.

Ellerbe graduated from Bowie in 1981, and attended college at Rutgers. He was a four-year starter as a guard on the Rutgers basketball team, finished his career with

979 points, and placed second on the school's list of assist leaders. He also holds the school record for career three-point field-goal percentage and assists in one game. Ellerbe is among the school's career leaders in several other categories and led Rutgers to the NIT tournament his freshman year and the NCAA Tournament his sophomore year. He also played alongside future NBA performers John Battle and Roy Hinson. Any hopes Ellerbe might have had for his own NBA career, however, were dashed by a shoulder injury he suffered midway through his senior season.

Ellerbe earned his degree in urban planning from Rutgers in 1985, and took a one-year position as a graduate assistant basketball coach for Rutgers. The following season Ellerbe moved on to Bowling Green State University, where he served as an assistant coach for the next two seasons. At the time, he was the youngest full-time assistant coach in the United States, and he helped the Falcons become a vastly improved team. His roommate at Bowling Green was assistant football coach Terry Malone, who would later also coach at Michigan.

During the 1988-89 season Ellerbe coached at George

At a Glance . . .

Born Brian Hersholt Ellerbe, September 1, 1963, in Capitol Heights, Maryland; married to Ingrid; children: Brian Jr., Morgan Ashleigh. *Education:* Rutgers University, bachelor's degree in urban planning, 1985.

Career: Graduate assistant coach, Rutgers University, 1985-86; assistant coach, Bowling Green University, 1986-88; assistant coach, George Mason University, 1988-89; assistant coach, South Carolina University, 1989-90; assistant coach, University of Virginia, 1990-94; head coach, Loyola (Maryland) College, 1994-97; assistant coach, University of Michigan, 1997, interim head coach, 1997-98, head coach, 1998-.

Addresses: *Office*—University of Michigan Athletic Department, 1000 South State Street, Ann Arbor, Michigan, 48109.

Mason, where the Patriots compiled a 20-11 record, won the Colonial Athletic Association title, and went to the NCAA Tournament for the first time in school history. The following year Ellerbe coached at South Carolina, where he recruited future NBA player Jamie Watson. In 1990, he became assistant coach at Virginia and stayed for the next four years. While serving as coach Jeff Jones' assistant, Ellerbe helped the Cavaliers to an 80-48 record, three NCAA Tournament appearances, and the 1991 NIT championship.

In 1994, Ellerbe was named head coach at Loyola College in Maryland. Ellerbe's strongest asset as a coach, his recruiting abilities, served him well. In three seasons at Loyola, he brought in the Metro Atlantic Athletic Conference's top recruiting class twice and placed at least one player on the league's all-rookie team each year. During the 1996-97 season, Loyola had its best conference record in school history (10-4), but finished only 13-14 overall. At the end of the season, Ellerbe resigned as head coach.

On May 29, 1997, Ellerbe landed an assistant coaching job at the University of Michigan. During this time, Michigan's basketball program was plagued by allegations that it had violated NCAA rules. As a result of the scandal, head coach Steve Fisher was fired on October 4. Initially, Michigan athletic director Tom Goss intended to hire a big-name coach from another university to replace Fisher. However, because a new season was about to begin, Goss felt that it would be unethical to hire a coach away from another team. As a result, Ellerbe was named interim

coach for the season. He took a positive approach to his new job, telling Bob Wojnowski of *The Detroit News,* "It's the opportunity of a lifetime. It's five months of scrutiny but it also can be five months of fun and adventure. It's not like I shut the door, looked in the mirror and said, 'What have I gotten myself into?' I'm going to keep it fun for the players. It's not fair to put a burden on them. All I'm asking is that they compete." Early in the new season,

Ellerbe told *The Detroit News* that he definitely wanted an opportunity to earn the job on a permanent basis, "It would be great. My wife really likes Ann Arbor. It's a very good place to raise a family. There's some business opportunities for my wife (vice-president of Boxer Learning, an educational software company) that's conducive to what she's doing. And obviously, Michigan is one of the marquee programs in the country. So that total environment makes it special."

Very little was expected from the Wolverines during the 1997-98 season, but Michigan had some surprises up its sleeve. It started the season with an upset of No. 1-ranked Duke and defeated previously unbeaten Syracuse to capture the Puerto Rico Holiday Classic tournament. In the Big Ten, they upset conference powerhouses Indiana and Minnesota. The Wolverines finished the season 25-9 overall and 11-5 in the Big Ten. The team's greatest triumph, however, occurred during the Big Ten conference's first championship tournament. The Wolverines won three games in a row, defeated Purdue in the championship game, and secured an automatic berth in the NCAA Tournament.

In the NCAA Tournament, Michigan won its first game before losing to UCLA in the second round. Although the Wolverines had exceeded all expectations, Ellerbe was not immediately offered the head coaching job on a permanent basis. Goss again considered hiring a big-name coach, but he quickly changed his mind and decided that Ellerbe was the best man for the job. On March 20, 1998, Ellerbe was officially named as Michigan's head coach. He told the *Detroit Free Press,* "I feel very, very fortunate and very, very blessed to have the situation finish the way it did. Tom told me from day one I would have an opportunity, and here we are." Goss later implied that he decided to hire Ellerbe after the coach excused himself in the middle of his interview with Goss to telephone a potential recruit. Goss remarked to *The Detroit News,* "When I compared all the candidates, I thought I had a bright, energetic young man right here. So I said, 'Let's take a chance.'"

The 1998-99 campaign marked a rebuilding year for Michigan. Despite several wins over ranked opponents, the Wolverines finished with a losing record and were not invited to a post-season tournament. Following the season, Ellerbe was able to sign several top recruits and appeared to secure his future as head coach of one of the most prestigious programs in college basketball.

Sources

Detroit Free Press, March 21, 1998, sec. B, p. 1; August 15, 1998.

The Detroit News, October 27, 1997, sec. D, p. 1; January 15, 1998, sec. C, p. 1; March 22, 1998, sec. D, p. 1.

The Sporting News, November 17, 1997, p. 54.

The University of Michigan 1998-99 Men's Basketball Media Guide, p.30.

—Michael Eggert

Darryl Evans

1961—

Executive chef

Darryl Evans, executive chef at Villa Christina in Atlanta, Georgia, is one of the top culinary artists in the nation. In 1988, as the first African American member of the U.S. Culinary Olympics team, he won two individual gold medals, and team gold and silver medals. His numerous other culinary awards include winning first prize in the National Taste of Elegance recipe contest in 1994, and being named Chef of the Year by the Greater Atlanta Chef's Association in 1996.

Evans began his career as a chef's apprentice in 1983. Seven years later, he was an executive chef, a position he has held at several restaurants and country clubs in the Atlanta area. "I would recommend my job to young people—it's a valuable career," Evans said in an interview with CBB. "It's taken me all around the world. I've traveled to South Africa, to China—I've stood on the Great Wall—to England, all over. Food can take you all around the world."

In 1998 Evans accepted the job of executive chef at Villa Christina, an Italian restaurant and banquet facility. That same year, Villa Christina was one of just 15 American eateries to be recognized by the Italian government for serving genuine Italian cuisine. "Evans owns a soft voice, a slender frame and an absurdly youthful appearance for one who has risen so far," Henry Chase wrote in American Visions, one of several national publications that have featured articles on Evans.

"It's tough to tell exactly how busy Darryl Evans is, because he'll be speaking softly and deliberately, cool as a cuke, regardless of the fray," wrote Kerri Conan in Restaurant Business. One reason for Evans' calmness is his attitude toward customer satisfaction. "Since I set my goals so high, I don't have to worry about cooking to satisfy 'the guest' or the style of the restaurant," Evans was quoted as saying in Nation's Restaurant News. "I just go all out—and cook for myself."

While eating delicious food is an enjoyable experience, the role of food is more significant than that, Evans believes. "Being exposed to good food can better your home life," he told CBB. "Eating together can bring a family together. Food initiates everything we do. Throughout history and culture, food has played an important part—whether as part of signing a peace treaty, or blessing an event or ceremony."

Won Medals at Culinary Olympics

Darryl E. Evans was born on November 24, 1961, in Columbus, Georgia. The youngest of three boys, he gained a great deal of experience working in the kitchen. "My father was a schoolteacher, and my mother was a housewife, so when my two older brothers were in school, I stayed home with my mother and did 'girly' things, like baking cakes," Evans told Henry Chase of American Visions.

At a Glance . . .

Born Darryl E. Evans, November 24, 1961 in Columbus, Georgia; married to Deborah, an IRS employee, 1991; children: Branford-Michael and Brandon. *Education:* Studied business administration at Chattanoochee Valley Community College, 1981-83; National Apprenticeship Program, American Culinary Foundation, 1983-86; became Certified Working Chef, 1991. *Religion:* Baptist.

Career: Apprentice, pastry chef, sous chef, Cherokee Town and Country Club, Atlanta, GA, 1983-90; executive chef, Azalea Restaurant, Atlanta, GA, 1990-91; executive chef, Athens Country Club, Athens, GA, 1991-92; executive chef, The Vinings Club, Atlanta, GA, 1992-94; executive chef, Grand Hotel Atlanta, 1995-97; executive chef, Four Seasons Hotel, Atlanta, GA, 1997-98; executive chef, Villa Christina, 1998-.

Selected awards: Gold medal, Atlanta Food Show, 1987; Three gold medals, one silver medal, International Culinary Olympics, Frankfurt, Germany, 1988; Chef's Hall of Fame, 1989; Gold medal, Culinary Olympics, Frankfurt, Germany, 1992; Culinarian of the Year, Greater Atlanta Chef's Association, 1991-92, 1992-93; First Place, National "A Taste of Elegance" Competition, 1994; Chef of the Year, Greater Atlanta Chef's Association, 1996.

Addresses: *Home*—Stone Mountain, GA. *Office*—Villa Christina, 45 Perimeter Summit Blvd., Atlanta, GA.

As a child growing up in western Georgia, Evans idolized Dr. Martin Luther King Jr. "We observed Dr. King's birthday even when there weren't celebrations elsewhere in the country," he was quoted as saying in American Visions. "Oscar Robertson and Dr. J were [also] big heroes, though I wasn't a big athlete—I preferred playing the drum in the marching band." In several interviews, Evans mentioned that his years in the ROTC band shaped his work habits. "I learned about precision from music," he told Jack Hayes of *Nation's Restaurant News.* "ROTC put rhythm in my step," he remarked to Henry Chase of *American Visions.* "We used to march three steps for every five yards, and even now, when I want to speed things up, I put myself in that cadence."

At the age of 21, Evans moved from Columbus to Atlanta,

where he took a job clearing tables in a restaurant. After meeting a young man who was a chef and a graduate of the Culinary Institute of America, Evans thought, "I could do that," he later recalled in an interview with Henry Chase of *American Visions.* His next job was in the purchasing department of the Cherokee Town and Country Club. This department was located across the hall from the club's pastry area, and whenever Evans had a chance, he wandered over. "Pastries set the tone for everything in my career," he remarked in *American Visions.* "Because I had done cakes at home in Columbus, I understood what the chef there was doing, and when he let me help him, I knew what to do."

Evans landed a full-time position in the pastry shop in 1983, and began a three-year apprenticeship with executive chef Thomas Catherall. "I just stuck by his side and did whatever he did," Evans told *American Visions.* "I didn't care about money, just about learning." In 1986, Evans was named Atlanta Apprentice of the Year. He stayed at the Cherokee Club for eight and a half years, honing his culinary skills. After his apprenticeship ended, Evans spent two years as pastry chef, and later was promoted to sous chef.

By 1987, Evans had begun to win local food competitions, including a gold medal at the Atlanta Food Show and second place in Atlanta's Seafood Challenge. The following year, he became the first African American member of the U.S. Culinary Olympics team. "It's held every year in conjunction with the regular Olympics," Evans explained to *CBB.* "You're given a basket of food, and you have four and a half hours to come up with the menus." At the 1988 Olympic competition in Frankfurt, Germany, Evans won two individual gold medals, and team gold and silver medals.

Participated in World Tour for Hunger

In 1990, Evans left the Cherokee Club. In partnership with Thomas Catherall, he opened the Azalea Restaurant in Atlanta. "I owned only a tiny, micro piece of the place," he remarked to Henry Chase of *American Visions.* Evans was given the position of executive chef, with responsibility for managing the kitchen as well as preparing food.

The following year, Evans was appointed executive chef of the Country Club in Athens, Georgia. "Being an executive chef requires more than just cooking skills," Evans told *CBB.* "You also have to have management skills, and to know about labor and food costs. There's a lot of pressure, because you're making something out of nothing, but when it works it's great." In 1992, he competed on the American Culinary Federation's southeast regional team at the Culinary Olympics in Frankfurt, Germany, and won another gold medal.

In 1993, Evans took a job as executive chef at the Vinings Club, a business and athletic facility with three food-service venues featuring heart-healthy "spa cuisine." That same year, he spent several weeks in South Africa, as a participant in the World Cooks Tour for Hunger. During the event, teams prepared fund-raising dinners, shared culinary skills and nutritional tips with those who feed the hungry, or cooked meals for local communities in need. "I feel like we had an impact," Evans remarked to Kerri Conan of *Restaurant Business*. "The chefs gave all they had. We worked harder at the food than during competition."

Meanwhile, Evans continued to win awards for his culinary ability. In 1994, he was awarded top honors in the national Taste of Elegance recipe contest, which was sponsored by the National Pork Producers Council and the National Pork Board. Evans took home the $5000 first prize for his recipe, Apple Smoked Pork Loin with an Apple, Dried Cherries, Smoked Gouda and Walnut Strudel.

Despite his success in culinary competitions, Evans believes that his restaurant work is the true measure of his ability. When the Vinings Club wanted to build a case to display the trophies he had won, Evans declined. "You're only as good as your last meal," he told Henry Chase of *American Visions*. "My meals will be the trophies of my work."

Served "Genuine Italian Cuisine"

In 1995, Evans accepted the position of executive chef at the Grand Hotel Atlanta. Two years later, he moved to a similar position at the Four Seasons Hotel. In 1998, Evans became executive chef at Villa Christina, a restaurant and banquet facility that is surrounded by eight acres of manicured lawns and nature paths. "We have an open kitchen here, so I can look out and see the happiness on people's faces," Evans told *CBB*. "It's instant satisfac-

tion. It's very rewarding."

"I try to cook as light as possible, using indigenous ingredients from Italy," Evans explained to *CBB*. "It's not the cream sauces or heavy tomato sauces that people in this country think of as typical of Italian food. I think of it as taking the lightness of California cuisine, and marrying it with the intense flavors of Italian cuisine. The result is modern Italian cuisine." The restaurant's eclectic menu features dishes such as roast petite chicken with creamy risotto, and grilled tenderloin with Tuscan beans and wild mushrooms. "We change our menu four times a year, in season with Italy," Evans told *CBB*. "We travel over there a lot too. But we're not trying to be a carbon copy of another Italian restaurant."

Despite the demands of his job, Evans makes time in his schedule to give back to the community. "I'm currently very involved with Taste of the Nations, which is a countrywide organization to feed the homeless," he remarked to *CBB*. "I'm very involved with my church, and feeding the homeless there—not just for one meal, but as a day-to-day thing." Evans told Henry Chase of *American Visions* that, in his spare time, he enjoys "doing yard work, cutting grass and listening to music. And...collecting Prince paraphernalia."

Sources

Periodicals

Essence, July 1998, p. 112.
Nation's Restaurant News, Oct. 3, 1994, p. 49.
Restaurant Business, Nov. 1, 1993, p. 134.
Restaurant Hospitality, June 1994, p. 74.

Other

Additional information for this profile was obtained from a *CBB* interview with Darryl Evans on May 28, 1999.

—Carrie Golus

Faith Evans

1973(?)—

Vocalist, songwriter

A multi-talented singer and musician, Faith Evans experienced tragedy when her life was touched by the violence that plagued the hip-hop music community through the mid-1990s. She became widely known as the woman who was married to rapper The Notorious B.I.G., who was murdered in March of 1997. Her performance on "I'll Be Missing You," the smash hit tribute to the slain rapper recorded by Evans and Sean "Puffy" Combs, made her voice identifiable even to Americans who were unacquainted with hip-hop. However, Evans had worked hard to develop her music career before marrying The Notorious B.I.G., and her two solo albums gained wide acclaim and garnered strong sales. By the late 1990s, it seemed clear that her solo career would outlast the controversies in which she had become embroiled.

Evans was born in Florida around 1973. Both of her parents had a background in music. Her mother, Helene, was singing backup in a rock band when Faith was born, and her father was a white musician in the same band. When her parents broke up six months after her birth, Evans was brought to Newark, New Jersey, to be raised by a cousin, Johnnie Mae Kennedy. Her mother also moved into the Kennedy house. Both women, as well as Kennedy's husband Orvelt, became important people in Evans's life.

Could Listen Only to Gospel

Evans's upbringing was strongly religious. She told *Interview* magazine writer Dimitri Ehrlich that she was not allowed to listen to the radio unless gospel programming was featured. It was at Newark's Emanuel Baptist Church that she began to develop her love of performing, singing for the first time there at the age of four. "When she got older and sang, people would just stand up and shout," Helene Evans told *Essence* writer Valerie Wilson Wesley. Later, Evans would credit the Clark Sisters and Shirley Murdock as the gospel singers who had a major influence on her own vocal style.

Evans was an honors student at Newark's University High School. She studied jazz and classical music and appeared in school musicals. She also competed in beauty pageants and won the title of Miss New Jersey Fashion Teen. Evans won a scholarship to New York's Fordham University and planned to work toward a marketing degree. However, she dropped out of Fordham after one year to pursue a musical career. Evans also gave birth to her daughter,

At a Glance . . .

Born in Florida ca. 1973; daughter of Helene Evans, a singer; hnnie Mae Kennedy, and Kennedy's husband Orvelt. Married Christopher Wallace, also known as Biggie Smalls, 1994; widowed 1997; children Chyna, Christopher Jordan, Joshua. *Education:* graduated with honors from University High School in Newark; attended Fordham University in New York. *Religion:* Baptist.

Career: Hip-hop vocalist and composer. Performed backup vocals for R&B stars Mary J. Blige, Al B. Sure, and others, early 1990s; signed to Bad Boy label, 1994; released debut album, *Faith,* 1995; with Sean "Puffy" Combs recorded "I'll Be Missing You," tribute song in honor of Smalls, 1997; released *Keep the Faith,* 1998.

Addresses: *Record label*–Bad Boy Records, 8 W. 19th St., New York, NY 10011.

Chyna, during this time.

Met the Notorious B.I.G.

As a talented vocalist, Evans was quickly able to find work in the music industry. A distinctive songwriter who has composed many of the pieces found on her own albums, she wrote music and did backup vocal work for such major talents of the early 1990s as Mary J. Blige and Al B. Sure. In 1993, her studio vocal work gained the attention of Bad Boy Records chief executive Sean "Puffy" Combs, whose own career was just beginning its meteoric rise. Evans met with Combs and became the first female vocalist signed to the Bad Boy label. At a Bad Boy event in July of 1994, she met The Notorious B.I.G., whose real name was Christopher Wallace, and who often went by the name Biggie Smalls. After dating for only two weeks, Smalls and Evans were married.

Evans contributed vocals to Smalls's first hit single, "One More Chance," and her debut album, *Faith,* was released in 1995. From the start, Evans's romantic stylings were a stark contrast to the combative nature of hip-hop. As Ehrlich remarked in *Interview* magazine, "her music balances the rawness and aggression of hip-hop with old school arrangements; she makes sexuality elegant in a way none of her peers can." Evans began work on a second album, and her life and career seemed to be firmly on

track.

It didn't take long, however, before the problems that plagued the "gangsta" rap community began to engulf Evans. In October of 1995, she worked with Death Row Records rapper Tupac Shakur. Rumors circulated by Shakur and his friend, Death Row chief executive Suge Knight, linked Evans and Shakur romantically. Shakur also claimed that he was the father of Evans's second child, a son. These rumors added fuel to an escalating war of words between Smalls and Shakur, who were the focal point of a much-publicized feud between East Coast and West Coast rap artists. Evans and Smalls saw little of each other, and their marriage soon deteriorated. On September 7, 1996, Shakur was murdered in Las Vegas, and Smalls met the same fate on March 9, 1997. It is unknown whether the enmity between Shakur and Smalls led directly to their deaths. Asked by Ehrlich in *Interview* whether Smalls's murder was related to the feud, Evans answered, "I doubt that very seriously."

Added Voice to Tribute

Stunned by the death of Smalls and the demanding task of managing his estate, Evans put her music career on hold. She did contribute vocals to "I'll Be Missing You," a song created by Evans and Combs as a tribute to Smalls. The recording, an imaginative recasting of the 1982 Police hit "Every Breath You Take," ended with Evans breaking into an old gospel hymn, "I'll Fly Away." "I'll Be Missing You" was one of the biggest hits of 1997, and soared to the top of the black and pop music charts.

Evans slowly began to put her life back together. A blossoming relationship with record company executive, Todd Russaw, brought her the stability she needed. Russaw and Evans married and he became the father of her third child, Joshua, who was born in 1998. A heart-shaped tattoo that read "B.I.G." was refashioned into a rose with her new husband's name. Evans also returned to the recording studio and completed work on her second album, *Keep the Faith,* which was released in October of 1998.

Keep the Faith, which referred indirectly to the trials Evans had experienced, was a huge commercial success. Critics loved the music and noted a new depth in Evans's voice, with some even comparing her to legendary soul divas Minnie Riperton and Chaka Khan. The album rose to Number Three on *Billboard* magazine's Top R&B Albums chart and to Number Six on its overall Top 200. In the spring and summer of 1999, Evans embarked on a tour with leading acts Dru Hill and Total. *Washington Post* writer Craig Seymour reveled in Evans's "angelic yet hearty soprano," and noted that "her rendition of 'Soon As I Get Home' was an awe-inspiring melismatic ride that had hands in the air and cries of 'Sing it, girl' coming from every part of the hall." Evans's life itself had been an awe-inspiring and often terrifying ride, but it once again seemed to be on an upward trajectory.

Selected discography

Faith, Bad Boy, 1995.
Keep the Faith, Bad Boy, 1998.

Sources

Books

Larkin, Colin, ed., *The Guinness Encyclopedia of Popular Music,* Muze U.K., 1998.

Periodicals

Ebony, April 1999, p. 52.
Essence, December 1997, p. 74.
Interview, December 1998, p. 112.
Washington Post, April 12, 1999, p. C5.

—James M. Manheim

Laurence Fishburne

1961—

Actor

Since his stage debut at age ten, Laurence Fishburne has spent his life acting. "He's the kind of actor you can't wait to say action on-- because you can't wait to see how he's gonna take it and deal with it," director Abel Ferrara said of Laurence Fishburne in a *Film Comment* interview. The roles Fishburne have chosen have been equally unpredictable, from psychopaths to activist lawyers, from the solid, hands-on father he played in *Boyz N the Hood* to the troubled cop of *Deep Cover*. "For every thug, for every nut, I try and do somebody who's a reasonable person, who's an educated person," the actor told Tom Perew of *Black Elegance*. Perew quoted a casting agent who praised Fishburne's selectivity and dedication: "I get the feeling he's more interested in the quality behind the work than the money."

Fishburne was born in 1961, in Augusta, Georgia. His father, a corrections officer, frequently took him to the movies, but it was his mother, a schoolteacher, who introduced him to the stage. The family moved to a middle-class neighborhood in Brooklyn, New York, when Laurence was young, and soon he was auditioning for parts in local plays. "I've always been an actor," he remarked to James Ryan of *Premiere;* he informed *New York* magazine that his first role was in the second grade: "I was Peter Pan, the boy who never grows up. I still am--I play make-believe for a living." At age ten he appeared in the play In *My Many Names and Days* at the New Federal Theater. "I played a little 10-year-old baseball freak from Brooklyn who used to dig going to Ebbitts Field and watching Jackie Robinson," Fishburne recalled to *Washington Post* correspondent David Mills.

Fishburne next landed a role in the 1972 television film *If You Give a Dance, You Got to Pay the Band,* which led to a part on the soap opera *One Life to Live* when he was 11 years old that lasted three years. One year after joining the daytime series, he appeared in the dramatic film *Cornbread, Earl and Me.* Fishburne told Patrick Pacheco of the *Los Angeles Times* that after *Cornbread's* release, "My father took all the guys at this juvenile correction facility in the Bronx to see it. Afterward, we got together and they told me that I was doing good, that I had something really fine going on for myself and that if I ever [messed] up, they'd be waiting. That kept me in line." The actor earned a part in a Negro Ensemble Theater production and was accepted into the prestigious High School of Performing Arts in New York City. Then, at 15, Fishburne

At a Glance . . .

Born Lawrence Fishburne III, in July 30, 1961, in Augusta, GA; son of Larry (a corrections officer) and Hattie (a teacher) Fishburne, Jr.; married Hajna Moss (casting agent and producer), c. 1987; divorced; two children.

Career: Actor appearing in motion pictures, including, *Cornbread, Earl and Me*, 1974, *Apocalypse Now*, 1979, *Death Wish 2*, 1982, *Rumble Fish*, 1983, *The Cotton Club*, 1984, *The Color Purple*, 1985 *Red Heat*, 1985, *Gardens of Stone*, 1987, *A Nightmare on Elm Street 3: Dream Warriors*, 1987, *Red Heat*, 1988, *School Daze*, 1988, *Cadence*, 1989, *King of New York*, 1990, *Boyz N the Hood*, 1991, *Class Action*, 1991, *Deep Cover*, 1992, *Searching for Bobby Fischer*, 1993, *What's Love Got to Do With It*, 1993, *Higher Learning*, 1995, *Bad Company*, 1995, *Just Cause*, 1995, *Othello*, 1995, *Fled*, 1996, *Event Horizon*, 1997, *Hoodlum*, 1997, *The Matrix*, 1999; in stage productions, including *Two Trains Running*, 1992, *The Tuskegee Airmen*, 1995, *Miss Evers' Boys*, 1997, *Always Outnumbered*, 1998; and on television, including *If You Give a Dance, You Got to Pay the Band*, 1972, *One Life to Live*, 1973-76, *A Rumor of War*, 1980, *For Us the Living*, PBS American Playhouse production, 1988, *Riff Raff*, 1995, *The Lion in Winter*, 1999, *Pee-Wee's Playhouse*, *Decoration Day*, and episodes of *Hill Street Blues* and *Miami Vice*.

Selected awards: Tony Award for best featured actor in a play, Outer Critic's Circle Award, Drama Desk Award, and Theater World Award, all 1992, all for *Two Trains Running*.

Addresses: *Agent*–Michelle Marx, Inc., 8756 Holloway Dr., Los Angeles, CA 90069.

embarked on the acting experience that would utterly transform him: a role as a member of the boat crew in Francis Ford Coppola's Vietnam epic *Apocalypse Now*.

Grew up on Apocalypse Set

Pacheco quoted Fishburne as saying that shooting *Apocalypse* was "the most formative event" of his life. He had a chance to observe several luminaries of American film acting--Marlon Brando, Robert DuVall, Martin Sheen, and others--and to consult them for advice. Coppola taught Fishburne that acting "could be taken seriously, as art, with potential for educating, entertaining and touching people." And in the drenching rain and chaos of the filming in the Philippines, Fishburne lived a sporadically unsupervised fantasy of adolescence: "I was smoking reefer like everybody else," he told Pacheco. "My mother was there with me, but she couldn't control me so she called in the big guns, my father. Everybody in the company referred to him as 'the jailer,' but all he had to do was say, 'OK, that's enough of that,' and I'd come around."

Recalling his return to the United States, Fishburne recounted to Ryan, "I figured I was one of the baddest motherf---ers on the planet. And I came to L.A. and nobody gave a shit. I was really pissed off about that. I couldn't get work. I think a lot of people thought I was crazy, and I probably was." Fishburne made the second of what would be a series of appearances in Coppola films, portraying Midget in *Rumble Fish*, before playing a heavy in *Death Wish II*. "I was only getting work playing bad guys, and I wanted to be an actor and didn't want to wait tables," he said to Perew. "But I would have [done so, if necessary]." In what Mills called Fishburne's "least dignified professional moment," the actor's *Death Wish* character "shielded his head with a boom box while fleeing vigilante Charles Bronson."

Fishburne was concerned with balancing the roles he portrayed and combating Hollywood stereotypes. He succeeded by appearing in two more Coppola films, *Gardens of Stone* and *The Cotton Club*, as well as in Steven Spielberg's *Color Purple*. He also participated in the PBS drama *For Us the Living*, based on the story of Medgar Evers, a crucial figure in the civil rights movement of the late 1950s and early 1960s. Fishburne explained in the *Los Angeles Times* that "this is a gig where I had to put myself up and pay my own transportation, but to be involved with Roscoe Lee Browne, Howard Rollins, Dick Anthony Williams, Irene Cara. Well, that was my ancestors saying to me, 'OK, here's some work we can do.'" He further confided that "I work with somebody on what is called 'ancestral memory,' and I find it a source of spiritual strength," since the struggles of the past "are not something to be embarrassed by, but a resource to be valued and respected."

Took Diverse Film Roles

In the meantime, an ambitious young director had been keeping an eye on Fishburne. One day in the mid-1980s, reported Mills, Fishburne was watching a street performance when someone tapped him on the shoulder. "I don't know who this guy is. He says, 'You're Larry Fishburne.... You're a good actor.' So he introduced himself and said he was from Brooklyn and he was making movies." The Brooklyn filmmaker was Spike Lee, who wanted Fishburne to appear in a film called *Messenger*. The movie was never made, but Lee utilized Fishburne in *School Daze;* the actor played the campus activist Dap in that collegiate musical comedy.

Fishburne later passed up the role of Radio Raheem in Lee's 1988 smash *Do the Right Thing,* criticizing the film's plot for straying from reality. "I'm from Brooklyn too," he told Mills. "And I didn't grow up in that kind of Brooklyn." Though Fishburne experienced some friction with Lee, the actor's refusal of roles in subsequent Lee films has evidently had more to do with Fishburne's desire for a starring part than any lingering hard feelings.

While working on *School Daze,* Fishburne met Hajna Moss, a casting agent and producer. The two eventually married and had two children, settling in the Bedford-Stuyvesant section of Brooklyn. Fishburne accepted the role of an orderly in the horror film *A Nightmare on Elm Street 3* in order to make the down payment on a house. "My wife likes horror movies, we wanted to buy a house, and they offered me a gig," he explained to Ryan. "[The film's supernatural villain Freddy Krueger] and I never met." He and Hajna have since divorced. Fishburne also played a cop in the thriller *Red Heat,* and, starting in the late 1980s, had the recurring role of the lovable Cowboy Curtis on the Saturday morning television series *Pee-Wee's Playhouse.* Among his other television projects were the film *A Rumor of War* and guest appearances on episodes of *Hill Street Blues* and *Miami Vice.*

In 1990 Fishburne landed an important role playing "New Jack Gangster" Jimmy Jump in Ferrara's *King of New York,* co-starring Christopher Walken and Wesley Snipes. Though the part was originally written for an Italian-American, Fishburne lobbied for it. "This cat was funny, enjoyed what he did," he said of the character in his interview with Smith, "he didn't deal drugs, he just killed people--the kind of lovable badman any actor would love to do. I talked to them for about four hours and I said, 'Look, young black people who saw *School Daze* in particular recognize me; there's at least two million of them living in New York, and if you put me in this role, a million of them will go see it, guaranteed, and they'll tell the other million." His extravagant performance was evidently as much fun for him to perform as it was for his audience to watch. "I took some liberty," he admitted to Smith. "For some people it may seem exaggerated, overblown, like I'm going way over the top with it. But that's real stuff." Fishburne also began working with

playwright Lanford Wilson in 1990, to develop the character of Sterling in Wilson's *Two Trains Running.*

True to his commitment to balance the cinematic "nuts" with responsible characters, Fishburne played an attorney working for activist lawyer Gene Hackman in Michael Apted's 1991 film *Class Action. People* correspondent Ralph Novak felt that Fishburne and the rest of the supporting cast were "first teamers." *Sight and Sound* praised "a perfectly formed performance from Larry Fishburne, a great black actor spoiling for a part in something really big." Fishburne also appeared in Martin Sheen's *Cadence,* a military drama co-starring Sheen and his son Charlie. "Fishburne, as leader of the black stockade residents, has a sly Jack Nicholson-like way of ingratiating himself," opined Novak.

Gained Recognition With Boyz

Fishburne's next big project was *Boyz N The Hood,* a film directed by then-23-year-old John Singleton, who had been a production assistant on *Pee-Wee's Playhouse.* As Furious Styles, the entrepreneur-activist father who guides his son out of trouble and into responsibility, Fishburne earned rave reviews. *Sight and Sound* declared, "Larry Fishburne continues to be a matchless screen presence in the central role of Furious," while Stanley Kauffmann of the *New Republic* wrote that the actor "brings an even-tempered, unforced authority to the role."

Even critics who disliked the film's tone admired Fishburne's work. Novak noted that Fishburne "acts his way through most of Singleton's verbiage, conveying the determination of a father trying to give his son a chance." Edmond Grant of *Films in Review* lamented that "the finest actor in the film ... gets the corniest role." While admitting that Fishburne "does bring some depth to the role," Grant was disturbed that Furious functioned primarily as "an obvious mouthpiece for Singleton's concerns." Christine Dolen of the *Detroit Free Press* observed that with *Boyz* Fishburne "seemed to leap, like a major movie star at the height of his power, from the screen into our startled and appreciative consciousness." Yet Fishburne is quoted in the same piece as saying that "*Boyz N The Hood* did take my career to a different level. But I did what I've been doing for the last 20 years. I think it was the power of the whole film. I give the credit to the writing and the execution of that film."

Won Awards for Stage Role

In his next role in Lanford Wilson's stage play *Two Trains Running,* which opened on Broadway in 1992, Fishburne won a Tony Award for best featured actor in a play and also picked up Outer Critic's Circle, Drama Desk, and Theater World awards. As Sterling, an ex-convict espousing the black empowerment philosophy of civil rights activist Malcolm X, Fishburne once again stunned the critics. Frank Rich of the *New York Times* wrote that the actor "greets each of Sterling's defeats with pride and heroic optimism" and called Fishburne and his co-star Roscoe Lee Browne "the jewels of the production."

Perew claimed that Fishburne's work in *Two Trains Running* "should convince any doubters that Larry Fishburne will forever play lead roles" and added, "watching the play, you get black history the way Sterling has seen it. Fishburne is quirky, insightful, often humorous and, finally, a profound Sterling." Of the role, the actor himself stated in his interview with Pacheco that "Sterling's a man with an idea, and that's what makes him dangerous," and that the character has "just got out of jail, he's got no money and he's got no job. When a brother's got to get himself a hustle, that makes him dangerous." He told Dolen that working with Browne, Wilson, and director Lloyd Richards was a bigger thrill than winning a Tony: "This is the longest time I've worked in the theater. It's the most exciting; it requires real discipline and develops your concentration to a level that I know when I come off this, no matter what the part is in what movie, I'll be able to do it. Because I feel like a bona fide actor now."

Played a Deep Character in Deep Cover

Returning to film in 1992, Fishburne portrayed a genuinely challenging character in *Deep Cover*: Russell Stevens, Jr., an undercover cop who gets drawn into the world of drug-dealing and begins to lose his moral bearings. Director Bill Duke found Fishburne's subtlety and range perfect for the part: "Larry can show a side of himself that will do whatever is necessary to get what he wants. He becomes as ferocious a bad guy as [he does] a cop. Looking in Larry's eyes, you don't see a lie, and that's what you want in an actor," Duke observed to Ryan, adding that he found Fishburne "confident but not egotistical." Commenting on Duke's improvisational, actor-centered approach, Fishburne observed in an *Entertainment Weekly* profile, "It's collaborative here. Everyone throws in his two cents." Duke contended in the same article that Fishburne was at first uneasy with the director's approach: "Larry hated working with me in the beginning. He's used to rehearsing a scene the way it's going to be shot. I said, 'Larry, that's not how I work.' It always made him nervous, but he started to trust me and we had a good collaboration."

Fishburne himself found playing Stevens a rich opportunity. "What makes Stevens special for me," he told Ryan, "is

he's a cop and he's a criminal at the same time. He has to do bad in order to do good. White actors get to play this type of stuff a lot, and we don't. It's an opportunity to show up and be a man on the screen--not a black man, not a white man, not a superman, just a man." Owen Gleiberman of *Entertainment Weekly* pointed to Fishburne's performance as one of the strengths of a film he judged inconsistent: "Fishburne, with his hair-trigger line readings and deadly reptilian gaze, conveys the controlled desperation of someone watching his faith unravel."

Gives Multi-Layered Performances

In 1993, Fishburne again played a character with a dark side when he starred opposite Angela Bassett in the movie version of singer Tina Turner's autobiography, *What's Love Got to Do With It*. Although he initially turned down the role of Turner's abusive husband, Ike, because it was too one-sidedly evil to be realistic, the opportunity to work with Bassett again (they acted opposite each other in *Boyz N the Hood*) proved to be too much of a draw. But rather than accept the flat character, Fishburne reworked his portrayal of Ike to demonstrate the humanizing charm which made Ike so attractive prior to his descent into drug abuse and violence. Rita Kempley of the *Washington Post* said, "Fishburne's performance is astounding for the humanity he brings to the thinly-drawn Ike." That same year he stepped down from star billing in order to play a streetsmart chess player in *Searching for Bobby Fischer*. Fishburne's character mentors a young chess prodigy who resists outside pressure to play chess competitively.

The year 1995 was a full one for the actor as six of his projects came to life. In a career move not unlike his decision to act in *For Us the Living*, Fishburne took a pay cut in order to lend the weight of his celebrity to the HBO movie *The Tuskegee Airmen*. He played Hannibal Lee, a pilot who endures racial prejudice in the course of his flying career with the all-black 99th Squadron of the 332d Fighter Group of the U.S. Air Force during World War II. Fishburne earned an Emmy nomination for his performance in this dramatization of the real-life elite fighting unit.

For the movie *Higher Learning*, Fishburne once again teamed up with director John Singleton to play a West Indian professor at an American university that is a racial and ideological war zone. Although the role of Professor Phipps is a smaller one in the film, critic Roger Ebert remarked that Fishburne's portrayal is "all the more effective because it is so subtle." While some critics found Singleton's characterizations rigidly stereotypical and the plot overblown, Fishburne was singled out in reviews time and again as outstanding.

Neither did critics fault Fishburne for the flaws of two 1995 thrillers *Bad Company* and *Just Cause,* in which he plays men immersed in illegal activities. In *Bad Company,* also starring Ellen Barkin, he is the newest recruit in an underworld company that specializes in industrial spying. The betrayals come fast and furious, but critics were largely unimpressed with the complicated plot and the emphasis on sex and violence. While commenting that "the film is a bore, a brute, a dullard," *Washington Post* critic Hal Hinson also noted, "with his panther glide and lounge-lizard eyes, Fishburne has become one of film's most mesmerizing stars." *Just Cause,* a suspense thriller about a law professor's investigation of a murder conviction in a Southern backwater town, was likewise criticized for being all plot and no substance. However, Fishburne's performance as the sadistic police chief who beats a confession out of the suspect, inspired Mike LaSalle of the *San Francisco Chronicle* to write, "Fishburne is scary enough in his own right. His performance, the most complex and fascinating in the film, never stops revealing layers of a character who on first glance seems a standard villain."

Plays First Black Othello on Screen

Fishburne generated a cinematic "first" when he became the first African American to play Shakespeare's Othello on the silver screen. Following in the footsteps of such legendary actors as Sir Laurence Olivier and Orson Welles, Fishburne brought the Moor Othello to life in the 1995 production which also starred Kenneth Branagh as Iago and Irene Jacob as Desdemona. While critics debated the merits of this version which cut the play by a third, Fishburne received good reviews for a role he admitted scared him initially. "It's definitely scary before you start. And harder to shake off afterwards. After all, Othello has been around for almost 400 years," he remarked in an interview with *Insight on the News.* Even though some critics faulted his inexperience with Elizabethan English for the diminished impact of his lines, the sheer charisma of Fishburne's screen presence won over audiences. Janet Matlin of the *New York Times* wrote, "With no previous Shakespearean experience, he at first displays an improbable loftiness, sounding very much the rarified thespian beside Mr. Branagh's deceptively regular Joe. But Mr. Fishburne's performance has a dangerous edge that ultimately works to its advantage, and he smolders movingly through the most anguished parts of the role."

Takes Stage Roles

But not content with film and television, Fishburne expanded his acting credits to include the stage when his own play, *Riff Raff,* appeared at the Off-Broadway Circle Repertory Theater. Fishburne wrote the script about two half-brothers hiding from the law in a friend's apartment in just eight days while filming *Just Cause,* and earned praise for its sharp dialogue and compelling story. In an enthusiastic review, *New York Times* critic Ben Brantley wrote "It is a relief to learn that Mr. Fishburne doesn't need a big screen or someone else's script to tell a story compellingly." Fishburne also directed and starred in the production. In 1999, he returned to the stage when he starred in the play *The Lion in Winter* at the Roundabout Theater Company in New York City.

Returns to Film with Fled

In 1996, Fishburne's participation in the buddy movie, *Fled,* was universally acknowledged as a step down in the quality of films the actor typically chose as critics lambasted the movie as brainless, cliched, and violent. Fishburne played the convict Piper, who escapes from a chain gang while manacled to fellow convict, Dodge. Together, they must elude the pursuing authorities and underworld figures in order to retrieve millions of dollars Dodge stole from the Cuban-American Mafia. Once again critics distanced the actor from the faults of the movie; after dwelling on improbable plot developments and poor dialogue, Roger Ebert commented that "Laurence Fishburne brings an authority to his role that the screenplay doesn't really deserve."

In 1997, Fishburne became involved with another HBO movie based on historical facts when he starred with Alfre Woodard in *Miss Evers' Boys.* The story is based on an actual medical experiment conducted by the government between 1932 and 1972, in which African American men suffering from syphilis were left untreated so that the effects of the disease could be studied. Woodard played the nurse, Miss Evers, who acts as friend and confidante to the men while, at the same time, she is aware of the deception her participation in the experiment necessitates. Fishburne played one of the victims of the experiment who becomes Miss Evers' romantic interest.

Violent Movies Take Critical Hit

Two graphically violent movies finished off 1997 for Fishburne: *Event Horizon* and *Hoodlum.* Neither movie was a darling of the critics who complained about the poor plots and gratuitous bloodletting. *Event Horizon,* a science fiction-horror movie about a space ship which disappears and mysteriously returns seven years later with the presence of pure evil on board, received special attention for its extreme gore, chaotic plot, and breathtaking special effects. In the movie, Fishburne played the commander of the crew sent to investigate the mysterious spacecraft. *Variety* critic Joe Leydon noted that the actor "perform[s] far beyond the call of duty, but to little avail," finding that "[the] initial promise of the offbeat premise...is rapidly dissipated by routine execution and risible dialogue." *Hoodlum* suffered much the same critical fate. The plot to that movie revolved around a Harlem gangster's attempt to thwart a white gangster's coup of the lucrative Harlem numbers game during the Depression. Fishburne, playing gangster Bumpy Johnson, lent an "instrinsic appeal" to a film which was described by Mike LaSalle of the *San Francisco Chronicle* as "an overlong gangster movie, a bloated and often laughable attempt at an epic."

Plays Positive African American Roles

Fishburne returned to the medium of some of his most lauded work when he played a compassionate ex-convict in the HBO movie *Always Outnumbered*. Based on stories by acclaimed African American author Walter Mosely, the story follows Socrates Fortlow–Fishburne's character–as he attempts to help his community after serving nearly thirty years in jail. The positive portrayal of African American men is particularly important to Fishburne who acknowledged in a *Jet* article the scarcity of such images in movies. "Socrates is a character who reminds people that not all [African American men] are ignorant, not all of us beat up women, not all of us are what you would think we are. Most of us are decent human beings."

Fishburne closed out the century in the reality-bending science-fiction thriller, *The Matrix*. Also starring Keanu Reeves, the cerebral action movie concerns a group of rebels who are trying to expose the matrix, a virtual reality which has been imposed on humanity by a machine to fool them into believing that they are free. Fishburne is Morpheus, the leader of this collection of renegades, who recruits Reeves's character to spearhead the rebellion. While the movie raised many philosophical issues, critics complained that it retreated from deeper explorations of the subjects of identity and reality in favor of high-gloss action sequences.

Fishburne has emerged in the 1990s as an African American actor of considerable talent whose name and reputation are worthy of top billing in whatever project he chooses. Unlike the black actors of yesteryear, Fishburne has proven that he does not need the support of a better-known white actor to draw in audiences, and, even when handicapped with less-than-average scripts, he manages to bowl over critics with his range and intelligence. As an advocate for positive African American images, Fishburne has successfully brought to life stories of significance to the African American community while breaking into roles not originally earmarked for black actors. With his versatility and depth, Fishburne will likely continue finding success as one of Hollywood's leading men.

Sources

Books

Current Biography Yearbook, 1996.

Periodicals

Back Stage, March 26, 1999.
Black Elegance, June/July 1992.
Chicago Sun-Times, January 11, 1995; December 29, 1995.
Detroit Free Press, June 2, 1992.
Entertainment Weekly, April 24, 1992.
Film Comment, July/August 1990.
Films in Review, February 1992.
Insight on the News, January 15, 1996.
Jet, July 15, 1991; February 24, 1997; March 23, 1998..
Los Angeles Times, January 12, 1992.
New Republic, September 2, 1991.
Newsweek, July 15, 1991.
New York, July 22, 1991.
New York Times, April 14, 1992.
Parade, June 28, 1992.
People, March 25, 1991; April 1, 1991; July 22, 1991.
Premiere, May 1992.
San Francisco Chronicle, August 4, 1995; August 27, 1997.
Sight and Sound, July 1991; August 1991; November 1991.
Time, May 11, 1992.
Variety, August 18, 1997.
Video Review, March 1992.
Washington Post, July 7, 1991; June 11, 1993; January 20, 1995; December 29, 1995.

Other

Additional information obtained from a press biography on Fishburne.

—Simon Glickman and Rebecca Parks

Josh Gibson

1911–1947

Professional baseball player

Josh Gibson, one of the most mysterious and revered figures of the Negro Leagues baseball era, was born on December 21, 1911. Some sources claim he hit over 900 home runs in his career, which spanned from 1930 to 1946 in the Negro National League and in leagues in Puerto Rico, the Dominican Republic, Venezuela, and Mexico. Although his exact statistics may never be known, Gibson led the Negro National League in home runs in nine of his 15 seasons. His father, Mark Gibson, lived in Buena Vista, Georgia, and worked as a sharecropper. He and his wife, Nancy Woodlock Gibson, had three children—Josh, Annie, and Jerry. The family moved to Pittsburgh in 1923. Gibson attended a vocational school and, by the time he was 15, began working in steel mines with his father. Already 6' 2" and 200 pounds, the hard physical labor further enhanced Gibson's already imposing physique. During this time, he also started playing baseball. Gibson played catcher for company teams such as Westinghouse Airbrake, Carnegie-Illinois, and Gimbel's department store.

In 1928 Harold Tinker, manager of a local professional team called the Pittsburgh Crawfords, first saw Gibson play at an Industrial League all-star game and immediately signed him to a contract. This chance meeting would alter Gibson's life and change the face of Negro League baseball. That same year, he met Helen Mason and the two were married on March 7, 1929. Gibson lived with his new in-laws on days when he didn't have scheduled games with the Crawfords, and worked as an elevator operator at Gimbels department store. This situation would soon change, however. Gibson's offensive power attracted the attention of the Homestead Grays, the professional Negro League team in Pittsburgh. On July 31, 1930, Gibson signed with the Homestead Grays. His professional success was soon dampened by personal tragedy. Gibson's wife, Helen, died while giving birth to twins. Gibson was so stunned by the death of his wife that he left the hospital before the children were named. He immediately rejoined the Grays and didn't tell anyone on the team what had happened. The children would eventually be raised by Helen's parents and took the names Josh and Helen.

Rejoined the Crawfords

As a member of the Grays, Gibson worked hard to

At a Glance . . .

Born on December 21, 1911 in Buena Vista, Georgia; died on January 20, 1947 in Pittsburgh, Pennsylvania; son of Mark and Nancy Gibson; married Helen Gibson; children: Josh Jr. and Helen.

Career: Played baseball for the Pittsburgh Crawfords, 1928-29, 1932-36; Homestead Grays, 1930-31, 1937-39, 1942-46; played for Club Azul in Vera Cruz, Mexico, 1940-41; throughout his career also played in Puerto Rico, the Dominican Republic, and Venezuela.

Awards: Led the Negro National League in home runs in nine of 15 seasons, started in nine East West All-Star Games; Won the Mexican League batting title and MVP award, 1941; Enshrined in the baseball Hall of Fame, 1972.

improve his baseball skills. He played various positions in the field, but was unable to displace the team's regular catcher. This situation changed when the Grays met the Lincoln Giants in a ten-game championship series in 1930. During the series, Gibson played so brilliantly that he replaced Buck Ewing as the team's catcher. The Grays won the series 6-4 and Gibson batted .368 in the series. After a solid 1931 season with the Grays, Gibson again signed with the team in February of 1932. The following day Gus Greenlee, the owner of the Crawfords, called Gibson and offered him a contract that would pay $250 per month. Gibson stunned the Grays by signing that contract. Although Grays owner Cumberland Posey resorted to threats in an attempt to retain his services, Gibson reported to the Pittsburgh Crawfords spring training camp. Gibson missed the first three weeks of the season with appendicitis, but was fully recovered when the Crawfords opened their new stadium in Pittsburgh on April 30, 1932. Gibson was behind the plate and the legendary Satchel Paige was on the mound for the Crawfords inaugural game. Lena Horne threw out the first pitch and Duke Ellington's band played after the game, which the Crawfords lost 1-0. Paige and Gibson soon became good friends, although Gibson did not have Paige's taste for the nightlife. Paige was known to pitch for other teams while under contract with the Crawfords, and soon began to bring Gibson with him when he moonlighted with other clubs. The duo even played a game for the Homestead Grays. When the 1932 season ended Gibson headed to Puerto Rico to play winter ball, a practice he continued throughout his career. In 1933, Gibson enjoyed another fine season and appeared in the first Negro League All-

Star Game. That same year, he met Hattie Jones and entered into his first serious relationship since the death of his wife. Gibson and Jones lived together and then bought a house in the spring of 1934.

Gibson played for the Crawfords during the 1934 season. Following the conclusion of the season, Gibson and Paige barnstormed against an all-white team of Major League All-Stars led by pitcher Dizzy Dean. Gibson played exceptionally well and frustrated his white opponents. After Gibson hit a massive home run, Dean became so upset that he threw up his hands and decided to play outfield for the remainder of the game. Gibson's play also caught the attention of other Major League greats, such as Hall of Fame pitcher Walter Johnson. Patrick Butters, in an article for *Insight on the News,* included Johnson's comment that it was "too bad" Gibson wasn't white. "He can do everything. He hits the ball a mile and he catches so easy, he might be in a rocking chair." remarked Johnson. In 1935, Paige refused to sign with the Crawfords because they would not give him a large pay raise, but Gibson and his teammates prospered without him. Gibson led the Crawfords to the Negro National League pennant and he began to be referred to as the "Black Babe Ruth." Paige returned to the Crawfords in 1936, but the team did not enjoy the success of the previous season. Gibson had one of his best seasons, however, batting .457 with 14 home runs.

Returned to the Grays

In 1937, Gibson held out for more money and refused to join the Crawfords. He also began to spend time with Sam Bankhead, a former teammate in Pittsburgh and in Puerto Rico. Gibson became more assertive under Bankhead's guidance, but he also began to drink heavily. When Gibson refused to accept the Crawford's final salary offer, he was traded back to the Homestead Grays on March 27, 1937. The Grays were reinvigorated by Gibson's return and quickly became the top club in the league. During the middle of the Grays season, however, Gibson decided to leave the team in order to play with other Negro National League stars in the Dominican Republic. During his stint in the Dominican Republic, he was paid $2,000 dollars for seven weeks of work and led the league in hitting with a .453 batting average. By the end of the 1937 season, the political situation in the Dominican Republic had greatly deteriorated. Gibson and other American stars were housed in jails for their own protection and often played their games before rifle-toting soldiers. Following the completion of the season in the Dominican Republic, Gibson returned to the Grays. In his first game back with the club, he belted three home runs. Gibson's exceptional play earned him the attention of both the black and white media of the time. As his fame and public stature increased, Gibson began to abuse alcohol more frequently. In fact, he missed the 1938 Negro League All-Star Game because he had gotten drunk the night before he was to leave and missed his train to Chicago.

Stayed South of the Border

In 1940, Gibson's personal life began to spin out of control. His drinking escalated and he began to use marijuana. His relationship with Hattie Jones also began to deteriorate. During 1940, Gibson opted to play baseball in Mexico and Venezuela. Many observers believed that Gibson had stayed out of the United States in order to escape his domestic troubles. After the conclusion of play in Mexico and Venezuela, Gibson returned to the United States and signed a new contract with the Grays that paid him $500 a month. In 1941, the Negro Leagues and its stars were receiving an increasing amount of attention from the white-dominated media. Legendary *Washington Post* sports writer Shirley Povich gave his opinion of the Negro Leagues, "There's a couple million dollars worth of baseball talent on the loose, ready for the big leagues, yet unsigned by any Major League. There are pitchers who would win 20 games a season ... and outfielders who could hit .350 ... and there's at least one catcher who at this writing is probably superior to (New York Yankee's catcher) Bill Dickey—Josh Gibson." Before the start of the 1941 season, Gibson shocked fans when he decided to renege on his contract with the Grays in order to play for Club Azul, the Mexican team he had played for previously. Deeply angered by Gibson's defection, Gray's owner Cumberland Posey sued Gibson for $10,000. The judge in the case also ruled that if Gibson did not return from Mexico within six days, his house would be in foreclosure. After securing a promise from Gibson that he would return to the Grays for the 1942 season, Posey dropped the lawsuit. During his season in Mexico, Gibson led his team to a championship and received the league MVP Award and home run title.

Health Faltered

In 1942, Gibson signed with the Grays for $250 a month plus bonuses. He also reconciled with Hattie Jones. The Grays enjoyed a spectacular season and met the Kansas City Monarchs, led by Satchel Paige, in the Negro League World Series. Paige dominated Gibson throughout the series. In game two, Paige intentionally walked the bases loaded to pitch to Gibson and struck him out on three straight pitches. This humiliating episode provided a graphic illustration that Gibson, the most feared hitter in the Negro Leagues, was a shadow of his former self.

Gibson tried to rest after the season, but was plagued by increasingly severe headaches. On New Years Day in 1943, Gibson collapsed and had a seizure. He was rushed to a hospital, where he fell into a coma. Upon regaining consciousness, Gibson's doctors informed him that he had a brain tumor. Gibson refused to have the tumor removed and did not notify the Grays management regarding his condition. A newspaper reported that Gibson had been hospitalized for nervous exhaustion.

Gibson started the 1943 season stronger and slimmer. He had such a good season that he was honored with a "Josh Gibson Night" and was featured in a *Time* article. Gibson also led the Grays to a Negro World Series victory over the Birmingham Black Barons. Despite enjoying one of the finest seasons of his career, Gibson's drinking problem worsened and his behavior became more erratic. On several occasions, Gibson's teammates put him in a cab and sent him to a hospital to dry out after games. These hospital stays usually lasted only one or two days, but some of the stays lasted a week or more.

Gibson played baseball in Puerto Rico during the winter of 1943. When he returned to the Grays for the 1944 season, he was out of shape and skipped spring training. However, despite the obvious decline of his skills, fans still flocked to stadiums across the east coast to watch Gibson play. During this time, he began a relationship with Grace Fournier, who was married to a solider stationed in the South Pacific. The pair lived a very raucous lifestyle, were often drunk, and rumored to be abusing heroin. Some former teammates believed that Fournier was a drug addict who had contributed greatly to Gibson's continued decline. In 1944, the Grays again won the Negro World Series against the Birmingham Black Barons in five games. Although his skills as a catcher remained sharp, Gibson struggled at the plate. During the series, he only hit three singles.

During the 1945 season, Gibson led the Negro Leagues with a .393 batting average. However, he only hit four home runs. That same year Jackie Robinson was signed by the Brooklyn Dodgers, becoming the first African American to play in the major leagues. This event marked the beginning of the end for the Negro Leagues, as many of its best players left for the majors. In 1946, Gibson played well in his last season with the Homestead Grays. He batted .361 and hit 18 home runs. It was becoming evident, however, that years of overindulgence and alcohol abuse had taken their toll on Gibson. By January of 1947, his health had declined dramatically. His weight slipped to 180 pounds and he suffered from liver disease, bronchitis, and nervous exhaustion. These health problems were worsened by Gibson's continued abuse of alcohol. He eventually became unable to care for himself and moved in with his mother. On January 20, 1947, Josh Gibson died. The cause of death has been attributed to either a stroke or a brain tumor. On August 7, 1972, Gibson was inducted into the major league baseball Hall of Fame.

Sources

Books

Ribowsky, Mark. *The Power and the Darkness: The Life of Josh Gibson in the Shadows of the Game.* Simon & Schuster: NY. 1996.

Periodicals

Insight on the News, September 21, 1998.
The Tribune-Review, January 19, 1997.

Other

Additional material for this essay was found on the worldwide web at http://www.majorleaguebaseball.com/nbl/nl13.sml.

—Michael Watkins

JoJo and K-Ci Hailey

Vocalists

Black music in the 1990s displayed a fascinating tension between traditional R&B, steeped in gospel roots, and newer and very streetwise hip-hop sounds. The brother duo of K-Ci and JoJo balanced on that razor's edge, mixing soulful vocals and harmonies with hip-hop attitudes and sounds. As part of the group Jodeci and as a solo act that emerged with great success in 1997, they were among the rhythm-and-blues field's most consistent album sellers and live concert draws over the entire decade. With a career that took them from pure gospel to the tutelage of the wildly successful hip-hop impresario Sean "Puffy" Combs, K-Ci and JoJo drew on the best of sharply different traditions.

K-Ci was born Cedric Hailey on September 2, 1969, and JoJo was born Joel Hailey on June 10, 1971. The brothers were born in Charlotte, North Carolina, and grew up in the nearby town of Monroe. The sons of gospel singers, they were raised in a strictly religious household. When the two brothers headed for New York to seek their musical fortune, their parents disapproved. "They weren't crazy about us leaving Monroe, North Carolina, to try to make it in the business," JoJo told *Ebony* magazine. "It was like, 'Why, baby?'," he continued.

Grew Up On Classic Gospel

K-Ci and JoJo grew up hearing the classic gospel sounds of Shirley Caesar, Sam Cooke, and the Winans, but also absorbed influences from soul vocalists such as Bobby Womack and Donny Hathaway. They performed together with their father in a group called Little Cedric & The Hailey Singers, and by the time the brothers had reached their teenage years, the group had already recorded three gospel albums. As with so many other acts in the history of R&B, the brothers' musical style was based in gospel: their intricately layered yet explosive vocal harmonies were already nearly perfected when they entered the secular music business.

In 1989 they joined with another pair of gospel-singing brothers, Dalvin and Donald DeGrate (now known respectively as Mr. Dalvin and DeVante Swing) to form Jodeci; the group's name was formed by combining syllables from three of its members' stage names. The group headed for New York, demo tape in hand. They landed an appointment with MCA's new urban label, Uptown, and although the representative they had first contacted gave thumbs down to their demo, they struck gold when it was overheard by rapper Heavy D. A live audition with Uptown CEO Andre Harrell turned into a contract, guest appearances on albums by Father MC and Jeff Redd, and finally Jodeci's debut album release, *Forever My Lady*, in 1991.

Uptown's gradual buildup of its young new group proved a wise strategy, for *Forever My Lady* rose to number one on the R&B charts and cracked the pop Top Twenty. Three singles—"Come & Talk to Me," "Stay," and the title track topped the R&B singles charts. The album, which sold well

At a Glance . . .

Born Cedric Hailey (K-Ci), September 2, 1969; Joel Hailey (JoJo) born, June 10, 1971; both brothers born in Charlotte, North Carolina; parents were gospel singers; children: K-Ci, a son; JoJo, a daughter. *Religion:* Baptist.

Career: Performed with Mr. Dalvin (Dalvin DeGrate) and DeVante Swing (Donald DeGrate, Jr.), formed group Jodeci, 1989; group signed to MCA subsidiary Uptown label, 1989; Jodeci released debut album *Forever My Lady*, 1991, *Diary of a Mad Band*, 1994, and *The Show, The After Party, The Hotel*, 1995; K-Ci and JoJo sang vocals on Tupac Shakur single, "How Do You Want It," 1996; K-Ci & JoJo debut release as duo, *Love Always*, 1997; *It's Real*, 1999.

Awards: Platinum sales levels for all Jodeci and K-Ci & JoJo releases; American Music Award, 1999.

Addresses: *Record company*—MCA, 1755 Broadway, New York, NY 10019.

over two million copies, showed the persistence and resiliency of traditional R&B romantic ballad singing, and its adaptability to a new era. As a *Vibe* magazine commentator had it, "The Jodeci sound—lush love songs with lots of whispered sweet nothings and declarations of need—is characteristic of the piningly sincere R&B balladry that rap would seem to have all but obliterated. Yet rather than seeming obsolete or old-fashioned, Jodeci have made that sound hip again."

Adopted Bad Boy Image

Jodeci's new hipness was a matter not just of music but also of fashion and style. Harrell immersed his gentle young Southerners in big-city culture, sending them to live in the rough Bronx neighborhood in which he grew up. It is probable that Jodeci's image was forged largely by the man who has succeeded better than anyone else in marketing hip-hop to a wide audience: Sean "Puffy" Combs. Jodeci made a strong impression in concert and on video with their up-to-the-minute oversized boots and pants and their suggestive stage moves.

The combination of hip-hop style and expressive R&B balladry installed Jodeci in the top rank of the black

entertainment world, and also exerted a strong influence in the next few years on up-and-coming harmonizers like Boyz II Men, Shai, and Silk. They kept their hand in traditional R&B with a lovely cover of Stevie Wonder's "Lately," included on the predominantly acoustic *Uptown MTV Unplugged* collection of 1993. The song brought Jodeci substantial pop success (it rose to number four on the pop charts), and although K-Ci and JoJo would themselves achieve major pop sales on their own a few years later, they claimed convincingly that they had never undertaken a specific crossover effort.

Jodeci released *Diary of a Mad Band* in 1993 and *The Show, The After Party, The Hotel* in 1995, increasing the proportion of rap music in their output and continuing to enjoy great success with their presentation, in which hip-hop attitude transformed romance into sexuality. *Ebony* reported that the group had become known as the "Kings of Do-Me R&B." K-Ci's voice was compared to that of Bobby Womack and to that of another master of stage sensuality, Teddy Pendergrass; his rendition of Womack's "If You Think You're Lonely Now" was included in the soundtrack of the film *Jason's Lyric*.

K-Ci and JoJo began to define an independent identity when they were centrally featured in Tupac Shakur's 1996 rap hit, "How Do You Want It." Though the brothers insist that Jodeci had not broken up and planned future releases as a group, they clearly were seeking new challenges. "Jodeci has been at it for almost ten years now," K-Ci explained to *Ebony*, "and even a mule takes a water break." Their label MCA supported the emergence of K-Ci and JoJo as a solo act, but the brothers still felt trepidation: Jodeci had been a true creative team, with each member making unique contributions. "We had MCA looking at us saying, 'We know you can do it,' but we were asking ourselves, Can we do it?" JoJo told *Essence*.

Song Catapulted Duo to Multiplatinum Success

The debut K-Ci and JoJo album, *Love Always*, was released in June of 1997. Its sales in the weeks after its launch were modest, its first two singles ("You Bring Me Up" and "Last Night's Letter") scored well among urban audiences but failed to match Jodeci's pop success. However, the third single, "All My Life," a song written by JoJo and addressed to his seven-year-old daughter, launched the album into multiplatinum sales and pop music history. The song was premiered by a Honolulu radio station, and spread rapidly through the playlists of both urban and pop radio outlets. A romantic ballad that became the theme song for countless couples, the song tied a record set by the Beatles in 1966 by leaping from

Number Fifteen to the top slot in successive pop charts. *Love Always* eventually topped the three-million sales mark.

K-Ci and JoJo were no mere extension of Jodeci. As the genesis of "All My Life" might imply, they carved out a very different image, one that emphasized romance and toned down the sexual suggestiveness the group had communicated. "You can listen to this in the car, riding with the folks, and not be embarrassed," K-Ci (also a father, of a seven-year-old son) told *Ebony*. The brothers composed most of the music for the album, and seemed to have set out on a new path as they neared their thirtieth birthdays. The album, said *People,* was "remarkably understated if not downright polite." "We had this 'bad boy' image, and we're trying to get around that," JoJo told *Jet.* "We don't get as much attention as we used to get now that we're doing right," he added ruefully. But K-Ci and JoJo found themselves very busy in 1998 and 1999, working with hitmaker Babyface as part of a group called Milestone that propelled the *Soul Food* film soundtrack to platinum status, and contributing songs to the soundtracks of films *The Prince of Egypt* and *Life.* The second K-Ci and JoJo album, *It's Real,* was slated for release in June of 1999.

Selected discography

(with Jodeci)

Forever My Lady, Uptown, 1991.
Uptown Unplugged, Uptown, 1993.

Diary of a Mad Band, Uptown, 1994.
The Show, The After Party, The Hotel, Uptown, 1995.

(as K-Ci and JoJo)

Love Always, MCA, 1997.
It's Real, MCA, 1999.

Sources

Books

Contemporary Musicians, volume 13, Gale, 1995.
Graff, Gary, Josh Freedom du Lac, and Jim McFarlin, *MusicHound R&B: The Essential Album Guide,* Visible Ink, 1998.
Larkin, Colin, ed., *The Encyclopedia of Popular Music,* Muze UK, 1998.
Romanowski, Patricia, and Holly George-Warren, eds., *The New Rolling Stone Encyclopedia of Rock and Roll,* Fireside, 1995.

Periodicals

Ebony, October 1998, p. 80.
Essence, August 1998, p. 58.
Jet, November 24, 1997, p. 57.
People, July 21, 1997, p. 21.
Playboy, October 1993, p. 17.

—James M. Manheim

Kadeem Hardison

1966—

Actor, television director, producer

A mainstay of the NBC comedy series *A Different World,* actor Kadeem Hardison helped co-star Jasmine Guy anchor the series during its six-year run. From 1987 to 1992, Hardison developed his fast-talking, somewhat nerdy character Dwayne Wayne into what the *Washington Post* aptly described in 1990 as "a hip Phi Beta Kappa who hides his sensitivity" behind trademark flip-up shades. It is the role for which he is best known, and it earned him an NAACP Image Award in 1989 and an Image Award nomination in 1992.

Theatre-trained—he appeared in several productions at the Eubie Blake Theatre—Hardison has worked steadily since his television debut in the early eighties, making numerous guest appearances on several television series and specials. His work on *A Different World* was decisive in the show's ability to soon stand on its own, well beyond the shadow of *The Cosby Show.* Hardison has also had many supporting and central roles on his list of film credits, including parts in *School Daze* (1988), *White Men Can't Jump* (1992), *Panther* (1995), and *The Sixth Man* (1997). In addition to acting, Hardison has directed episodes of *A Different World,* and also served as co-executive producer on the CBS-TV Schoolbreak Special *Words Up!* in 1992.

Acting Classes Directed Career

The son of Bethann Hardison, a former fashion model, and Donald McFadden, an art collector, Kadeem Hardi-
son was born July 24, 1966 in Brooklyn, New York. He was an only child whose parents were married for only a short time, and was raised in Brooklyn by three women: his mother, his aunt Marta, and his late grandmother, Sophie. The constant travel demands of her career meant he would see his mother less frequently than his aunt and grandmother in his first ten years, but Hardison told *People Weekly* in 1992 that he credits her with being "the driving force, the one I got ambition from." Although she would encourage him to pursue modeling, Bethann Hardison enrolled her son in acting classes at the age of nine.

When he was 14, Hardison landed his first role in *The Color of Friendship,* an ABC After School Special. He also appeared in the ABC After School Specials *Amazing Grace* and *Don't Touch.* In 1984, at the age of 17, he appeared as Royal in the PBS production *Go Tell It on the Mountain,* and also won a recurring role on *The Cosby Show* as a friend of *Cosby* son Theo. His efforts were rewarded in 1987 with the regular part of wisecracking Dwayne Wayne on the *Cosby* spinoff, *A Different World.*

Helped Steer Show to Success

Set at fictional Hillman College, the show initially featured *Cosby* daughter Denise, played by actress Lisa Bonet. The show lacked conviction and focus in its first season. Donna Britt wrote in the *Washington Post* in 1990 that

At a Glance . . .

Born Kadeem Hardison, July 24, 1966, in Brooklyn, New York; son of Bethann Hardison (owner of a modeling agency) and Donald McFadden (an art collector). *Education:* Studied acting with Earl Hyman and at H.B. Studios, New York.

Career: Actor, television director, producer. Television: *A Different World,* 1987-92; numerous guest appearances on television series and specials; host, *For Our Children: the Concert,* 1993. Made-for-television movies: *Go Tell It on the Mountain,* 1984; *Dream Date,* 1989; *Words Up!* 1992; *Drive,* 1997; *Blind Faith,* 1998. Films: *Beat Street,* 1984; *Rappin',* 1985; *I'm Gonna Git You Sucka,* 1988; *School Daze,* 1988; *Def by Temptation,* 1990; *White Men Can't Jump,* 1992; *Renaissance Man,* 1994; *Gunmen,* 1994; *Vampire in Brooklyn,* 1995; *Panther,* 1995; *Drive* 1997; *The Sixth Man,* 1997. Television director: episodes of *A Different World.* Co-executive producer: CBS-TV Schoolbreak Special *Words Up!* 1992. Video recording: *The Imagination Machines,* 1992.

Memberships: Screen Actors Guild.

Awards: Recipient, NAACP Image Award for Best Performance by an Actor in a Comedy Series or Special, for <u>A</u> *Different World,* 1989; Emmy nomination for *Words Up!* 1992; NAACP Image Award nomination for *A Different World,* 1992.

Addresses: 19743 Valleyview Drive, Topanga, CA 90291.

ensemble sitcom about the insular nature of campus life. In their book, *Harry and Wally's Favorite TV Shows,* Harry Castleman and Walter Podrazik noted the crucial addition of former *Fame* star Debbie Allen, who joined the show in 1988 as producer-director and writer. Lisa Bonet also left the show that year. The result, according to Castleman and Podrazik, was "a more truly balanced ensemble." In a cast that included DawnnLewis as Jaleesa, Darryl Bell as Ron, and Sinbad as Walter, Hardison and Guy emerged as the two main co-stars. Britt also noted that once Allen joined the production, the scripts improved significantly, broadening their scope to deal with real-life college student concerns such as date rape, unprotected sex, and drug use.

It is unfortunate that *A Different World's* favorable time slot was often credited for the show's success, causing many, including Hardison, to speculate that perhaps NBC's lackluster promotion of the show was based on racial issues. Additionally, the shadow of the show's poor first season continued to unfairly color subsequent evaluations. Nevertheless, beginning with its second season, *A Different World* received very favorable reviews of its own, and consistently placed in the Nielsen ratings' top ten shows. Hardison himself was so popular as Dwayne Wayne that he was voted favorite actor in a poll conducted by Canada's *TV Guide.* According to *Jet,* Hardison "won by a landslide." Following a successful six-year run, *A Different World* was cancelled by NBC in 1992.

Films Earned Good Reviews

In 1992 Hardison starred in *Words Up!,* a CBS Schoolbreak Special. Playing Henry, an illiterate dropout who returns to high school to get an education, his performance was called "attractive, funny and thoughtful" by the *Los Angeles Times.* Hardison also served as co-executive producer for *Words Up!* and received an Emmy nomination for his excellent work on the film. "I was proud to contribute information about a problem that greatly affects our community," he told *Essence* in 1995.

Hardison has also received favorable reviews for his acting in other films. In a review of Keenen Ivory Wayans's 1988 blaxploitation parody *I'm Gonna Git You Sucka, Variety* pronounced him "hilarious" in his supporting role. His performance as K in the 1990 all-black horror film *Def by Temptation* was called "a delight" by a *Los Angeles Times* reviewer. Although the film itself received great reviews in limited release, it was not highly publicized and performed poorly at the box office.

Hardison landed a role in the comedy *White Men Can't Jump* in 1992. Initially, Shelton did not realize Hardison

"critics bashed the show's unfunny scripts and then-star...Bonet's lackadaisical acting; black viewers wondered why so many white kids were enrolled in what was supposed to be a Howard University-type school." Hardison noted in the same article that the show "just wasn't black," and added, "The problem was the producers and the scripts. The humor wasn't true to us. We were acting like. . .high school kids from Kansas." Despite an uncertain start, the show's first season was buoyed by its favorable time slot on Thursday night, sandwiched between the wildly popular *Cosby Show* and *Cheers.*

In its second season, *A Different World* settled into a solid was a legitimate actor, and cast him in a bit part as a pick-up player. Assuring Shelton that he could handle the challenge, Hardison was given a larger role. "The result," according to *People Weekly,* was "an ad-libbed, in-your-face insult-and-hoops scrimmage that has audiences roaring." In 1994, he played Izzy in *Gunmen* and Jamaal Montgomery in the Danny DeVito film *Renaissance Man.* *Variety* called him "a hoot" in *Renaissance Man,* as one of the eight student recruits "who bring the film an inordinate amount of energy."

In 1995, Hardison starred in *Panther,* which was directed by Mario Van Peebles from a script written by his father, Melvin Van Peebles. The film is a fictionalized account of various events in Black Panther history, and Hardison plays the central character named Judge who, while sympathetic to the Panther cause, is also tapped by the authorities as an informant. *Variety* described Hardison as very effective in his role as "the classic man in the middle, someone through whom the audience presumably can. . . view the more extreme behavior of the activists on both sides." "I wanted to do this part," Hardison told *Seventeen* in 1995, "...not only because I thought it was something I could relate to, but because it's an important story."

In 1997's *Vampire in Brooklyn,* Hardison co-starred with Eddie Murphy as Julius, the vampire's ghoulish chauffeur whose limbs keep falling off. Although *Entertainment Weekly* pronounced the film "a lethally leaden horror comedy," Hardison is singled out in reviews as a scene-stealer. That same year, he co-starred with Marlon Wayans in the Disney film, *The Sixth Man.* In this basketball comedy, Hardison played Antoine Tyler, a self-serving college star who unexpectedly dies from a heart ailment. He returns from the dead to help his brother lead the Washington Huskies to the NCAA title. *Variety* reviewer Joe Leydon praised Hardison's performance, calling him "very funny as a swaggering, trash-talking spirit," as well as skilled at conveying his character's darker aspects. Leydon added, "Together, Hardison and Wayans give the comedy a bit more depth and texture than it might otherwise have had."

Although he has lived in the Los Angeles area for much of his career, Hardison's heart remains in New York, where the rhythms and energy of the city stimulate him. Described by an *Essence* interviewer in 1991 as being as "introspective and analytical" as he is outgoing and talkative, Hardison's personal tastes run to sleek motorcycles, rap, jazz, and funk. He reserves admiration for acting icons such as Eddie Murphy, Denzel Washington, Robert DeNiro, and Wesley Snipes. Having successfully made the transition from television to film, Hardison is aware of his position as an African American celebrity. "I'm an African-American," he told *Essence* in 1995, "and my role in the entertainment industry is to entertain—and to educate."

Sources

Books

Brown, Les. *Les Brown's Encyclopedia of Television,* 3rd Edition. Detroit: Gale, 1992, p.153.

Castleman, Harry, and Walter J. Podrazik. *Harry and Wally's Favorite TV Shows.* New York: Prentice Hall Press, 1989, p.129.

International Motion Picture Almanac, 68th Edition. Edited by James D. Moser. New York: Quigley Publishing Company, Inc., 1997, p.159.

Who's Who Among African Americans, 11th Edition. Edited by Shirelle Phelps. Detroit: Gale, 1999, p.541.

Who's Who in Hollywood, Vol. 1. Edited by David Ragan. New York: Facts on File, 1992, p.696.

Periodicals

Entertainment Weekly, April 19, 1996, p.86; October 24, 1997, p.72.

Essence, February 1993, p.49; June 1995, p.48.

Jet, April 16, 1990, pp.59-60; April 19, 1991, p.52; October 19, 1992, p.56; May 10, 1993, p.60; February 2, 1998, p.46.

Los Angeles Times, December 1, 1992, p.F9.

People Weekly, April 27, 1992, pp.101-102; May 22, 1995, p.17; November 13, 1995, p.26.

Playboy, July 1995, p.20.

Seventeen, June 1995, p.110.

Variety, March 31, 1997, p.86.

Variety's Film Reviews 1987-1988, Vol. 20. New Providence, RI: R.R. Bowker, 1991.

Variety's Film Reviews 1989-1990, Vol. 21. New Providence, RI: R.R. Bowker, 1991.

Variety's Film Reviews 1993-1994, Vol. 23. New Providence, RI: R.R. Bowker, 1995.

Variety's Film Reviews 1995-1996, Vol. 24. New Providence, RI: R.R. Bowker, 1997.

Washington Post, September 20, 1990, p.D1.

—*Ellen Dennis* French

Marques Hayes

1926—

Basketball player

Marques Haynes used the basketball court as a stage from which to entertain generations of fans. As the "World's Greatest Dribbler," Haynes delighted basketball crowds spanning over four decades with his ball handling wizardry. Haynes performed in over 12,000 games during the course of his legendary career with the Harlem Globetrotters and various other teams specializing in comedic basketball.

Haynes, the youngest child of Matthew and Hattie Haynes, was born in a modest shack in Sand Springs, Oklahoma, on October 3, 1926. His father, a domestic laborer, left the family four years later. All of the Haynes children played basketball, so it was no surprise that Marques took up the sport at an early age. He learned to shoot primarily from an older sister, Cecil. A brother, Wendell, taught him how to dribble. Ball handling became Marques' specialty. Of the family's early basketball exploits, Haynes told William Nack of *Sports Illustrated* in a 1985 interview, "We'd take economy-size food cans and cut the bottoms out and tack them to the outhouse, then ball rags and tie them together and shoot baskets. Sometimes we'd find a barrel hoop on an empty lot and tie a feed 'n' graingunnysack to it for a net and use that for a basket." Marques went on to star at Booker T. Washington High School, leading his team to an Oklahoma state championship in 1942.

Like his siblings, Haynes attended Langston University. He led the Langston basketball team to an impressive record of 112 wins, three losses and two conference titles.

Langston also scored a victory over the touring Harlem Globetrotters. After that game, Haynes was offered a contract by the Globetrotters, but he turned it down in order to finish his education. "My mother would have killed me if I had left school," he remarked to *Sports Illustrated*. In 1946, he earned a bachelor's degree in industrial education.

Shortly after his graduation, Haynes signed with a barnstorming team called the Kansas City Stars. The Stars were, in essence, a farm team for the Globetrotters. In 1947, the Globetrotters signed Haynes to a contract. For the next seven years, he traveled across the United States with the Globetrotters. Billed as the "World's Greatest Dribbler," Haynes quickly became one of the team's main attractions along with Reece "Goose" Tatum, who provided most of the comic relief. Haynes' ball handling skills were amazing. His stunts included bouncing the ball three times per second, at a height as low as one inch off the floor. He could perform his wizardry in almost any position, including lying on his stomach.

When he first signed with the Globetrotters, Haynes earned $250 a month. His salary had escalated to $10,000 a year by 1953, but it still paled in comparison to what his peers earned in the NBA. The NBA's Philadelphia Warriors offered him a contract in 1953 and, two years later, the Minneapolis Lakers did the same. However, Haynes declined both offers. He left the Globetrotters during a financial dispute in 1953 and, along with Goose

At a Glance . . .

Born Marques Oreole Haynes on October 3, 1926 in Sand Springs, OK; son of Matthew (a domestic employee) and Hattie Haynes; married Joan (a model); children: Marsha Kaye and Marquetta; *Education:* Langston University, BS, 1946.

Career: Began playing career with Kansas City Stars, 1946; Harlem Globetrotters, player, 1947-53; Fabulous Magicians, owner, coach, player, 1953-72; second stint with the Globetrotters, 1972-79; Meadowlark Lemon's Bucketeers, player, 1979-81; Harlem Magicians, owner, player, 1983-88.

Awards: Elected to Naismith Basketball Hall of Fame, 1998.

Addresses: *Residence*—Dallas, TX.

Tatum, formed his own touring team known as the Fabulous Magicians. Haynes practically ran the organization singlehandedly, serving as the team's owner, president, booking agent, coach, and star player.

The Fabulous Magicians became a very profitable organization. In the team's first year of operation, it grossed $700,000. It earned even more money the following year. For the next two decades, Haynes toured with the Magicians and retained his title as the "World's Greatest Dribbler." In 1972, Haynes rejoined the Harlem Globetrotters. Since his departure in 1953, the Globetrotters had become internationally famous, performing on every continent and in front of many heads of state and members of royalty.

Although Haynes had achieved financial security, he was keenly aware of the financial inequities that African American basketball players faced in comparison to their white counterparts. He was equally appalled by the growing disparity between what members of the Globetrotters made—$37,000 average for a nine-month, 300-game season—and salaries being paid to NBA players, who made an average of $100,000 for 82 games over six months. He soon became president of a player's union that represented members of the Globetrotters.

When the Globetrotters fired Haynes in July of 1979, he claimed that it was because of his union activities. The Globetrotters, Haynes argued, were using him as an example to discourage other players from supporting the union. The National Labor Relations Board (NLRB) apparently agreed, and awarded Haynes a settlement based on his complaint. In spite of the NLRB ruling, members of the Globetrotters charged that the team continued to engage in anti-union activities. Gerald Smith, who was fired from the team in 1980, told *Jet,* "I was in favor of what the union represented...but I wasn't actively involved in anything. My problem stems from socializing with Haynes, which was against management's wishes."

After being fired by the Globetrotters, Haynes joined the Bucketeers, a team run by another former Globetrotter great, Meadowlark Lemon. Two years later, he was back with the Globetrotters for another stint, which lasted until 1983. That year, he left the Globetrotters again to form his own squad, the Harlem Magicians. Haynes retired as an active player in 1988, having played in more than 12,000 professional games. In June of 1998, he was elected to the Naismith Basketball Hall of Fame.

Sources

Periodicals

Chicago Tribune, July 1, 1998, sec. 4, p. 1.
Jet, May 15, 1980, p. 52; December 4, 1980, p. 49.
Sports Illustrated, April 22, 1985, p. 78.
Washington Post, June 30, 1998, p. B2.

—Robert R. Jacobson

Anna Arnold Hedgeman

1899–1990

Civil rights advocate, writer, educator

Anna Arnold Hedgeman began life in a small, white, Midwestern community unaware of the discrimination African Americans faced in the United States. However, her curious mind and hunger for information and experiences exposed her to the realities of her time, and she made it her life's work to balance the scales. From her work with the Young Women's Christian Association (YWCA) in the 1920s and 1930s to her duties with the Commission on Religion and Race of the National Council of Churches in the 1960s, Hedgeman's goals were singular. As the first African American female member of a mayoral cabinet, her example surpassed the city limits in which she worked. It began in her childhood which was marked with the influences that would last her lifetime. "Four ideas dominated our family life," she wrote of her youth in *The Gift of Chaos*. "Education, religion, character, and service to mankind."

Born Anna Arnold in Marshalltown, Iowa she moved with her family to Anoka, Minnesota when she was very young. Her father created an insular world for Hedgeman and her sisters. "I grew up in Anoka, Minnesota, in a small, comfortable Midwestern town with the traditional main street," she wrote in her book *The Trumpet Sounds*.

"There was no poverty as I have come to know it in the slums of our urban centers. I had not realized that a man could need bread and not be able to get it."

The only African American family in an area dominated by European immigrants, the Arnolds were very much a part of the community and the young Arnold children were never made to feel different. Hedgeman's father created a nurturing environment that stressed education and a strong work ethic. In that environment, however, there was also a strictness and high level of expectation for Hedgeman and her two sisters. She learned to read at home, but wasn't permitted to attend school until she was seven years old.

An Education In Mississippi

Following her graduation from high school, Hedgeman prepared to attend Hamline University, a small Methodist college. She would become the first African American student at Hamline. One of the highlights of her college years was a lecture given by author and NAACP president W.E.B. DuBois in St. Paul. Hedgeman recalled in *The*

Gift of Chaos, "The audience gave rapt attention and I returned to the campus with the image of black men of poise, dignity, and intelligence, who were determined to be free."

In 1922, armed with a degree and a deep conviction to serve, Hedgeman chose to teach at the small black Rust College in Holly Springs, Mississippi. Having never been to the South nor having heard of some of the greater indignities African Americans suffered there, Hedgeman was in for a rude awakening. On the train from Chicago, the conductor informed Hedgeman that she would have to switch to the "colored" coach at Cairo, Illinois because African Americans couldn't ride in the "white" coach beyond that point. She recalled in *The Gift of Chaos,* "When we reached Cairo a Negro porter escorted me from my comfortable seat to the "colored" coach. This coach was just behind the engine, and soot and dirt filled the air, soiling both the seat and my lovely new traveling costume. I was indignant; how could the railroad company permit such disgraceful service to any American?"

When she arrived in Holly Springs, Hedgeman saw poor African Americans and experienced the humiliation of segregation for the first time. She also realized that her students, mostly poor children of sharecroppers, were forced to work for a wage at the expense of their education. "It did not take long for the love of the soil, which had been my heritage, to turn into hate," she wrote in *The Gift of Chaos.* "For it was the soil and its demand that its crop be harvested which brought my bright, eager students late to the classroom, and it was the same soil which claimed them for spring planting, just when they were beginning to progress."

After two years at Rust College, Hedgeman decided she'd had enough. The circumstances in which she was forced to teach and the attitudes of Southern whites became too much to endure. Also, as a Northerner, she was resented by both blacks and whites in the South and could accomplish little without meeting stiff resistance. Her future, Hedgeman reasoned, lay in the North where opportunities to influence change were greater. "I decided that I must return North and organize the Midwest," she recalled in *Trumpet,* "to help eliminate the cruelty of the Southern part of my country.

Began Association With YWCA

However, Hedgeman faced difficulty when she returned to Minnesota in 1924. Unable to find a teaching job because she was African American, she went to work for the YWCA where she experienced a great deal of racial prejudice. After accepting a position in Springfield, Ohio she found that her branch, which was located in an African American neighborhood, had no gymnasium, swimming pool, cafeteria, or an adequate staff. Although the central branch had all of these amenities, African Americans were not allowed to use them. Hedgeman was also not allowed to eat in the central branch's cafeteria, even though she was a YWCA employee.

Despite the prejudice Hedgeman experienced, the YWCA was one of the first organizations to have African American executives and Hedgeman continued her ties with the association, becoming executive director of an African American branch in Jersey City, New Jersey. In 1927, she became membership secretary of the West 137th Street branch in New York City's Harlem neighborhood. Hedgeman welcomed the Harlem assignment because it had adequate facilities and was an environment free of racism. "I would have equipment with which to work and the challenge of the largest Negro community in the nation," she wrote in *The Gift of Chaos*. "The walls of segregation had done its work. I was completely free of and through with white people."

As the Great Depression hit Harlem residents especially hard, Hedgeman and other YWCA staffers were called upon to redouble their efforts and provide essential social services. Seven-day work weeks were not uncommon and, after five years, Hedgeman decided that it was time for a change. In the late summer of 1933, she resigned her position in Harlem to become executive director of an African American branch in Philadelphia. Working in a more racially-mixed environment than Harlem, Hedgeman was forced to break her isolation from white people. "I knew this [position] would involve, in addition to the branch program, continuous contact with white Association and other community leaders," she reminisced in *Trumpet*. "I could no longer merely talk at white people. I had to work with them."

Fair Employment Practices Commission

In November of 1933 Hedgeman married her husband, Merrit, who was an interpreter of African American folk music. The following year, she returned to New York to be with her husband and took a job as a supervisor and consultant to the Emergency Relief Bureau, now called the Department of Welfare. She would remain in that position until 1938 when she went back to the YWCA as director of the African American branch in Brooklyn. Disillusioned with the blatant segregation policies of the national Association, Hedgeman resigned and went to work as an assistant in race relations for the National Office of Civilian Defense.

In 1944, Hedgeman served as the executive director of the newly-formed National Council for a Permanent Fair Employment Practices Commission. This organization initiated national legislative programs to ensure that minority groups would have access to education and jobs. The main goal of the organization was to secure passage of the FEPC bill, which would have guaranteed the right to work without regard to race, creed, or color. Passage of the bill was defeated in 1945.

In 1949, after working on Harry Truman's presidential campaign, Hedgeman went to work as an assistant to the administrator of the Federal Security Agency, which was later known as the Office of Health, Education and Welfare. This position enabled her to spend three months in India as an exchange leader for the Department of State. Upon returning to New York, Hedgeman became involved in city politics and, following the election of Mayor Robert F. Wagner, Jr. in 1954, became the first African American woman to hold a mayoral cabinet position in the city's history. In this position, Hedgeman was responsible for corresponding with eight city departments and served as a liaison for international guests visiting New York.

Disenchanted with the back room bureaucracy of city hall, Hedgeman resigned in 1958 to take a job as a public relations consultant for the Fuller Products Company, a cosmetics firm. At Fuller Products, she made contacts with church and civic groups and gave daily lectures to salesmen. When company president S.B. Fuller bought the *New York Age*, the nation's oldest African American newspaper, Hedgeman was asked to serve as associate editor and columnist. Due to dwindling circulation, the paper ceased production in 1960. That same year, Hedgeman was the keynote speaker at the first Conference of the Woman of Africa and of African Descent held in Ghana.

Helped Plan March On Washington

In 1963, Hedgeman was asked to serve as Coordinator of Special Events for the Commission of Religion and Race of the National Council of Churches. Her first task was to locate 30,000 white Protestants from across the country who were willing to participate in a March on Washington scheduled for August 28, 1963. Hedgeman played a major role in what is considered one of the greatest civil rights moments in history. When she noticed that there were no women scheduled to speak at the Lincoln Memorial, Hedgeman moved swiftly to correct the oversight. She also worked with the National Council of Churches to ensure passage of the Civil Rights Bill of 1964, a descendant of the FEPC bill proposed twenty years earlier.

In 1965, Hedgeman ran an unsuccessful candidacy for City Council President in New York. Two year later, she retired from the National Council of Churches. Along with her husband, she founded Hedgeman Consultant Services. With the consulting firm serving as a home base,

Hedgeman spent the 1970s lecturing, teaching, and consulting on race relations and black studies to educational centers, colleges and universities, and public school teachers. Following the death of her husband in 1987, Hedgeman moved to the Greater Harlem Nursing home where she lived until her death on January 17, 1990.

Sources

Books

Hedgeman, Anna Arnold, *The Gift of Chaos: Decades of American Discontent,* Oxford University Press, 1977.

Hedgeman, Anna Arnold, *The Trumpet Sounds: A Memoir of Negro Leadership,* Holt, Rinehart and Winston, 1964.

Periodicals

Jet, February 12, 1990, p. 17.
New York Times, January 26, 1990, p. D-18.

Other

Additional information for this profile was obtained from the Rare Books and Manuscripts division of the Schomburg Center for Research in Black Culture.

—Brian Escamilla

Freeman A. Hrabowski

1950—

Educator, author

Freeman A. Hrabowski has built his impressive reputation as an educator by challenging minority students to reach their full potential. As president of the University of Maryland Baltimore County, he oversees an institution of 10,000 students from all races and backgrounds. However, he is best known as the co-founder of the university's Meyerhoff Scholarship Program, which is designed to encourage African American men to pursue high-level academic work in science and engineering. By 1998, 112 students had graduated from the program, and 95 percent of them had gone on to pursue graduate work.

In 1998, Hrabowski wrote about these top scholars in *Beating the Odds: Raising Academically Successful African American Males*. To research the book, Hrabowski and his co-authors interviewed participants in the Meyerhoff Program, along with their families, to determine what parenting methods had helped the sons to succeed.

"Beating the Odds is undoubtedly one of the most important tools the African American parent can possess," Kweisi Mfume, president of the NAACP, was quoted as saying on the book's jacket. "This inspirational text reconceptualizes the falsely perpetuated image of the black male and introduces us to the fundamental elements needed to help our young men achieve academic excellence." While parental involvement is critical in raising African American men to become successful, schools and universities also must play a role. "The critical question is what commitment will the administration and faculty of

each institution make to ensure that in spite of legal obstacles, we continue to educate large numbers of minority young people," Hrabowski noted in *Black Issues in Higher Education*. "If the commitment is there, we can do it."

Jailed with Dr. Martin Luther King

Freeman Alphonsa Hrabowski III was born on August 13, 1950, in Birmingham, Alabama. His parents, Freeman and Maggie Hrabowski, were both teachers and they expected their children to perform well in school. In fact, Hrabowski did so well in his studies that he was able to skip two grades, graduating from high school when he was just 15 years old. "No one was more critical to my development than my parents and family," Hrabowski wrote in *Beating the Odds*. "Both my father and mother made me feel that I was the most special part of their lives and that my future would be bright....My parents taught me by example the importance of work, faith, family, and being the best."

As well as focusing on his education, Hrabowski was involved from a very young age in the civil rights movement. At the age of 12, when he was in his first year of high school, he took part in a demonstration led by Dr. Martin Luther King Jr. When the march was stopped, allegedly because the marchers did not have a permit, the demonstrators were arrested. Hrabowski spent a week in jail,

Born Freeman Alphonsa Hrabowski III, Aug. 13, 1950, Birmingham, AL; son of Maggie Hrabowski and Freeman Hrabowski; married to Jackie; children: Eric. *Education:* Hampton Institute, B.A., 1970; University of Illinois, MA, 1971; University of Illinois, PhD, 1975.

Career: Assistant dean for student services, University of Illinois, Urbana-Champaign, IL, 1974-76; associate professor of statistics and research and associate dean for graduate studies, Alabama A&M University, Normal, AL, 1976-77; professor of mathematics and dean of arts and sciences, Coppin State College, Baltimore, MD, 1977-81; vice president for academic affairs, Coppin State, 1981-87; vice provost, University of Maryland Baltimore County (UMBC), 1987-90; executive vice president, UMBC, 1990-92; interim president, 1992-93; president, 1993–.

Awards: Educator Achievement Award from the National Science Foundation; the first U.S. Presidential Award for Excellence in Science, Mathematics, and Engineering Mentoring (awarded in recognition of the Meyerhoff Scholarship Program).

Member: American Council on Education, Baltimore Community Foundation, Maryland High-Technology Council, Joint Center for Political and Economic Studies. Past president, Maryland Humanities Council.

Addresses: *Office—*5401 Wilkins Avenue, Baltimore, MD 21228.

along with King.

After graduating from high school, Hrabowski enrolled at the Hampton Institute—now Hampton University—in Hampton, Virginia. Despite the fact that he had performed well in high school, he found the transition to higher education difficult. "After my first week of college, I was devastated," Hrabowski recalled in a lecture at the University of California at Davis that was quoted in the *California Aggie.* "I found out I was mediocre. People from private, integrated and preparatory schools were used to working harder." At the same time, Hrabowski found that his instructors were not always a source of support or encouragement. "Often, professors didn't ex-

pect me to do well," he remarked in *Sun Spot Black History Month,* "or they made discouraging comments." During his time at the Hampton Institute, Hrabowski spent a year studying abroad in Cairo, Egypt. At Cairo University, he took courses in mathematics, physics, and Arab culture. In 1970, at the age of 19, he graduated from Hampton with highest honors in mathematics.

The following year, Hrabowski went on to pursue graduate work at the University of Illinois at Urbana-Champaign. In addition to his studies, he established a tutorial center that offered mathematics instruction for minority students. In spite of all the hours he devoted to the tutoring program, Hrabowski was able to complete all the requirements for his master's degree in just one year and graduated in 1971.

Hrabowski remained at the University of Illinois to complete his PhD, writing his dissertation on college-level mathematics instruction for African American students. Even before he had finished his research, Hrabowski's talents for teaching and working with minorities gained the attention of the university. In 1974 he was named assistant dean for student services, with responsibility for two programs: Project Upward Bound, which encouraged low-income high school students to attend college, and the Educational Opportunities Program, which provided support for minority students after they had arrived at college. In 1975, Hrabowski earned his PhD in higher education administration and statistics.

In the fall of 1975, Hrabowski moved back to Alabama. He accepted positions at Alabama A&M University as associate professor of statistics and research and associate dean for graduate studies. The following year, he was appointed professor of mathematics and dean of arts and sciences at Coppin State College in Baltimore, Maryland. By 1981, he had become vice president for academic affairs, the second highest administrative position at Coppin State.

Co-Founded Meyerhoff Scholarship Program

In 1987, Hrabowski joined the University of Maryland Baltimore County (UMBC) as vice provost. In this new position, Hrabowski continued to pursue the goal of increasing minority enrollment in higher education, especially in science and engineering. In 1988, with assistance from the Robert and Jane Meyerhoff Foundation, he cofounded the Meyerhoff Scholarship Program. Initially, the goal of the Meyerhoff Program was to encourage and support African American males who had chosen to study science and engineering. The focus of the program eventually shifted to increasing the number of African

Americans earning doctorates, in order to bolster the numbers of African American college faculty members in engineering, medicine, and the sciences. "The challenge we face is creating role models of smart black males who can help other little boys to want to be like them," Hrabowski told Joan Morgan of *Black Issues in Higher Education.*

In 1990, Hrabowski became executive vice president of UMBC. After a year of serving as interim president, he was appointed president of the university in 1993. In addition to his duties as president, Hrabowski continued to work closely with the Meyerhoff Program. "Dr. Hrabowski takes time to have a lot of personal contact with us," Meyerhoff participant Tove Goldson noted in *Black Issues in Higher Education.* "He meets with each Meyerhoff class individually and does things like stop us to talk if he sees us while out on the campus. He does that for other students, too. You can tell he really cares."

The Meyerhoff Program was an immediate success, gaining national attention for attracting high-achieving minority students to the sciences. In recognition of his work with the program, Hrabowski was presented with the first U.S. Presidential Award for Excellence in Science, Mathematics, and Engineering Mentoring. Because the program receives some federal funding, and similar programs have come under legal scrutiny for discrimination, it was expanded to include African American women, as well as students from across the country, in 1990. Six years later, the program was opened to all ethnic groups. However, African Americans remain the focus of the Meyerhoff Program. In 1996, the year the program was expanded, 55 percent of the participants were African American males, and 85 percent were African American students. "The idea here is that we need to educate people who are not African-American about the issues we face," Hrabowski told Joan Morgan of *Black Issues in Higher Education.* "So when these people graduate, they will not only have a degree in science or engineering, they will have had time to reflect and become comfortable with issues of race and gender in our country."

In addition to the Meyerhoff Program, UMBC offers several other innovative programs aimed at reaching students who might otherwise drop out of school. These programs include UMBC's Choice Program, a mentoring program for troubled youth, and Upward Bound, which works with low-income high school students of all races. "Those of us who are fortunate need to take greater responsibility to help the underprivileged," Hrabowski was quoted as saying in *Sun Spot Black History Month.* "Many children are not in an environment that helps them develop academically and intellectually."

Wrote Book on Raising Black Males

In 1998 Hrabowski teamed up with Kenneth I. Maton, a UMBC psychology professor, and Geoffrey L. Greif, a professor of social work at the University of Maryland Baltimore, to write *Beating the Odds: Raising Academically Successful African American Males.* The book, published by Oxford University Press, was based on interviews with 60 Meyerhoff scholars and their families. The parents of program participants explained the strategies they had used to keep their sons out of trouble, while encouraging them to excel at school. "Much of the previous literature on African American families has focused on their deficiencies and weaknesses," Hrabowski and his co-authors wrote in the book's preface. "Our book complements the growing body of literature that looks at the strengths of these families." Based on their findings, the authors advocated a number of parenting strategies: demonstrating love through involvement in the children's education, establishing an environment with strict limits, and encouraging children to struggle against adversity, whether it be racism or poverty. In addition, schools should create an environment that offers rewards for academic achievement, while providing opportunities for African American males to meet and talk about their performance in school.

As president of UMBC, Hrabowski continues to focus on improving the university's academic competitiveness. "This place is like a dream fulfilled, a place that doesn't have to be rich or be 300 years old to offer a top quality education," Hrabowski told Fern Shen of the *Washington Post.* At the same time, increasing the number and quality of minority students who attend the college is a top priority. "We are now in the top ten in the country among universities sending African-Americans to science PhDs," Hrabowski told Tamara Henry of *USA Today* in 1998. "We are hoping to become number one."

In addition to his academic and administrative duties at UMBC, Hrabowski serves as a consultant to the National Science Foundation, the National Institutes of Health, the National Academy of Sciences, the U.S. Department of Education, and universities and school systems nationally. He is a member of numerous boards, including the American Council on Education, Baltimore Community Foundation, Maryland High-Technology Council, and the Joint Center for Political and Economic Studies. Hrabowski also makes time in his schedule to give lectures and speeches throughout the country. "In the sciences, to be a success, a student must marry the work," Hrabowski told a group of students at the University of California at Davis (quoted as saying in the student newspaper, the *California Aggie).* "You can't miss your classes. You have to develop the level of discipline and focus to push you to be the best....Learn to love to read. Learn to think out of the box. Word problems and story problems are at the heart of life."

Sources

Periodicals

Black Issues in Higher Education, October 3, 1996, p. 16.
California Aggie, November 23, 1998.
Jet, June 7, 1993, p. 22.
USA Today, April 9, 1998, p. 9D.
Washington Post, September 17, 1996, p. D2.

Books

Beating the Odds: Raising Academically Successful African American Males, by Freeman A. Hrabowski III, Kenneth I. Maton and Geoffrey L. Greif, Oxford University Press, 1998.
Distinguished African American Scientists of the 20th Century, by James H. Kessler et al., Oryx Press, 1996.

Other

Additional information for this profile was provided by the *California Aggie* web site at www.californiaaggie.com/archive/98/11/23/hrabowski.html; the Meyerhoff Programs web site at www.umbc.edu/Programs/Meyerhoff/Undergrad/dream.html; the Sun Spot Black History Month web site page at 208.241.241.244/news/special/blackhistory/profiles/hrabowski.shtml and the UMBC web site at www.umbc.edu/AboutUMBC/Welcome/freemanbio.html

—Carrie Golus

Billy Hunter

1943—

Union executive

Billy Hunter has always prided himself on being a streetfighter, literally and, especially, figuratively. His tough struggles for justice have been waged at all levels of society, but since 1996 they have been waged at their most visible level, as executive director of the National Basketball Association's players union. Hunter has brought the same drive and conscience to this role he has brought to all the others in which he has found himself since the mid-1960s.

Hunter was born George William Hunter in 1943, and was raised by his mother's parents, John and Loretta Holmes, in Cherry Hill, New Jersey, across the river from Philadelphia. It was a poor, black environment, but Hunter had a lot of contact with his white peers, and was the first black youngster to play in the local Little League.

"Although I lived in a segregated community, a lot of my friends were white," he told the New York Times. "So I was like the black kid who got to leave the black neighborhood to go into the white neighborhood and play with all the guys. My athletic ability opened a lot of doors."

Sports dominated much of Hunter's childhood, but one sidelight which interested him early on was black history. He used to listen to his great-Uncle Ben tell stories about William Still, a great-great-grandfather who helped run the underground railroad in Philadelphia.

"As a young kid growing up in the 1940s and 1950s, you never really thought about it," he told the New York Times. "Black history hadn't come into fruition or being. It wasn't taught, so there was no relevance. No one was promoting black contributions to America. But then the '60s came along and Alex Haley's 'Roots.' It made you think about your past."

Hunter attended Syracuse University, where he was the captain of the football team. He was expected to be a first-round draft pick in the National Football League, but he suffered an injury in his senior year which damaged his value to pro scouts. While at Syracuse he organized his teammates into a boycott of Southern schools with segregated stadiums. He also became friends with future NBA Hall-of-Famer Dave Bing, an association which would land him a job one day.

Hunter overcame his injury to scrap out a three-year NFL

At a Glance . . .

Born George William Hunter in 1943; raised by grandparents John and Loretta Holmes in Cherry Hill, New Jersey. *Education:* Attended Syracuse University, 1962-66; law degrees from Howard University and the University of California.

Career: Named U.S. Attorney for Northern California by President Jimmy Carter, 1977; prosecuted members of Jim Jones' Peoples' Temple and the Hell's Angels; instrumental in the pardoning of Patty Hearst; entertainment lawyer, represented rapper Hammer, among others; ran for U.S. House of Representatives against longtime incumbent Ron Dellums (lost); executive director, National Basketball Association Players' Assn., 1996-.

Addresses: National Basketball Association Players Association, 1700 Broadway, Suite 1400, New York, New York, 10019.

career with the Washington Redskins and Miami Dolphins, but he knew football was not going to be his meal ticket, and injuries forced him out of the game in the late 1960s. He returned to school and quickly earned law degrees from Howard University and the University of California. While at Howard he led a protest that locked up the law school and resulted in replacement of the dean. "My first child was born while I was in the school behind the chains," he told the *Chicago Tribune.* Early in his law career Hunter wrote briefs supporting Huey Newton and the Black Panthers.

In 1977 President Jimmy Carter appointed Hunter to the U.S. Attorney's office for Northern California, and in that position Hunter was involved in a number of high-profile cases. He prosecuted members of Jim Jones' Peoples' Temple in the aftermath of the mass suicide in Guyana, and he also prosecuted members of the Hell's Angels motorcycle gang. Perhaps the most visible case he was involved with on that job was in his role as Carter's emissary in his review of the Patty Hearst conviction. Hunter convinced Carter to pardon the heiress. He could not help but reflect on the irony of the two of them coming together from such different backgrounds, and recalled to the *New York Times:* "At one point I said to her: 'I can't believe I'm the one who makes a recommendation whether you go free. Here I am, a kid who came from a very poor, black environment. And here you are, on the opposite end. I mean, your grandfather is William Randolph Hearst. How do we intersect at this point and time?' She just

chuckled, and said, 'That's amazing, isn't it.'"

Hunter went into private practice after leaving the prosecutor's office, and worked on a wide variety of cases. He had some entertainment clients, including rapper Hammer. He was involved in litigation and some white-collar defense work. He represented a few athletes, but tried to steer clear of that for the most part, and he took on a number of pro-bono cases. "He would take cases of young guys that had recently been arrested for one thing or another and represent them," one of his partners, Bill Webster, told the *New York Times.* "They were always someone's kids he knew or a member of the church. Sometimes, he was loyal to a fault." His scrappiness shone through on occasion, too, as during his years in private practice he came to blows with a lawyer who called him a racial epithet, and with rapper Bobby Brown.

In 1996 Bing convinced Hunter to give up his resistance to get into sports law and take the position as executive director of the NBA players' union. The union had been plagued by problems for years and did not get much respect, even from many of its own members. There was even a rumor that circulated that the union made Hunter swear an oath that he would not back down from management. Hunter said that was not true, but told the *Los Angeles Times,* "They (the players) wanted someone to stand up, and someone that they felt would be committed to them. I think that was the issue. There was the perception among the membership that Simon Gourdine (Hunter's predecessor, who also had been NBA deputy commissioner) was in the back pocket of the ownership....They wanted to know, did I have any other agenda....I just said, 'I've always prided myself on being fair, being a hard worker, objective and professional. And if I accept you as a client, it's always been my position to give you 110 percent.' And I also assured them that I could hang in there if I had to, that I could be tough."

Hunter took over with a definite agenda, which including strengthening union solidarity, bettering the position of the union's "middle-class," or mid-range salary players, and organizing the players of the Women's National Basketball Association. The first time the sports world took much note of him in his new job came early in the 1997-98 season, when Golden State Warrior Latrell Sprewell was suspended for attacking his coach. The punishment of a one-year suspension and forfeiture of his contract was unprecedented, and many observers expected Hunter and the union would invoke race in their defense of Sprewell. Those observers were impressed that Hunter never raised race as an issue in the case, even when it was publicly suggested by others, but rather used past precedents to successfully convince an arbitrator to reduce the suspension.

The big issue which loomed, however, came at the beginning of the following season, when the owners shut down the league to rewrite the labor agreement they had with the players. The issues were myriad and complex, and Hunter's objectives were to gain a few advantages for the union while giving up as little as possible. The lockout was announced as soon as the 1997-98 season ended, and the pressure tightened as the deadlines passed for a settlement by the start of training camp, the start of the exhibition schedule, the start of the regular season, and finally, the drop-dead date when the season would be canceled altogether. Hunter held firm throughout, until the very end, but in the final few weeks before the impending cancellation of the season the union's membership wavered, with several members calling for an immediate vote to accept or reject whatever proposal management currently had on the table. Just when it appeared the only two possible conclusions to the matter were the union caving in and accepting whatever deal it could get or the cancellation of the season, Hunter met with league commissioner David Stern in a secret, all-night meeting in league offices in New York and hammered out an agreement.

Some of the key points on which the union won in the settlement involved saving some loopholes in the salary cap rules, especially exceptions which would benefit some of the mid-level salaried players. The owners won out by keeping the percentage of revenues devoted to players' salaries to 55 percent, imposing for the first time in any sport an individual salary cap to augment the team salary cap, and pushing back the date at which players can become unrestricted free agents to the end of their fifth season. While experts agreed that both sides had won some concessions and given up others, most agreed that the union had given up more than the owners had. Most of the union's membership just wanted what remained of the season—and that season's salary—to be salvaged, however, and the union overwhelmingly approved the new contract.

Despite the poor taste the lockout left in many players' mouths, Hunter's security as executive director seemed sound a year after the start of the lockout. The union had clearly found the tough negotiator it had been looking for for so long, and a story he told the *New York Times* he had related to numerous union members during the lockout seemed best to define his resolve. He recalled, "I can remember when I was a young kid, ten or 11 years of age, there were guys in my neighborhood who, if they started something, said something to my relatives, I would always go in there and fight. And many of them I fought because I knew I could beat them. But as soon as they fought me back, and they had demonstrated they were willing to fight—and I wasn't so sure that it was going to be a slam dunk—then I was more reluctant to fight. And I wanted to find some other way we could reach an accord. I became a negotiator, man. I wanted to befriend them. When I realized they were throwing punches, too, it wasn't so easy."

Sources

Periodicals

Chicago Tribune, October 10, 1998, sec. 3, p. 1.
Fortune, February 1, 1999, p. 28.
Los Angeles Times, October 30, 1998, sec. D, p. 1.
New York Times, August 2, 1998, sec. 8, p. 1; Jan. 7, 1999, sec. 1, p. 1.

—Michael Eggert

Jonathan Lee Iverson

1976—

Circus ringmaster

Johnathan Lee Iverson is the first African American ringmaster in the history of the Ringling Brothers and Barnum & Bailey Circus. He is also the youngest person to be chosen as ringmaster. Iverson is responsible for controlling the pacing of the show, performing musical numbers and introducing circus acts as they enter the ring. Indeed, the role of ringmaster is an extremely difficult job. As Iverson told *USA Today,* "It takes a lot of sleep and a lot of energy. I'm the image of the circus. It's up to me to initiate the energy of the show and keep you awake." Iverson became ringmaster of the Ringling Brothers and Barnum & Bailey Circus through talent and hard work. He also exhibits a quiet self-confidence that does not admit the possibility of failure. In an interview with *Contemporary Black Biography,* Iverson described the secret of his success, "You have to keep believing in the dream, you have to live it into existence."

Iverson was born in Manhattan, New York, in 1976, the son of a firefighter and a secretary for the postal service. His parents were not married when Iverson was born and his father spent very little time with him. Despite the fact that he rarely saw his father, Iverson harbored no bitterness. "I never had any animosity against him," he told

People magazine, "When I was born, he wasn't ready to be a man yet."

Iverson developed an early interest in show business and, as a child, always wanted to perform. At the age of 11, he auditioned for the Harlem Boys Choir. To his delight, he was accepted into the choir. As a member of the Harlem Boys Choir, Iverson received intensive training in classical, hip hop, jazz, and gospel music. He also had the opportunity to travel throughout the United States, as well as Singapore, France, Spain, and the Netherlands. During a visit to Japan, the Harlem Boys Choir appeared in concert with opera star Placido Domingo. "I saw other people getting his autograph," Iverson recalled to *CBB,* "I didn't know who he was. But when he opened his mouth to sing, I was amazed at what the human voice could do." Watching Domingo perform inspired Iverson to work hard to develop his own singing voice.

After six years with the Harlem Boys Choir, Iverson left to attend Fiorello H. LaGuardia High School of Music and Art and Performing Arts in Manhattan. He thrived at LaGuardia and was chosen to appear for a two-week engagement on Broadway. He also won second place in

At a Glance . . .

Born Jonathan Lee Iverson on January 30, 1976. Education: Graduated from the Hartt School of Music, 1998.

Career: Ringling Brothers and Barnum & Bailey Circus, ringmaster, 1998-.

Awards: Lena Horne Vocal Jazz Scholarship.

Addresses: 8607 Westwood Center, Vienna, VA 22182.

the Lena Horne Vocal Jazz Scholarship competition. Iverson's second place finish earned him a scholarship to the Hartt School of Music at the University of Hartford. As one of America's finest music conservatories, Hartt was known for training opera and classical singers. Although many Hartt graduates have become famous opera stars, Iverson had no interest in becoming an opera singer. He told CBB, "I was bent on a career as a singer, and I had noted that a classical training seemed to lead to longevity as an artist. That is why I pursued a classical training."

Following his graduation from Hartt in 1998, Iverson had planned to continue his musical studies. However, he could not afford to pay the tuition fees. He traveled to Fort Atkinson, Wisconsin, to audition for a part in a new show at the town's Fireside Dinner Theater. Iverson landed the part and his excellent performances soon attracted the attention of the show's director, Phil McKinley. McKinley was also the director-choreographer for the Ringling Brothers and Barnum & Bailey Circus and he felt that Iverson's commanding stage presence and beautiful singing voice made him an excellent candidate for ringmaster of the circus. Iverson agreed to attend the ringmaster auditions and, from a field of 28 candidates, was selected as the new ringmaster of the Ringling Brothers and Barnum & Bailey Circus.

Iverson quickly discovered that being a ringmaster is an extremely demanding job. It requires a great deal of energy and physical stamina to perform at least one show a day and, on weekends, two or three shows. "The children demand a lot of you," Iverson told People magazine, "They draw the energy out of you, so by the end of the day, you're dead." Also, the ringmaster is given a tremendous amount of responsibility. In his book Ringmaster! My Year on the Road with the Greatest Show on Earth, former ringmaster Kristopher Antekeier noted that "the responsi

bility of the job was enormous. It was possible that an announcement uttered at the wrong time could hurl the entire show into disarray. Someone could even be injured. An instant of confusion might cause a performer to miss a hold and fall to his death." Iverson is keenly aware of his responsibilities and is confident that he and his fellow cast members can handle any last-minute change or unexpected glitch. As he remarked to CBB, "I work with very smart people and very seasoned people. Together, we give our public an all-star event."

When Iverson first began rehearsing with the circus in late 1998, he quickly earned the admiration and respect of the other cast members. "The first time Johnathan sang in rehearsal, everybody stopped," circus owner Kenneth Feld told the St. Petersburg Times. "They listened, and then they broke into applause." In the same article, horse and elephant trainer Catherine Hanneford remarked, "We didn't see anybody who looked like a ringmaster. You only could see this tall kid in jeans standing there. But then the music starts, and you hear the ringmaster, and the most beautiful voice you've ever heard in your life. And you look out again and see this big kid turn into just an amazing ringmaster."

Iverson has been unfazed by the tremendous attention he has received as both the youngest and first African American ringmaster of the Ringling Brothers and Barnum & Bailey Circus. He is a man who relies heavily on his faith to see him through. As Iverson told the St. Petersburg Times, "I come from a very God-oriented family, and I want to live my life by that hymn I used to hear when I was younger: Oh, What Needless Sorrows We Bear. It's true. It's not my place to worry about it. I know the tension it would bring. I can only do the best job I can do."

Sources

Books

Antekeier, Kristopher, and Greg Aunapu, Ringmaster! My Year on the Road with the Greatest Show on Earth. New York, E.P. Dutton, 1989.
Culhane, John, The American Circus: An Illustrated History. New York, Henry Holt, 1990.

Periodicals

Buffalo News, February 24, 1999, p. 4A.
Milwaukee Journal Sentinel, January 28, 1997, p. 5.
New York Times, December 18, 1998, p. B1.
People, April 19, 1999, p. 167.
St. Petersburg Times, December 29, 1998, p. 1D.
USA Today, March 26, 1999, p. 3E.

Other

Additional information for this profile was obtained from an interview with Johnathan Lee Iverson on May 17, 1999.

—Gillian Wolf and David G. Oblender

Alexine Clement Jackson

1936—

Organization executive

Alexine Clement Jackson is the national president of the Young Women's Christian Association (YWCA), an organization which has long been at the forefront of progressive gender and racial issues. Continuing a family tradition that began with her grandmothers, Jackson has been involved with the YWCA for over 25 years. As head of this venerable organization, she has been able to concentrate her energies on empowering women and helping to end racism. Jackson has referred to herself as a "professional volunteer." In addition to her work with the YWCA, she is affiliated with organizations that champion the arts, education, health, and fashion.

Excelled in Academics

Born in 1936 in Sumter, South Carolina, Jackson was four when her birth mother, Frances, died of breast cancer. From the age of five, she was raised by her father, William A. Clement, Sr., and her stepmother, Josephine Dobbs Clement. Jackson's family stressed education and public commitment, and she was encouraged to cultivate her intelligence and leadership skills. Her stepmother also served as a strong role model.

Jackson's father was a senior executive for North Carolina Mutual Life Insurance Company. Founded nearly a century ago, the enterprise was for many years the largest African American-owned company in the United States. Both of Jackson's parents were deeply involved in civic affairs and politics. Her father was Grandmaster of the Prince Hall Masons of North Carolina and served as chairman of the board of the Raleigh-Durham Airport Authority. Her stepmother co-chaired Governor James Hunt's election campaign in the Durham area in 1980 and 1984.

While a student at Spelman College, she met Aaron G. Jackson, a Morehouse College student from Jackson, Mississippi, and the two eventually married. Her husband attended medical school at Howard University and did a two-year stint in the U.S. Navy. Jackson graduated magna cum laude from Spelman and was valedictorian of her class. She also earned a master of arts degree in speech pathology and audiology from the University of Iowa.

During her husband's service in the Navy, the Jacksons lived on the Marine base at Camp Pendleton, California. Jackson worked as a speech pathologist for a year, but

At a Glance . . .

Born Alexine Clement June 10, 1936, in Sumter, South Carolina; daughter of William A. Clement, Sr. and Frances Clement; married Aaron G. Jackson; five children. *Education:* Graduated magna cum laude from Spelman College; University of Iowa, M.A. in speech pathology and audiology.

Career: Former president of the YWCA, National Capital Area; national president of the YWCA, 1996–.

Member: Has been involved as volunteer, administrator, and leader in numerous other organizations. Board member of: The National Museum for Women in the Arts; Medical Education for South African Blacks; Cancer Research Foundation of America; Black Women's Agenda; National Campaign to Prevent Teen Pregnancy; National Assembly of Human Service and Health Organizations; and Advisory Board of Pfizer Women's Health Initiative.

Awards: *Washingtonian* Magazine, Washingtonian of the Year, 1994; Cultural Alliance, Founders' Award in the category of Distinguished Service to the Arts, 1996; *Washington Woman* Magazine, Woman of the Year, 1985. Community Service Awards from Potomac Valley Chapter of Delta Sigma Theta sorority, Arlington Chapter of Links, Inc., and Junior Citizens' Corps, Inc.; Honorary doctorate of humane letters, Spelman College, 1998.

Addresses: *Home*—11815 Piney Glen Lane, Potomac, MD 20854.

took time off to have children. She gave birth to a set of twins and then had three more children. As her five children were growing up, Jackson stayed home to attend to their needs and actively supported their participation in dance classes, school plays, and sports.

Witnessed Civil Rights Struggle

The Jacksons moved to Mississippi in 1963 and her husband set up a medical practice in Greenwood, becoming the only African American doctor within a 50-mile radius of the city. When the Jacksons moved to Green-

wood, the civil rights movement was in full swing and Mississippi was noted for its fierce opposition to desegregation and its extreme violence against African Americans. In an interview with *CBB*, Jackson remarked, "There were some frightening situations. When really violent things would happen, or someone was shot, people would come to our door looking for him [her husband]. He was the one called to treat the civil rights protesters who were beaten or hurt while jailed." Mississippi was also notorious for its backward attitudes. As Jackson told *CBB*, "It was like stepping back in time about 25 years. The struggles were just as basic as getting people to call you `Mrs.' Whites wanted to call you by your first name. Because my husband was a physician in town, and I wasn't working, they couldn't quite figure out how I had the free time during the day to shop downtown."

Greenwood became a hotbed of civil rights activity and served as the headquarters of the Student Nonviolent Coordinating Committee (SNCC). Many people visited Greenwood for activist training at the SNCC or to witness the civil rights struggle first-hand. As Jackson described to *CBB*, "I found it very rewarding—it was a beehive. There were lots of visits; people wanted to come and see the situation. Times were tense, with demonstrations and everybody trying to outmaneuver each other."

Jackson demonstrated her support for the civil rights movement by getting involved in community service. As she told *CBB*, "With time, I got involved in the community. The high school would call me to be judge of different events, such as oratorical contests, music festivals, etc. I served more as a mentor for some of the high school kids. Then we became very involved in organizing and funding a daycare center at our church, and I really took that project on. We started it just before Head Start came into being. By the time we finished the project, the center was eligible to be a Head Start school."

The Jacksons moved to Iowa City in 1968, where Jackson's husband began a residency in urology at the University of Iowa. Living in predominantly-white Iowa City proved to be a mixed experience for the family. As Jackson described it to *CBB*, "It was a university town, so there's an intellectual atmosphere. The University of Iowa was also one of the first universities that was open to blacks, way back in the 1930s. But...my children were never called `nigger' till we moved to Iowa. They were the only black kids in their school. They really suffered more direct racism once we left Mississippi than when we were there. Because [in Mississippi] you were protected by the racial lines. There was a totally separate community." In 1973, the Jacksons moved to Washington, D.C. Jackson's husband took a position at the Howard University Hospital, where he eventually became chief of the urology department.

Became Active in YWCA

When Jackson moved to Washington, D.C., she became actively involved as a volunteer with the YWCA. As she related to *CBB*: "When I moved to Washington, someone asked me to join [the YWCA administration]. Both of my grandmothers were involved in the YWCA—in Charleston and Atlanta. My mother was also on the board of the YWCA in Durham. In those days in the South, the YWCA was segregated....In other parts of the country, integration had already begun to happen. In 1940s the YWCA passed a new charter, advocating for racial justice, and that's been an integral aspect ever since."

In 1970 the YWCA passed the One Imperative, which sought to eliminate racism by any means necessary. For some, the phrase "by any means necessary" evoked memories of speeches by Malcolm X and the militant tones of the Black Power movement. Jackson remarked to *CBB* that "The phrase is within the context of our mission. Of course, there's nothing violent in our history. But still, there are some within the YWCA that have some problems with the wording.

Many people do not realize that the YWCA has always been radical in its way. By 1909, they were inserting sex education in their health classes. Also, the YWCA organized the first interracial conference in the South."

In 1965, the YWCA established a National Office for Racial Justice, which was headed for many years by Dorothy Height. Jackson remarked to *CBB*, "[Height] created many of the training materials we use today. She's certainly a woman that I admire greatly." The YWCA continues to create new programs to combat the poison of racism. In the wake of the Los Angeles riots, for example, it started an annual national day of commitment to eliminate racism. Other programs included the five-kilometer `Race Against Racism' and a partnership with the President's Initiative on Race to organize dialogues on racism with governors in nearly 40 states.

In addition to working against racism, the YWCA provides crucial services for women, such as shelters for victims of domestic violence and childcare centers. In an interview with *CBB*, Jackson described the YWCA's approach to childcare. "We take care of about 750,000 children a day. Our centers are designed to have a nonbiased curriculum: no war toys, for example. We try to teach kids how to resolve conflicts without violence. We think it is very important to teach them how to work through their anger, even at three and four years old. We also run some centers

for other groups, such as corporations or churches. Some associations even certify childcare centers for the state."

In addition to providing services for women and children, the YWCA focuses on the underlying economic issues that cause some women to struggle economically. Jackson told *CBB*, "Our concerns center around fair wages, housing, jobs, and health care—trying to achieve parity. I think there's been a lot of progress, of course, but I don't think we're there yet. Especially in terms of economic empowerment. There is a glass ceiling. There are differences in wages. And virtually no ownership of resources. We don't have women in the boardrooms. Women are still struggling to become economically independent....Women bear 100% of the world's children, perform more than 60% of the world's work, and constitute more than 50% of the population. However, they earn 10% of incomes, and own 1% of the world's resources."

Jackson remarked to *CBB* that the YWCA offers a resounding message of unity and inclusiveness to women everywhere. "We are strengthening ourselves as a movement. And we're learning that we are connected. I travel around to the local associations, and help them see that they're linked to a national movement. This gives us a very strong voice for advocacy. Plus, we do things intentionally: Local affiliations' membership is contingent on how well they fulfill the mission. This is reviewed on cyclical phases. It's not just about paying dues."

In an article in *Ebony*, Jackson related that in her travels abroad on behalf of the YWCA, she learned that empowerment means having an active role in the decision-making process. "We met women in these communities [in the 'developing world'] who were so proud to take charge of their lives. When women organize themselves, there is this spirit that is so inspiring. The thing that was life-changing for me was understanding the concept of membership and what it means to belong, to have the freedom to make decisions about your own life."

During her tenure as YWCA president, Jackson has focused on building relationships and gathering resources. She told *Women's Enterprise* that strong relationships are essential to a healthy organization, "When you have national and local affiliates, there are tensions. We needed to develop relationships not only with our associates but also with long-time YWCA members and board members who have contributed to what we are today." With regard to gathering needed resources, Jackson told *Women's Enterprise* that, "Women tend to shy away from major fund raising, because they consider it too unladylike or too aggressive, but we need to learn to step up to the plate and stand up for our beliefs. ... I am trying to encourage the belief that as an organization we can be strong in financial resources as well as human resources."

Survived Cancer

Jackson is passionately involved in the Washington, D.C. community. She has served on countless boards and committees for organizations promoting opera, ballet, and other performing arts; fashion shows; events at Howard University; and hospitality accommodations for the families of diplomats. Among Jackson's most cherished awards are those that she has received from local publications such as the *Washingtonian* and *Washington Woman* magazines.

In addition to her many other accomplishments, Jackson is a survivor of breast cancer. After undergoing surgery, chemotherapy, radiation treatments, and hormonal therapy, Jackson became a staunch advocate for early breast cancer detection and treatment. "I've always been very open about it [cancer] and announced it most places I go," Jackson told *CBB*, "because I want to remind women about the importance of mammography and early detection. I've been very happy to be a spokesperson, in a way, for that." She also serves on the board of the Cancer Research Foundation of America and the advisory board of Pfizer Inc.'s Women's Health Initiative.

Jackson enjoys her position as national president of the YWCA. As she told *CBB*, "I enjoy the position; it's very full, very time-consuming. I travel a lot, but it's energizing, as well as offering me the opportunity for personal growth." In *Ebony*, Jackson described the YWCA's vision for the future as one "where we have peace, justice, freedom, and dignity for all people. That's a very lofty vision, but when we talk about peace, we're not just talking about Bosnia and the Middle East. We're talking about peace right here within ourselves and within our towns. I'm often reminded of Gandhi's statement that `We must be the things that we see.'"

Sources

Periodicals

Ebony, March 1999, p. 101.
Women's Enterprise, November/December 1998, p. 31.

Other

Additional information for this profile was obtained from an interview with Alexine Clement Jackson on June 2, 1999 and from the YWCA web site at http://www.ywca.org.

—Mark Baven

Hazel Johnson

1927—

Military official, nurse, educator

When Hazel Johnson, an operating room nurse, joined the U.S. army in 1955, she had no idea she'd make military history. Initially searching for a way to stay in her profession and see the world, Johnson would eventually rise through the ranks to become the first black woman general in 1979. "I always wanted to move about and to experience different philosophies," she told *Ebony* in 1980. "The army offered me a chance to do that while continuing to advance in level of responsibility." Throughout her tenure in the army, Johnson also taught, not only by example, but in the classroom as well. Following her retirement from the army and a stint as government affairs director of the American Nursing Association, Johnson became a professor of nursing, first at George Washington University in Washington, DC, then George Mason University in Virginia.

Born in 1927 in Malvern, Pennsylvania, Johnson was one of seven children raised on her father's farm in nearby West Chester. Early on Johnson looked toward nursing as a career and began her training at New York's Harlem Hospital in 1950. While working at a veteran's hospital in Philadelphia, a former army nurse who knew of Johnson's desire to see the world, urged her to consider a career in the military. After just one meeting with a recruiter in 1955, Johnson enlisted. Five years later, she received a direct commission to the Army Nurse Corps as a first lieutenant.

In The Army

Timing had much to do with Johnson's success in the military as she entered the Army shortly after President Harry Truman banned segregation and discrimination in the armed services. "I think the nurse corps has been more progressive as far as human rights" Johnson admitted to *Ebony*. "When I came in there were no problems that I encountered so far as being black. I was very fortunate that I was given assignments that allowed me to demonstrate my ability and potential for greater ability." Additionally, Johnson was afforded educational opportunities in the Army and went on to earn a bachelor's degree in nursing from Villanova University, a master's degree in nursing education from Columbia University, and a Ph.D in education administration from Catholic University.

Like most good soldiers Johnson was rewarded with promotions and posts of responsibility during her service in assistant dean of the undergraduate program of the School of Nursing at the University of Maryland where she was responsible for the training of students who were sent to military health facilities around the world.

A New Post, A New Rank

While the list of credentials Johnson accumulated was impressive, her responsibilities were all consuming and left little time to pursue other avenues of life, including marriage. "Well, when I went into nursing you were not allowed to be married," she told *Ebony.* "But I also found that it is very difficult for a woman to find a man who can cope with the problems inherent in a busy and time-consuming schedule. From my point of view, I had to decide what was more important, marriage or my career." A decision rewarded in 1979 when Johnson was named the first black woman general in the United States Army and the first black chief of the Army Nurse Corps at the age of 52.

As chief of the Army Nurse Corps, Johnson oversaw 7,000 men and women nurses in the Army, Army National Guard and Army Reserves. Additionally, it was her charge to set policy and monitor the operations of eight Army medical centers, 56 community hospitals, and 143 free-standing clinics in the U.S. and abroad. Shortly after beginning her four-year term as chief of the nurse corps, Johnson indicated she hoped to make her mark by improving training and educational programs in the organization. "Positive progress towards excellence, that's what we want," she told *Ebony.* "If you stand still and settle for the status quo, that's exactly what you will have."

Back To Civilian Life

In 1983, at the completion of her term as chief of the Army Nurse Corps, General Johnson retired from the Army. From 1984 to 1986 she was director of government affairs for the American Nursing Association in Washington, DC, while simultaneously teaching nursing at George Washington University. In 1986 she became a professor of nursing at George Mason University in Virginia. Additionally, the demands of teaching being somewhat less rigorous than running health operations for the U.S. Army, Johnson found time to marry in the 1980s.

"I've really done what I wanted to do," she reflected to *Ebony.* "In fact, I've done more than I ever expected to do." Since she made that statement in 1980, Hazel Johnson—now Hazel Johnson-Brown—has still done more. And she continues to have enormous achievements every time someone walks out of George Mason University

the army. From first lieutenant to captain, then major, lieutenant colonel and by the mid-1970s, Johnson was colonel and the highest ranking black woman in the armed services. Positions she held included Surgical Directorate at the U.S. Army Medical Research and Development Command in Washington, DC, dean of the Walter Reed Army Institute of Nursing, chief nurse of the U.S. Army Medical Command in Korea, and special assistant to the chief of the Army Nurse Corps. Additionally, she was with a nursing degree.

Sources

Books

Carnegie, Mary Elizabeth, *The Path We Tread: Blacks in Nursing Worldwide, 1954-1994*, National League for Nursing Press, 1995.

Hine, Darlene Clark, et. al., *Black Women in America: An Historical Encyclopedia*, Indiana University Press, 1993.
Sammons, Vivian Ovelton, *Blacks in Science and Medicine*, Hemisphere Publishing, 1990.

Periodicals

Ebony, August 1977, p. 76; February 1980, p.44.
Jet, July 17, 1980, p. 60; September 23, 1983, p. 30.

—Brian Escamilla

Roy Jones, Jr.

1969—

Professional boxer

Countless journalists, fans, trainers, managers, and other boxers have termed Roy Jones "the best pound for pound fighter in the world.'' This middleweight champion from Pensacola, Florida, is known for lightning hand speed, thunderous knockout power, and astonishing agility in the ring. He even improvises with his technique, launching punches from unlikely angles and surprising opponents with unexpected moves and flurries of blows. Quoted on Jones' website, former heavyweight champion George Foreman said Jones "hits like a heavyweight and moves like a lightweight,''

In addition, Jones is one boxer who has provided a positive role model for young people. He is totally disciplined in his approach to training, avoids drugs and drink completely, is highly involved in his hometown community, and dedicates much of his time to charitable organizations and projects. Jones has been especially involved in working with teenagers: by speaking in public to many groups, warning young people about taking drugs, and providing a training program and facility for local youths. A man with strong religious convictions—which he expresses without any self-righteousness—Jones never bothers with the trash-talking so many boxers use to "psyche out''

opponents.

With his supremacy in the middleweight and light heavyweight range, it is surprising that "Roy Jones'' does not have universal name recognition. Part of the reason probably is his refusal to market himself as a spectacle—merely as a spectacular fighter. In many ways, he has refused to play the game by rules established by the media and starmakers such as Don King.

But the biggest reason is the lack of any fighters in Jones' weight division who can push him to his limits. The 1980s, by contrast, was a middleweight heyday, with a crop of sensational fighters at the top of their form, such as Sugar Ray Leonard, Marvin Hagler, Roberto Duran, and Thomas Hearns. These boxers incited and pushed each other; many of their fights were epic battles. But Jones has found no credible, champion-grade warriors to take on. In fact, many of his fights have been serious mismatches. While Jones is certainly a great boxer to watch, his matches are usually too one-sided to make for a good fight. This is a shame, because Jones' potential has hardly been tested; it is quite likely that he would have prevailed over all the other great middleweights.

Often compared favorably with the Sugar Rays—both

At a Glance . . .

Born Roy Jones Jr., January 16, 1969, in Pensacola, FL. Son of Roy Sr. and Carol Jones. Father, an ex-fighter, was Roy Jr.'s boxing teacher. *Education:* Graduate from Washington High in Pensacola in 1987. Attended Pensacola Junior College.

Career: Widely considered best pound-for-pound boxer in the world. Won National Junior Olympics title before he was 15. Won Golden Gloves in 1986 and 1987. As amateur, record was 121-13. Won Silver Medal at 1988 Olympic Games. Captured IBF middleweight crown in 1993. Won IBF super middleweight title in 1994. Earned WBC light heavyweight title in 1996. Lost (by disqualification), then regained, WBC light heavyweight crown in 1997. Captured WBA light heavyweight crown in 1998; defended it in January 1999. Won IBF belt in June of 1999 to become the first undisputed light heavyweight champion since 1985.

Selected awards: *Ring Sports* Magazine—1993 Fighter of the Year; 1995 Man of the Year; 1996 Sportsman of the Year. *Ring, Boxing Illustrated,* and *Boxing Scene* magazines—1994 Fighter of the Year. International Boxing Federation—1995 Fighter of the Year and 1995 Fighter of Unlimited Potential. ESPN ESPY Award—1995 Boxer of the Year. Boxing Illustrated's Budweiser ratings, June 1995 onward—Best Pound-for-Pound Fighter in the World. March of Dimes—1995 Honorary Chairman. *KO*—1996 Best Pound-for-Pound Fighter in the World and 1996 Best Fighter in the World (in poll of boxing experts). Congress of Racial Equality—1996 Outstanding Achievement Award. Amer. Assn. for the Improvement of Boxing (the Marciano Foundation)—1996 Humanitarian of the Year. *Boxing 1996*—Best Pound-for Pound Fighter in the World. Harlem Globetrotters—Honorary Ambassador of Goodwill (1997). Escambia-Pensacola Human Relations Commission—1997 Olive Branch Award, for humanitarianism.

Addresses: *Online*—http://www.RoyJonesJr.Com. Promotion–Square Ring, Inc., 200 West LA RUA Street, Pensacola, FL 32501. *Manager*—Richard Pope, 704 West Michigan Ave., Pensacola, FL 32505.

"were there for Leonard and Hagler and Hearns and Duran in their prime. I think Roy Jones gets in a ring and beats them all. I've never seen that kind of punching power and speed in one man.'' In 1996, *High Frequency Boxing's* John DiMaio wrote "The early evidence points toward the real possibility that Jones is the greatest talent this sport has ever seen. His skill so dwarfs that of his nearest ranked opposition...that providing competitive opponents is a more challenging dilemma than the fights themselves.'' The expert opinion of *Boxing* magazine's editor, Bert Sugar, is provided on Jones' website: "He possesses the fastest hands in boxing with lightning fast moves and explosive power in both hands.'' After lost the World Boxing Council light heavyweight crown to Jones in a 1996 unanimous decision, Mike McCallum called Jones "the greatest fighter of all time.''

Jones' mastery extends beyond mere strength and speed, however. He also has the ability to outthink other fighters, to anticipate and counter their moves before they even know what they are. Olympic team coach Alton Merkerson, whom Jones hired in the early 1990's as his trainer, said in *Sports Illustrated,* "Roy's not only got the quickest hands in boxing, but the quickest mind.''

Life With Father Was Trial By Fire

Roy Jones, Jr., was born in Pensacola, Florida, to two very different parents. His mother, Carol, was warm and easy-going, whereas his father, Roy Sr., was much like a Marine drill sergeant with respect to his son. A decorated Vietnam veteran, ex-club fighter, and retired aircraft engineer who had taken up hog farming, Roy Sr. was hard on his son from early on, taunting the child, "sparring'' with him, enraging Roy Jr., yelling at him, and beating the child, often for 20 minutes at a time. This behavior never really changed; if anything it became more brutal as Roy Jr. grew up. Many people would call the father's treatment out-and-out abuse, but he believed he had a good reason for it: to make Roy Jr. tough enough to be a champion. In this pursuit, he was relentless, and Roy Jr. lived in constant fear of his father's verbal and physical violence against him.

Jones described his childhood in *Sports Illustrated:* "After a while I didn't care about gettin' hurt or dyin' anymore. I was in pain all day, every day, I was so scared of my father. He'd pull up in his truck and start lookin' for something I'd done wrong. There was no escape, no excuse, no way out of nothin'. ... Getting' hurt or dyin' might've been better than the life I was livin'. ... Used to think about killin' myself anyway.'' There's no way to know whether or not Jones would have become a world champion fighter without this extremely punitive upbringing, but there's little question it toughened the young man.

Leonard and Robinson—Jones is believed by many to be the greatest boxer of all time. As Ross Greenburg, executive producer of HBO Sports, was quoted in a *Sports Illustrated* feature, he and the other HBO commentators

Roy Sr. ran his own boxing gym, to which he devoted all his available time and financial resources. He offered direction and useful discipline to numerous youths, and steered many of them away from trouble. Roy Sr. did everything possible to expand the program and help more kids. But towards his own son he was merciless, driving Roy Jr. to the brink of exhaustion, screaming at him in front of all the other fighters, assaulting him. Roy Sr.'s father had been a hard-working laborer, and had been tough on him the way he was on Roy Jr. But Jones, the world champion boxer, will not continue this line of treatment. He is very attuned to others' anguish; on his web site, he says, "What gets [me] down?" is "...watching other people be hurt and mistreated." It is a feeling he has known very well.

Using his fighting birds as an image for his own predicament, Jones said in the same *Sports Illustrated* piece: "I spent all my life in my dad's cage. I could never be 100 percent of who I am until I left it. But because of him, nothing bothers me. I'll never face anything stronger and harder than what I already have." Jones' father, with his overbearing and overwhelming personality, had created a powerful craving in the boxer—the need to become his own man.

Robbed of Gold in Olympics Scandal

Going into the 1988 Olympic games in Seoul, Korea, Jones had amassed an extraordinary record of 106-4. (His final tally as an amateur would be 121-13.) In the final, championship bout for his division, Jones thoroughly dominated his opponent, South Korean Park Si-Hun, with 86 punches to Park's 32—and a standing eight count to boot. But the judges decided against him, 3-2. The boxing world was stunned by this outrageous decision. As Kevin Monaghan, NBC's boxing correspondent at the games, said in *USA Today*, "It was an absolute joke. It was obvious Roy had won the fight. He was so fast, the guy couldn't lay a glove on Roy." The same article includes a quote from U.S. Olympic Committee director of media services Bob Condron: "It was not, in any sense of the word, close." The decision was such a blatant injustice that 50 Korean Buddhist monks went to Jones to express their shame.

An investigation ensued, and evidence surfaced indicating corruption—i.e., bribes. Ultimately, two of the three judges who ruled against Jones were permanently barred from boxing. At the time of the games, Jones reacted with dignity, accepting the silver medal despite the gross affront that had occurred. Since then, he has waged a campaign to get the medal he deserved. But the International Olympic Committee has refused to overturn the scandal-

ous decision. The Committee presented Jones with the Olympic Order in September 1997, but this belated consolation prize was no substitute for the medal that was stolen.

Despite Jones' preeminent stature, the Olympic incident still vexes him deeply. Millions of people believe Jones obviously won the Gold Medal. But for him, vindication can come only when the decision is officially overturned. And he still keeps a flame burning: "I will die with a little hope in me," Jones said in a *USA Today* piece.

Broke With Dad; Demolished Toney

The early days of Jones' professional career were very controversial. His father's style of management was one of absolute control, and many of Jones Sr.'s decisions at the time were considered perverse—especially his choices of opponents for his son. He refused to set up matches against any serious contenders, and stuck instead with second- or third-raters. Roy Sr. claimed he was just trying to carefully cultivate his son's career and his character. As he asserted in a *USA Today* article: "I don't care what nobody thinks. You don't give a kid $2 million and the prestige of a world title. Otherwise, you wind up with a Mike Tyson." But the boxing establishment saw this as merely padding Jones' record with easy wins. The phenomenal Olympic boxer was rapidly falling into obscurity.

Jones' loyalty to his father was intense, and so he passed up numerous offers from managers and handlers to guide him to greatness. But in denying his son any decision-making capacity, Roy Sr. was stoking the fighter's frustration. Finally, he went too far; he crossed the line. The incident involved a dog, which had bitten Jones' younger sister in fear. Roy Sr. went onto his son's land and shot the dog numerous times while it was tied to a tree.

"The final act of disrespect," was what Jones called it in a *New York Times* piece. "There's certain things you don't do to a man. ... My father didn't raise me to be a pushover, not even to him." Shortly after, he hired Alton Merkerson. Jones also took on Stanley Levin, a trusted friend and mentor, to handle the business side of things. Roy Sr. has never forgiven his son: He refuses to talk with Roy Jr. As he said in *Sports Illustrated*, "Once you break the plate at my table, you can never eat there again."

Jones' career finally started to soar. He took on the most challenging fighters out there, and trounced most of them in a few rounds. Finally, in November 1994, Jones got his chance for a truly sensational match, against James "Lights Out" Toney. Toney, an admitted former crack dealer who talked enough trash to fill a city dump, had gone undefeated in 46 bouts and was rated the best in the world. The Jones/Toney fight was ultra-hyped, and Jones for the first time in his career was the underdog. The world was eager to see whether he really had what it takes.

Over the course of the 12-round unanimous decision, Jones demonstrated his greatness. He danced circles around Toney, knocked him down hard in the third round, and blasted the big man repeatedly. *Ring* magazine called Jones' performance the most dominant of any big fight in 20 years.

Since then, Jones has faced few true challenges. His only "loss" was the result of a foul. In a March 1997 fight against Montell Griffin, Jones had to work hard to gain an edge. Griffin was proving himself a tough adversary, and it had gotten to Jones. Around the seventh round, though, Jones started to prevail. By the ninth, he was bashing Griffin hard, and forced the challenger down to one knee. Since the ref did not tell him to halt his attack, Jones hit Griffin with two more punches, the second one hard enough to knock him out. Jones was disqualified for the infraction. In the August 1997 rematch, Jones KO'd Griffin in the first round, and with that regained the World Boxing Council title he had forfeited in the earlier fight. That was the end of that controversy.

In June of 1999 Jones became the first undisputed ight heavyweight champ since 1985 (when Michael Spinks relinquished that distinction to fight at the heavyweight level). to unify the belts, Jones easily overwhelmed International Boxing Federation (IBF) belt-holder Reggie Johnson in a unanimous decision, with Johnson bleeding heavily down several times, and in trouble the entire fight. At one point Jones looked over at Michael Jordan in the front rows and yelled, "Watched this!" He tattooed Johnson with a series of blows too rapid to see clearly even on slow-motion replay.

Cultivated Other Interests

Jones leads an extraordinarily active life. Boxing is his profession, but he has loads of other passions. These include cock-fighting, which Jones has pursued avidly his whole life. He even raises birds himself, though he does not necessarily fight them. Jones credits the gutsy roosters for helping teach him about being a valiant and shrewd fighter.

Jones also loves the game of basketball, and he even played professionally with the United States Basketball League's Jacksonville Barracudas during the summer of 1996. In fact, to keep things interesting for himself, Jones became the first man to play a game of pro basketball and defend a boxing title in the same day—June 15, 1996. His opponent that day, Canada's Eric Lucas, was widely considered easy pickings for Jones, so a fatiguing basketball game was one way to even the field a little. *Knight-Ridder/Tribune News Service* quoted Jones as saying, a little defensively perhaps, "At least this gives the guy a chance." Clearly, basketball is far more than a casual hobby to Jones. But no one suggests that the 5'11" Jones should switch sports.

In addition, Jones has done a lot of motivational speaking, primarily to younger people. He has raised money for a number of charitable causes, including his injured friend Gerald McClellan. Jones visits hospitals to offer hope and inspiration to severely ill and injured patients. He also runs a youth program in Pensacola. And the list goes on; Jones is as involved in community-building and humanitarian work as any fighter ever.

A boxer with Jones' skills and genius easily could rack up a string of victories every year, and expand his visibility to the public. Many people in the boxing industry would love to see him do exactly that. But Jones does not fight just for the sake of fighting. In fact, he usually keeps it to three or four matches per year. Jones aims to select matches that carry big purses, and he has expressed frustration that his weight class is paid is so much less than the heavyweights are. But part of the reason Jones fights infrequently is because there are no fighters with comparable talent. He has even considered bulking up to take on the heavyweights or trimming down to fight the welterweight champions.

Jones has made clear many times that he has conflicted feelings about boxing, mostly because of the sport's inherent danger—for both combatants. Even a great fighter gets hit sometimes, and the human brain was not designed to endure much battering within the skull. Jones has seen up close the effects of one severe knockout punch on a friend of his: Gerald McClellan, whose eyesight, hearing, and speech were badly damaged. As he said to *USA Today,* "I care about my well-being after boxing. This game is dangerous. It doesn't take an accumulation of punches to mess you up. Gerald didn't have any hard fights before Benn. And look what happened." A year later, he was quoted in the same paper: "This game is not a good game for anyone—me or anyone else. Look at the history of the guys who were great. Look at their condition 10 years after they're done. This game doesn't usually deal you a good hand, not in the long run."

It is very rare for a fighter to discuss the long-term effects of the sport, but Jones is honest about the risks entailed. In addition to being a great athlete, Jones is intelligent and sensitive—and he does not want those qualities diminished.

> "He hits like a heavyweight and moves like a lightweight."
> —George Foreman

The other side of the issue is that Jones does not want to maim anyone. He has a well-developed conscience, and would hate to inflict a terrible injury. Sometimes when Jones fights opponents who are far below his caliber, he has to look out for the other man's well-being. For instance, when pressure from promoters and the challenger pushed Jones into taking on Vinny Pacienza in June 1995, he was not happy about it. He knew Pacienza was past his prime but also had the kind of grit that would keep him going even if the going got dangerously self-destructive. In that fight, Jones' intent to avoid hurting Pacienza prompted the referee to issue a warning. Then, as he steadily bloodied and rocked Pacienza at will, Jones all but pleaded with the ref to halt the fight. After six rounds, a TKO finally was called.

"I cried after the Pazienza fight," said Jones in the *New York Times*. "It tore me up inside. It really made me wonder about what I do automatically."

For Jones, fighting is a means to an end, but it is not how he chooses to approach life outside the ring—or indefinitely in it either. Not many boxers are tough enough to admit, as Jones did in *USA Today,* that his real desire is "to be loved and feel wanted." On another occasion, in *Sports Illustrated* Jones discussed the idea of "living large," in the ring and out: "Sure, I'll do some show-boating in the ring—I'm the only true performer in the ring today. But not outside of it. People assume every boxer wants to live the fast life. That's an escape, not a life. I want a person-to-person life."

Sources

Periodicals

High Frequency Boxing, February 1, 1996.
Knight-Ridder/Tribune News Service, June 14, 1996.
New York Times, August 3, 1997, magazine, p. 23.
Sports Illustrated, May 24, 1993, p. 56; June 26, 1995, p. 78.
USA Today, August 29, 1990, p. 1C; June 13, 1996, p. 14C; September 26, 1997; April 30, 1998, p. 14C.

Other

Roy Jones Jr.'s web site: http://www.RoyJonesJr.Com.

—Mark Baven

Eddie Kendricks

1939–1992

Vocalist

Eddie Kendricks's silken falsetto vocals were integral to the success of the Temptations, one of the musical groups that brought Detroit's Motown label to national prominence in the 1960s. He often sang lead vocal in the group's songs, many of which relied structurally on the contrast between his gentle, graceful high tenor and the southern-gospel growl of groupmate David Ruffin. Kendricks would have been assured of a place in posterity for his virtuoso performance on his final single with the Temptations, the breathtaking "Just My Imagination," but he went on to a successful solo career after leaving the group.

Like the other members of the Temptations, Eddie Kendricks was a native of the South. He was born in Union Springs, Alabama, on December 17, 1939, and grew up in Birmingham. Along with his school friend, Paul Williams, he headed North in the mid-1950s to seek fame and fortune in the music business. The two men had honed their skills while singing doo-wop music in Birmingham. They settled first in Cleveland, and hooked up for a time with a group called the Cavaliers. While they were in Cleveland, a booking agent told them about the live music scene that flourished in Detroit's African American neigh-borhoods.

Sister Group Evolved Into Supremes

In 1959, Kendricks and Williams moved to Detroit and joined with Otis Williams (no relation to Paul), Elbridge Bryant, and Melvin Franklin to form the Primes. This group, which went by the name of the Elgins for a time, gained a strong following in Detroit's nightspots. The popularity of the Primes led to the formation of a "sister" group, the Primettes. The Primettes were headed by a whispery-voiced singer named Diane Ross. She later changed her name to Diana Ross and the group became known as the Supremes.

In 1960 the Primes, later renamed the Temptations, signed a recording contract with the Miracle label. This label was one of the first imprints established by the visionary African American recording executive, Berry Gordy. The Temptations continued recording, first for the label that bore Gordy's own name, and later for the newly-christened Motown label. They also opened for Gordy's star act, Smokey Robinson and the Miracles. This association with Robinson finally helped the Temptations

At a Glance . . .

Born Eddie Kendricks in Union Springs, AL, on December 17, 1939; Died October 5, 1992, in Birmingham; went by name Eddie Kendricks until 1980s; began using original form of name by early 1980s. *Education:* attended high school in Birmingham.

Career: R&B vocalist. Helped form group the Primes, 1960; signed to Miracle label, owned by Motown Records creator Berry Gordy, 1961; name of group changed to Temptations, ca. 1961; worked with Motown songwriter Smokey Robinson, 1963–64; recorded and performed with Temptations, 1961–70; solo vocal career, 1971–92; recorded for Arista and Atlantic labels; appeared in reunions with Temptations and individual Temptations vocalists, 1982–92.

crack the charts for the first time. Their first charted single was "The Way You Do the Things You Do," which was written by Smokey Robinson and featured a new group member, David Ruffin.

Sang Lead on Temptations Singles

The Temptations became wildly popular with both rhythm-and-blues and pop audiences, placing twenty-one singles in the Top Twenty pop charts between 1964 and 1971. Kendricks sang lead vocal on several of those hits, including the upbeat "Get Ready," and sang in harmony with Ruffin on many more. He stayed with the Temptations during several personnel changes, but when the Temptations came under the direction of writer-producer Norman Whitfield in the late 1960s, Kendricks's role in the group was reduced. In 1970, after singing lead on one of the Temptations few ballads, "Just My Imagination," Kendricks decided to strike out on his own. Many critics considered "Just My Imagination" as Kendricks's finest performance with the group. He had already left the Temptations when the song spent three weeks atop *Billboard* magazine's pop chart in 1971.

Kendricks moved to Motown's sister label Tamla, and his solo career got off to a respectable start with "Girl, You Need a Change of Mind (Part I)," which was released in 1972. His 1973 proto-disco hit "Keep On Truckin'" reached Number One on the R&B charts, crossed over to pop, and eventually sold an estimated three million copies. Kendricks followed up this hit with "Boogie Down" and other singles drawn from his nine Tamla albums, and

remained a presence on the music charts throughout most of the 1970s. Songs such as "Son of Sagittarius," "Tell Her Love Has Felt the Need," "One Tear," "Shoeshine Boy," "Get the Cream Off the Top," "Happy," and "He's a Friend" all hit the R&B Top Ten.

Although he had anticipated the disco movement in some respects, sales of Kendricks's records plummeted toward the end of the 1970s. Moves to the Arista and Atlantic labels failed to improve sales. In 1982, the Temptations' reunited for a tour and a new album, which scored a hit single, "Standing On the Top." Although the Temptations reunion did not last, Ruffin and Kendricks continued performing together.

Recorded with Ruffin and Edwards

In 1984 Ruffin and Kendricks recorded an album together, *Live at the Apollo with David Ruffin and Eddie Kendrick,"* and performed at the Live Aid charity concert the following year. They also collaborated with the Philadelphia "blue-eyed soul" hitmakers Daryl Hall and John Oates, who modeled their restrained soul vocals on Kendricks's style. During the early 1990s Kendricks teamed with another ex-Temptation, Dennis Edwards, on the song "Get It While It's Hot." Kendricks, Ruffin, and Edwards also toured together with a Temptations-themed show.

In 1991, Kendricks was diagnosed with lung cancer and doctors removed one of his lungs in an effort to save his life. The surgery seemed to improve Kendricks's health and he was able to tour in Europe and Japan in the summer of 1992. He also sued Motown Records, claiming that royalties owed to him had been withheld. Before the case could be settled, Kendricks's cancer reappeared and he returned to Birmingham, where he died on October 5. At the time of his death, Kendricks did not have health insurance and soul singer Bobby Womack organized two benefit concerts to help Kendricks's family with their financial burdens.

Selected discography

(solo albums)

All by Myself, Tamla, 1971.
People . . . Hold On, Tamla, 1972.
Eddie Kendricks, Tamla, 1973.
Boogie Down, Tamla, 1974.
For You, Tamla, 1974.
The Hit Man, Tamla, 1975.
He's a Friend, Tamla, 1976.
Goin' Up in Smoke, Tamla, 1976.
Slick, Tamla, 1978.

At His Best, Tamla, 1978.
Vintage '78, Arista, 1978.
Love Keys, Atlantic, 1981.

(with David Ruffin)

David Ruffin and Eddie Kendricks, RCA, 1987.

(with David Ruffin, Daryl Hall, and John Oates)

Live at the Apollo with David Ruffin and Eddie Kendrick, RCA, 1985.

(with the Temptations)

Anthology (greatest hits), Motown, 1973.
Reunion, Motown, 1982.

Sources

Books

Contemporary Musicians, volume 3, Gale, 1990.
Romanowski, Patricia, and Holly George-Warren, *The New Rolling Stone Encyclopedia of Rock and Roll,* Fireside, 1995.
Stambler, Irwin, *Encyclopedia of Pop, Rock & Soul,* St. Martin's, 1989.
Williams, Otis, and Patricia Romanowski, *Temptations,* Putnam's, 1988.

Periodicals

Billboard, October 17, 1992, p. 12.
Jet, October 26, 1992, p. 53.
New York Times, October 7, 1992.
Rolling Stone, November 26, 1992, p. 24.

—James M. Manheim

Barbara King

19(?)(?)—

Cleric

Barbara Lewis King creates quite a presence standing upon the podium. Possessing a flair for flamboyant clothes and dramatic gestures, she exhorts her congregation to love themselves and to find the Father-Mother God within each of them. Raised by a grandmother who emphasized spirituality, King has inspired others with her message of positive action and leads a congregation exceeding 5,000 worshipers.

King was born in Houston, Texas to parents who divorced shortly after her birth. Her father, Lee Andrew Lewis, was an activist who fought to bring African American motion picture operators into the AFL-CIO, pressed for equal wages for African Americans, and became the first African American motion picture operator in Texas. While her father's example of dignity in the face of struggle continued to influence her significantly, King moved in with her grandmother, Ida Bates Lewis. Despite the fact that King lived in poverty and sometimes went to school with cardboard stuffed into the bottom of her shoes, her grandmother stressed the pleasures of dressing well and the satisfaction of making the best of one's situation. She was further bolstered by her grandmother's strong faith and the teachings of the Baptist church. This combination of spiritual and emotional

fulfillment worked to strengthen King's self-confidence in the face of adversity.

As King explained to *Women Looking Ahead,* "I saw the working of the spirit in my grandmother. She demonstrated religious and spiritual principles through her actions and how she lived; not through talk…Her affirmation [that "The Lord will make a way"] moved me as a child; gave me the will and courage to pursue my calling." She also remarked to Donita Rolle in *Femme* that her grandmother often told her to "Never say you can't do something. You can do what you have to do."

Soon after enrolling at Texas State University in 1948, King was diagnosed with tuberculosis. Instead of attending college, she found herself in a sanatorium for the next four years. While convalescing at the sanatorium, King was introduced to the Unity School of Christianity, a belief system whose central tenet states that because all people are created in the image of God, all are potentially divine. The Unity message of personal power strongly appealed to her. Although doctors were skeptical that King would recover from her disease, she claimed that she was miraculously healed after following a radio preacher's

At a Glance . . .

Born Barbara Lewis; daughter of Lee Andrew Harris; married and divorced three times; children: Michael. *Education:* Texas Southern University, BA in sociology; Atlanta University, MSW in social work administration.

Career: Program director, Henry Booth House, Chicago; program consultant, Church Federation of Greater Chicago; executive director, South Chicago Community Services Association, 1966-68; dean of community relations, Chicago City College, Malcolm X Campus, 1967-69; instructor, Atlanta University School of Social Work, 1971-72; director, South Central Community Mental Health Center, Atlanta, 1971-73; dean of students, Spelman College, Atlanta, 1974-76; founder and minister, Hillside Chapel and Truth Center, Inc., Atlanta, 1971-; founder and president, Barbara King School of Ministry, Atlanta, 1977-.

Memberships: Chair, Community Relations Commission, Atlanta; vice-president, International New Thought Alliance; member, Atlanta Women's Network; member, Women's Chamber of Commerce of Atlanta; member, American Management Association.

Addresses: Hillside Chapel and Truth Center, 2450 Cascade Road, SW, Atlanta, GA 30311.

instruction to put her hands on the radio and pray with him. She has often recounted that when she removed her hands from the radio, a voice within her declared that her lungs were clear. In 1951, King convinced her physicians to allow her to return to college, and she remained free of tuberculosis.

Called to the Ministry

From the age of 13, King felt called to the ministry. She often taught Sunday school classes as a teenager and, at the age of 15, was the youngest Woman's Day speaker in the history of Houston's Antioch Baptist Church. King recalled that she would envision herself standing at the pulpit during church services. However, she was repeatedly discouraged by male church leaders from pursuing the ministry and told that she should become a missionary. Setting aside her dream of becoming a minister, King

earned a bachelor's degree in sociology from Texas Southern. In 1955, she moved to Atlanta to pursue a master's degree at Atlanta University's School of Social Work. Upon completing her degree, she moved to Chicago and found employment as a social work administrator, heading a $3 million-a-year settlement project within the city's housing bureaucracy.

While living in Chicago, King married Moses King in June of 1966 and gave birth to her son, Michael, on March 15, 1967. In 1968 she met the Rev. Johnnie Colemon, the first female African American minister that she had ever encountered. At the time, Colemon was the full-time minister of Christ Universal Temple, one of the largest churches in Chicago, and she inspired King to establish her own ministry. King served as Colemon's director of administration while Coleman concurrently guided her ministerial training. King also studied at the Baptist Training School in Chicago and at Missouri's Unity Institute of Continuing Education. She completed her training and was ordained by the Rev. Roy Blake in 1971.

In 1971, King returned to Atlanta and joined the faculty of Atlanta University (later known as Clark Atlanta University) as a professor of social work before becoming dean of students at Spelman College. In addition to her university responsibilities, King started a Bible study group. The group blossomed into what Virginia Holland-Davis of *Reflections* termed "a sort of 'underground' religious-social women's organization" that networked and served as an umbrella to other woman-led underground ministries. From this small, dedicated group of 12 people, King began to create a ministry.

Founded Hillside Chapel and International Truth Center

By 1974, the Bible study group had grown into a church-sized gathering. King left Spelman, bought a building to house the congregation, and named her new church the Hillside Chapel and International Truth Center. She remarked in *Women Looking Ahead* that shortly after the church's founding, "verbal attacks and allegations that we were a cult, that we were non-religious because a woman was the pastor," began to surface. King is quick to point out that her ministry is not feminist-centered although, as she noted in the *Atlanta Journal and Constitution*, "I don't believe any woman ought to be put in a position where she has to depend on a man for paying the bills....I just grew up in a family of strong women who taught that whatever you can be you ought to be that."

Despite its critics, the Hillside Chapel's membership continued to multiply. By 1985 the congregation had outgrown its facilities, and church members embarked on a massive fund-raising campaign to build a "church-in-the-round" on the nearly 12-acre property next door. The new facility was completed in 1991, and its circular configuration eliminated the need for a pulpit so that King could be closer to the congregation. The church center also includes a preschool, elementary school, ministers' school, and bookstore. King's message is broadcast locally twice every Sunday morning, and she has hosted her own television show, *A New Thought, A New Life.*

King remains unaffiliated with any particular Christian denomination, but maintains ties with the International New Thought Alliance. Blending humor, positive thinking, and health tips into her sermons, she preaches love of oneself as a vehicle to loving God and one's neighbor. King also preaches about the 12 spiritual gifts of man as embodied in each of Jesus's 12 disciples. Each disciple is represented by a color and honored on a designated month. King wears a robe to match the color of the disciple honored and preaches about the spiritual gifts of that disciple during his particular month.

Formalized Church's Philosophy

In an interview with Susan Howard of the *Atlanta Journal and Constitution,* King explained the appeal of her ministry, "I still bring in the emotion, the feelings that evolve from out of the traditional black church. But I teach that God is within. I teach that life is consciousness, that when you're loving you, you're loving God in you. God is not someone who is way off sitting at a throne looking down on you." As a practitioner of the New Thought church, she goes beyond a literal interpretation of the Bible. "We go beyond to the spiritual translation," she explained to Myrian Richmond of *Aquarius,* "because we are mindful of the historical and cultural contexts within which the Bible was written…The New Thought Movement has always recognized the threefold nature of man, that he is mind, body and emotions and that there must be balance among all three aspects if we are to perfectly unfold as spiritual beings." The majority of Hillside's congregation is between the ages of 18 and 45. Employing a message designed to appeal to this age group, King encourages her members to utilize the Hillside "Treasure Map," a guide for visualizing one's goals. The map includes categories for education, the perfect mate, and the ideal car, and members are asked to attach a photograph of their goal to the map so that they may forever see immediately before them the goals they hope to attain.

Critics charge that King's philosophy overly emphasizes the material instead of the spiritual. She counters these negative comments by stressing that her church speaks to current issues, to the concerns of her specific community, and always within a spiritual context. As King noted in the *Atlanta Journal and Constitution,* "People need to feel good about themselves, and when a church gives that kind of support and reinforcement, it will attract people. . . . At Hillside, we teach that you should have whatever you want. . . . You can have your Volvo. . .whatever you want, but you better have God with it. Recognize God as the source of everything you have…You don't have to be poor and singing the blues all the time to be a Christian."

Expanded Personal Mission

King's stature in Atlanta extends far beyond the walls of her church. Preaching her message of faith in God, belief in self, and the power of positive thinking, she is the first female chaplain for the Atlanta Police Department. In an interview with the *Atlanta Journal and Constitution,* the Rev. Robert L. "Jackey" Beavers remarked, "When people talk about black leaders, they have to include Dr. King. That's evident at election time. When people are running for office, they go to see Dr. Barbara King. Anybody who has that much of a following, well, you definitely want them on your side. She has earned herself a place in Atlanta's black power structure whether no one else wanted her to have it or not." Responding to Beavers's comments, King told the *Atlanta Journal and Constitution,* "I see power as something that comes from within. A powerful person gives his best and motivates people to exercise their own personal power. If that makes me powerful, then that's what I'm about."

> "I teach that God is within. I teach that life is consciousness, that when you're loving you, you're loving God in you."

The Hillside Center ministry has continued to expand. The church opened a holistic health center in 1997 and, one year later, celebrated the establishment of A Quiet Place, a meditation and prayer center in downtown Atlanta. The Hillside Center also has satellite congregations throughout the United States, and has established a church in South Africa. Apart from her ministry, King has opened an exclusive boutique which caters to women who require speciality sizing. Her goal is to franchise the store across the United States and abroad. King also remains focused on traveling throughout the world and preaching her message of healing and spiritual fulfillment. As she told

Aquarius, "I just look forward to being led by Spirit and to being open to the guidance I will receive."

Selected writings

Transform Your Life, DeVorss, 1989.
Do I Need a Flood, CSA Press, 1983.
What Is A Miracle? CSA Press, 1981.
Love Your Body Temple.
Giving Is Receiving.
The Church: A Matter of Consciousness.
Prosperity That Can't Quite.

Sources

Periodicals

Aquarius, January 1998, p. 8.
Atlanta Business Journal, Fall/Winter 1997, pp. 66-67.
Atlanta Journal and Constitution, September 26, 1985; June 9, 1987, p. 1-B, 4-B; December 26, 1992, pp. B1, 10; June 6, 1995, p. F1.
Ebony, December 1996, p. 40.
Essence, June 1998, pp. 84-89.
Femme, October 29, 1983.
Heart & Soul, March 1997, pp. 85-86.
Newsweek, March 4, 1996, pp. 50-52.
Recovery Network, October 1992.
Reflections, September 1995, pp. 3, 6.
Upscale, January 1999, p. 41.
Women Looking Ahead, November 1996, pp. 16-17.

Other

Additional information for this profile was obtained from Hillside Chapel & Truth Center press releases and the Hillside Chapel & Truth Center web site.

—Lisa S. Weitzman

Regina King

1971—

Actress

Regina King's versatility as a performer and down to earth good looks have made her one of Hollywood's most in-demand young actresses. Equally adept at comedy and drama, King has appeared in a wide range of films, most notably *Jerry Maguire,* the 1996 box-office smash starring Tom Cruise, *Boyz N the Hood,* a 1991 drama of gang warfare, and *How Stella Got Her Groove Back,* a glossy 1998 romance starring Angela Bassett. Usually King plays a supporting role as a wife, sister, or friend. Though she would like larger parts, King sees some advantages in not being a big name. "I've gotten much more life span in roles because I'm not the flavor of the month," King told Joan Morgan of *Essence.*

King was born in Los Angeles in 1971. Her father, Thomas, was an electrician, and her mother, Gloria, was a special education teacher. After her parents divorced in 1979, King and her younger sister, Reina, lived with their mother and were given an assortment of lessons. "Everything—tap dancing, baton twirling, ice skating," King told Tom Gliatto of *People.* Acting lessons were also on the agenda. Her remarkable dramatic talent was so apparent that a professional career was encouraged. King began acting professionally at age twelve in local theatre produc-

tions and on televisions shows, including *The Cosby Show* on which she appeared as a friend of Tempestt Bledsoe's character, Vanessa. Being on television did not change King's upbringing much. "I came from a very grounded family...Even though everyone on our block was well off, there were drug dealers around the corner selling. I grew up knowing what it was like to be around gangstas and superrich kids. That's why I've never been the type to ignore someone just because they're not like me," King explained to Morgan.

In 1985, at age 14, King landed a regular role on the NBC series *227,* a situation comedy about working class neighbors in a Washington, DC apartment building. King played Brenda, the often petulant teenage daughter of the show's star, Marla Gibbs. King and Gibbs, along with several other members of the show's cast, had earlier performed in a Los Angeles stage version of *227.* "Regina took pride in what she was doing," Gibbs said of King to Gliatto. Though never a television ratings powerhouse, *227* drew enough of a following to last for five seasons. During her years on the show, King attended a regular high school whenever her shooting schedule permitted, and was even on the track team. "I wanted to be in tune with normal

At a Glance . . .

Born in Los Angeles, CA, the daughter of Thomas (an electrician) and Gloria (a special education teacher). Married to Ian Alexander (a recording company executive), 1997-; one child, Ian, Jr. *Education:* Westchester High School, Los Angeles, CA, class of 1988.

Career: A professional actress since 1984. Film appearances in *Boyz N the 'Hood*, 1991; *Poetic Justice*, 1993; *Friday*, 1995; *Higher Learning*, 1995; *Jerry Maguire*, 1996; *A Thin Line Between Love and Hate*, 1996; *How Stella Got Her Groove Back*, 1998; *Enemy of the State*, 1998; *Mighty Joe Young*, 1998. Television appearances include a regular role on the series *227*, NBC, 1985-90; recurring roles on *Living Single*, Fox, 1993-94; and *New York Undercover*, Fox, 1994-95; guest appearances on *The Cosby Show*, *Silver Spoons*, *Northern Exposure*. Also appeared on the special programs *BET's Voices Against Violence*, 1995; *Why Colors?*, 1995; and *Rituals*, 1998. Co-owner of the restaurant Paio, Los Angeles, CA.

Awards: Acapulco Black Film Festival nomination for best actress for *A Thin Line Between Love and Hate*, 1996; National Association for the Advancement of Colored People (NAACP) Image Award nomination for *Enemy of the State*, 1998.

Addresses: *Home*—Los Angeles, CA. *Agent*—Chuck James, Gersh Agency, 232 N. Canon Drive, Beverly Hills, CA 90210.

people," King told Gliatto.

Soon after *227* left the air, King made her film debut in *Boyz N the Hood*, a gut-wrenching depiction of a young man's coming of age in a tough section of Los Angeles. Directed by John Singleton and starring Laurence Fishburne, the well-received 1991 drama featured a cast made up of future screen notables including Cuba Gooding, Jr., Angela Bassett, and Nia Long. King did not personally associate with the difficulties of the characters in the film. "Fortunately, I've never had serious trauma. I haven't had somebody die from drugs. I haven't been caught up in drugs, and I don't have a mother or father who didn't have jobs or education. The *Boyz N the Hood* story was not my story. That I can't give you that story is a nice story to tell,"

King said to Morgan.

King went on to appear in two more films directed by Singleton—*Poetic Justice* and *Higher Learning*. Released in 1993, *Poetic Justice* starred Janet Jackson and Tupac Shakur as a beautician and a mailman finding romance amidst the poverty and violence of South Central Los Angeles. King was part of a large cast including Fishburne, Tyra Banks, Ice Cube, Omar Epps, Michael Rapaport, and Jennifer Connolly in 1995's *Higher Learning*, a drama about racial and romantic problems at a contemporary university. Returning to lighter fare, King appeared in A *Thin Line Between Love and Hate*, a 1996 comedy written and directed by Martin Lawrence about a Lothario who finds himself the object of a wronged woman's vengeance.

In the comedic drama *Jerry Maguire*, Tom Cruise portrayed a ruthless sports agent who decides to walk a more virtuous path only to find himself abandoned by all his clients save one, Rod Tidwell, a second-string wide receiver played by Cuba Gooding, Jr. King played Tidwell's forthright and strongly supportive wife, Marcee. Written and directed by Cameron Crowe, *Jerry Maguire* was one of the most popular films of the year and originated the catch phrase "Show me the money!" The smash picture brought fame to Gooding, who won the best supporting actor Oscar for his exuberant performance as Rod Tidwell, and to Renee Zellweger, who played Cruise's love interest. The film did not do as much for King's career. "I signed with a really huge publicity company and I felt like just got lost. They didn't care about my career. And I was never really into the whole publicity thing, so it was kind of new to me...I couldn't dwell on being disappointed. I was so happy to play a role that got to show a functional Black family. Plus the response I got from people--from the streets to the industry--was just incredible," King said of the *Jerry Maguire* fallout to Morgan.

In January of 1996, shortly before commencing work on *Jerry Maguire*, King gave birth to a son, Ian Alexander, Jr. "I was nursing Ian between takes," King told Gliatto. King and the child's father, Ian Alexander, Sr., an executive at Quincy Jones' Qwest Records, were married in 1997. King said of her husband to Morgan – "Ian is a very secure person. He knows who he is and knew it long before we got together. He works in the entertainment industry, so it's cool because we can respect and understand the demands of the business."

After a respite from acting to devote herself to motherhood, King returned to the screen in three films released in 1998. *How Stella Got Her Groove Back* was a film adaptation of Terry McMillan's novel about a forty year old stockbroker who finds love with a much younger man while on a trip to Jamaica. The film starred Angela Bassett and newcomer Taye Diggs. King played Vanessa, Bassett's smart-mouthed ambulance driver sister. "Regina is smart and funny. She's got the snap we wanted," said McMillan, who also wrote the film's screenplay, to Gliatto. In the political conspiracy thriller *Enemy of the State,* King played the wife of Will Smith. King moved away from the sister and wife roles to play wildlife researcher Dr. Cecily Banks in *Mighty Joe Young,* a Christmastime release from the Disney studio. A remake of a 1948 film of the same name, *Mighty Joe Young,* which also starred Bill Paxton and Charlize Theron, tells the story of giant gorilla brought a California animal sanctuary. "I'm really excited about this movie. It's the first film I've done that *every* single person in my family, no matter what age, can come and see. This is a fun family film," King told the *Los Angeles Sentinel.*

King's professional interests are not restricted to show business. In August 1998, King and other investors opened a restaurant in Los Angeles called Paio (Italian for pair), featuring nouvelle American cuisine. "It's my way of giving back to L.A., which is long overdue for a place that has great atmosphere and good food and is not about

the industry," King explained to Morgan.

King has completed filming of *Love and Action in Chicago,* in which she co-stars with Courtney B. Vance, Kathleen Turner, and Jason Alexander. Future projects include the film *Quest for Atlantis.* Though King continues with a busy career and has not ruled out the possibility of someday being a major star, she tries to keep her life in balance. As she told Morgan—"I stay in tune with my family and God...I want to live a full life—period."

Sources

Periodicals

Essence, October 1998, p. 98.
Los Angeles Sentinel, January 6, 1999, p. B6.
Los Angeles Times, August 14, 1998, pp. F1, 22.
Newsweek, January 12, 1998, p. 58.
People, August 31, 1998, pp. 103-104.
Tri-State Defender, June 11, 1997, p. B2.

—Mary Kalfatovic

Annie Frances Lee

1935—

Artist

Painter and decorative artist, Annie Lee is well known for her realistic and humorous portrayals of contemporary and historical African American family life. "My paintings are of everyday life. I try to paint things that people can identify with," Lee told *Contemporary Black Biography (CBB)*. Identify they did. Since her first gallery show in 1985, during which her paintings sold out in the first four hours of the show, Lee has enjoyed resounding success. In particular, her paintings "Blue Monday" and "Six No Uptown" struck a chord with viewers. They have been consistent best sellers and a springboard to Lee's wide-ranging artistic endeavors.

Lee was born in Gadsden, Alabama in 1935 and raised in Chicago. She grew up in a family that expected girls and boys alike to learn survival skills, so her mother, a seamstress, taught her and her older brother Tony to cook, wash, clean, and sew. While listening to the popular radio shows of the time, like *The Lone Ranger* and *The Shadow*, Annie also learned to knit, crochet, and draw. At age ten, she took up painting. Immediately she demonstrated talent, winning recognition at art contests and several free semesters of lessons at the Art Institute of Chicago.

On Sundays Lee and her family often went to church. They then enjoyed eggnog ice cream at the corner drug store and sometimes a movie matinee. While a high school student, the energetic Lee both honed her artistic skills and urged on the Wendell Phillips High School football team as part of the cheerleading squad. Although she was offered a four-year scholarship to study art at Northwestern University, Lee opted to marry and raise a family. "At the time, it wasn't a hard decision to make," Lee told *CBB*.

Resumed Painting

Busy with family life, Lee did not resume painting until she was 40 years old. By then she had lost two husbands to cancer and raised a daughter from her first marriage and a son from her second. While working as the chief clerk at Northwestern Railroad, in the department that ensures the safety of the train tracks, Lee decided to study art at night. Although she never intended to teach, after eight years of night classes, she earned a masters degree in interdisciplinary arts education from Loyola University. Lee told *CBB*,

"Getting my masters degree was the best thing I ever did for myself. It reopened my mind."

Painting at night was Lee's haven and release from the pressures of everyday life. Her railroad job inspired one of Lee's most popular paintings, "Blue Monday," which depicts a woman struggling to pull herself out of bed on a Monday morning. Living in such close proximity to her art caused new challenges for Lee. She developed tendinitis and spinal problems from painting so much. Even worse, the fumes from the acrylic paints she used made her sick. Despite these problems, she continued to paint, having her first gallery show in 1985. The show was so successful that Lee allowed prints to be made of four of the paintings, so that she could meet the demand for her work.

Launched Career

In December of 1986 tragedy befell Lee when her son died in an automobile accident. While on leave from work to grieve, she decided to take a risk: she would give up the financial security of her day job to pursue her dream of painting full-time. "I prayed I could make my living by painting. I felt I was supposed to paint. Now that my son was gone, I didn't need such financial resources," Lee remembered to *CBB*. "God did this through me," she continued. "I never thought I would leave the railroad, but it was the best thing I ever did. It was hard to leave the security, but you have to take a leap of faith."

Lee's risk paid off. In 1990, after showing her work in other galleries, Lee opened her own shop, Annie Lee and Friends Gallery. There she initially displayed 49 original paintings of her own, as well as the works fellow artists. Lee quickly demonstrated her business acumen. Her gallery proved to be a success, so she moved it to a new location in the southeastern suburbs of Chicago in order to have more floor space. When several of her paintings appeared in the sets of popular television shows—on Bill Cosby's *A Different World*, for instance—the exposure helped make her work even more popular.

Painted "Black Americana"

For her use of two-dimensional figures that are set in scenes of everyday life, art commentators dubbed Lee's style "Black Americana." For example, "Gimme Dat Gum" shows a mother demanding her children's bubble gum as they sit in a church pew. In "Max-ed Out" a young woman reclines on a sofa after a clothes shopping trip. In "Al Ain't Here," a group of men play cards. "In Control" depicts a man lounging in his favorite chair, with the newspaper on his lap and the television remote control in hand. Ballet dancers, card players, women primping and at a beauty shop, dancing couples, a baby sitter, a girl taking a bubble bath, a boy eating watermelons out of the patch--all flowed from Lee's paint brush. A hallmark of Lee's work is that the figures she paints are faceless. "You don't need to see a face to understand emotion," Lee explained to *CBB*. "I try to make the movement of the body express the emotion. And people can use their imaginations." Using her unique designs, Lee also developed figurines, high fashion dolls, decorative housewares, and kitchen tiles.

After many years, Lee left the Windy City for the Southwest. It was a natural decision, because to protect her health Lee needs to paint outdoors or under an exhaust fan. Although she regularly receives numerous requests for public appearances, Lee prefers to appear at gallery shows. She enjoys chatting one on one and signing prints for buyers. She also likes to visit schools, where, as she told *CBB*, she encourages students to "concentrate on something you like. You're going to be working all of your life, so just do what makes you happy! And, if you are able to make others happy while doing what makes you happy, what more could you ask?"

Sources

Periodicals

Jet, May 3, 1999, p. 14.
Upscale, April, 1999, pp. 68-69.

Other

Additional information was provided via an interview with Annie Lee." May, 1999.

"Wilson Brown Gallery." http://www.wbgallery.com/catalog/cgi/goto.cgi?FILE=artists/a_lee.html (14 April 1999).

—Jeanne M. Lesinski

Hughie Lee-Smith

1915–1999

Artist, educator

Like his paintings, artist Hughie Lee-Smith presented a riddle. Although his works were exhibited at museums, schools, and galleries around the United States, earned him many honors and awards, and were hung on the set of *The Cosby Show*, Lee-Smith did not enjoy a major solo exhibition of his work until fifty years after he began painting. His first retrospective exhibit—at the New Jersey State Museum in Trenton in 1988–occurred when he was 73 years old.

often confronted viewers with a world where African American and white people maintained a cautious or uneasy distance from one another. Secondly, his work was mainly shown in African American art exhibits and for many years remained largely unrecognized in mainstream art circles. Thirdly, he chose to paint figuratively at a time when abstract expressionism was at its height.

Unlike his contemporary, painter Jacob Lawrence, Lee-Smith didn't receive much attention as a young artist. However, he slowly gained national recognition as he produced a steady stream of oil paintings. He created an impressive series of lithographic prints and was commissioned by the U.S. Navy to paint several murals. Lee-Smith's works, which often featured the fantastic elements of magical realism and surrealism, are well known for their hard-hitting social commentary. Many critics have observed that his paintings bear a strong resemblance to the works of Italy's Giorgio de Chirico and American artist Edward Hopper.

Lee-Smith did not receive a great deal of attention during his lifetime for a number of reasons. Firstly, his paintings

Lee-Smith's artistic career did not pass completely unnoticed, however. During the 1980s, he was awarded a day in his honor in Cleveland, Ohio and given the key to the city of Hartford, Connecticut. He also received honors from the Maryland Commission on Afro-American History and Culture, and prizes from the National Academy of Design and Audubon Artists. In 1996, the Lotos Club awarded Lee-Smith with its Medal of Merit and, that same year, he was presented with the Benjamin West Clinedinst Medal from the Artists Fellowship Inc. His works have been included in the Evans-Tibbs collection in Washington, D.C., and were displayed in museums such as the Cleveland Museum of Art, the Whitney Museum of American Art, and the Museum of Modern Art in New York City, as well as in galleries, including New York's

At a Glance . . .

Born September 20, 1915, in Eustis, FL, died in Albuquerque, NM; son of Luther and Alice (Williams) Lee-Smith; married Mabel Louise Everett, 1940 (divorced, 1953); married Helen Nebraska, 1965 (divorced, 1974); married Patricia Thomas-Ferry, 1978; children: Christina. *Education:* Graduated from Cleveland Institute of Art, 1938; Wayne State University, B.S. 1953.

Career: Worked for the Ohio Works Progress Administration and the Ford factory in River Rouge during the 1930s and 1940s; did a series of lithographic prints; painted murals at the Great Lakes Naval Station in Illinois; taught art at Karamu House, Cleveland, late 1930s, the Grosse Pointe War Memorial in Michigan, 1955-56, Princeton Country Day School, NJ, 1963-65, Howard University, Washington, DC, 1969-71, the Art Students League, New York City, 1972-87, and elsewhere. Works shown in museums, schools, galleries, and collections across the U.S., including the American Negro Exposition, Chicago; Detroit Artists Market; Cleveland Museum of Art; Whitney Museum of American Art; Museum of Modern Art; the June Kelly Gallery, New York City; and the Evans-Tibbs collection, Washington, DC. *Military service:* Served in the U.S. Navy during World War II.

Selected awards: Bronze Plaque, Maryland Commission on Afro-American History and Culture, 1981; October 19, 1984 declared Hughie Lee-Smith Day, Cleveland, OH; key to Hartford, CT, 1984; awarded the Ralph Fabri, 1982, the Emily Lowe, 1985, and the Len Everette Memorial, 1986, all from Audubon Artists, Inc.; National Academy of Design's Clarke Prize, 1959, and Ranger Fund Purchase, 1963 and 1977; Lotos Club, Medal of Merit, 1996; Artists Fellowship, Inc., Benjamin West Clinedinst Medal, 1996.

June Kelly Gallery.

In 1988, a retrospective of Lee-Smith's works were shown at the New Jersey State Museum. Works selected for the exhibit included his depictions of alienated youth during the 1940s, his desolate landscapes of the 1950s and 1960s, and his paintings of isolated African American and white people confronting or refusing to confront one another. While allusions to the isolation of African Americans are present, the paintings also portrayed the inability of some human beings to make contact with each other. According to some art critics, what made Lee-Smith unique was his ability to fuse theAfrican American experience with his own brand of surrealism.

In her essay for the *Hughie Lee-Smith Retrospective Exhibition* catalogue, Lowery S. Sims, an associate curator of twentieth century art at the Metropolitan Museum of Art, wrote of the settings and images used in the Lee-Smith's works: "Lee-Smith's dramas unfold on desolate beaches, or vacant lots bordering on a lake, or tenement buildings and disengaged, crumbling walls. Balls, balloons, ribbons, wires, poles, antennae, rotten piers, bricks and rocks, labyrinths and, more recently, antique sculpture fragments and mannikins [sic] are the accouterments that charge these scenes with metaphorical and allegorical content that eludes definitive interpretations."

Elsa Honig Fine, writing in *The Afro-American Artist: A Search for Identity,* described the Lee-Smith's work as "captur[ing] the loneliness and alienation of contemporary urban life through the emotive devices associated with the Surrealists--a sharply converging perspective and an 'ambiguous sense of nearness and distance' between figure and background. Lee-Smith's people are alienated from each other and from the space that encloses them." And in *American Artist* magazine, Carol Wald characterized Lee-Smith's paintings as "haunting" and "memorable," adding, "Figures in them move silently across the stage of a barren universe and seem to be teetering on the very edge of another kind of reality ... perhaps that of sleep. Often the subject is a desolate, dark landscape occupied by one or a few solitary figures related somehow by their proximity but nevertheless adrift in separate worlds of being and action."

Whatever qualities may be attributed to Lee-Smith's paintings, the artist offered his own analysis of his work in *American Artist,* "I think my paintings have to do with an invisible life--a reality on a different level." And in an interview with Inga Saffron for the *Philadelphia Inquirer,* he noted that his paintings "deal with alienation, which is a fact of life ... separation of the races ... and of races coming together."

Lee-Smith's paintings also reflected the psychological uncertainty he experienced as a child. After his birth in Eustis, Florida, on September 20, 1915, his family moved to Atlanta and then to Cleveland. His parents divorced when he was still quite young, and his mother raised him during the Great Depression. "I was already aiming at perfection," he told Wald, "at being good at whatever I was doing.... I drew all the time, and it became a natural thing. I breathed it; I dreamed it. Art was my whole being, and I knew from an early age that it was my mission." Lee-Smith's mother encouraged him in his artistic pursuits and helped him gain admission to a class for gifted children at the Cleveland Museum of Art.

When he was twenty years old, Lee-Smith won a *Scholastic* magazine competition that enabled him to study on a one-year scholarship at the Art School of the Detroit Society of Arts and Crafts. Later, he taught art at Karamu House in Cleveland and studied at the Cleveland Institute of Art on another scholarship, this time from the Gilpin Players, the resident company of the Karamu Theatre.

In addition to attending the Cleveland Institute of Art, from which he graduated in 1938, Lee-Smith also studied at Wayne State University in Detroit, where he received his bachelor's degree in art education in 1953. His early works were shown mostly in Chicago and Detroit, at the Southside Community Art Center, the Snowden Gallery, and the Detroit Artists Market. His work was also displayed at a 1940 exhibit of art at the American Negro Exposition in Chicago.

Gravitated Toward Artistic Group

Lee-Smith was still a child during the Harlem Renaissance, a period of heightened literary and artistic activity among African Americans centered in New York City's Harlem during the 1920s. In the 1940s, he gravitated toward an artistic group that met at the Southside Community Art Center in Chicago. It included painter Rex Goreleigh, as well as poet Gwendolyn Brooks. Around the same time, Lee-Smith met artist Joseph Hirsch, who has seen the young painter's work in Chicago and later saw to his admission to the prestigious National Academy of Design. Lee-Smith served on the academy's council over forty years later.

To support himself as an artist during the 1930s and 1940s, Lee-Smith worked for the Ohio Works Progress Administration (WPA) and at the Ford factory in River Rouge while turning out a series of lithographic prints. He received an award from the Cleveland Museum for freehand drawing in 1938 and for his lithographs in 1939 and 1940. Commenting on the style of the lithographs, James Porter wrote in *Modern Negro Art*, "Lee-Smith takes huge delight in his expert ability as a draftsman, and for him line and form are the essence of the picture. Into this mold he pours all the exciting experience that his mind can call up—sometimes with startling results."

Painted Murals for the U.S. Navy

Lee-Smith continued working on his art while serving as a seaman in the U.S. Navy during World War II. The Works Progress Administration assigned him to paint murals with patriotic subjects at the Great Lakes Naval Station in Illinois. "They were on the theme of the Negro in U.S. history [and] were intended to build morale with black recruits," he recalled in the *Chicago Free Weekly*. Having spent his time in the service stationed in the Chicago area, the city served as an inspiration for his early paintings. "I have always thought that this part of the Midwest affected the character of my palette," he said in the *Chicago Free Weekly*. "The climate, the weather—dark, dreary lugubrious days that darkened the colors. Those years in Chicago ... also affected the way I see things politically, socially, philosophically."

Style Evolved From Realism to Surrealism

For Lee-Smith, art reflected common daily life experiences. During the 1930s and 1940s he expressed himself through a kind of social realism, as illustrated by his dark, serious *Portrait of a Boy* (1938). From there his work became "primitivist," as reflected in his painting *Girl with Balloon* (1949-50), in which the elongated figure of a yearning girl stands in front of a simple shack. By the early 1950s, according to Sims, Lee-Smith's style reflected the use of surrealist devices similar to those used by Giorgio de Chirico. She observed that such paintings as *The Scientist* (1949), *Impedimenta* (1958), and *Woman in Green Sweater* (1950s) "evoke de Chirico's celebration of the enigma."

From the 1950s through the 1980s, Lee-Smith divided his time between the Midwest and Northeast, teaching art in Michigan, New Jersey, Washington, D.C., and New York City. His works were exhibited at various galleries, academic institutions, and museums, including the Museum of Modern Art and the Whitney Museum. Meanwhile, he steadily amassed awards, among them several from the National Academy of Design and Audubon Artists.

Captured Racial and Urban Isolation

Before and during the civil rights movement of the 1960s, Lee-Smith often painted African American figures set against the backdrop of inner cities. Such is the case in *Boy with a Tire* (1952), *The Walls* (1952), *Slum Song* (1962), and *Ballplayer* (1970). Aside from the more obvious symbols of racial separation in America, his paintings from this period portrayed subtle psychological tensions between blacks and whites.

Before 1970, Lee-Smith was known as an elder statesman of African American art. He told Douglas Davis of *Newsweek*, "We are concerned with communications, with glorifying our heroes, contributing to black pride. We look upon this as our historical mission." However, Lee-Smith had mixed feelings about art shows that contain only the works of African American artists. "There was a time during the 1960s when it was necessary to bring the reality of black artists into the consciousness of the mainstream. But there's a time limit on that sort of thing," he explained to Joy Hakanson Colby of the *Detroit News*. "If you're black, people can see that. But I guess that kind of label is part of the American racial fabric, and I just don't allow it to hinder me in any way."

Throughout the 1980s, Lee-Smith's works often focused on African Americans and whites attempting to relate to each other. In *Counterpoise II* (1989), a puzzled, angry young African American woman is left standing on a stage while a white woman walks away from her and blends in with the set in the background. In *End of Act One* (1987), a African American woman walks away from a white counterpart, leaving her with a headless mannequin. Other paintings from this phase in Lee-Smith's career highlighted the artist's ongoing use of solitary figures to depict loneliness and alienation in contemporary life.

While there had been no major changes in Lee-Smith's style after the 1950s, several art critics contended that subtle variations had emerged in his works from the late 1980s. Vivien Raynor wrote in *ARTNews*: "He seems to stand closer to his subjects, incorporating more foliage and architectural detail; and perhaps there is more menace in his mystery. The color may be colder and harsher, too. But the imagery continues to be beautiful and the mood fatalistic." In an interview with the *Detroit News*, Lee-Smith commented on his artistic style, "I've always felt a need to communicate on an emotional level with people. My paintings don't tell stories. they are about expressing emotion by means of form and color."

In 1994, the City of New York commissioned Lee-Smith to paint the official portrait of David Dinkins, the former mayor of New York City. The portrait was completed and hung in City Hall. In 1999, Lee-Smith died in Albuquerque, New Mexico after battling cancer.

Selected works

Paintings

Portrait of a Boy, 1938.
The Scientist, 1949.
Girl with Balloon, 1949-50.
Bouquet, 1949.
Boy with a Tire, 1952.
The Walls, 1952.
The Piper, 1953.

Landscape with Black Man, 1953.
Impedimenta, 1958.
Woman in Green Sweater, 1950s.
Interval, 1960.
Man with Balloons, c. 1960.
Slum Song, 1962.
The Juggler #1, c. 1964.
Man Running, 1965.
The Other Side, 1960s.
Man Standing on His Head, 1970.
Ballplayer, 1970.
Trio, 1973.
Hard Hat, 1980.
Industrial Landscape, c. 1980.
Acropolis II, 1984.
Merry Go Round I, 1984.
Desert Elegy, 1987.
End of Act One, 1987.
Waiting, 1987.
Silent Riddle, 1988.
Curtain Call, 1989.
Counterpoise II, 1989.
Crossroads, 1991.
Temptation, 1991.
A Summer Spell, 1992.

Commissioned works

Idyllic Landscape (mosaic tile mural), Prudential and Deansbank Investment Corporation, McPherson Building, Washington, DC; *Cityscape* (mural painting), New Jersey State Council on the Arts, New Jersey State Commerce Building, Trenton; and *Navy Black History* (oil painting), U.S. Navy, Washington, DC, 1974; Portrait of New York City Mayor David Dinkins, 1994.

Sources

Books

African-American Artists 1880-1987: Selections from the Evans-Tibbs Collection, Smithsonian Institution Traveling Service, in association with the University of Washington Press, 1989, pp. 78, 80, 120.

Cederholm, Theresa D., *Afro-American Artists: A Bio-Bibliographical Directory,* Boston Public Library, 1973, pp. 174-76.

Fine, Elsa Honig, *The Afro-American Artist: A Search for Identity,* Holt, Rinehart & Winston, 1973, pp. 97-98, 142-45, 280.

Hedgepeth, Chester M., Jr., *Twentieth-Century African American Writers and Artists,* American Library Association, 1991, pp. 193-95.

Locke, Alain, *The Negro in Art: A Pictorial Record of the Negro Artist and of the Negro Theme in Art,* Associates in Negro Folk Education, 1940, pp. 126, 135.

Porter, James A., *Modern Negro Art*, Dryden Press, 1943, pp. 160-64.

Sims, Lowery S., essay in *Hughie Lee-Smith Retrospective Exhibition* (catalogue), New Jersey State Museum, 1988, pp. 1-35.

Periodicals

American Artist, October 1978, pp. 48-53, 101.

Art in America, February 1990, p. 168.

ARTnews, December 1987, pp. 156, 158; March 1989, pp. 124-31; March 1990, p. 176.

Arts New Jersey, Summer 1987.

Black Enterprise, December 1986, pp. 86, 88, 92.

Chicago Free Weekly, February 24, 1989, sec. 1, p. 6.

Detroit News, October 15, 1989, 1M, 4M.

Ebony, May 1986, p. 50.

Emerge, May 1992.

Jet, March 22, 1999, p. 17.

Newsweek, June 22, 1970, pp. 89-90.

New York Times, October 17, 1987; December 4, 1988; March 12, 1989, p. 34; July 28, 1989.

Philadelphia Inquirer, December 19, 1988, pp. 1E, 4E.

Time Off, January 21, 1987, p. 21; October 3, 1990; October 24, 1990.

Village Voice, June 21, 1988.

—Alison Carb Sussman

Gerald Levert

1966—

Vocalist, songwriter, producer

The son of one of the classic soul era's best-loved group leaders, Gerald Levert demonstrated the staying power of R&B vocal styles in an era when technologically driven musical genres such as hip-hop gradually gained ascendancy. His father was Eddie Levert, lead vocalist and organizer of the O'Jays, themselves an R&B act of unusual staying power. Levert came onto the music scene in the middle 1980s as part of the trio LeVert, and embarked on a solo career in 1991. By the late 1990s he was still a leading album seller and concert headliner, and although he worked widely as a producer and was keenly aware of contemporary musical trends, in his own music he kept the focus where it had always been—on the vocals.

Levert was born on July 13, 1966. Although his father and the rest of the O'Jays worked primarily in Philadelphia, Gerald and his siblings spent their formative years in Cleveland, Ohio. He and his brother Sean hooked up with a school friend, Marc Gordon, who sang and played keyboards. Growing up in a musical environment had its advantages. In addition to enjoying their father's encouragement, the Leverts and Gordon could perfect their music skills in the fully equipped studio that was part of the Levert household. Toward the end of their high school years the group, performing under the name Le-Vert, made appearances at Ohio nightclubs.

Signed to Atlantic Label

In the mid-1980s, the group landed a contract with the independent label Tempre. Despite the waning influence of small independent labels in the 1980s, LeVert's album *I Get Hot* and its lead single "I'm Still" gained regional popularity in the influential R&B market of Baltimore and Washington, D.C. As a result, the group came to the attention of Atlantic Records and was signed to that label. LeVert became an overnight success, hitting Number One on the R&B charts with the single "(Pop, Pop, Pop, Pop) Goes My Mind," from their Atlantic debut album, *Bloodline*. Observers of the music scene noticed that Levert's voice closely resembled his father's. The group, moreover, was clearly steeped in the classic soul harmonies of the O'Jays. However, the sophisticated production work on the LeVert albums gave them a contemporary style.

LeVert's second album, *The Big Throwdown*, was released in 1987 and sold more copies than *Bloodline*. The debut solo album, *Private Line,* in 1991.

Private Line was a resounding commercial success, reaching Number Two on the R&B charts. Four of the album's singles: "School Me," "Can You Handle It," "Baby Hold On To Me," and the title track were widely played on R&B radio stations in 1992. Levert, in collaboration with Tony Nicholas, wrote most of the music on the album. "Baby Hold On To Me" reached Number One on the R&B charts and featured a duet with Levert and his father, Eddie. The two also recorded an album, *Father and Son,* for the East West label and jointly established a national scholarship fund under the administration of 100 Black Men, a public-service organization in which Eddie Levert was an active member.

Levert appeared in the 1991 film *New Jack City* and continued with his own production work. In 1994, he released his second solo album *Groove On.* This album attempted to recreate the atmosphere of 1960s soul and included a full horn section on many of the tracks. *Groove On* also featured several soulful romantic ballads. The album's lead single, "I'd Give Anything," had originally been recorded as "She'd Give Anything (To Fall in Love)" by the country group Boy Howdy. "When his peers were speaking of relationships as an unnecessary evil," wrote Sonia Murray of the *Atlanta Constitution,* "Levert, in his big, palpable baritone, proclaimed 'I'd give anything and everything to fall in love.'"

By the late 1990s, Levert seemed firmly enshrined in the pantheon of classic rhythm-and-blues and soul performers. He teamed with vocalists Keith Sweat and Johnny Gill in 1997 to produce the album *Levert Sweat Gill.* In 1998, he released the solo album *Love & Consequences.* Like its predecessors, *Love & Consequences* was a commercial success and sold more than one million copies. In 1999, Levert toured with classic soul diva Patti LaBelle.

Selected discography

(with group LeVert)

I Get Hot, Tempre, 1985.
Bloodline, Atlantic, 1986.
The Big Throwdown, Atlantic, 1987.
Just Coolin', Atlantic, 1988.
Rope-a-Dope, Atlantic, 1990.
For Real Tho', Atlantic, 1992.
The Whole Scenario, Atlantic, 1997.

(solo albums)

Private Line, Atlantic, 1991.
Groove On, Atlantic, 1994.

album's lead single, "Casanova," reached Number One on the R&B charts and crossed over to the pop charts. Several other singles from the album became hits, and LeVert earned even more mainstream exposure with the song "Addicted to You," from the soundtrack of the 1988 film *Coming to America.* "Addicted to You" also rose to Number One on the R&B charts. In 1988 LeVert released *Just Coolin',* which featured rapper Heavy D and included a groundbreaking R&B/hip-hop combination on its title track. They also released *Rope-a-Dope Style* in 1990 and *For Real Tho'* in 1992. In 1997, the group released *The Whole Scenario,* an innovative work that included both rapping and classical orchestral instruments. Several of the LeVert albums sold 500,000 copies or more.

Launched Solo Career

By the late 1980s, Levert began taking steps toward developing a solo career. Also, realizing that producers and writers were controlling the musical direction of R&B, he and Marc Gordon formed their own production company. This company, Trevel Productions, worked with such acts as Anita Baker, Men at Large, the O'Jays, and Miki Howard. The success of Trevel Productions solidified Levert's position at Atlantic and paved the way for his

Love & Consequences, East West, 1998.

(with Keith Sweat and Johnny Gill)

Levert Sweat Gill, East West, 1997.

(with Eddie Levert)

Father and Son, East West, 1995

Sources

Books

Graff, Gary, Josh Freedom du Lac, and Jim McFarlin, *MusicHound R&B: The Essential Album Guide,* Visible Ink, 1998.

Larkin, Colin, ed., *The Guinness Encyclopedia of Popular Music,* Muze U.K., 1998.

Romanowski, Patricia, and Holly George-Warren, *The New Rolling Stone Encyclopedia of Rock & Roll,* Fireside, 1995.

Periodicals

Billboard, August 6, 1994; p. 18; September 16, 1995, p. 11.

Scripps Howard News Service (in Bergen County [N.J.] Record), April 2, 1999, p. 5.

—James M. Manheim

Frankie Lymon

1942–1968

Vocalist

Frankie Lymon's short and tragic life took him from modest beginnings, to international stardom at the age of thirteen, to a long descent into the nightmare of drug addiction and an early death. He was the first African American teen heartthrob and inspired a host of other young musicians, such as Michael Jackson. Lymon's career was born at the very beginning of the rock and roll era and the song with which he remains identified, "Why Do Fools Fall in Love?, is considered a classic. However, Lymon was an ill-fated pioneer who could not cope with his sudden fame and who spent the final years of his life battling drug addiction.

Lymon was born in Harlem on September 30, 1942. His father sang gospel music in a group called the Harlemaires, and Lymon became a talented singer of the street-corner harmony known as doo-wop. During the early 1950s, Lymon and his friends sang for donations on New York's streets and Lymon's distinctive, high-pitched voice led to the creation of a quartet known at various times as the Ermines, the Coupe de Villes, and the Premiers. The group was eventually dubbed the Teenagers and its other members, Sherman Garnes, Joe Negroni, Herman Santiago, and Jimmy Merchant, were all about a year or two older than Lymon.

In 1955, a chance encounter propelled Frankie Lymon and the Teenagers to a higher level. Richard Barrett, a member of the successful vocal group, the Valentines, heard Lymon's group performing on the street. The Valentines had recorded for Gee Records, a small independent label that had cashed in on the rapidly growing popularity of doo-wop music. Barrett brought Lymon and his group to the attention of the label's executives. Upon hearing Lymon and the Teenagers perform, they rushed the group into the recording studio. The executives were particularly impressed with a song entitled "Why Do Fools Fall in Love?" and asked Lymon for the sheet music to the song. According to an account in Irwin Stambler's *Encyclopedia of Pop, Rock & Soul,* Lymon replied, "Nope, we don't know anything about written-down music."

Substituted in Lead Vocal Slot

"Why Do Fools Fall in Love?" was released in January of 1956 and shared the upper levels of the charts with such luminaries as Elvis Presley and Carl Perkins. The song reached Number One on the R&B charts and Number Six on the pop charts. It became a hit in England as well, reaching Number One there. "Why Do Fools Fall in Love?" exemplified the best in doo-wop music, with its graceful vocal line from Lymon and its rhythmic and precise harmonies. Although the group is said to have worked to perfect some of their songs in rehearsals, "Why Do Fools Fall in Love?" coalesced spontaneously—Lymon filled in on lead vocals for the ailing Santiago, who had been scheduled to perform.

Despite competition from cover versions by white singers, "Why Do Fools Fall in Love?" topped the charts for several weeks. Gee Records crafted an innocent, old-fashioned image for Lymon and the Teenagers—they were often seen wearing collegiate-style school letter sweaters—and the song's durability worked to prolong the group's moment in the spotlight. They appeared in two movies, *Rock Rock Rock* (which included a song called "I'm Not a Juvenile Delinquent" that hit both American and British charts) in 1956 and *Mr. Rock and Roll* in 1957. Their debut album, *The Teenagers Featuring Frankie Lymon*, included several other hit singles, such as "I Want You To Be My Girl," "I Promise to Remember," and "The ABCs of Love."

Split from the Teenagers

Due to the success of their recordings in England, Lymon and the Teenagers were invited to tour the country and appeared at London's famed Palladium. During this time, Lymon began to distance himself from the Teenagers. He recorded a solo single while in England, "Goody Goody," which enjoyed moderate success. Lymon split from the group when they returned to the United States and attempted to launch a solo career. However, his distinctively youthful voice was changing and his popularity soon vanished. While the Teenagers struggled to survive with a succession of new lead vocalists, Lymon began experimenting with drugs and eventually entered a drug rehabilitation program at Manhattan's General Hospital in 1961.

Lymon worked hard to resurrect his career. He took drumming lessons, and reunited briefly with the Teenagers in 1965. However, his attempts at a musical comeback continued to be overshadowed by his abuse of drugs. In 1964, he was arrested on drug charges. Lymon married Emira Eagle, a Georgia schoolteacher, in 1967 and it appeared that the marriage had offered Lymon another opportunity to get his life back on track. He began playing in small Southern clubs, and planned to embark on a European tour with other 1950s music stars. In February of 1968, Lymon departed for New York to make a quick publicity appearance. When his wife tried to contact him in New York, she was unsuccessful. On February 28th, Lymon was found dead of a heroin overdose in his grandmother's Harlem apartment.

Song Ownership Contested in Court

Following Lymon's death, a bitter court battle ensued to determine ownership rights to "Why Do Fools Fall in Love?" All of the Teenagers filed suit and two of the members, Herman Santiago and Jimmy Merchant, eventually won the case. At the same time, two women who claimed to have been married to Lymon battled his widow, Emira, for rights to his estate. The court determined that Emira was the sole heir to Lymon's fortune. Following resolution of the case, Emira Lymon's attorney William McCracken told *Ebony*, "You could teach a class in domestic law on nothing but this case. It's just been a battle royale all the way."

Despite Lymon's troubled life and tragic death, the popularity of "Why Do Fools Fall in Love?" has not diminished. It is considered a rock and roll standard and many artists, including Diana Ross, have recorded versions of the song. The song also appeared on the soundtrack of George Lucas's 1973 hit film *American Graffiti*. A host of doo-wop high tenors emulated Lymon throughout the 1950s, and the sweet-voiced male vocalists who recorded for Berry Gordy's Motown label owed much to Lymon's style. In 1993, the Teenagers were inducted into the Rock and Roll Hall of Fame. In 1998, Lymon's life became the subject of a movie, "Why Do Fools Fall in Love?," which showcased both his years of stardom and the mysteries of his later life.

Selected discography

The Teenagers Featuring Frankie Lymon, Gee, 1957.
The Teenagers at the London Palladium, Gee, 1958.
Rock 'n' Roll Party with Frankie Lymon, Guest, 1959.
Frankie Lymon and the Teenagers: For Collectors Only,
    Murray Hill, 1987.
Why Do Fools Fall in Love and Other Hits, Rhino, 1989.
The Best of Frankie Lymon and the Teenagers, Roulette,
    1990.
Frankie Lymon and the Teenagers: Complete Recordings,
    Bear Family, 1994.

Sources

Books

Erlewine, Michael, et al, eds., *The All-Music Guide to Rock,* Miller/Freeman, 1998.
Larkin, Colin, ed., *The Guinness Encyclopedia of Popular Music,* Muze U.K., 1998.
Romanowski, Patricia, and Holly George-Warren, eds., *The New Rolling Stone Encyclopedia of Rock & Roll,* Fireside, 1995.
Stambler, Irwin, *The Encyclopedia of Pop, Rock & Soul,* St. Martin's, 1989.

Periodicals

Ebony, December 1998, p. 68.

—James M. Manheim

Bella Marshall

1950—

Real estate executive

At the age of just 32, Detroiter Bella Marshall became one of the youngest women—and one of a handful of African Americans—to head the finance department of a major American city. Marshall spent over a decade as director of Detroit's fiscal activities, responsible for the financial health of a city that seemed at first to be tottering on the brink of budgetary collapse. By the time she left the post in the early 1990s, Detroit was well on its way to a spectacular rebound, and Marshall and her husband, Don Barden, had become one of the city's most well-connected and socially-active partnerships, involved in both luxury home development projects and the casino industry. Marshall is one of the richest African American women in the country, according to *Essence* magazine, who estimated her net worth at about $25 million.

Marshall was born across the border in Windsor, Canada, but grew up on the east side of Detroit. When she was eight, her father suffered a series of strokes that left him disabled, and he died when she was 19. Marshall's mother, Lillian, was an energetic woman, a clerical worker who strove to keep Marshall and her two siblings challenged intellectually. As a youth Marshall was enrolled in numerous youth organizations and activities, including the Girl Scouts, cheerleading, church athletics, basketball, and baseball. "My mother kept me in every organization known to modern man," Marshall told *Detroit Free Press* reporter Patricia Edmonds. "I didn't have time to go out and get pregnant."

Inspired by a novel about a female attorney, Marshall decided on a career in law at a young age. She won two scholarships to Wayne State University in Detroit, and then earned her law degree from the University of Michigan. Hired by the Detroit office of the Michigan State Housing Development Authority in 1975 as staff counsel, she became its first female director as well as the youngest in the agency's history just three years later.

Marshall's rising star attracted the attention of Detroit Mayor Coleman A. Young, who was searching for someone to fill the post of city finance director that had been vacant for several months. The colorful mayor took Marshall out to dinner at an Italian restaurant, and as she later recalled in the interview with Edmonds, "I don't know whether I talked him to death, or he was dieting, but he did not finish his food. So he offered me his leftovers, and I took them home."

Young also offered Marshall the job, and at the age of just 32 she became the first woman to hold the post in Detroit history. As finance director, she was given an enormous amount of responsibility: Marshall headed a staff of 500, was responsible for all of the city's banking and investments, and also was charged with reforming its beleaguered property-tax department. Furthermore, she battled tenaciously to upgrade the rating that Wall Street gave Detroit's municipal bonds, considered a reliable sign of a city's financial health.

At a Glance . . .

Born c. 1950 in Windsor, Ontario, Canada; daughter of Lillian (Simpson) Marshall; married Don Barden (a media and gaming-industry entrepreneur), 1988. *Education:* Earned undergraduate degree from Wayne State University; graduated from the University of Michigan Law School, c. 1975.

Career: Michigan State Housing Development Authority, Detroit, MI, staff attorney, 1975-78, director, 1978-82; City of Detroit, finance director, 1982-93; Waycor Development Co., president and chief executive officer, 1994-, and chief operating officer of Barden International, Inc.

Addresses: *Home*—Detroit, MI.

During the 1980s, Marshall became involved in a bitter fight, along with the Young Administration, to raise funds for, build, and operate a greatly contested trash-burning plant. Marshall also worked to arrange financing for a massive new Chrysler automotive plant on Detroit's east side, where North America's Jeep Cherokees are built. It was an $82,000 a year job, but as Marshall told Edmonds at the time, "I work hard for my money." She regularly put in 14-hour days.

But Marshall's job also had its perks, and she moved inside Detroit's circle of accomplished African American young professionals. In the mid-1980s she began dating Don Barden, at the time a cable-television system owner campaigning to win the lucrative contract for Detroit's cable franchise. Both kept running into one another at the same civic and social functions, and they married in 1988. Barden later sold his Barden Cablevision and delved further into the real-estate and casino industries.

Marshall lost her job with the election of a new mayor, Dennis Archer, in 1993. The following year her husband appointed her president and chief executive officer of Waycor Development Company, a real-estate developer building new luxury homes in Detroit—ironically, a terrific sign of Detroit's overall financial prosperity and symbolic of just how far it had come since 1982. Marshall's executive duties are not limited to the Detroit area, however: Waycor builds in St. Louis and other cities, and she is also chief operating officer of one of her husband's other business interests, an automobile manufacturing plant in Namibia.

While her husband is a generous contributor to the Democratic Party coffers, the couple are renowned local philanthropists as well, giving back to the community in which both were raised. TheDetroit Symphony Orchestra and the city's acclaimed Museum of African-American History have been beneficiaries of their largesse, and Marshall is active in numerous area institutions. In 1997 she was tapped to serve on team of community leaders given the task of reviewing the Detroit Public School system's troubled finances.

In 1998 Don Barden entered into a media and political battle with the Archer administration over casino ownership; Barden was unhappy with the mayor's picks by which several other entrepreneurs received three lucrative licenses. As a result of Barden's efforts, a referendum was held that allowed county residents to vote for what became known as the "Barden Proposal," that would have allowed one black-owned casino enterprise. Voters chose the mayor's plan, however, though Barden had enlisted the help of pop singer Michael Jackson.

Marshall, who had her first child at the age of 41, lives in a palatial stone home in a mansion-lined street in northwest Detroit. The area is now home to many of the city's most prominent names in politics, business, and sports. Marshall is described as warm, energetic, a stylish dresser with a penchant for the highest heels, and a rapid-fire talker. Despite her list of achievements, Marshall always planned to stay in Detroit: "I would like for my children to look at Cobo Hall or the Chrysler Jefferson Avenue plant, which I had a part in, and say, `Isn't this a neat thing.' It would be like my children touching the tips of their noses and saying, `Gee I've got a great nose—it's like my mother's nose.'"

Sources

Detroit Free Press, October 2, 1982, p. 1C; November 9, 1983; November 23, 1986; November 18, 1990, p. 3J; June 30, 1993, p. 1A; April 16, 1997.
Detroit News, January 5, 1997; February 20, 1997; October 10, 1997; June 24, 1998; October 9, 1998.
Essence, October, 1998.

—Carol Brennan

Robert McGruder

1942—

Journalist

Detroit Free Press executive editor Robert McGruder is one of the top African American editorial executives in the American newspaper industry. He oversees a paper with a daily circulation of 400,000 readers spread across a diverse metropolitan area. Professionalism and a marked calmness under fire have helped fuel McGruder's rise at the *Free Press*. "He is known as principled, resolute and—unusual in his profession—soft-spoken," reported Jim Naughton after interviewing several of McGruder's colleagues, past and present, for a profile on him in the *Detroit Free Press*.

McGruder was born in 1942 in Louisville, Kentucky, and had an unusually trying childhood. His parents divorced when he was five years-old and, one year later, he was stricken with polio. McGruder was hospitalized and also spent time in a rehabilitation facility. He attended a school for disabled children and later moved with his mother and younger brother to Campbellsburg, Kentucky. His mother, who was a school teacher, took a teaching job at Campbellsburg's school for African American children and enrolled McGruder in the fourth grade.

Eventually, the McGruder family moved to Dayton, Ohio. In addition to working on a library science degree, McGrud-er's mother took a second job so that her two sons could attend private schools. In 1959, McGruder graduated as salutatorian from Chaminade Catholic High School and enrolled at Kent State University. His career in journalism began when he started working at Kent State's student newspaper. "There were all of these smart, fun people, who welcomed me in and showed me how to write stories, take pictures, lay out pages" McGruder recalled in an interview with John Carroll of *American Editor*. "Then I became the editor and they actually paid me to do it."

Two days after his graduation from Kent State in 1963, McGruder landed a job as a cub reporter at the *Dayton Journal-Herald*. Three months later, he was hired by the *Cleveland Plain Dealer* as its first African American reporter. In 1964, McGruder was drafted into the U.S. Army and served for two years as a public information specialist in Washington, D.C.

Vietnam and Race Riots

McGruder returned to the *Plain Dealer* in 1966 and,

At a Glance . . .

Born Robert Grandison McGruder Jr., March 31, 1942, in Louisville, KY; son of Robert Sr. and Nancy (a teacher) McGruder; married Annette Cottingham, December 7, 1968. *Education:* Kent State University, B.A., 1963.

Career: *Dayton Journal-Herald,* Dayton, OH, reporter, 1963; *Cleveland Plain Dealer,* Cleveland, OH, reporter, 1963-66, and 1966-71, assistant city editor, 1971-73, reporter and editor, 1973-78, city editor, 1978-81, managing editor, 1981-86; *Detroit Free Press,* Detroit, MI, deputy managing editor, 1986-87, managing editor for news, 1987-92, managing editor, 1993-96, executive editor, 1996—. *Military service:* U.S. Army, 1964-66;

Awards: William Taylor Distinguished Alumni Award, Kent State University School of Journalism, 1984; member of nominating juries for the Pulitzer Prize in Journalism, 1986, 1987, 1990, 1991, and 1998; Knight-Ridder Duke University fellow, 1991-92.

Member: American Society of Newspaper Editors; Associated Press Managing Editors; American Press Institute; National Association of Black Journalists; National Association of Minority Media Executives; Michigan Press Association; Knight Foundation; Foundation for American Communication; Institute for Minority Journalism at Wayne State University.

Addresses: *Home*—Detroit, MI. *Office*—Detroit Free Press, 600 W. Lafayette, Detroit, MI 48226.

because of his years of military service at the Pentagon, became the paper's military reporter. During the Vietnam War, this assignment was particularly difficult for McGruder because he had to interview people throughout the Cleveland area who had lost loved ones in the war. He also reported on the violent anti-busing battles and urban riots that plagued many American cities during the 1960s. Eventually promoted to the city hall beat, McGruder made a name for himself during a fiery, scandal-ridden era in Cleveland city politics. Along with a colleague at the *Plain Dealer,* McGruder investigated the city's financial records and wrote a series of articles that exposed Cleveland's dire financial circumstances. Eventually, Cleveland became the first major American city to declare bankruptcy.

Despite his successful career at the *Plain Dealer,* McGruder encountered many difficulties as one of the nation's few African American journalists. "There were no senior black editors to go to," McGruder recalled in an interview with *American Editor.* "There was no [National Association of Black Journalists]. I was on my own." Nevertheless, he was named the assistant city editor of the *Plain Dealer* in 1971. McGruder also co-authored a political biography of Cleveland's Carl B. Stokes, the first African American mayor of a major city. The book, *Promises of Power,* was published in 1973.

Moved to Detroit

Between the years 1973 and 1978, McGruder served as both reporter and editor at the *Plain Dealer* and was promoted to city editor in 1978. In 1981, he became the *Plain Dealer's* managing editor. McGruder left the *Plain Dealer* in 1986 to become the deputy managing editor of the *Detroit Free Press.* One year later, he was named managing editor.

During the next several years at the *Free Press,* McGruder would face adversities that were greater than any he had faced in Cleveland. In the late 1980s, the *Free Press* was attempting to implement a controversial Joint Operating Agreement with the other Detroit daily, the *Detroit News.* The agreement, which went into effect in late 1989, merged the business, advertising, production and delivery sides of the two papers; the news and editorial areas remained independent.

An Embattled Executive

In 1993, McGruder was named managing editor of all *Free Press* operations. During this time, tensions between management and staff at both newspapers had increased dramatically. In the summer of 1995, a bitter labor dispute evolved between the management of the *Detroit Free Press* and the *Detroit News* and several labor unions. McGruder served on the negotiating committee that worked with the unions in an attempt to avoid a newspaper strike. However, the talks were unsuccessful and thousands of employees at both newspapers, including typesetters, delivery drivers, and columnists, walked off the job at midnight on July 13, 1995.

McGruder and other members of the management teams at the *Detroit Free Press* and the *Detroit News* worked with an extremely limited staff to produce a newspaper each day of the strike. During the early days of the strike, the two papers published a joint edition newspaper. However, as large numbers of replacement workers were brought in from around the country, the *Detroit Free Press* and the *Detroit News* resumed publishing separate editions.

The strike, which became Detroit's most contentious labor dispute in decades, was resolved over a period of several months. During the strike, McGruder was named executive editor of the *Free Press*. Reflecting on the devastating effects of the newspaper strike, McGruder told Carroll in an interview in *American Editor,* "Many of us could not understand the forces that got us into such a horrible situation. We lost some of our best people; many of our best have returned. We have tried to keep people focused on journalism."

Crusader for Increased Diversity

McGruder is involved in numerous professional activities. In 1995, he became the first African American president of the Associated Press Managing Editors group. He is an active member of the American Society of Newspaper Editors, the National Association of Black Journalists, and several other organizations. McGruder has also served on the nominating juries for the Pulitzer Prize in Journalism on several occasions.

As a highly respected journalist, McGruder has used his position to speak frankly about the need for increased minority representation in the newsroom. Although America's urban centers have become more racially diverse, the staffing of most newspapers does not reflect this trend. McGruder and other executives in the industry are attempting to correct this shortcoming. In *American Editor,* McGruder remarked that "editors need to work harder at developing minority journalists....Hiring is not enough. Training, retention and listening are vital." The *Free Press* features a mentoring program, and McGruder sits on the advisory board of Institute for Minority Journalism at Wayne State University. "I've been at the *Free Press* long

enough now to see kids who used to come around my office when they were in high school, talked to when they were in college, and now are working here and elsewhere as professional journalists," McGruder told *American Editor.* One former protege, Jim Crutchfield, later became the executive editor of the Long Beach (Calif.) *Press-Telegram.* "I flourished under him," Crutchfield said of McGruder in an interview in the *Detroit Free Press.* "He gave me the chance to just expand as I could."

McGruder, who lives with his wife in a high-rise waterfront complex within walking distance of his *Free Press* office, has been nicknamed "Darth Vader" for his quiet intensity. However, he is widely admired and respected by his colleagues and subordinates. For relaxation, he enjoys old Western films on television, Cohiba cigars and Jamaican holidays.

Selected writings

(With Allen Wiggins)

Promises of Power, 1973.

Sources

Periodicals

American Editor, June 1998, pp. 22-24.
Detroit Free Press, October 23, 1995, p. 1A; August 18, 1996, p. 3E; September 22, 1996, p. 3F.

Other

Additional information for this profile was provided by the *Detroit Free Press.*

—Carol Brennan

Steve McNair

1973—

Professional football player

The starting quarterback for the National Football League's (NFL's) Tennessee Titans (formerly the Houston, and then Tennessee, Oilers), Steve McNair continues to develop into a major force in the sport. Following a spectacular college career, McNair has progressed smoothly as a pro player. He adopted a dependable and workmanlike approach rather than go for the high-risk "big plays." McNair has the power to rocket the ball 75 yards downfield with pinpoint accuracy and is also one of the league's best scramblers, both inside and outside of the pocket. Given the right receivers, McNair's prowess, intelligence, leadership, and guts could propel his team to glory.

McNair's life is a classic American success story. His inspiration and support in his early years came from his tight-knit family and community. Selma McNair left the family when Steve was young, leaving the five brothers to be raised by their single mother, Lucille, in a ramshackle house in rural Mount Olive, MS. She toiled as a factory worker, and money was scarce. But despite material hardships she instilled an unshakable set of values in her sons—including loyalty, fairness, an appreciation for education, and a strong work ethic. Fred, the oldest brother

and star athlete, served as the family's father figure, and carefully instructed Steve in every aspect of sports. Quoted in *Sports Illustrated*, McNair said, "Fred has taught me absolutely everything I know. I can't thank him enough for giving me a map and then showing me how to take the short road when he's taken the longer one." Steve's nickname, "Air McNair," is another version of Air II; Fred was the original Air.

Showed Early Signs of Greatness

In a family with deep athletic gifts, Steve McNair was especially blessed—and not only with extraordinary talent (as well as huge hands), but also the determination and discipline to cultivate it. He had multiple options for pursuing a professional sports career. He starred in three sports at Mount Olive High: baseball, as a shortstop and outfielder, all-state four years running; basketball, at point guard; and football, in which he played both offense and defense. As cornerback, McNair set a state record for single-season pass interceptions (15) and tied the career mark (30). In 1989, he quarterbacked Mount Olive to a small-school state title when he was a junior. A strapping 6'2, 220-pounder who could run 40 yards in 4.6 seconds

At a Glance . . .

B orn Steve McNair, February 14, 1973, in Mount Olive, MS; son of Selma McNair (an off-shore oil rig worker) and Lucille McNair (a factory worker); raised with four brothers including Fred McNair, quarterback with CFL's Toronto Argonauts (1991) and London Monarchs of the World League (1992); married Mechelle Cartwright, June 21, 1997. *Education:* Attended Alcorn State University, Lorman, MS.

Career: Football player. Starred in three sports in high school, playing two separate positions in both baseball and football; as quarterback, led Mount Olive High Pirates to Class A state title in 1989; set NCAA's all-time record for total offense (16,823 yards); set record for average yards total offense (400.6); chosen by Houston Oilers in first round (third pick overall) of 1995 NFL draft, and signed by the team July 25, 1995; became starting quarterback for Oilers for 1997 season, when the team moved to Tennessee, team name changed to Tiatan at end of 1998.

Awards: Named SWAC Offensive Player of the Year four straight years at Alcorn; unanimous All-America choice.

Addresses: Tennessee Titans, Baptist Sports Park, 7640 Hwy. 70 South, Nashville, TN 37221.

and hurl a baseball 90 mph, McNair had both the strength and speed to play a multitude of positions.

McNair was strongly tempted when the Seattle Mariners baseball team picked him in the 14th round of the amateur draft, but with some guidance from Fred and Lucille he opted to pass it by, as well as several college basketball offers.

The next pivotal decision concerned his choice of college. Many of the powerhouse schools courted McNair, including Louisiana State, Miami, Ohio State, Nebraska, and Mississippi State. But they all wanted him as a defensive back, whereas he was determined to be a quarterback. Again, Fred's counsel helped him set a course, this time to Alcorn State, in Lorman, MS, where Fred had starred as a quarterback and where Steve was guaranteed a shot at the position.

Alcorn, a predominantly black school, was the country's

first black land-grant institution, the first black state-supported school, and the first to provide the NFL with a black player—Jack Spinks, drafted in 1952 as a fullback by the Pittsburgh Steelers. It is a member of the Division I-AA Southwestern Athletic Conference (SWAC), which comprises other mostly black schools and has produced several football immortals, including all-time touchdown leader Jerry Rice (Mississippi Valley) and all-time rushing leader Walter Payton (Jackson State). It was virtually a foregone conclusion that attending a Division I-AA school, rather than an I-A, would seriously impair or even scuttle McNair's shot at a Heisman Trophy and potentially hurt his chances for the NFL. But the assurance of a quarterback role and the proximity to home were major pulls for him, and he decided to take the chance.

Attained College Glory

McNair's college career became the stuff of legend, a true story of the all-conquering hero. As a mere freshman, McNair set nine records and was named Southwestern Athletic Conference player of the year. In his sophomore year, he led the nation in total offense, with an average of 405.7 yards. McNair racked up numerous 500-plus-passing-yard games, and many times he added another 100 or so rushing.

After his junior year, McNair again faced a choice—shoot for an NFL contract or stay for his senior year of college. Once he found out his draft status was first- or second-round, the enticement was especially strong to try for the kind of deal that Tennessee quarterback Heath Shuler got when he left school early to sign with the Washington Redskins—$19.25 million over eight years. Steve wanted to take care of his mother and family financially and to get on with his professional career. But both Lucille and Fred urged him to finish his education—as well as strengthen his hand even further with one more outstanding college season.

McNair opted to remain in school, as he was quoted in *Jet:* "I am an Alcornite and will continue to be an Alcornite. I want my degree.'' During his senior year his game improved in several capacities. He learned how to hang in the pocket longer and find his receiver, while his rushing grew even more devastating. Among his other accomplishments that season, he finished with a phenomenal 44/17 touchdown/interception pass differential.

Though McNair had a great year, his team fared poorly in post-season play. (Historically the SWAC champs had racked up an appalling 0-15 record in the I-AA playoffs.) In the first round of the playoffs, defending champion Youngstown (Ohio) State College destroyed Alcorn, 63-

20. McNair showed great heart in playing with a badly-pulled hamstring. His rushing ability crippled, he still nailed 514 passing yards and three touchdowns. The game did not hurt his stature as a potential NFL draft pick, but it did not enhance his shot at clinching the coveted Heisman Trophy either.

Steve's brother Tim, an Alcorn wide receiver, told *Sports Illustrated*, "That was not Steve McNair out there. He was maybe 60 percent." In the same article, Steve said, "I hope I'm still in the hunt and I'm at least one of the candidates for the Heisman."

Faced The Heisman Question

In pursuit of the Hiesman Trophy, McNair faced many obstacles, including poor visibility as an athlete at a small college, and rumors of an NFL prejudice against black quarterbacks. However, he had the backing of numerous coaches who recognized his extraordinary talent. Team offensive coordinator Rickey Taylor said in *Sports Illustrated*, "Steve has the intelligence of a Montana, the release of a Marino, the scrambling ability of an Elway. … I haven't seen anybody yet I can compare this kid with." Ultimately, McNair came in a strong third, matching the highest-ever finish for a small-school player.

Signed with Oilers

The next step was the Senior Bowl, which is considered essentially an exhibition game for pro scouts. Players are given a mere week to train with a whole new team of all-star college players, and both North and South teams showcase two quarterbacks. McNair completed 8 of 19 passes for 88 yards, a reasonable showing for this type of game, but far below his average numbers. Most important, though, he carried himself like a born quarterback. As Washington running back Napolean Kauffman said in the *New York Times*, "He handled everything well. He showed today how good he's going to be in the pros."

All that remained before the draft itself was the mid-February NFL scouting combine in Indianapolis—private workouts where prospects are drilled and grilled for the benefit of the scouts and coaches. McNair was tested on every conceivable type of pass, and some scouts grilled him on his defense-reading ability. He impressed the recruiters mightily with his super-accurate cannon arm and intelligence.

On April 22, 1995, the Houston Oilers drafted McNair as the third pick of the first round. Clearly, playing I-AA ball had not impeded McNair's standing. He became the highest-drafted black quarterback ever—a berth previously occupied by Andre Ware, who was chosen seventh in 1990 by the Detroit Lions. When the negotiations were finalized in August of 1995, McNair signed a contract for $28.4 million over seven years. At 22, he had become the Oilers' highest-paid player–not bad for the guy who had told *Jet*, "No matter what happens, I'm just Steve, the country boy from Mount Olive."

Progressed Steadily as a Pro

Quarterbacks usually develop more gradually than other players. Not only is it the highest-profile position, with the most pressure, but it is also the most mentally challenging. NFL playbooks are vast, and reading the opposition's defense to make split-second play changes is incredibly complex. Plus, the pace of NFL play is far faster than in college ball and even the finest quarterback athletes can be intimidated by the speed of the action surrounding the pocket. As ESPN draft analyst Mel Kiper, discussing the development curve, said in *USA Today*, "With any quarterback, you really need to figure three years."

Oiler management made sure to cultivate McNair carefully; they did not want to rush him into play abruptly and expose him to damaging and unnecessary pressure. He was tutored intensively throughout the off-season by offensive coordinator Jerry Rhome, a premier quarterback teacher. Later, Les Steckel took on this role. During the 1995 and 1996 seasons, McNair's primary mission was to absorb knowledge and make the leap from the shotgun offense at Alcorn to the far more elaborate and turbo-charged conditions in the NFL.

Some of McNair's first games were rough initiations indeed, with the Arizona Cardinals blitzing him mercilessly in an exhibition game with as many as five pass rushers. But this merely fortified McNair's will; he knew this was part of his initiation. When starting quarterback Chris Chandler was injured late in McNair's first season, the rookie went into action. The results were impressive: in the December 11, 1995, game against the Detroit Lions, McNair entered after halftime with the Oilers down 17-7 and played out the game. He completed 16 of 27 passes for 203 yards, including a touchdown. In fact, McNair nearly pulled off a come-from-behind upset. There was little question in anyone's mind as to whether he could hack it as a pro. He started the next two games, helping the Oilers end the season with back-to-back victories over the New York Jets and the Buffalo Bills.

In the 1996 season McNair played in ten games (as the starter in four), and completed an impressive 88 of 103 pass attempts for 1197 yards and six touchdowns. The team went 8-8, missing the playoffs by one game.

In his first six starts, McNair threw seven touchdown passes with only two interceptions. However, his leadership most impressed the coaches. In a *Sports Illustrated* piece Steckel said, "Even though he's the most humble athlete I've encountered in pro sports, he's also a leader who exudes extreme confidence." Head coach Jeff Fisher said in the same article, "If you were going to put together a list of all the things you can't coach—poise, ability to lead, competitiveness, responsibility—he has them all."

In February of 1997, the Oilers traded Chandler to the Atlanta Falcons, and McNair's career as a starter began in earnest. Meanwhile, the franchise relocated to Tennessee that same year. With big changes afoot, there was a lot more pressure on McNair, including constant demands for interviews.

McNair steadily accrued impressive stats on third-down conversions and pass completions, touchdowns per starts, and rushing, among others. In the 1997 season, for example, his 674 yards rushing was the third-highest in NFL history. By the end of that season, McNair had garnered the second-best overall rating of any quarterback drafted in the previous six years (trailing only the Jacksonville Jaguars' Mark Brunell).

According to Bob Sherwin of the *Knight-Ridder/Tribune News Service*, McNair is "a quarterback on the cusp of greatness"—one who "is beginning to make his impact on the NFL." In the article, McNair said: "The last part of the [1997] season it finally clicked for me."

At the end of the 1998 season, the Titans—the Oilers' new name—had placed second in the AFC Central. McNair continued to show toughness—playing in pain through a series of injuries—as well as power, maturing judgment, and calm leadership. Few football analysts and fans would be surprised to see 'Air McNair' take flight and guide his team to victory.

Sources

Periodicals

Jet, January 31, 1994, p. 50; September 26, 1994, p. 49.

Knight-Ridder/Tribune News Service, November 27, 1998.

New York Times, September 28, 1994, p. B11; January 22, 1995, p. 2.

Sports Illustrated, August 30, 1993, p. 76; September 26, 1994, p. 40; December 5, 1994, p. 85; September 1, 1997, p. 188.

The Sporting News, August 22, 1994, p. S8; November 28, 1994, p. 6.

USA Today, April 12, 1995.

—Mark Baven

Florence Mills

1896–1927

Entertainer

Before her untimely death in 1927, Florence Mills was considered the preeminent female jazz dancer of the Harlem Renaissance. With top billing in musical reviews such as *Shuffle Along* and *Blackbirds of 1926*, she earned critical praise as a graceful dancer and confident comedienne with a delightful voice. A favorite with African American audiences, Mills also possessed a popularity that crossed over to mainstream Broadway theatergoers as well at a time when color lines were only beginning to vanish. She was nicknamed "Blackbird" herself from her signature song, "I'm a Little Blackbird Looking for a Bluebird," and enjoyed considerable success in Europe as well.

Mills was born on January 25, 1896, in Washington, D.C. at her family home on K Street. Her parents, John and Nellie Winfree, were originally from Lynchburg, Virginia. When Virginia's tobacco economy worsened, the family relocated to Washington, D.C. and Mills's father found work as a carpenter and day laborer. The neighborhood surrounding K Street was pleasant and stable, but the Winfrees fell upon hard times and were forced to move to a far more dangerous area of Washington called Goat Alley. Despite the family's hardships, Mills showed excep-

tional talents as a singer and dancer from a very young age.

A Child Prodigy

Mills began entering dance contests at local theaters and won several medals and other prizes. At the age of four, she performed for the first time at Washington's Bijou Theater. In 1903, she sang "Miss Hannah from Savannah" in the touring production of an African American musical comedy entitled *Sons of Ham*. The star of the show, an accomplished performer named Aida Overton Walker, taught Mills the song, and soon took her under her wing. Walker's guidance helped make Mills a stage phenomenon by the age of eight. In 1905 she was hired by a vaudeville company, Bonita and Hearn, and made her professional debut. Because the vaudeville company was operated by whites and played to segregated audiences, Mills, like other black vaudeville performers of the day, often performed in degrading "pickaninny" numbers that fostered racist stereotypes of African American culture.

As a teenager Mills joined with her sisters, Maude and Olivia, to form a touring vaudeville troupe known as "The Mills Sisters." However, the group enjoyed only minor

At a Glance . . .

Born January 25, 1896, in Washington, D.C.; died in New York City of paralytic ileus and general peritonitis, November 1, 1927; daughter of John (a carpenter) and Nellie (Simon) Winfree; married James Randolph, c. 1912 (divorced); married Ulysses S. Thompson (a dancer), 1923.

Career: First public performance at Washington's Bijou Theater, c. 1900; appeared in *Sons of Ham*, 1903; made vaudeville debut with her two sisters as "The Mills Trio," c. 1910; made stage musical debut in *Shuffle Along*, New York City, 1921; made Broadway debut in *Plantation Review*, 1922.

success. Around 1912 Mills married a man named James Randolph, but the union was short-lived. Tired of the constant travel of the vaudeville circuit, Mills settled in Chicago in 1915 and began working at the infamous Panama Café. The Café, located in South State Street's red-light district, was notorious for its freewheeling atmosphere. Blacks and whites often danced together there, which was considered very scandalous at the time, and the Café was eventually shut down by the Chicago vice squad. While working at the Panama Café, Mills sang as a member of the club's "Panama Trio."

Shuffle Along

For a time, Mills performed with the Keith vaudeville troupe as a member of its "Tennessee Ten," and soon became involved with a fellow performer, Ulysses S. Thompson. They were married in 1923. Mills eventually began moving out of vaudeville and into the more stable—and lucrative—cabaret and nightclub circuit. In 1921, while performing in Harlem at the Barron's Club, she received an offer to replace one of the leads in the groundbreaking production of Noble Sissle and Eubie Blake's musical *Shuffle Along*.

Shuffle Along, which was the first legitimate African American musical comedy and a tremendous hit with white audiences as well, made Mills a star. In sold-out performances at New York's 63rd Street Music Hall, *Shuffle Along* showcased African American song and dance numbers and is considered the work that introduced jazz rhythms and dance to mainstream America. The title of the musical referred to a dance step that is considered the predecessor of tap. *Shuffle Along* "marked the begin-

ning of the Black Renaissance," noted Lynne Fauley Emery in *Black Dance from 1619 to Today*.

Mills performed for five months in *Shuffle Along*, and received rave reviews. She sang with an unusually high-pitched voice that was sometimes described as birdlike, and her petite, lithe frame was well-suited to the energetic score. "Mills's performances were memorable," wrote Richard Newman in *Notable Black American Women*, "for her charismatic effectiveness in presentation. Demure and modest personally and in her private life, on stage she was assured, vivacious, and as capable of intimate mutual interaction with her audiences as a black preacher."

Success in London

Following her success in *Shuffle Along*, promoter Lew Leslie hired Mills to perform at his Plantation Club, a black-themed cabaret on Broadway that played to white audiences. Her performance in the club's "Plantation Review" was such a success that Leslie created a full-scale Broadway show of the same name, which opened at the 48th Street Theater in July of 1922. Mills's performance in *Plantation Review* received rave reviews from New York stage critics, who "liked her energy and vitality, her sinuous dancing, her lack of self-consciousness," wrote Newman in *Notable Black American Women*. The essay also explained that *Plantation Review* was a groundbreaking show because it attracted white audiences to an entirely African American-themed work: "...There was real appreciation for the authenticity of black song and dance, and the realization that Negro portrayals by blackface performers like Al Jolson and Eddie Cantor were only imitations of the real thing," noted Newman.

In 1923, Mills was invited to appear in London in a stage work entitled *Dover Street to Dixie*. The show was a critical success, but the British cast considered Mills an outsider and treated her badly. It was also feared that the appearance of an African American on stage would cause London audiences to boycott the show. However, midway through the show, Mills mesmerized the audience with her beautiful singing of "The Sleeping Hills of Tennessee" and "any threat of opposition vanished, and for the rest of that night and the remainder of the show's run, she received a fervent ovation before every song she sang," wrote Newman.

Dover Street to Dixie soon evolved into a New York stage show, *From Dixie to Broadway*, which became the first African American musical comedy in an established Broadway theater. It opened in New York in October of 1924, and Mills's rendition of "I'm a Little Blackbird

Looking for a Bluebird" was a showstopper. Theater scholars point out that musical reviews such as *From Dixie to Broadway* gave African American performers like Mills an opportunity to showcase their talents and did much to eradicate vaudeville-era racial stereotypes. Stars such as Mills now became box-office draws, but their success depended upon remaining true to African American musical forms and the rhythms of jazz.

Blackbirds of 1926

In June of 1925, Mills became the first African American woman to headline at a Broadway venue with her engagement at the Palace Theatre. "Other blacks had been in Palace programs," explained Newman in *Notable Black American Women*, "but as a headliner Mills received money, billing, the best dressing room, and courtesy from management—real and symbolic achievements for a black American woman." For six weeks, Mills starred in *Blackbirds of 1926* at Harlem's Alhambra Theatre. The show—featuring her signature tune, "I'm a Little Blackbird Looking for a Bluebird"—was such a hit that it opened in Paris, London, and several other British cities. At London's Pavilion Theatre the Prince of Wales, who later became King Edward VIII, reportedly saw *Blackbirds* over twenty times. During her time abroad, Mills was a celebrated guest at the glittering parties of young aristocrats and creative types and Evelyn Waugh reportedly based a character in his *Brideshead Revisited* on Mills.

A Fatal Workload

The heavy touring schedule for *Blackbirds* took a devastating toll on Mills's health and she was forced to withdraw from the show. After a stay at a spa in Germany failed to restore her health, Mills sailed back to New York City in the fall of 1927. Upon her arrival in New York, she became seriously ill and was admitted to New York's Hospital for Joint Diseases for an appendectomy. On November 1, 1927, Mills died of an intestinal obstruction known as paralytic ileus.

The number of mourners at Mills's funeral at Harlem's Mount Zion African Methodist Episcopal Church was estimated at 5,000, while 150,000 lined the streets outside. She was buried in Woodlawn Cemetery in the Bronx. As Newman wrote in *Notable Black American Women,* "Mills was one of the most popular people in Harlem during the 1920s. Blacks understood that she had never forgotten her roots, that she never put on airs, that she affirmed over and over again the heritage—and the struggle—they shared together. In appreciation for everything she meant to them, the people of Harlem gave her the grandest funeral within their considerable power, an outpouring of affection and recognition, music and flowers, tears and drama."

Sources

Emery, Lynne Fauley, *Black Dance from 1619 to Today,* second revised edition, Dance Horizons, 1988.

Encyclopedia of African-American Culture and History, edited by Jack Salzman, Volume 4, Macmillan, 1996, p. 1801.

Negro Almanac, 4th edition, Wiley, 1976.

Notable American Women 1607-1950, edited by Edward T. James, Belknap Press, 1971, pp. 545-546.

Notable Black American Women, Book I, edited by Jessie Carney Smith, Gale, 1992, pp. 752-756.

—Carol Brennan

Olusegun Obasanjo

1937—

Nigerian president

Nigeria, located on the west coast of Africa, is the continent's most populous nation, and potentially its richest. Since it gained independence from Britain in 1960, however, it has been plagued by political instability and economic problems. Olusegun Obasanjo, a Nigerian military officer, first came to international prominence in 1975, when he co-engineered the bloodless coup of General Yakubu Gowon, Nigeria's head of state. The following year, Obasanjo took over as the country's leader. In 1979, after implementing a wide range of governmental reforms, Obasanjo stepped down from office and restored civilian rule. In doing so, he became the only Nigerian military leader to voluntarily hand power to a democratically-elected government. Following two decades of corrupt political leadership, Obasanjo presented himself as a candidate for president, and was elected in March of 1999.

As president, Obasanjo faced some daunting problems. In the 20 years since he was last in office, the country's annual per capita income has dropped from $788 to $679. Its currency, the naira, was worth almost $2 then; today it trades for just over a cent. The economy, already damaged by high-level corruption, is dependent on oil for 98.9 percent of its export earnings—and the price of oil has continued to drop.

"Top of his agenda should be three issues," the *Economist* advised, "corruption, weaning the economy off its dependency on oil, and finding a more democratic federal system that spreads power and money more evenly through the country." Whether Obasanjo can undo the damage of years of mismanagement remains to be seen.

Rose Through Ranks of Nigerian Military

Olusegun Obasanjo was born on May 5, 1937, in Abeokuta, Ogun State, in southwest Nigeria. He was educated at Abeokuta Baptist High School and Mons Officers Cadet School in Aldershot, England. In 1958, Obasanjo enlisted in the Nigerian army. He was commissioned in 1959, and served in the Congo (now Zaire) the following year.

During his military career, Obasanjo frequently studied in Britain, receiving training at the Royal College of Military Engineering in Chatham and at the School of Survey in Newbury. At the British Royal Engineers' Young Officers

At a Glance . . .

Born Olusegun Obasanjo, May 5, 1937, Abeokuta, Ogun State, Nigeria; married Oluremi Akinbwon; two sons, four daughters. *Education:* Abeokuta Baptist High School; Mons Officers' Cadet School, Aldershot, England; Royal College of Military Engineering, Chatham, England; School of Survey, Newbury, England; British Royal Engineers' Young Officers School, Shrivenham, England; Indian Defence Staff College; Indian Army School of Engineering; Royal College of Defence Studies, London.

Career: Enlisted in the Nigerian Army, 1958; served in 5th Battalion, Kaduna and the Cameroons, 1958-59; second lieutenant, 1959; lieutenant, 1960; captain and commander of Nigerian Army's Engineering Unit, 1963; major and commander of Field Engineering Unit, 1965; lieutenant-colonel, 1967; commander of Ibadan Garrison, 1967-69; colonel, 1969; commander of 3rd Marine Commando Division, 1969-70; accepted Biafran surrender ending Nigerian Civil War, 1970; federal commissioner for Works and Housing, 1975; led coup to overthrow head of state Yakubu Gowon, 1975; head of state and commander in chief of the Nigerian Armed Forces, 1976-79; founder, Obasanjo Farms Nigeria Ltd. in Otta, Ogun State, 1979-; elected president of Nigeria, 1999.

Author, *A March of Progress: Collected Speeches* (1979), *My Command: An Account of the Nigerian Civil War,* (1980), *Africa in Perspective: Myths and Realities* (1987), *Africa Embattled* (1988), *Constitution for National Integration and Development* (1989), *Not My Will* (1990); many articles for periodicals, including *Foreign Policy, Foreign Affairs, Review of International Affairs,* and *New Perspectives Quarterly.*

Selected awards: Grand Commander of the Order of the Federal Republic of Nigeria, 1980; Africa Prize for Leadership for the Sustainable End of Hunger, 1990; several honorary degrees.

Addresses: *Home*—Abeokuta, Nigeria.

In his two decades in the military, Obasanjo advanced steadily through the ranks. From 1958 to 1959, he served in the 5th Battalion in Kaduna and the Cameroons. In 1959, he was commissioned second lieutenant. The following year, he was promoted to lieutenant, and served in the Nigerian contingent of the UN Force in the Congo. In 1963, he became commander of the only engineering unit of the Nigerian Army; the same year, he was promoted to captain. He became a major in 1965, lieutenant-colonel in 1967, and colonel in 1969.

Meanwhile, in 1960, Nigeria gained its independence from Britain, and a period of intense political instability followed. In 1966, the military seized power. In 1969, Biafra—the country's eastern, predominantly-Christian region—seceded from Nigeria, and civil war broke out. During the civil war, Obasanjo served as commander of the 3rd marine commando division. Under his leadership, federal troops split the Biafran Army into two enclaves, and forced a surrender less than a month later.

In his autobiographical work, *My Command: An Account of the Nigerian Civil War*, Obasanjo described this tumultuous period in Nigerian history: "Within a space of six months I turned a situation of low morale, desertion, and distrust within my division and within the Army into one of high morale, confidence, co-operation, and success for my division and for the Army....A nation almost torn asunder and on the brink of total disintegration was reunited and the wound healed."

Following the war, Obasanjo returned to his former position as chief of army engineers. After he was promoted to brigadier-general in 1972, he enrolled in an advanced training course at the Royal College of Defence Studies in London. Two years later, he returned to Nigeria, and was appointed federal commissioner for works and housing.

Took Over as Head of State

The political situation in Nigeria, then under military rule, continued to be unstable. In 1974, the Nigerian head of state, General Yakubu Gowon, declared that a return to civilian rule would be postponed indefinitely. Opposition to Gowon's rule grew, and in 1975 Obasanjo, along with Murtala Muhammed, led a bloodless coup that overthrew him.

The following year, Muhammed was assassinated, and Obasanjo was appointed head of state and commander-in-chief of the Nigerian Armed Forces. He assured Nigerians that he would follow a strict program to return

School in Shrivenham, he won first prize and a citation as "the best Commonwealth student ever." In the mid-1960s, Obasanjo studied at the Indian Defence Staff College and the Indian Army School of Engineering.

Nigeria to civilian rule.

During his time in office, Obasanjo proved himself to be a tough leader, unafraid to stand up to colonial powers. At one point, British Prime Minister Margaret Thatcher refused to restore British authority in Rhodesia (now called Zimbabwe) after the country's white population usurped power. In response, Obasanjo nationalized British Petroleum's interests in Nigeria, and threatened to boycott British imports. Thatcher eventually relented, and began the process that led to free elections and majority rule in Zimbabwe.

In 1979, after three years as Nigeria's leader, Obasanjo handed power to elected president Shehu Shagari. In doing so, he became the only military ruler in Nigeria's history to voluntarily step down in favor of a democratically-elected government. While Obasanjo was widely praised for adhering to his promise, many Nigerians were glad to see him go. "Students and journalists remember his years in office as a time of repression and lack of tolerance," Barnaby Phillips wrote in the *Daily Telegraph*.

While in office, Obasanjo oversaw the creation of a new constitution for Nigeria, and implemented a wide range of governmental reforms. However, the newly-elected civilian government suffered from corruption, and collapsed in just five years, when the military once again seized power. According to the *Economist*, "the army, once seen as the only institution capable of running the country, turned instead to looting, and destroyed it. Nigeria's descent into chaos accelerated."

Dedicated Himself to Farming, Writing

Having retired from the armed forces as a general in 1979, Obasanjo started a company called Obasanjo Farms Nigeria Ltd. in Otta, Ogun State. According to Jonathan Power, writing in the *Los Angeles Times*, "Obasanjo was so obsessed by his countrymen's refusal to come to terms with economic chaos, not least the running down of the country's precious agricultural base, that he decided to show what could be done with the land." He supervised the construction of the farm closely, often choosing to spend the night in the half-built structures. "I call myself a chicken farmer," he told Rushworth M. Kidder of the *Christian Science Monitor*. "Some of my friends don't like that, but some do!"

Obasanjo also became a fellow at the University of Ibadan's Institute of African Studies. During the 1980s and 1990s, he wrote prolifically, publishing *My Command* and numerous books and articles on African development. He served on a variety of policy research and advisory committees concerned with the future of African countries. "Democracy, farming, and disarmament are Obasanjo's passions," Jonathan Power wrote in the *Los Angeles Times*, "and he has relentlessly promulgated them."

"The improvement of living standards and the wealth of nations are more of a journey and less of a destination," Obasanjo was quoted as saying in the *Los Angeles Times*. In his view, it would take three or four generations for Africa to transform its centuries-old culture to fit with the demands of the global marketplace; but at the same time, African culture should not be devalued. "What, for example, is wrong with our traditional society, which respects age, experience, and authority?" he was quoted as saying in the *Los Angeles Times*. "Or the norm that everybody is his brother's keeper? Or the practice of stigmatizing and ostracizing evil-doers and the indolent?"

In 1993, a civil election was held in Nigeria, but the country's military ruler, General Ibrahim Babangida, refused to hand over power to the winner. "We demand that the Babangida administration be terminated forthwith," Obasanjo was quoted as saying in the *Boston Globe*. In protest, the European Community suspended aid to Nigeria, but the military government held on.

By 1995, leadership had passed to General Sani Abacha, who jailed Obasanjo and other military officers on charges of plotting a coup. Obasanjo strongly denied the charges, and—after international pressure was applied—he was soon released from prison, although he was restricted to his hometown indefinitely.

In the summer of 1998, Abacha, whom the *Economist* once called "the worst ruler Nigeria has ever had," died suddenly—whether from natural or unnatural causes is still uncertain. In his place came General Abdulsalam Abubakar, who quickly announced his intention to restore Nigeria to civilian rule after 15 years of army dictatorship. He set out a timetable for the formation of political parties and for democratic elections, and released a number of political prisoners, including Obasanjo. Almost immediately, rumors began circulating that he would run for office. In November of 1998, Obasanjo confirmed the rumors, arousing both interest and controversy.

"More than issues, however, the election is about the complex balancing of hundreds of ethnic interests," Anton La Guardia wrote in the *Daily Telegraph*. Although Obasanjo is from southwestern Nigeria, critics claimed that he was a pawn of the northern-dominated military establishment, which bankrolled his campaign. "He is not a true democrat, and having a former soldier in power does not provide the clean break with the past that Nigeria needs," one prominent politician was quoted as saying in the *Daily Telegraph*. However, his years spent in house arrest were a definite asset for his campaign: "Mr. Obasanjo's aura as a political martyr is expected to help him to overcome the handicap of his uniform," La Guardia observed.

Elected President of Nigeria

During the ill-fated 1993 election, Obasanjo criticized General Yakubu Gowon—whom he had earlier ejected from office—for seeking the presidential nomination. "What did you forget to take from the State House that you have to go back?" the *Daily Telegraph* quoted him as saying. Five years later, Obasanjo denied that he was vulnerable to the same criticism, telling the *Daily Telegraph*, "I have not forgotten anything. I do not regret leaving power. What I left behind and should have been taken care of has all been destroyed."

Obasanjo also rejected accusations that he would perpetuate decades of military rule in the guise of a civilian government. He told the *Daily Telegraph* that he had to return to power to "bring Nigeria out of the mess it has been put into" by a succession of corrupt army dictators. "I believe I have something to offer. If someone has something to offer, he should say so and let the electorate decide," he was quoted as saying.

On March 1, 1999, Obasanjo was formally proclaimed Nigeria's new civilian president. According to the final tally, Obasanjo, heading the People's Democratic Party, won by 63 percent of the vote, while Chief Olu Falae, head of a coalition of the Alliance for Democracy and the All People's Party, captured 37 percent.

However, Obasanjo's opponents, as well as international observers, questioned the result, alleging that there had been widespread election fraud. Jimmy Carter, the former U.S. president and head of one of several foreign monitoring groups, was quoted as stating in the *Daily Telegraph*, "There was a wide disparity between the number of voters observed at the polling stations and the final results that have been reported from several states .... it is not possible for us to make an accurate judgement about the outcome of the presidential elections." In setting up the timetable for the elections, current ruler Abubakar had allowed for such a possibility; he planned to remain in power until at least May of 1999, in part to give time for any legal challenges.

Obasanjo admitted that irregularities had occurred, but blamed "ignorant" people, rather than planned election fraud. "I don't believe there is anywhere in the world where elections are conducted by human beings that are perfect," he was quoted as saying in the *Daily Telegraph*. "Democracy, under my leadership, will continue."

Sources

Periodicals

Boston Globe, July 14, 1993, p. 13.
Christian Science Monitor, March 18, 1987.
Daily Telegraph, March 2, 1999; February 17, 1999; February 22, 1999.
Economist, March 6, 1999, p. 44.
Los Angeles Times, April 4, 1995, p. B7.
New York Times, March 24, 1995, p. A5.

—Carrie Golus

Teddy Pendergrass

1950—

Vocalist

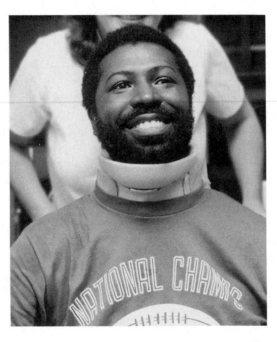

The consummate African American sex symbol of the 1970s music scene, Teddy Pendergrass gained unparalleled adulation from female fans for his suggestive crooning and his women-only concerts at which teddy bears were passed out to audience members. Prior to his solo career, he had already been in the spotlight for many years as the lead vocalist of one of the most lyrical and distinctive of the Philadelphia soul groups, Harold Melvin and the Blue Notes. In 1982, Pendergrass was in an automobile accident that left him a paraplegic. However, he was able to successfully resume his career.

Pendergrass was born in Philadelphia on March 26, 1950. His mother named him Theodore, which means "gift from God," because she had suffered six previous miscarriages. His father Jesse, who had left the family and moved in with another woman, was murdered when Pendergrass was 12. As a young man, Pendergrass was ordained as a minister and he followed a religious lifestyle. His first exposure to secular music occurred in his early teens when his mother, who worked at a Philadelphia supper club, let him play some of the club's musical instruments. Pendergrass soon taught himself to play several instruments and he joined several local musical groups in Philadelphia.

Blue Notes Drummer and Vocalist

In 1969, Pendergrass received his first big break when he signed on as the drummer for Harold Melvin and the Blue Notes, a Philadelphia soul group. When the Blue Notes' lead vocalist left the group the following year, Pendergrass replaced him and brought a new level of fame to the group. The Philadelphia soul sound pioneered by producers Kenny Gamble and Leon Huff during the 1970s combined a down-to-earth intensity with a more lyrical, mellow side. Pendergrass's baritone voice was vigorous, yet smooth, and was well-suited to the Philadelphia soul sound. Blue Notes hits such as "If You Don't Know Me By Now" and "The Love I Lost" made Pendergrass a singing sensation and helped to launch his solo career.

Pendergrass released his debut solo album, *Teddy Pendergrass*, in 1977. Two singles from the album, "I Don't Love You Any More" and the ballad "The Whole Town's Laughing at Me," were modest hits. However, it was only when Pendergrass began to be marketed as a sex symbol that his career really took off. When he performed in concert, Pendergrass would launch into spectacular vocal outbursts that delighted throngs of adoring female fans.

At a Glance . . .

Born Theodore Pendergrass on March 26, 1950, in Philadelphia; married Karen Still, in June of 1987; children: Theodore Jr., Tamon, Tisha Lazette, and La-Donna.

Career: R&B vocalist. Joined Harold Melvin and the Blue Notes as drummer, 1968; lead vocalist for the group, 1970-77, featured on major Blue Notes recordings such as "If You Don't Know Me By Now"; solo performer, 1977-; suffered permanent paralysis in auto crash, 1982; returned to recording and performing, mid-1980s; released *You & I*, 1997; released *This Christmas, I'd Rather Have Love*, 1998; wrote autobiography with Patricia Romanowski, *Truly Blessed*, 1998; active in disabled-welfare organizations.

Awards: Received numerous civic awards; Image Award, NAACP, 1973 and 1980.

Addresses: *Agent*—Dream Street Management, 1460 Fourth St., Suite 205, Santa Monica, CA 90401.

Many of these fans threw underwear on stage and reveled in his tank-top attire and seductive stage routines. Concerts were often billed as "Ladies Only" affairs and, in one notorious incident, one woman shot another after a struggle over Pendergrass's sweat-soaked head scarf.

Permanently Paralyzed by Crash

For a time, Pendergrass was arguably the most popular male star in R&B music. However, his life would be changed forever on the night of March 18, 1982, when the brakes on his Rolls-Royce failed, causing the car to hit a metal guardrail, cross into oncoming traffic, and ram into a tree. Pendergrass suffered a broken neck, a crushed spinal cord, and damage to vital nerves. He was unconscious for eight days and, when he regained consciousness, he realized that he was paralyzed below the waist and would be confined to a wheelchair for the rest of his life.

Following his accident, Pendergrass contemplated suicide. In his 1998 autobiography, *Truly Blessed*, he remarked that he had once asked his wife to give him an overdose of sleeping pills. Pendergrass suffered severe depression and insomnia for years after the accident, but his road to recovery began when he gingerly tried out his voice by singing along with a coffee commercial on television. Although he had been warned that he might never sing again, Pendergrass found that his voice was still in working condition. "Nothing ever sounded as sweet to my ears as my version of that silly damn jingle," he wrote in *Truly Blessed*. Pendergrass sought help from a quadriplegic therapist, who helped him exorcize thoughts of suicide through the staging of a mock funeral.

In addition to his disability, Pendergrass had to defend himself against rumors that his accident had been caused by excessive alcohol and drug use. Although Philadelphia police cited Pendergrass for reckless driving, they found no evidence that alcohol or drugs had contributed to the crash. Another rumor circulated that Pendergrass's passenger at the time of the accident, Tenika Watson, was actually a transsexual nightclub entertainer. Pendergrass denied any involvement with Watson, stating that he had simply offered a late-night ride to a woman with whom he had been casually acquainted.

Returned to Recording and Performing

His voice weakened by the crash but imbued with new emotional depth, Pendergrass slowly returned to work. In 1984, he released his first album since the accident. The album, *Love Language*, thrilled and inspired his many fans, and was certified platinum for sales of one million copies. Pendergrass made a live appearance at the Live Aid charity concert in 1985 and his 1988 album, *Joy*, put him back atop the R&B charts. Ron Wynn, in his review of *Joy* for the *All-Music Guide*, observed that Pendergrass "sang in a slower, somber yet appealing way quite different from the swaggering, openly sexual, macho posturing of the late 1970s and early 1980s. This was a weary but not beaten Pendergrass, whose manner and delivery underscored the resilient theme in *Joy's* lyrics."

With the constant support of his wife and his mother, Pendergrass has far exceeded the expectations of his doctors, who had predicted that Pendergrass would live only ten years after the accident. He kept up a moderate schedule of recording and touring, releasing the albums *Truly Blessed* (1991), *You & I* (1997), and *This Christmas, I'd Rather Have Love* (1998), and touring with the traveling company of the gospel musical *Your Arms Too Short to Box with God* in 1996. He founded the Pendergrass Institute for Music and Performing Arts to assist aspiring performers, and also supported causes that championed the rights of the disabled.

Selected discography

Life Is a Song Worth Singing, Philadelphia International, 1978.
Teddy, Philadelphia International, 1979.

T. P., Philadelphia International, 1980.
Live Coast to Coast, Philadelphia International, 1980.
It's Time for Teddy, Philadelphia International, 1981.
Teddy Pendergrass, Philadelphia International, 1982.
This One's for You, Philadelphia International, 1982.
Heaven Only Knows, Philadelphia International, 1983.
Greatest Hits, Philadelphia International, 1984.
Love Language, Asylum, 1984.
Workin' It Back, Asylum, 1985.
Joy, Asylum, 1988.
Truly Blessed, Elektra, 1991.
You & I, Elektra, 1997.
This Christmas, I'd Rather Have Love, Elektra, 1998.

Sources

Books

Contemporary Musicians, volume 3, Gale, 1990.

Erlewine, Michael, et al, eds., *The All Music Guide to Rock,* Miller-Freeman, 1998.
Graff, Gary, Josh Freedom du Lac, and Jim McFarlin, *MusicHound R&B: The Essential Album Guide,* Visible Ink, 1998.
Pendergrass, Teddy, with Patricia Romanowski, *Truly Blessed,* Putnam's, 1998.
Romanowski, Patricia, and Holly George-Warren, *The New Rolling Stone Encyclopedia of Rock and Roll,* Fireside, 1995.

Periodicals

Billboard, October 31, 1998, p. 23.
Entertainment Weekly, March 18, 1994, p. 112.
Jet, November 9, 1998, p. 56; April 5, 1999, p. 48.

—James M. Manheim

Dottie Peoples

19(?)(?)—

Gospel vocalist

Gospel vocalist, songwriter, producer, tour director, businesswoman, and spokesperson Dottie Peoples has been a star in the gospel music industry for more than 30 years, since she was nine years old. Called the "Songbird of the South" by Atlanta WAOK radio announcer Brother Esmond Patterson, Peoples won the top four honors at the 1995 Stellar Awards with her album, *On Time God.* Since then she has perpetually won or been nominated for many awards.

The firstborn of ten children, and the only singer in the family, Peoples was born in Dayton, Ohio. Her father worked two jobs, one at General Motors, to support the large family. According to Richard Gincel of the *Atlanta Constitution,* Peoples well remembers "walking a mile to school in snow up to our heads" because her family could not afford bus fare.

During her summer vacations, Peoples would stay with her grandmother in Birmingham, Alabama and would attend church with her all day on Sundays. The singers fascinated Peoples. She pictured herself as another Mahalia Jackson and went on to sing in her church choir and her high school concert choir. After high school, she toured

briefly with gospel singer Dorothy Norwood and then with Shirley Caesar. Peoples' mother did not want her daughter to go on tour.

Started With Jazz

Despite her mother's objections about touring, Groove Holmes gave Peoples the opportunity to join his ensemble and for five years she performed in jazz clubs. When she married, Peoples stopped performing, but she could not stay away from singing. Not only did she want to serve God with song, Peoples had the voice to inspire. In fact, with a vocal range of soprano to alto to tenor, she has been compared to Patti LaBelle. The *Philadelphia Tribune* called Peoples a "vocal powerhouse." But singing was not the most important thing in her life. She told writer Jimmy Stewart, "I love singing, but it's my personal relationship with Jesus that inspires me to do it."

In the seventies, while working at Salem Baptist Church in Atlanta, Peoples persuaded Reverend Doctor Jasper Williams, Jr. to start Church Door Records. Peoples became the general manager. The record label produced albums for the pastor and the church choir, and later, in 1984, Peoples's first solo effort, *Surely God Is Able.* In 1987,

At a Glance . . .

Born Dottie Peoples in Dayton, OH.

Career: Vocalist with jazz ensemble and Groove Holmes, five years; Church Door Records, 1979-91, general manager; "The Dottie Peoples' Showcase," WAOK Atlanta, 1990-96, host, director, producer; Atlanta International Records, 1991-; Harry's Jazz Symphony, 1996, vocalist; producer for Rev. Dreyfus Smith and The Wings of Faith Mass Choir; producer for Rev. Andrew Cheairs and The Songbirds of Byhalia, MS; *WOW Gospel*, 1999, vocalist.

Awards: Atlanta Gospel Choice Award Winner, 1994, for Song of the Year, "Pure Love," and Female Soloist Traditional; Atlanta Gospel Choice Award Winner, 1995, for Song of the Year, "On Time God"; Gospel Music Workshop of America/Gospel Excellence Awards, 1995, Album of the Year-Traditional, Female Vocalist of the Year, Song of the Year, "On Time God"; Vision Awards Recipient, 1995, Bobby Jones Gospel; Stellar Awards Winner, 1995, Female Vocalist-Traditional, Choir of the Year-Traditional, Album of the Year, *On Time God*, Song of the Year, "On Time God"; Atlanta Gospel Choice Award Winner, 1995, Best Choir of the Year, Song of the Year, "Everybody Ought to Know Who Jesus Is"; Stellar Awards Winner, 1996, Top Female Vocalist; First Annual NAACP Phoenix Awards Winner, 1996, Female Vocalist of the Year; Gospel Music Workshop of America/Gospel Excellence Awards, 1997, Traditional Album of the Year, Traditional Female Vocalist of the Year, Song of the Year, "Count On God"; National Association of Independent Record Distributors (Indie Award), 1997, Gospel Album of the Year.

Addresses: *Office*—Atlanta International Records, 881 Memorial Drive, S.E., Atlanta, GA 30316; Dottie Peoples Productions, PO Box 1705, Red Oak, GA 30272.

People's *Is It Worth It All* nourished the spiritual world on the same label. Two other albums followed.

Exploded in the Nineties

Gospel music exploded in the nineties. In 1990, "The

Dottie Peoples' Showcase" on radio station WAOK of Atlanta helped this explosion. In 1991, a year after Peoples started hosting, directing, and producing the show, she signed with Atlanta International Records. In 1993 her album, *"Live" at Salem Baptist Church*, garnered her a Stellar Award nomination for Best Female Solo Performance of traditional music. More nominations—for the Gospel Excellence Awards, Soul Train "Lady of Soul" Awards, and Dove awards—would follow with other albums. Peoples's success with her *"Live"* album allowed her to leave her position with Church Door Records and sing full-time.

Peoples's 1995 album, *On Time God*, would change her role in gospel music. At the Stellar Awards, she won Female Vocalist of the Year for traditional music, Choir of the Year for traditional music, Album of the Year, and Song of the Year for "On Time God." That same year, Peoples would receive a Vision Award by Bobby Jones Gospel of *Black Entertainment Television* and *Gospel Today Magazine*. ``On Time God'' would also win the Atlanta Gospel Choice Award for Song of the Year.

Throughout the nineties, Peoples toured with many gospel artists, among them Shirley Caesar, Kirk Franklin, and the Jasper Williams Crusade for Christ Ministry. Her vocals have also been featured on many other albums, such as the *Women of Worship '98* album.

Once described as "single, saved, and successful," Peoples continues to win awards and inspire. She not only sings, but writes many of her songs, such as "On Time God" and "Testify" from her 1996 album of the same name. *Testify* won numerous nominations for awards. In 1999, *God Can and God Will: Live In Atlanta* became her ninth album. She sang songs from the new release to an audience of 4,500 at the New Birth Missionary Baptist Church in Decatur, Georgia. An inspiring 225-member choir backed her performance.

Considered a Leader

Besides writing and singing gospel music, Peoples tours with a five-piece band consisting of guitar, keyboards, bass, synthesizer, and drums. She produces her own music, plus that of Reverend Dreyfus Smith, her pastor, and The Wings Of Faith Mass Choir, her home church. Peoples also produces the music for Reverend Andrew Cheairs and The Songbirds of Byhalia, Mississippi.

Though considered a traditional singer, Peoples appeals to all ages by incorporating contemporary songs and styles, such as rap, with her concerts. Her dynamic personality and faith keep her connected to others. Another way

Peoples connects is through her business acumen. Though her heart remains with gospel music, she has allowed herself to branch out, first as a spokesperson for Lustrasilk, a hair product of the Gillette company, and then as a spokesperson for a southern women's clothing store, Colbert's. She can be seen and heard in television commercials. She has sung the National Anthem at the Atlanta Hawks basketball games and at the Centennial Summer Olympics. Also, in 1996, Peoples performed with "Harry's Jazz Symphony" and the Atlanta Symphony Orchestra, the first time a gospel singer had been featured.

Already considered a leader among the future's female gospel greats, Peoples maintains, "Gospel has to change a bit for the new generation because young people need gospel, need to hear a word from the Lord, now more than ever. By the time I leave the stage, I want to have an impact on somebody's life." In 1997, Peoples won the James Cleveland Lifetime Achievement Award. That award emphasized that Peoples has made an impact on the world and will continue to do so as she sings in the twenty-first century.

Selected discography

(On Church Door Records)

Surely God Is Able, 1984.
Is It Worth It All, 1987.

(On Atlanta International Records)

"Live" at Salem Baptist Church, 1991.
On Time God, 1994.
Christmas With Dottie, 1995.
Testify, 1996.
The Collection: Songs of Faith, Hope & Love, 1998.
God Can & God Will, 1999.

Sources

Periodicals

Atlanta Constitution, October 21, 1993, p. 6.
Billboard, August 19, 1995, p. 45; August 15, 1998, p. 19.
Cleveland Call and Post, February 20, 1997, p. C1.
Los Angeles Sentinel, August 27, 1998, p. 4E.
Philadelphia Tribune, August 15, 1997, p. 4E.
Washington Post, February 23, 1998, p. B8.

Other

Additional information obtained from Atlanta International Records and found on the *Charisma* Website, URL: http://www.strang.com/cm/stories/cu297220.htm; *The Psalmist* Website, URL: http://www.praiseplace.com/psalmist/peoples.html.

—Eileen Daily

Glenda Price

1939—

College president

Named president of Detroit's Marygrove College in 1998, Glenda Price made her mark on the small Catholic institution almost immediately. Harrison Blackmond, a member of the school's board of trustees, remarked to the *Detroit Free Press* that Price " has brought a new level of excitement to this campus. She has this can-do spirit." That spirit had already provided the underpinnings for a distinguished academic career, and promised great things for an urban university whose sense of mission had been renewed by Price's leadership.

Glenda Dolores Price was born in York, Pennsylvania, on October 10, 1939, and grew up in nearby Harrisburg. She graduated from Temple University with a bachelor of science degree in 1961, and earned master of education and Ph.D. degrees from the same institution, in 1969 and 1979 respectively. Price's progress toward her graduate degrees took some time because she had worked to support herself all through her educational career—an experience that later would help her relate to Marygrove's student body, comprised largely of older individuals who juggled multiple commitments. "She . . . worked her way through college, she returned to graduate school after working and she worked and earned graduate degrees," colleague Freddye Hill told the *Detroit Free Press* when Price moved to Marygrove from Spelman College. "I think she will say to the Marygrove women, 'It's possible!'"

Price's field of study was medical technology and, after receiving her master's degree at Temple, she worked there

for ten years as a professor of clinical laboratory science. Her master's and doctoral degrees were in education, and her dual background in science and education made her a natural for an administrative career. After finishing her doctorate Price was named assistant dean at Temple's College of Allied Health, remaining there until 1986. Her career continued its upward track when she became dean of the School of Allied Health Professions at the University of Connecticut and served in that post for six years. In addition to her administrative responsibilities, Price remained actively involved in her field. She authored or co-authored over twenty articles in academic publications, served as president of the American Society for Clinical Laboratory Sciences, and received many professional awards.

In 1992 Price was named provost at Spelman College in Atlanta, an all-female school and an institution with elite status among the ranks of America's historically black colleges. She served as Spelman's top administrative officer, managed the day-to-day affairs of the school, and gained key national contacts by joining the board of a health professions commission established by the prestigious Pew Charitable Trusts in Washington, D.C. Price also played a critical role in Spelman's successful $114 million fundraising drive. The amount raised was the largest in the college's history and was remarkable in an era when many similar schools were facing difficult financial straits.

Price's fund-raising prowess attracted the attention of the

At a Glance . . .

Born October 10, 1939, in York, Pennsylvania; raised in Harrisburg, Pennsylvania. *Education:* Temple University, B.S., 1961, M.Ed., 1969, and Ph.D., 1979; graduated from the Harvard University Management Program. *Religion:* Baptist.

Career: Professor of clinical laboratory science, Temple University, 1969–79; assistant dean, College of Allied Health, Temple University, 1979–86; dean, College of Allied Health Professions, University of Connecticut, 1986–92; provost, Spelman College, 1992–97; president, Marygrove College, Detroit, 1998–;. author of numerous scholarly articles.

Awards: Pennsylvania Society for Medical Technology, Member of the Year, 1979; SUNY-Buffalo Warren Perry Allied Health Leadership Award, 1982; Temple University Alumni Fellow, 1992; University of Connecticut Medallion Award, 1992.

Addresses: *Office*—Marygrove College, 8425 W. Mc-Nichols, Detroit, MI 48221.

board of trustees at Marygrove College in Detroit, a Catholic liberal-arts school with about 1,000 undergraduates. Enrollment at the college had traditionally consisted of affluent, white Catholic women. The school became coeducational during the 1970s and, by the 1990s, the student body closely reflected Detroit's predominantly African American population. Unanimously selected by Marygrove's board, Price assumed the office of president in July of 1998, and was inaugurated the following April. She became the first African American and the first non-Catholic to hold the position of Marygrove president.

Within two weeks of taking office, Price established a program called Marygrove Griots (the word, pronounced Gree-oh, is a West African one meaning a respected storyteller). The program was designed to increase the number of African American males entering the teaching profession. "We recognize that there is a tremendous need to increase the number of men [in teaching] because there are too few mentors for young men particularly, as well as for young women in public education," Price told the *Detroit News.* Valuing the college's small-school, liberal-arts heritage, Price made plans to reopen its sole residence hall, reinstate a quaint tradition of Sunday teas, and

attract students from beyond the Detroit area. At the same time, she clearly stated that she planned to fulfill Marygrove's commitment to an urban mission and expressed a desire to enter into new relationship with Detroit civic leaders, businesses, and social groups.

The Detroit Public Schools had long been plagued by a variety of problems. In 1999 Michigan's Republican governor, John Engler, took action to remove the city's elected school board from office. He asked Detroit mayor Dennis Archer to name a replacement "reform" board, and Price was one of the nine members selected. Archer remarked in the *Detroit Free Press* of the "settling effect that she [Price] can bring to the school board." The new board met with considerable resistance and its meetings were disrupted by protesters. Price, who offered the Marygrove campus as a sanctuary for the board's meetings, was puzzled by the intensity of the anger she had encountered. "As a relative newcomer to Detroit," she wrote in the *Detroit Free Press*, "I cannot state with any certainty that I understand the political dynamics surrounding the Detroit public schools controversy." She went on to criticize those who launched rhetorical attacks on the reform board, "because they divert time and energy away from solving problems."

As the twenty-first century approached, Price seemed to be emerging as an educational leader in her adopted city of Detroit. She appeared to have won a place in the hearts of Marygrove students and served as an effective role model. "I want to be just like her," a Marygrove student told the *Free Press.* "I adore her." In addition to her career as an educational administrator, Price enjoyed reading, gourmet cooking, and international travel.

Sources

Periodicals

Detroit Free Press, February 3, 1998, p. 1B; July 9, 1998, p. 1B; February 27, 1999; April 14, 1999.
Detroit News, February 3, 1998, p. D1; February 12, 1998, p. C1; July 15, 1998, p. S3; April 7, 1999, p. S4; April 18, 1999, p. C1; April 23, 1999, p. C6.

Other

Additional information for this profile was provided by the Office of the Director of Communications, Marygrove College, Detroit.

—James M. Manheim

Sharon Robinson

1950—

Baseball administrator, author

Sharon Robinson grew up in the public eye as the daughter of Jackie Robinson, the famous baseball player who broke the major league color barrier in 1947. She has worked as a nurse midwife for twenty years, served as a trustee for the American College of Nurse-Midwives Foundation, and taught at Yale University School of Nursing, Columbia, Howard, and Georgetown universities. She has also served as a top official in Reverend Jesse Jackson's Operation PUSH organization, and as an executive member to the board of directors of the Jackie Robinson Foundation. In 1997, Robinson became the director of educational programming for Major League Baseball. She developed "Breaking Barriers—It's a Complete Game," a program that focused on human values and women's issues. The program was widely popular and used as an educational tool in thousands of classrooms across the United States.

a nursing degree, but was a full-time homemaker while her husband played major league baseball. At the time of Sharon's birth, Jackie Robinson had been scheduled to go to Hollywood to film *The Jackie Robinson Story*. He traveled to Hollywood after the birth and Robinson and her mother eventually flew out to California to be with Jackie during the filming. Her father starred as himself in the movie, while actress Ruby Dee played the part of her mother.

Robinson's childhood was lived in the public eye, and the media took many photos of the family. They were also featured in national magazines such as *Life*. The Robinson family lived in the St. Albans section of Long Island, and reporters and fans often came to the door unannounced for autographs or to take pictures. Robinson discussed this situation in her book *Stealing Home: An Intimate Family Portrait by the Daughter of Jackie Robinson*, "All I knew was that my dad was a famous baseball player on the Brooklyn Dodgers and that people loved to tell stories about his feats."

Childhood Lived in Public Eye

Robinson was born in New York City on January 13, 1950, the middle child and only daughter of Rachel (Isum) Robinson and Jack Roosevelt Robinson. Her mother held

When Robinson was two years old, her parents decided to move from Long Island. They desired a large country home in an area where the schools were integrated and where their children could receive a quality education. The family decided to live in North Stamford, an all-white community in Connecticut. Upon their arrival in Stamford, the Robinsons experienced some racial discrimination and prejudice. However, they were eventually able to purchase some property and built a new home. Despite the fact that her parents wanted her to attend an integrated school, the school that Robinson and her brother attended was all white. Robinson's brother became the first African American child to attend school in North Stamford.

When she was six years old, Robinson saw the movie about her father's life for the first time while she was attending a summer camp. In her book *Stealing Home* Robinson remarked that, at the time, she was largely unaware of her father's accomplishments. "By the time I was born the major trauma of the first few years in baseball were behind my parents. I did not grow up hearing horror stories of my father's pioneering efforts...now, I was watching this story about my father for the first time...[and] I saw a story about his playing, a story of racism and one brave attempt to end an aspect of it. It would have been a peculiar situation for an adult to deal with. It was certainly beyond the powers of comprehension of a six-year-old." She remembered being upset during parts of

the movie, but also felt a deep sense of pride. "I felt ready to burst, or blossom, and I think I knew even then that something inside me had changed, and just as my father had changed the larger world, my own little world would never look quite the same again."

Jackie Robinson retired from baseball in 1956. Although her brothers were disappointed that their father was leaving baseball, Robinson was glad because she could spend more time with her father. Even though Robinson's father had retired from baseball, the family remained in the public eye. While eating dinner at a restaurant, they were often interrupted by fans seeking autographs. Although her father dealt graciously with these fans, Robinson and her family knew that he was greatly displeased that their dinner was interrupted.

Robinson's childhood years were filled with typical school and family activities. She belonged to Jack and Jill, a national organization for the children of middle class African Americans. This organization offered opportunities for the children to socialize and participate in cultural and service activities. She also belonged to the Girl Scouts and attended summer camp. By the time she was finishing junior high school, the civil rights movement was in full swing. In 1963, Robinson and her family participated in the March on Washington and she heard Dr. Martin Luther King Jr. give his "I Have A Dream" speech. After the march, the Robinsons hosted a fund raising party at their home to benefit the civil rights movement and Dr. King attended. Robinson recalled in *Stealing Home,* "Ordinarily, I wasn't thrown by celebrities, but Dr. King was different .standing in his presence was as close to God as I figured I would ever get."

During Robinson's first year in high school, Stamford began to integrate their public schools. She was bussed across town to Stamford High School, even though a new school had been built closer to her home. It marked the first time that Robinson had attended school with other African Americans. She found that she enjoyed the experience and became actively involved in school sports.

Began Nursing Career

During her junior year, Robinson became a nursing assistant at a local hospital. She received her interest in nursing from her grandmother, who thought that it was a good way to meet and marry a doctor. Robinson would often spend time with her grandmother knitting and watching *The Doctors* soap opera. Her grandmother also read doctor-nurse romance novels and Robinson found that she enjoyed them too. At the age of sixteen, she became engaged and also made plans to attend nursing school.

After a nursing school accepted her into their program based, Robinson believed, on her father's celebrity rather than her application and test scores, she refused to attend. This experience reinforced Robinson's need to establish her own identity and she later told *Ebony,* "And my reason for getting engaged was to change my last name. I didn't realize it at that point but I wanted to be anonymous."

Robinson got married at the age of 18, but divorced one year later. She enrolled at Columbia University as a nursing student and met Joe Mitchel, who was enrolled in a pre-med program. They were married in 1968, but this marriage also ended in divorce. Robinson left Columbia and enrolled at Howard University, where she graduated with a degree in nursing in 1973. She began her nursing career and, at the age of 26, earned her master's degree in maternity nursing from Columbia University's School of Nursing. She also became certified in nurse-midwifery, where she said in *Stealing Home* that she " joined the modern version of an ancient order. Fascinated with birth from childhood, raised by my mother to nurture, fueled by observing my parents find fulfillment in a life of service, I accepted my calling when it came."

In 1977 Robinson gave birth to her son, Jesse Martin Robinson Simms, and raised him as a single parent. After sixteen years of nursing and midwifery and teaching positions at Columbia, Howard, and Yale Universities, Robinson left the medical field in 1989 to work as executive director of PUSH (People United to Save Humanity) for Excellence, Jesse Jackson's civil rights organization. In 1997, she left PUSH to resume teaching and practicing midwifery.

Became an Author

Robinson's book, *Stealing Home: An Intimate Family Portrait by the Daughter of Jackie Robinson* was published in 1996. It provided many intimate details about growing up with a famous father. The book illustrated that even though the Robinson's lived the American Dream and that her father was greatly admired, the family also had its share of problems and difficulties. *Publisher's Weekly* gave the book a favorable review.

Robinson left the nursing profession in 1997. That year marked the fiftieth anniversary of her father's entry into Major League Baseball and many activities were held to commemorate the event. She was also hired as the national director of educational programming for National League Baseball. This position allowed Robinson to continue her love of teaching and offered an opportunity to pay tribute to her father and his many accomplishments.

Sources

Books

Rampersad, Arnold, *Jackie Robinson. A Biography,* Alfred A. Knopf, 1997.

Robinson, Jackie, as told to Alfred Duckett, *I Never Had It Made,* G.P. Putnam's Sons, 1972.

Robinson, Rachel, with Lee Daniels, *Jackie Robinson. An Intimate Portrait,* Harry N. Abrams, 1996.

Robinson, Sharon, *Stealing Home. An Intimate Family Portrait by the Daughter of Jackie Robinson,* Harper-Collins, 1996.

Periodicals

Christian Science Monitor, October 14, 1997, p.15.
Ebony, November 1987, p. 62; October 1998, p. 45.
Jet, August 11, 1997, p. 48.
The Sporting News, August 24, 1998, p. 10.

—Sandy J. Stiefer

Spottswood W. Robinson, III

1916–1998

Judge, lawyer, educator

In his long and varied career, Spottswood W. Robinson III served as an educator, a lawyer, and a judge on one of the highest appellate courts in the United States. However, he is most remembered as the attorney who argued the case of *Brown v. Board of Education* before the US Supreme Court in 1954. The Court's historic ruling in that case led to the desegregation of public schools throughout the nation.

After the *Brown* case, Robinson went on to become dean of the law school at his alma mater, Howard University. He was the first African American to serve as a judge of the US District Court in Washington. Robinson was also the first African American to be named a judge on the US Court of Appeals for the District of Columbia. This court is the most important appeals court in the country, and is sometimes called the nation's second most influential court after the US Supreme Court. Robinson was Chief Judge of this court from 1981 until 1986. Jack Greenberg, an expert on civil rights law who worked with Robinson on the *Brown* case, remarked in Robinson's obituary in the *New York Times* that "He (Robinson) was a curious combination of a property lawyer, who knew the ins and outs of property law, and a constitutional lawyer, who knew the great

policies of the Constitution as they were expressed in the Fourteenth Amendment."

A few days after his death, the *Washington Post* ran an editorial praising Robinson for his contribution to the advancement of civil rights in the United States. "Because of the research and courtroom work of Judge Robinson and a handful of lawyers and students of his era, countless Americans today attend schools, ride buses, buy homes, use state parks, and enjoy the protection of the law without regard to their race or color. It was not always so for America."

Pioneering Civil Rights Lawyer

Robinson was born on July 26, 1916, in Richmond, Virginia. He was the son of Spottswood Robinson Jr., a lawyer, and his wife, Inez C. Robinson. As a young man, Robinson attended public schools in Richmond, which were segregated at the time, and graduated from Armstrong High School in 1932. Following high school, he studied at Richmond's Virginia Union University from 1932 until 1934 and from 1935 until 1936. Instead of completing work on his bachelor's degree, however, Rob-

At a Glance . . .

Born Spottswood W. Robinson III, July 26, 1916, Richmond, VA; died October 11, 1998; son of Spottswood Robinson, Jr. and Inez (Clements) Robinson; married Marian Bernice Wilkerson, Mar. 5, 1936; children: Spottswood W. IV, Nina. *Education:* Virginia Union University, Richmond, 1932-34, 1935-36; Howard University School of Law, Washington, DC, LLB, magna cum laude, 1939. *Religion:* Episcopalian.

Career: Teaching fellow, Howard University, 1939-48; Instructor, 1941-43; Assistant professor, 1943-46; Associate professor, 1945-48; Dean, Howard University Law School, 1960-63. Legal representative, Virginia NAACP Legal Defense and Educational Fund, 1948-50; Legal representative for Southwest Regional Council, NAACP, 1951-60; Member, US Commission on Civil Rights, 1961-63. Judge, US District Court, Washington, DC, 1964-66; US Court of Appeals, Washington, DC, 1966-92; Chief Judge, US Court of Appeals, 1981-86.

Selected awards: Honorary degrees from Howard University, Georgetown University, New York Law School.

inson entered Howard University School of Law in Washington, D.C.

According to the *Washington Post,* Robinson once said of Howard University's law school, "The turning point of my life was the day I put my foot in there." During his years at Howard, Robinson was strongly influenced by Charles Hamilton Houston, a pioneering African American lawyer who encouraged law students to fight for civil rights. "One of the things that was drilled into my head was ... 'This legal education that you're getting is not just for you, it was for everybody. So when you leave here, you want to put it to good use,'" Robinson was quoted as saying in *Jet.* Robinson studied incessantly in law school, developing a passion for detailed research that later would be indispensable in documenting arguments for civil rights cases. He graduated magna cum laude in 1939, having earned the highest grade point average in the school's history.

After graduation, Robinson was offered a teaching fellowship in law at Howard. He remained at the school for the next eight years, advancing steadily through the academic ranks. He became an instructor in 1941, an assistant professor in 1943, and an associate professor in 1945. He taught courses on a range of subjects, including bills and notes, business units, civil rights, constitutional law, real

property, and torts. Meanwhile, having been admitted to the Virginia bar in 1943, Robinson began to practice law in Richmond. During the 1940s, Robinson moved into the front lines of the emerging struggle for civil rights and soon rose to national prominence. He was "one of just a very small handful of practicing lawyers who handled civil rights cases in the late forties and early fifties in Virginia," Jack Greenberg remarked in the *New York Times.*

In 1947, Robinson took a leave of absence from Howard University. The following year, he resigned from the faculty in order to take a position as an attorney for the legal defense and educational fund of Virginia's NAACP. This fund provided legal assistance for needy African Americans whose civil rights had been violated. Working with his former mentor, Charles Houston, Robinson helped to win a Supreme Court ruling that outlawed restrictive covenants banning the sale of real estate to African Americans.

While Robinson would become famous for his civil rights victories, he also experienced significant losses. From 1949 to 1951, he was a member of an NAACP legal team that defended the Martinsville Seven, a group of African American men accused of sexually assaulting a woman in Martinsville, Virginia. Despite Robinson's valiant efforts, the men were eventually executed.

In 1951 Robinson was appointed southeast regional counsel for the NAACP fund, a job that required him to travel all over Virginia and the South. Years later, he recalled that he always had to pack a lunch for those trips because many southern restaurants refused to serve African Americans. "A Negro lawyer practicing in some of the outlying country courts had a hard time finding any place to eat," he was quoted as saying in his obituary in the *Washington Post.*

Desegregated American Schools

In his first year as southeast regional counsel, Robinson represented an African American student in Virginia's Prince Edward County. The student claimed that, at the high school for African American students, the textbooks, facilities, and buses were vastly inferior to what was available at schools for white students. Robinson filed suit on behalf of 100 parents of 450 students at Moton High School, convinced that their only chance of success lay in having the case heard by the US Supreme Court. The lawsuit was eventually combined with the *Brown v. Board of Education* case. The Supreme Court agreed to hear *Brown v. Board of Education* in 1954.

Robinson's contribution to *Brown v. Board of Education*

was to argue the constitutional history of the Fourteenth Amendment. In Robinson's view, the amendment called for equality for all people, regardless of race. African Americans, he argued, were denied equality because they attended segregated schools. As Robinson presented his arguments in front of the Supreme Court, "he was very calm and just absolutely brimming with facts and information and legal doctrine," recalled Greenberg in the *New York Times*. The Supreme Court, in an historic decision, agreed with Robinson and struck down the "separate but equal" doctrine that had prevailed in public education throughout the South.

Robinson argued many other civil rights cases, winning rulings that desegregated interstate buses and state parks. In an effort to protect segregation, the state of Virginia tried to restrict the NAACP's activities. A series of laws were passed that prohibited the solicitation or contribution of funds to pay for litigation of race-based court cases. In response, Robinson filed suit and a federal court declared the laws to be unconstitutional in 1956.

In 1960, Robinson gave up his law practice to become dean of Howard's law school, a position he held until 1963. In 1961, President John F. Kennedy named Robinson to the U.S. Commission on Civil Rights, a six-member bipartisan commission charged with studying civil rights violations in the United States. Although several Southern senators protested Robinson's nomination because of his activist background, he was confirmed by a vote of 73 to 17. During the 1960s, the commission focused attention on racial discrimination within labor unions and the National Guard, as well as police brutality directed against African Americans.

Served on Appellate Court

In 1964, President Lyndon B. Johnson appointed Robinson to a federal judgeship. Two years later, he became the first African American to serve on the U.S. Court of Appeals for the D.C. Circuit, a position he would hold until his retirement in 1992. From 1981 until 1986, Robinson was Chief Judge of the Court of Appeals.

As a judge, Robinson was known for his long, scholarly opinions, which often featured excessive numbers of footnotes—a subject of good-natured teasing from his former clerks, who had to painstakingly research each one. "I was taught to approach everything and get it done

conscientiously and thoroughly," he remarked to the *Washington Post*. "I really don't know of any other way to deal with it. It is just as easy to do it the right way as any other way."

In 1989, after 23 years on the US Court of Appeals for the DC Circuit, Robinson announced his retirement. This left an unprecedented three vacancies on the court. One vacancy was created by the resignation of Robert H. Bork, an unsuccessful nominee for the Supreme Court, and the other by the departure of Kenneth W. Starr, who became solicitor general. Many commentators and activists expressed concern that the court was becoming too conservative because older, more liberal judges such as Robinson were retiring, and the vacancies were being filled by Republican appointees. Robinson "was the court's last link to the pro-civil rights administrations of Presidents Kennedy and Johnson," Tracy Thompson and Saundra Torry wrote in the *Washington Post*. At an event preceding his retirement, Chief Judge Patricia M. Wald praised Robinson as "the quintessential judge—ultimately fair to all sides, intimately knowledgeable ... unwilling to cut any corners or slough over any uncomfortable facts or law."

For the next three years, Robinson kept an office at the U.S. Courthouse, and continued to hear cases on a reduced workload. In 1992, he took full retirement and returned home to Richmond, Virginia. Robinson died on October 11, 1998 at his home in Richmond. He had been in failing health for years and his death was attributed to a heart attack. Following Robinson's death, the editorial board of the *Washington Post* praised him as a man who helped to create a "much fairer and more just legal and social structure than the one he was born into 82 years ago. He had a large hand in making it this way."

Sources

Periodicals

Ebony Success Library, Southwestern Co., 1973.
Jet, November 2, 1998, p. 57.
Los Angeles Times, October 14, 1998, p. A18.
New York Times, July 28, 1961, p. 9; October 13, 1998.
Washington Post, August 12, 1989, p. A8; October 13, 1998, p. B6; October 17, 1998, p. A20.

—Carrie Golus

Chris Rock

1967(?)—

Comedian, actor

Chris Rock has worked as a stand-up comic in local New York comedy clubs since he was a teenager. It was in these clubs that he learned how to make people laugh, a skill that Rock has developed into a highly successful career. With a hip talk show on HBO, an enormously popular appearance as host of the *MTV Video Music Awards,* a comedy album, and numerous film appearances, Rock is definitely on a roll.

Rock was born in 1967 and grew up in the tough Bedford-Stuyvesant section of Brooklyn. The eldest of six children, he dropped out of school–he later obtained a general equivalency diploma–and went to work as busboy, a mental hospital orderly, and a laborer unloading trucks for the *New York Daily News,* where his father was employed. Rock's humor--sharp, political, and streetwise--cracked up his co-workers, and he took the act to the local comedy club circuit. After viewing Rock's performance at Manhattan's Comic Strip Club in 1986, actor-comedian Eddie Murphy found the young comedian a spot on his HBO special, *Uptown Comedy Express,* and gave him a small role in *Beverly Hills Cop II.* Rock's portrayal of a rib joint customer two years later in *I'm Gonna Git You Sucka,* a parody of a 1970s blackexploitation film, led to appearances on *The Arsenio Hall Show.* Rock soon attracted the attention of *Saturday Night Live*'s executive producer, Lorne Michaels, who asked him to audition for the show.

After a mass audition in Chicago in 1990, Michaels hired Rock as a featured player for the late-night show. Although he created such memorable characters as the militant talk-show host Nat X, Rock was dissatisfied with *Saturday Night Live* and left the show in 1993. In a 1996 Internet chat on *Up Close,* he remarked that during his stint with *Saturday Night Live* he "felt like the adopted [black] kid with great white parents." In 1994, Rock joined the cast of the predominantly black sketch show *In Living Color,* but the show was canceled that same year.

In addition to his work on *Saturday Night Live* and *In Living Color,* Rock developed a career as a film actor. In 1991, he received critical accolades for his performance in *New Jack City,* a film about a team of cops who bring down a Harlem drug lord. Directed by Mario Van Peebles, the film's cast included Wesley Snipes, Ice-T, Judd Nelson, and Rock as Pookie, a young African American man trapped in a world of drugs and violence. To prepare for the role, Rock spent several days on the streets with a

At a Glance . . .

Born c. 1967 in Brooklyn, NY, son of Julius (a truckdriver) and Rose (a schoolteacher); married Malaak Compton, (a public relations coordinator), 1996.

Career: Comedian, actor; cast member on *Saturday Night Live*, 1990-93, and *In Living Color*, 1993-94; host, The Chris Rock Show, HBO, 1996-. hosted the *MTV Music Video Awards*, 1997; co-produced the tv sitcom *The Hughleys*, 1998; appeared in the films *Beverly Hills Cop II*, 1987; *I'm Gonna Git You Sucka*, 1988; *New Jack City*, 1991; *Boomerang*, 1992; *CB4*, 1993; *Panther*, 1995; *Sgt. Bilko*, 1996; *Beverly Hills Ninja*, 1997; *Lethal Weapon 4*, 1998; *Doctor Dolittle*, 1998; *Dogma*, 1999; author of *Rock This!*, 1997.

Awards: CableAce Award for *Chris Rock: Big Ass Jokes*, 1995; Emmy Award for *Bring the Pain*, 1997.

Addresses: *Home*–Fort Greene, Brooklyn, NY. *Agent*–Michael Rotenberg, 3 Arts Entertainment, 9460 Wilshire Blvd., 7th Floor, Beverly Hills, CA 90212.

Brooklyn drug addict. The following year, he played the role of Bony T in the Eddie Murphy film *Boomerang*. In 1993 Rock also starred as Albert in the rap parody *CB4*, a film which he wrote and co-produced.

During the mid-1990s, Rock's career appeared to stall. Although he did several comedy specials for HBO and had a role in the 1995 film *Panther*, he had no offers to do an upcoming television series, which would offer an opportunity for steady work. Hoping to jump start his career, Rock left the William Morris Agency in search of a new agent. Leaving the William Morris Agency only made matters worse. "After I left," Rock told *Entertainment Weekly*, "no one wanted me. Literally every agent in town turned me down."

Undaunted by this rejection, Rock decided to work harder to become a better comic and actor. He carefully studied the comedic techniques of some of his heroes such as Bill Cosby, Eddie Murphy, Richard Pryor, Woody Allen, and Don Rickles and looked for ways to improve his performance. In 1996, Rock taped a comedy special for HBO entitled *Bring the Pain*. The show was a smash hit, earned Rock two Emmy awards and rekindled his career. HBO signed him to host his own show and Comedy Central's *Politically Incorrect* hired him to cover the 1996 presidential elections. He also landed a role in the film *Sgt. Bilko*. At the end of 1996, Rock married public relations execu-

tive Malaak Compton. In an interview with *Time*, Rock credited his career resurgence to the purchase of a new home, "People ask me how the change in my career came about...When I bought a new house I needed more money. So I had to work twice as hard. And in the work on the road, I got better."

During 1997, Rock's star continued to rise. He released the comedy album *Roll with the New* and a book entitled *Rock This!*, appeared with the late Chris Farley in the film *Beverly Hills Ninja*, and hosted the *MTV Music Video Awards*. Rock also appeared in commercials for Nike, where he was featured as the voice of the puppet Li'l Penny, and 1-800 Collect. In 1998, Rock landed roles in the films *Lethal Weapon 4* and *Doctor Dolittle*, where he delighted audiences as the voice of a guinea pig. That same year he co-produced the sitcom *The Hughleys*, which told the story of a successful African American family and their struggle to adjust to life in an all-white suburb. The show, which aired on ABC, received generally favorable reviews.

Rock appeared in the highly controversial 1999 film *Dogma*. This film featured Rock as Jesus' 13th apostle, Rufus, who is excluded from biblical history because he revealed that Jesus was an African American. *Dogma* was criticized as blasphemous and sacrilegious by the Catholic League for Religious and Civil Rights and the Ethics and Religious Liberty Commission of the Southern Baptist Convention.

Although he has achieved remarkable success, Rock remained modest. "It's a good time to be a young, black comedian," he told *Time*, "Of course, that's easy for me to say because I'm one of the people working. . . . No matter how good you are, you have to work hard–or you'll only be as funny as the next guy."

Sources

Books

Rooney, Terrie M., ed. *Newsmakers 98*, Gale, 1999.

Periodicals

Entertainment Weekly, May 21, 1999, pp. 50-51.
Time, July 20, 1998, pp. 56-59.

Other

Additional information for this profile was obtained from the "Meet Mr. Rock" *Up Close* Internet chat on June 6, 1996.

—Ann M. Peters and David G. Oblender

John L. Smith

1938—

College president

In March of 1999, John L. Smith became president of Fisk University, a predominantly African American institution in Nashville, Tennessee. Fisk is one of the oldest, and most prestigious, of the historically black universities, having been founded as a school to educate former slaves in 1866. Among its first alumni were W.E.B. DuBois, social critic and co-founder of the NAACP. The university is also famous for its singing group, the Jubilee Singers, who, beginning in 1871, introduced much of the world to the spiritual as a musical genre. In 1998, Fisk had 825 students.

Before his appointment as president of Fisk, Smith was a professor and administrator at the University of South Florida in Tampa for more than 26 years. Smith, a musician by training, served for 15 years in various management positions in the College of Fine Arts, including dean, assistant dean and assistant department chair.

"The school's choice [for president], John L. Smith Jr., might seem an odd one at first glance," Monique Fields wrote in the *Tennessean*. "Smith comes to Fisk from a large public institution, the predominantly white University of South Florida." Nevertheless, his appointment as president was well-received by Fisk's faculty and students, who both gave Smith a standing ovation when the appointment was announced. "While the contrasts are evident, Smith seems a good fit at Fisk ...," Fields wrote in the *Tennessean*. "The university needs a fundraiser and a solid administrator."

In the early years of his career, Smith taught at University of Missouri-Kansas City, Oklahoma City University, and Langston University in Oklahoma. He also achieved recognition as a gifted tubist, performing with orchestras in Florida and Oklahoma. "John L. Smith Jr. brings excellent qualities to his new position as president of Fisk University," the editorial board of the *Tennessean* wrote. "... Smith's background in music and the fine arts matches him perfectly to an institution that began with the strong voices of its choir. That's called harmony."

Visited Fisk as a Child

John L. Smith Jr. was born on Sept. 14, 1938, in Bastrop, Louisiana. At the age of 15, he first visited the Fisk campus, when his sister, Barbara Terry, began her freshman year there in 1953. According to Monique Fields, writing in the *Tennessean*, "he saw Jubilee Hall and the Fisk Memorial Chapel and was so impressed with their power that he never forgot them." Little did Smith suspect that one day he would become president of this historic university.

After high school, Smith enrolled at Lincoln University, a predominantly African American institution in Jefferson City, Missouri. He graduated with a bachelor's of music education in 1959. During the summers of 1959 and 1960, Smith had his first experience as an educator, teaching at Griffen High School in Lake Providence,

At a Glance . . .

Born John L. Smith, Sept. 14, 1938, Bastrop, LA; married Juel Shannon Smith, founding director of the Institute of Black Life at the Univ. of South FL; seven grown children. *Education:* B.A. in music education, Lincoln Univ., MO, 1959; M.A. in music education, Indiana Univ., 1961; Performer's certificate, Indiana Univ., 1961; PhD, Univ. of MS, Kansas City, 1979; Post-doctoral study, Institute for Educational Management, Harvard University, 1992.

Career: Taught at Griffen High School, Grambling State Univ., Oklahoma City Univ., and Univ. of MS, Kansas City. Asst. prof of music, Langston Univ., 1966-72; Chair, Dept. of music, 1969-72. Asst. prof. of music, Univ. of South FL, 1972-78; Asst. chair for the Dept. of music, 1973-74; Asst. dean, College of Fine Arts, 1977-86; Assoc. prof., with tenure, 1978-85; Full professor, 1985-98; Interim dean, College of Fine Arts, 1986-87; Dean, College of Fine Arts, 1988-98. President, Fisk University, 1999-.

Principal tubist and associate conductor with the Great Lakes Navy Band, 1963-66; Principal tubist with the Chicago Community Orchestra, 1964-66; Principal tubist with the OK City Orchestra, 1966-72; Adjunct and second tubist with the Florida Orchestra, 1972 to 1986; Principal tubist with the Florida West Coast Symphony, 1985-86.

Member: President, Intl. Council of Fine Arts Deans, 1996-98; Chair, FL Higher Education Arts Network, 1992-94; Natl. Assn. of State Universities and the Land Grant Colleges Commission on the Arts, 1992-94. boards of numerous organizations, including the Florida Orchestra, the African American Arts Council, the Museum of African American Art, and Habitat for Humanity in Tampa, as well as the Black Liberated Arts Center in Oklahoma City.

Addresses: *Office*—Fisk University, Nashville, TN.

Louisiana.

In 1961, Smith earned a master's degree in music educa-

tion from Indiana University, Bloomington; he also earned a performer's certificate, becoming the first tubist to do so. While he did well academically at the predominantly white institution, "he remembers so vividly how alienated he felt when he attended Indiana University," Monique Fields wrote in the *Tennessean*. Years later, when Smith became an administrator at the University of South Florida, one of his top priorities was to make sure that the African-American, Asian, and Hispanic students there felt at home.

In the early sixties, Smith pursued a career as a professional musician. He was the principal tubist and associate conductor with the Great Lakes Navy Band from 1963 to 1966, and principal tubist with the Chicago Community Orchestra from 1964 to 1966. In 1966, Smith moved to Oklahoma, taking a position as assistant professor of music at Langston University. In 1969, he became chair of Langston's music department, a position he held for three years; meanwhile, in 1971, the university awarded him tenure. In addition to his teaching and administrative load, Smith was also principal tubist with the Oklahoma City Orchestra.

Became Dean of Fine Arts at USF

In 1972, Smith left Langston University to take a job as assistant professor of music at the University of South Florida (USF). USF, located in Tampa, is Florida's second largest university, with more than 37,000 students.

Two years later, Smith was awarded a grant from the Florida State University system and USF to pursue a year of graduate study. Smith used the grant to do doctoral work at the University of Missouri in Kansas City, earning his PhD in 1979. Years later, in 1992, he would further his education at the Institute for Educational Management at Harvard University, where he pursued post-doctoral study.

Even with his teaching load and graduate work, Smith still found time to perform professionally: from 1972 to 1986, he was adjunct and second tubist with the Florida Orchestra, and from 1985 to 1986 he was principal tubist with the Florida West Coast Symphony.

At the University of South Florida, Smith rose steadily through the academic and administrative ranks. From 1973 to 1974, he served as assistant chair for the department of music. In 1977, he was appointed assistant dean for the college of fine arts, a position he held until 1986, when he was named interim dean. He became associate professor, with tenure, in 1978, and a full professor in 1985.

In 1988, Smith was named dean of the college of fine arts, serving in this role for ten years. As dean, he was responsible for more than 2,000 students, including 820 majors; 85 full-time faculty; 25 visiting and adjunct faculty; and a $13 million annual budget.

From 1992 to 1994, Smith served as chair of the Florida Higher Education Arts Network, a statewide university arts organization. From 1996 to 1998, he was president of the International Council of Fine Arts Deans, which has representation from 23 countries.

As dean, Smith distinguished himself as a talented fundraiser. In 1990, he persuaded the university to offer "endowed chairs" in the fine arts. Under this system, donors agree to give a certain sum of money, and in return an academic position at the university is named in their honor. Smith raised $1.2 million for the Stuart S. Golding African Art Chair, thought to be the only chair of its kind in the United States. He also raised $2.4 million for the British International Theatre Program, which brings British theater professionals to Florida to work with students in developing productions.

"Fundraising is a quiet, serious process," Betty Castor, USF president, was quoted as saying in the *Tennessean.* "Big gifts don't just happen. What he did for us is build those quiet, long-term relationships, and that's what really counts."

"His work at the University of South Florida undoubtedly caught the attention of Fisk trustees," wrote the editorial board of the *Tennessean,* in a piece that lauded Fisk's decision to appoint Smith as president. "In the course of that position, Smith raised large amounts of money— exactly what Fisk now needs to do to stay on top of its game and continue to attract top students to its campus."

Appointed President of Fisk University

In November of 1998, the Board of Trustees of Fisk University elected Smith to be the 12th president of Fisk University. "We...are delighted to find an educator and administrator of his caliber to lead the university into the next important stage of its growth and development," Ben R. Rechter, chairman of the Fisk University Board of Trustees, was quoted as saying in a university press release. "Dr. Smith brings more than 20 years of outstanding management and fundraising experience as a university administrator as well as 33 years of classroom experience. His leadership skills are vital to Fisk's growth and success over the next decade...."

"I am honored and humbled to accept the distinguished position of Fisk University's 12th president," Smith was quoted as saying in the same press release. "Fisk is at the forefront of American education, not just among historically black colleges and universities, but among all colleges as well....For years I have followed and admired the moving work of the Jubilee Singers, and for a musician to serve as president of their university is indeed a great honor." Smith took office on March 1, 1999.

Smith calls his vision for Fisk "TLC," which stands for "Total Learning Community." According to this plan, all formal and informal activities will be evaluated based on the amount of learning that takes place. TLC can be used as a guide to decide whether or not an activity is worthwhile, Smith told Monique Fields of the *Tennessean.* He also plans to embark on a major capital campaign, which may include expanding the campus and creating an endowed chair for the Fisk Jubilee Singers.

Smith also has high hopes for Fisk's academic program, envisioning a day when 100 percent of graduates either enter graduate school or professional school, or become leaders in the national or international arena, he told Monique Fields of the *Tennessean.* "I think the possibilities are enormous," Smith was quoted as saying in the *Tennessean.* "I think that it's possible for this institution to become recognized based on understood standards as one of the great liberal arts institutions in this country."

Smith has served on the boards of numerous organizations, including the Florida Orchestra, the African American Arts Council, the Museum of African American Art, and Habitat for Humanity in Tampa, as well as the Black Liberated Arts Center in Oklahoma City. He has delivered papers and addresses throughout the US, and in fourteen overseas conferences in Europe and Africa. Smith is married to Juel Shannon Smith, founding director of the Institute of Black Life at the University of South Florida; the couple have seven grown children.

Sources

Periodicals

Tennessean, Dec. 13, 1998, p. 1B; Nov. 24, 1998, p. 12A; Nov. 20, 1998, p. 1A.

Other

Curriculum vitae, John L. Smith Jr.
Fisk University webpage, www.fisk.edu.

—Carrie Golus

Darryl Strawberry

1962—

Professional baseball player

Darryl Strawberry was born on March 12, 1962 in Los Angeles, CA and would grow up to be one of the most controversial figures in Major League Baseball history. He was the middle child of Henry and Ruby Strawberry's five children. His parents divorced in 1974 when he was 12, and his father moved out of the house. Strawberry grew up two miles from Dodger Stadium and attended Crenshaw High School. He was a shy student, but he loved to play baseball. By his senior year he was the most highly regarded high school player in the country and the New York Mets made him their first pick of the 1980 free-agent draft. In 1981 Strawberry played Class A ball and was promoted to Double A in 1982. He led the Texas League with a .602 slugging percentage hitting .283 with 34 home runs, and 97 runs batted in (RBIs). He was named the Texas League's Most Valuable Player.

A Major-League Sensation

In 1983 he was called up to the Mets. Though he struck out his first three times at bat, the rest of his year was like a dream. Strawberry was named the National League (N.

L.) Rookie of the Year by the *Sporting News* and the Baseball Writers' Association of America. But off the field Strawberry was having trouble dealing with his success. He began to use alcohol and eventually he started to experiment with cocaine and amphetamines. Strawberry had been drinking beer casually since high school but started using drugs upon his arrival with the Mets as a way to fit in. It was easy to drink after the game as the team gave the players complimentary beer and then Strawberry and other Mets would continue the party often all night long. He began to use amphetamines to overcome his hangovers before games. Still his performance on the field was outstanding. He followed up his rookie season in 1984 batting .250 with 26 home runs and 97 RBIs and was named to the N. L. All-Star team.

Before the 1985 season Strawberry signed a six-year $7.2 million contract. He also married Lisa Andrews and the two endured a short and stormy marriage. Strawberry admitted to hitting his wife and to threatening her with a gun in his 1992 autobiography, *Darryl*. On the field Strawberry hit 29 home runs with 79 RBIs and a .277 average. In 1986 Strawberry and the Mets won the World Series. Though Strawberry put together another solid

At a Glance . . .

Born Darryl Eugene Strawberry on March 12, 1962 in Los Angeles, CA; son of Henry and Ruby Strawberry; married to Charisse Strawberry; children: Darryl Jr., Diamond Nicole, Jordan, and Jade. *Education:* Graduated Crenshaw High School, 1980.

Career: Selected by the New York Mets with the first overall pick, June 3, 1980; promoted to the Mets, 1983; signed by the Los Angeles Dodgers, 1990; released by the Dodgers and signed by the San Francisco Giants, 1994; released by the Giants, February 8, 1995; signed by the New York Yankees, June 19, 1995; signed by the St. Paul Saints, May 3, 1996; signed by the New York Yankees, July 4, 1996; placed on administrative leave from baseball, April 24, 1999.

Awards: Most Valuable Player in the Texas League, 1982; National League Rookie of the Year, 1983; holds New York Mets' records for most runs (662), most home runs (252), and most runs batted in (733); selected to the National League All-Star team, 1984-1991.

Addresses: *Residence*—Tampa, FL.

season, his behavior was becoming more and more erratic. He even charged the mound and started a brawl after a team mate was hit by a pitch. After the World Championship Strawberry received more attention, more adulation, and got into more trouble. By 1987 he was drinking virtually every night and was using more cocaine. Though he reached career highs in batting average (.283), home runs (39), and RBIs (104) he was starting to wear on the Mets organization. He skipped part of spring training and then missed a late-season game claiming he had a virus when he had cut a rap record earlier in the day.

Strawberry seemed to redeem himself in 1988 making the *Sporting News* N. L. All-Star team and the magazine's N. L. Silver Slugger team. He followed up that year with an embarrassing start to the 1989 campaign. During picture day with all the media present Strawberry and former friend and Mets first baseman Keith Hernandez got into a highly publicized brawl. The incident began the year poorly and it continued that way. Strawberry had the worst season of his career batting just .225, with 29 home runs, and 77 RBIs.

If 1989 was a disappointment, 1990 would be different. In

January Strawberry was arrested after a domestic violence complaint by his wife. Strawberry spent a short time in an alcohol rehabilitation center and admitted that he had a problem with alcohol, though he told no one at the center about his drug use. It was crucial he put together a good season in the final year of his contract. And Strawberry delivered. He improved in virtually every offensive category batting .276 with 37 home runs, and 108 RBIs. He was again named to the *Sporting News* N. L. All-Star team and its N. L. Silver Slugger Team. After the 1990 season it was clear that he was going to move on. In his autobiography he claimed that the Mets was a racist organization. He had always wanted to go back home to Los Angeles and also to play with his boyhood friend Eric Davis. Before the 1991 season he signed a five-year deal with the Los Angeles Dodgers worth $20.25 million. He left the Mets all-time leader in RBIs (733), home runs (252), and runs scored (662).

Life in Los Angeles

Strawberry's life appeared to be finally in order. In 1991 he became a born-again Christian and seemed to be living a sober life. He made the N. L. All-Star team and finished the season batting .265 with 28 home runs and 99 RBIs. Though the 1991 season seemed like a turning point in Strawberry's life, it would only be a brief break in the years of uninterrupted turmoil. On the field Strawberry hurt his back which eventually would require disc surgery. His back problems would limit him to just 75 games in the 1992 and 1993 seasons combined. At the end of the 1993 campaign the once Herculean hitter had only managed a .139 average in 100 times at bat. The only thing worse than his professional life was his private life. To cope with his injury and personal problems he resumed drinking alcohol and soon after he turned to cocaine. He had an altercation with a homeless man in September of 1993 and then divorced his wife in October. Later that year Strawberry uttered the infamous comment about his hometown. When informed that people were rioting and looting in Los Angeles he said, "Let it burn". Later Strawberry told *Sports Illustrated's* Richard Hoffer, "I regret it of course. I was just joking around on the telephone, not knowing how serious it was. I mean, I live here in L.A., grew up here; my children were born here. But it should never have been said anyway. I was wrong. I admit it." Then he was arrested for hitting his soon-to-be wife Charisse Simon. The two still got married in December of 1993. Strawberry also commented on his arrest and his status with the Dodgers in Hoffer's *Sports Illustrated* article: "I don't care about what happened before, because we weren't married then. All I know is that I love my wife... I'm excited now. I'm going to give Los Angeles a treat. Darryl owes the fans one. I just want to love everybody, be happy and bring the Dodgers a championship."

Strawberry began his season of redemption with the news that he was under investigation for tax fraud. The day before the 1994 season Dodgers manager Tommy Lasorda had a direct confrontation with Strawberry telling him he had to produce in 1994. Strawberry's reaction was to walk out. He did not return to Dodger Stadium the next day and missed the opener. Finally Strawberry came back to the Dodgers general manager's office with his lawyer Robert Shapiro and his family. He confessed that he was addicted to drugs. The Dodgers put him on the disabled list, and he entered the Betty Ford clinic. After his time in drug rehabilitation, his career with the Dodgers was over. The team paid him almost $5 million and released him.

He immediately signed with the San Francisco Giants on June 20, 1994. At 32 he was back in the majors on July 7th. Strawberry was making a contribution to the team and staying clean when the strike cut the season short. Just when it seemed events were turned around for the positive, on December ninth Strawberry was charged with tax evasion and income tax conspiracy for hiding $500,000 in earnings from baseball card shows. The government said Strawberry owed $146,000 in taxes on income he hadn't reported. Strawberry was facing jail time, his legal bills were bankrupting him, and he turned to alcohol, which led him to do a line or two of cocaine. His brief cocaine use caused him to fail a drug test. He was released from the Giants and received a sixty-day suspension from baseball. Suddenly Strawberry was broke, had no income, and was facing a trial. Strawberry was fully prepared to go to jail after pleading guilty to the felony, but the judge gave him three years probation, six months home confinement, 100 hours of community service, and he had to pay $350,000 in back taxes.

Back to the Big Apple

Strawberry made the most of his next chance at baseball signing with the New York Yankees before the 1995 season. After signing the troubled star Yankee owner George Steinbrenner tried to renegotiate Strawberry's contract to include payments to charity and more extensive drug testing. While the owner and Strawberry's agent argued, the former Mets leader spent 44 days in the minor leagues. Strawberry passed the time living with a Yankee vice president under house arrest in Columbus. On August 4th Strawberry was called up to Yankees. Because the Yankees were clogged with talent, Strawberry played sparingly. But unlike the old days, the newest Yankee was no distraction. Strawberry even met with manager Buck Showalter to assure him that he would not be disruptive

to the club. Despite his mounting frustration with the Yankees—a team that followed his every off-field move but then left him out of the line-up—Strawberry continued to stay clean through the 1995 season.

After the season the Yankees had to decide whether to release Strawberry or pay him $1.8 million for the 1996 season. The club sent him to play in Puerto Rico. Strawberry tore up the pitching south of the border, but Yankees released him anyway. Instead of throwing in the towel on his baseball career, Strawberry ended up signing with the St. Paul Saints of the Independent Northern League on May 3rd. Strawberry made the most of his time in Minnesota. He told Ross Newhan of the *Los Angeles Times*: "To play in that atmosphere brought me back to a totally different place involving what the game is all about… It helped shape my priorities. Gave me an appreciation for my life and family." Strawberry's .435 average with 18 home runs and 39 RBIs in 39 games proved to his old team that he could still play. In July the Yankees called again and Strawberry signed a minor league contract with the club for the rest of the 1996 season with an option for 1997. The day after his signing he agreed to pay his ex-wife Lisa $200,000 in back child support. The Yankees called him up in time for Strawberry to hit 11 home runs and 36 RBIs in 202 at bats in a World Series-winning season. In 1997 Strawberry battled a knee injury and only played in 11 games all year. Though he came back in 1998 the Yankees had brought in Chili Davis to replace him. After Davis was hurt, Strawberry made the most of his opportunity platooning in left field and as a designated hitter. The Yankees were on their way to the best record in baseball and another World Series victory, when Strawberry was set back again. This time his pain was not self-inflicted. During the second part of the 1998 season Strawberry had been losing weight and having stomach pains. He kept quiet until late September and then had the problem checked out. Strawberry and the rest of the Yankees learned on October 1 in the middle of a playoff series against the Texas Rangers that he had colon cancer. He had surgery soon after his diagnosis to remove a 2.4 inch tumor from his colon.

Strawberry spent the off-season recovering from his illness and receiving chemotherapy. In 1998 he had one of his best seasons since he played for the New York Mets. His battle with cancer made him an inspiration to his teammates and to many fans. He had been off drugs since his return to Major League baseball in 1995. He had reconstructed his image and was set to report to the Yankees AAA club in Columbus for rehabilitation to start the 1999 season. He had even signed a $2.5 million contract with the Yankees after his surgery. All these accomplishments came crashing down on him yet again on Wednesday April 15th when he was arrested for possession of .3 grams of cocaine after allegedly soliciting a prostitute, who turned out to be an undercover police officer. Baseball Commissioner Bud Selig put Strawberry on administrative leave, which meant he was not able to play or practice with the team. Strawberry claimed that the cocaine did not belong to him, and he was joking with the woman and would not have met her at a hotel. The Yankees kept him off the 40-man roster and some sources believe the team suspended his pay. In the roller coaster ride that has been Strawberry's career as a major league baseball player, this last indiscretion appears to be particularly serious for the 37-year-old outfielder's career.

Sources

Books

Klapisch, Bob. *High and Tight: The Rise and Fall of Dwight Gooden and Darryl Strawberry.* Villard: New York, 1996.

Periodicals

Los Angeles Times, October 13, 1996.
People Weekly, October 19, 1998.
The Sporting News, April 25, 1999.
Sports Illustrated, March 14, 1994.

Other

Additional material for this essay was found on the Worldwide Web at http://www.sportingnews.com/baseball/players/3216.
http://www.majorleaguebaseball.com/bios/021923.sml

—Michael J. Watkins

H. Patrick Swygert

1943—

College president

In the summer of 1995, H. Patrick Swygert became the fifteenth president of Howard University, the oldest historically Black university in the United States. For Swygert, the appointment was a homecoming as well. Thirty years earlier, he had received his undergraduate degree in history at Howard and also earned a law degree there. His ties to Howard University were strong and deep.

Founded in 1867, Howard is one of only two federally chartered colleges. The university has a long and impressive history of advocacy, and has educated a stellar list of African Americans who have made major contributions to research, to the development of civil rights, and to the arts. Distinguished African Americans who have been associated with Howard include Charles H. Houston, civil rights lawyer from the 1920s; Supreme Court Justice Thurgood Marshall; David Dinkins, the former mayor of New York City; novelists Toni Morrison and Zora Neale Hurston; actress Felicia Rashid and singer Roberta Flack. James Nasbrit Jr., president of Howard during the 1960s, was one of the attorneys who successfully argued *Brown vs. Board of Education*, the ground-breaking Supreme Court case that ended segregation in schools. The Howard University Law School during the civil rights movement was de-

scribed as the "West Point of the Civil Rights Movement."

Swygert became president of Howard University during a difficult period in the school's history. The university was experiencing severe financial problems, and was reported to be nearly 25 million dollars in debt. To cut operating expenses, over 400 campus employees were laid off in 1994. The Department of Education charged the university with poor financial management, amid reports that four departing administrators had been given overly generous severance packages. The Budget Committee of the House of Representatives voted not to approve the $200 million subsidy to Howard's annual operating budget. Since this subsidy constituted roughly 40 percent of the university's budget, Howard faced a full-blown crisis. To make matters worse, Khalid Abdul Muhammad, then a spokesperson for The Nation of Islam, incited a wave of negative publicity for Howard by making anti-Semitic statements in two speeches that he gave at the university in 1994.

The financial crisis and negative press that Howard received led to a dramatic decline in faculty and student morale and a change in leadership. Franklyn G. Jenifer,

At a Glance . . .

Born in Philadelphia March 17, 1943, son of Gus tina and LeRoy Huzzy. Married to Sonja E. Branson. Children: Hayward Patrick Jr, Michael B. Education: Howard University, BA, 1965; Howard University, JD, cum laude, 1968.

Career: Worked as a law clerk for Justice William H Hastie; served as an administrative assistant for Congressman Charles B. Rangel, 1971-72; Temple University, assistant professor of law, 1972, acting dean of law school, 1977, vice president administrative affairs, 1982-87, executive vice president, 1987; served as general counsel for the Civil Service Commission, 1977-79; president of State University of New York at Albany (SUNY-Albany), 1990-95; president of Howard University, 1995–.

Addresses: *Office*—Office of the President, Howard University, 2400 Sixth Street NW, Washington, DC 20059.

who had been hired as president of Howard in 1990, resigned. One of the deans was appointed as an interim president while a search for a new president began. According to an article in *Jet*, the search committee determined to find a new leader "who could pull Howard out of the doldrums."

Swygert became one of the top candidates to replace Jenifer as president of Howard University. He had applied for the position five years earlier, but Jenifer had been selected. Swygert then became president of the State University of New York at Albany. During his tenure at SUNY-Albany, minority enrollment, the recruitment of minority faculty, and graduation rates for minorities all increased. Swygert also spearheaded a $55 million fundraising campaign and rekindled alumni interest in the university. Because Howard University depended heavily on Congress for its budget, Swygert's experience in dealing with government bureaucracy was considered a great strength. Before becoming an educational administrator, he had worked for the Civil Service Commission and had held other government positions. All of these factors led to the selection of Swygert as Howard University's new president.

Before his inauguration as president of Howard University,

Swygert appeared before Congress and appealed for a reinstatement of the federal budget appropriation promising that, within a year, he would produce a plan to revitalize Howard and stabilize it financially. Within two months, he convened the first of fiveretreats in which faculty, students, and staff came together to develop a strategic plan for the university.

The five retreats that Swygert convened resulted in the creation of "The Strategic Framework for Action." This plan identified a set of core values and delineated a practical set of goals for the university. Key features of the plan included: creating a Center of Excellence in Teaching and Learning and a National Center for African American Heritage and Culture, making computers accessible to all teachers and students, increasing the university's endowment by soliciting more contributions from Howard alumni, attracting more high-performing African American students to Howard, and making needed repairs to campus buildings.

During the first two years of Swygert's presidency, implementation of the plan was well under way. In 1997 Swygert announced that 79 National Achievement Scholars had chosen to attend Howard, a clear indication that the school was again attracting top minority high school students. Over seven million dollars was spent to repair and upgrade campus buildings. The Fine Arts building, for example, was extensively renovated, new pianos were purchased, and a "smart" classroom for presentations was built. By early 1998, all faculty members had their own computers and students in each dorm were given access to computers. The percent of alumni contributing to Howard increased from five percent to over 12 percent. Lastly, the school's debt rating improved from a negative rating to an A+.

Swygert's management style is designed to be inclusive, not exclusive. He also promoted an air of tolerance. One of Swygert's former classmates, quoted in a *New York Times* article, said "He's a guy who has been elected president of every organization he's been a member of. He's a consensus builder."

Throughout his life, Swygert has developed his leadership abilities. He began his professional career as a clerk for the late Judge William H. Hastie, Chief Justice of the 3rd Circuit Court of Appeals, whom Swygert described in an interview with *CBB* as "a great legal scholar and a man of great character." When his clerkship was over, Swygert worked first as a law associate in a law firm and then as administrative assistant to New York representative Charles B. Rangel. In 1972 he began a long association with Temple University in Philadelphia, first as assistant professor, then as acting dean of the law school, and vice president of administrative affairs. By 1987, he was an executive vice-president at Temple. He also served as general counsel for the Civil Service Commission and taught law overseas as a visiting professor at Tel Aviv University in Israel, the University of Ghana, and the Hungarian Ministry of Higher Education.

Swygert has taken great interest in the educational status of minorities. As president of SUNY--Albany, he headed a state commission on education in New York. In the final report Swygert wrote, "Our public elementary and secondary schools--with notable exceptions--still sift and sort children along undeniable lines of social class." Along with other presidents of historically Black colleges and universities, he has spoken out about the erosion of affirmative action in the United States. Swygert is also concerned about the low number of minorities in positions of leadership at colleges and universities. From 1980 to 1996, the number of minority candidates pursuing doctoral degrees was quite small. These small numbers ensure that the number of minority faculty and administrators in higher education will continue to be limited unless changes are made.

Swygert has proven to be a capable and effective administrator of Howard University. In an interview for *Black issues in Higher Education,* he stated, "I think it's most appropriate that, at Howard University, we never lose sight of the fact that this is an African American institution. It's an African American institution that was created and charted by the United States Congress to speak to the needs and the aspirations of the larger African American community. That core value is something that has to inform all of our decisions."

Sources

Periodicals

Black Issues in Higher Education, March 5, 1998, p 24.
Jet, May 8, 1995, p. 9.
New York Times, January 15, 1997, p. C22; April 26, 1995, p. A17.
Washington City Paper, February 19-25, 1999, p. 1.

Other

Additional information for this profile was obtained from the Cox News Service at http://www.coxnews.com; the US Department of Education web site at http://www.ed.gov; Howard University "The Strategic Framework for Action" at http://www.howard.edu; a press release from the Office of University Communications at Howard University; and an interview with H. Patrick Swygert on June 11, 1999.

—Rory Donnelly

Annice Wagner

1937—

Judge

As chief judge of the District of Columbia Court of Appeals, Annice Wagner heads the highest court in the district. She has a reputation as a thorough, painstaking judge, who controls her trials with quiet confidence.

By the time Wagner was appointed chief judge in 1994, she had racked up decades of experience in public service. During the 1970s, she served as chief lawyer for the National Capital Housing Authority, and later as people's counsel for the District of Columbia, representing the interests of utility consumers. In 1977, she was appointed associate judge of the Superior Court of the District of Columbia. In 1990, she was appointed to the Appeals Court, becoming chief judge four years later.

Throughout her career, however, Wagner has had to struggle against public criticism of her abilities. When she was nominated as people's counsel in 1975, some D.C. consumer groups and politicians questioned her lack of experience in the utilities field. In 1994, when Wagner and another candidate were shortlisted for the position of chief judge, she was criticized for taking too long to decide her cases. Despite the opposition, Wagner managed to win both jobs.

Nominated People's Counsel for D.C.

Annice Wagner was born in the District of Columbia and attended public schools there. After graduating from high school, she moved to Detroit, Michigan, earning her B.A. and law degrees from Wayne State University. She was admitted to practice in Michigan and, later, in the District of Columbia.

After earning her law degree, she spent two years working as administrative aide to the president of the Barnstable County Mental Health Association in Hyannis, Massachusetts.

Later, Wagner moved back to the District of Columbia, where she was admitted to the bar in 1964. That year, she took a position in the D.C. law firm of Houston & Gardner, which specializes in civil cases. She was engaged in private practice in the district for nine years, working in a wide variety of legal areas: landlord-tenant disputes, probate, divorce, support and custody of juveniles, real property actions, conservatorships, contracts, and negligence.

In 1973, Wagner was appointed chief lawyer for the National Capital Housing Authority, which runs the District of Columbia's 11,000 public housing units. She was the first woman to serve as general counsel to the housing authority, which was then a federal agency.

In 1975, Mayor Walter E. Washington nominated Wagner to be the first people's counsel for the District of Columbia. The office had been created by Congress to represent the interests of utility consumers before the public service commission and the District of Columbia Court of Ap-

At a Glance . . .

Born Annice M. Wagner, 1937, Washington, D.C.; married. *Education:* B.A., law degree, Wayne State University, Detroit, MI.

Career: Lawyer with Houston & Gardner, beginning in 1964; General Counsel, National Capital Housing Authority, 1973-75; People's Counsel for the District of Columbia, 1975-77; Associate Judge, Superior Court of the District of Columbia, 1977-90; Judge, District of Columbia Court of Appeals, 1990-94; Chief Judge, District of Columbia Court of Appeals, 1994-.

Awards: Charlotte E. Ray Award of the National Bar Association; Honored at Turner Broadcasting System's Sixth Annual Trumpet Awards, 1988.

Member: Board of Trustees, United Planning Organization, Washington D.C., beginning in 1979; Vice president of UPO Board, beginning in 1988; Teaching team, trial advocacy workshop, Harvard University, beginning in 1986; Board of directors of the Conference of Chief Justices; Chair, Joint Committee on Judicial Administration; American Bar Association committee on mediation law.

Addresses: *Office*—500 Indiana Ave. NW, Washington, D.C. 20001.

peals.

At the time, Wagner's nomination was criticized by some D.C. consumer groups and politicians, who argued that Wagner had little experience in the utilities field. She also received some openly hostile press coverage, such as a *Washington Post* article with the headline, "Advocate Nominee Lacks Experience."

"I feel that I possess the qualifications that one would need in order to handle these kinds of (utilities) cases," Wagner was quoted as saying in the *Washington Post* article. She had dealt with a "wide variety of civil matters" and had the ability to analyze complex legal problems, she was quoted as saying during a press conference.

Wagner's nomination was defended by the only other people's counsel in the Washington area: Gary R. Alexander, people's counsel to the Maryland Public Service Commission. Alexander noted that he also had no

experience in utilities when he took office the year before, telling Stephen J. Lynton of the *Washington Post* that the criticism of Wagner was "unfair and unfounded." Wagner was able to weather the criticism, and eventually her nomination was approved by the city council. She served as people's counsel for the District of Columbia for two years.

Appointed to Superior Court, Appeals Court

In 1977, President Jimmy Carter appointed Wagner as an associate judge of the Superior Court of the District of Columbia, a position she would hold for 13 years. While in Superior Court, she served in all of its divisions—civil, criminal, family, probate and tax—and she was the presiding judge of the court's probate and tax divisions for two years.

During her years on the Superior Court, Wagner served as chair of the court's advisory committee on probate and fiduciary rules. She was largely responsible for the implementation of new rules that simplified and clarified procedures concerning people who were missing, protected or incapacitated. She also served as chair of the committee on selection and tenure of hearing commissioners. She was a member of the Superior Court rules committee and the sentencing guidelines commission, and she was chair of various subcommittees.

In addition to her judicial duties, Wagner found time for community service and teaching. In 1979, she became a member of the Board of Trustees of the United Planning Organization (UPO), which provides social service programs designed to improve the quality of life for the poor in the District of Columbia; these programs include day care, the Head Start program, food programs for children, and services for the elderly. In 1988, she was appointed vice president of the UPO board, helping to oversee all aspects of the organization. In addition, Wagner has been a member of a teaching team for the trial advocacy workshop at Harvard Law School since 1986.

In 1989, Wagner was among the candidates chosen by a D.C. commission to fill a vacancy on the district's Court of Appeals. According to the laws that govern the District of Columbia, the commission develops a short list of three candidates; the president of the United States then makes the final choice, who is subject to confirmation by the U.S. Senate. President George Bush selected Wagner, and she took her seat on the bench in 1990.

While on the trial bench, Wagner gained the respect of prosecutors and defense attorneys as a no-nonsense judge who did her homework and controlled her trials with confidence. "She didn't appear to need to flex her judicial muscles to let the boys know who is running the courtroom," one trial lawyer, Michele Roberts, was quoted as saying in the *Washington Post.* "Here she was, both black and a woman. If she had any concern about perceptions, you didn't see it."

In addition to her work as a judge on the Court of Appeals, Wagner served on numerous committees. She was chair of a task force on gender bias, which conducted a comprehensive study of bias in the courts. She also chaired the committee on arrangements for the District of Columbia judicial conference in 1992.

Became Chief Judge of D.C. Court of Appeals

In 1994, Wagner and another judge on the Court of Appeals, John M. Ferren, were shortlisted for the job of chief judge on the court. As Saundra Terry noted in the *Washington Post,* the work load in this position is extremely demanding: the chief judge handles a full load of cases, while also overseeing the court, dealing with budgets, and managing myriad other duties.

"Both are smart, respected by their peers, and considered thoughtful and pleasant to work for," Terry wrote in the *Washington Post.* "But because the court is saddled with a crushing backlog, some say the candidates' experience, speed in making decisions, and ability to inspire quick action by colleagues are crucial factors."

In the run-up to the final decision, Wagner was criticized for taking too long to decide her cases. According to a *Washington Post* survey, Wagner took an average of 14 months to decide a case. Under the court's own rules, judges are required to circulate their proposed opinions within 180 days after a case is argued orally or submitted on paper.

"Some Wagner admirers offered explanations for her backlog," Terry wrote in the *Washington Post;* they suggested that her additional duties, such as heading the task force on gender bias, had sapped her time and energy. In addition, unlike many appellate judges, Wagner insisted on drafting her own opinions, rather than relying on assistants. "She is incredibly thorough, considerate, and considered about everything she does," Karen Burke, one of Wagner's former law clerks, was quoted as saying in the *Washington Post.*

Wagner managed to overcome the criticism—just as she had earlier in her career—and was named chief judge for a four-year term. In doing so, she became the country's first African American woman chief justice.

The D.C. Judicial Nomination Commission, which made the final decision, explained that three factors had been critical to the decision: Wagner's experience as both a trial and appeals judge, her "continued commitment" to the district, and her "experience and ability in working with other agencies of government" (quoted as saying in the *Washington Post).* Wagner told the *Washington Post* that she looked forward to working with the other judges, court personnel, and the community "in our continuing effort to improve the administration of justice."

Wagner is a member of the board of directors of the Conference of Chief Justices, an organization of chief justices and judges from the 50 states, the District of Columbia and various federal territories. She also chairs the joint committee on judicial administration, the policy-making body for the District of Columbia Courts. In 1998, Wagner was chosen to be a member of an American Bar Association committee dedicated to developing a uniform mediation law throughout the country.

Wagner has received numerous awards for her accomplishments. In 1998, she, along with the five other black chief justices of state supreme courts, was honored at Turner Broadcasting System's Sixth Annual Trumpet Awards. She has also received the prestigious Charlotte E. Ray Award of the National Bar Association, in recognition of her outstanding contribution to the law and the community.

Sources

Periodicals

Washington Post, June 15, 1994, p. B3; June 11, 1994, p. A20; May 16, 1994, p. BIZ 7; Oct. 11, 1989, p. D5; Feb. 22, 1975, p. E2; Feb. 20, 1975, p. E3.

Other

Webpage, the National Conference of Commissioners on Uniform State Laws and the American Bar Association Section on Dispute Resolution. http://www.stanford.edu/group/sccn/mediation.

—Carrie Golus

Malcolm Jamal-Warner

1970—

Actor, director

As one of television's darling "Cosby Kids" in the 1980s, Malcolm-Jamal Warner could have sat back for the rest of his life and basked in the glow of early success. Instead, Warner has chosen to push his career in new directions. In the post-Cosby era, he has shaped himself into a polished and versatile actor, a skilled director, and a much sought-after host for television specials. Some child stars fall into a state of arrested development; Warner has managed to outgrow Theo.

Warner was born August 18, 1970 in Jersey City, New Jersey. He was named after two of his parents' African American heroes: Malcolm X and jazz pianist Ahmad Jamal. His parents, Robert and Pamela, divorced two years later. In 1975 Pamela and Malcolm moved to Los Angeles, her home town. Robert, meanwhile, moved to Chicago, where he earned a master's degree from the University of Chicago and became director of a drug intervention program. Throughout his childhood, Malcolm made regular summer visits to Chicago.

At first, Warner was more interested in basketball than in acting. At the end of the basketball season one year, however, his mother enrolled him in an acting class.

Before long, he was actively involved in community theater, where his talent captured the attention of casting agents and directors. With mother Pam serving as his agent, Warner began receiving calls from directors. Most of his early roles were street kids. "They'd always say, 'Pam, don't shine him up so much,'" Warner's agent/mom recalled in a 1987 *TV Guide* profile. "'He looks too clean-cut.'"

Hit Big Time With Cosby

Warner began finding steady work, both on the stage and in television, beginning at about age 9. In the early 1980s he landed guest spots on the TV series *Matt Houston*, *Fame*, and *Call to Glory*. His big break did not come until 1984, following the first dry spell of his young career. Warner was one of hundreds of kids who auditioned for the role of Bill Cosby's son Theo in *The Cosby Show*. "I was scared to death," Warner was quoted as saying in the 1987 *TV Guide* piece. "I knew they were looking for a bigger kid, like Bill's own son, Ennis, who was 6-feet-2. I was only 5-feet-5 then. But I got it."

While landing the role of Theo changed Warner's life

At a Glance . . .

Born August 18, 1970, in Jersey City, NJ; son of Pamela (his manager) and Robert (director of a drug intervention program) Warner.

Career: Began acting in community theater at age 9; appeared in commercials for Walt Disney World; played Theo Huxtable on *The Cosby Show,* NBC, 1984-92; appeared in NBC movie *The Father Clemens Story,* 1987; various television appearances on numerous series and specials, 1984- ; made directing debut in episode of *The Cosby Show,* 1990; starred in own series, *Here and Now,* NBC, 1992; plays role of Malcolm in UPN series *Malcolm and Eddie.*

Awards: NAACP Image Award, best performance by an actor in a comedy, 1986, for *The Cosby Show;* Emmy Award nomination, 1986, for *The Cosby Show.*

Addresses: *Agent*—Artists First, 8230 Beverly Blvd., Suite 23, Los Angeles, CA 90048.

dramatically, one thing did not change. Pamela remained his manager. Their relationship, while undergoing a certain amount of strain, understandably, remained strong throughout. "When I started managing him, he took an attitude," Pam was quoted as saying in a 1994 *People Weekly* feature. "It could be very unpleasant....By the time he was 18, we were in great shape." She was also forced to learn the business side of the TV game on the fly. "That first night, when the numbers went through the roof," she told *New York Times* reporter Stephen Henderson in 1997, "I didn't even know what 'numbers going through the roof' meant."

Overnight, Warner was a star. *The Cosby Show* became a huge hit, and Warner and his fellow Cosby kids became America's little darlings. For the show's first two seasons, Warner and his mother commuted from their California home to Brooklyn, New York, where the series was shot. It was immediately apparent to everyone involved in the show that the young Warner was mature beyond his years. He managed to thwart the problems and temptations that have been the undoing of many a child star. Bill Cosby became Warner's mentor, educating him in the ways of stardom. Cosby would coach Warner on everything from cars to romance to school to career moves. "He talks in a subtle way; he makes a joke, and hiding in there is the advice," Warner was quoted as saying in a 1990 *TV Guide*

interview.

Pam Warner characterized Cosby's influence as being even more profound. "He taught Malcolm to function in this business as an African American male," she told *TV Guide's* Mary Murphy. "He taught him when to compromise and when not to compromise, how to use power and how not to abuse it."

Starred Opposite Gossett as Adoptee

Along with stardom came scads of offers. After turning down several, Warner finally came across one—not counting bit parts on specials—that appealed to him. In 1987 he starred opposite Louis Gossett, Jr. in "The Father Clemens Story," a TV movie about a priest's efforts to adopt a street kid in order to publicize the disparity in adoption rates between white and black children. Like Cosby, and virtually every other adult with whom Warner worked, Gossett was impressed by both his talent and his character. "He's a terrific kid," Gossett told Rick Kogan of *TV Guide,* "and he is the finest young actor I've seen in years, with a great potential to be a great talent."

In 1988 Warner penned a book, *Theo and Me: Growing Up Okay,* in which he imparted his admittedly modest wisdom on his legions of fans. While the book was generally well-received for its honesty and sincere approach to the hazards of stardom and the worship that accompanies it, Warner was also criticized for his blunt appraisal of such sensitive topics as racism in show business.

As the seasons went on, Warner began preparing for life after *Cosby* by learning how to direct. In 1990 he directed an episode of *Cosby* called "Off to See the Wretched." His behind-the-camera work continued with a number of music videos, including one for the popular R&B group New Edition. He also directed several episodes of *Sesame Street,* and co-produced four television specials for young people. Eventually, Warner's directing career expanded into other sitcoms, including *The Fresh Prince of Bel-Air.*

Entered Post-Theo Era

Cosby went off the air in 1992 after eight spectacularly successful seasons. Shortly after the show's demise, Warner was cast as a graduate student in his own Cosby-produced NBC series, *Here and Now.* Unfortunately, the series failed to find much of an audience, and it was soon pulled from the lineup.

Disappointed with NBC's handling of *Here and Now,*

Warner turned to the stage and the big screen. He starred in Chicago in a gritty crime drama called *Freefall,* by Chicago playwright Charles Smith. Warner's portrayal of a drug dealer contrasted sharply with his clean cut TV image. "The first time I say the F-word, I can hear the hearts stop," he was quoted as saying in a 1993 *Jet* article.

In 1994 Warner made his motion picture debut in the action-adventure *Drop Zone,* in which he played the brother of star Wesley Snipes. Warner stretched his acting chops further the following year, taking on his first "bad-guy" role as a no-good friend of boxer Mike Tyson in the HBO movie *Tyson.* 1995 also brought a feature role in another HBO movie, *Tuskegee Airmen,* along side Laurence Fishburne and Cuba Gooding, Jr.. Meanwhile, Warner's interest in children's programming continued to occupy a significant space on his calendar. He had an ongoing role as the voice of the producer in the animated educational series *The Magic School Bus.* He also hosted such specials as "Kids Killing Kids/Kids Saving Kids" and the "The Kids' Choice Awards."

Warner finally broke through with a new series of his own in 1996, with *Malcolm and Eddie,* in which he stars as an aspiring commentator opposite comedian Eddie Griffin, who plays his tow-truck driving roommate. The series is broadcast on the upstart UPN network.

In the minds of a generation of TV viewers, Warner will always be Theo Huxtable. As time goes on, however, a larger and larger share of the public will recognize that there is much more to Malcolm-Jamal Warner than what rubbed off of Bill Cosby.

Sources

Books

Warner, Malcolm-Jamal, *Theo and Me: Growing Up Okay,* Dutton, 1988.

Periodicals

Essence, August 1995, p. 56.
Jet, April 9, 1990, p. 54; May10, 1993, p. 38.
Hollywood Reporter, January 28, 1999, p. 19.
New York Times, March 30, 1997, sec. 2, p. 36.
Money, Spring 1993, p. 22.
People Weekly, December 12, 1994, p. 89.
Teen Magazine, June 1985, p. 61.
TV Guide, December 12, 1987, p. 49; November 24, 1990, p. 15.

—Robert R. Jacobson

Dinah Washington

1924–1963

Vocalist

Known as "The Queen" or "Miss D," vocalist Dinah Washington emerged one of the most versatile cross-over artists of the post World War era. Her gospel-trained voice--noted for its rhythmical precision and tonal clarity—performed blues, jazz, and ballads with equal authority. Arnold Shaw, in his book *Honkers and Shouters: Golden Years of Rhythm and Blues,* stated "She had a flutelike voice, sinuous, caressing, and penetrating. Master of all devices of the blues and gospel shadings-- the bent notes, the broken notes, the slides, the anticipations, and the behind-the-beat notes—she handled them with intensity that came from her early church training." Between 1948 and 1961 Washington made over 400 sides with the Mercury label, recordings that reveal her diversity and popular acclaim. Renown for her offstage brashness and erratic behavior, Washington spent these years struggling to maintain a successful music career while overcoming the affects of numerous marriages and sporadic crash dieting. Until her death in 1963 she toured nationally playing nightclubs and large venues such as Las Vegas and Carnegie Hall—a 20-year career that influenced younger singers from Ruth Brown to Nancy Wilson.

Dinah Washington was born Ruth Lee Jones in Tusca-loosa, Alabama, on August 29, 1924. At age three Ruth's parents Ollie Jones and Alice Williams took her to Chicago. By age 11 Jones performed as a gospel vocalist and often appeared with her mother (who served her first music instructor) at church recitals across the country. In 1938 the 15-year old vocalist won first prize at an amateur contest at Chicago's Regal Theatre. She married at 17 and subsequently worked in local nightclubs. Jones studied vocals with renown gospel singer Sallie Martin and became her piano accompanist. Around 1943 she left the gospel field and sang in various Chicago nightclubs, including the Rhumboogie and the Down Beat Room. Jones worked as washroom attendant at a downtown lounge, the Garrick, often singing with the house band led by trumpeter Walter Fuller.

With Lionel Hampton

In 1943 Jones' performances at the Garrick gained the attention of music manager Joe Glaser who informed bandleader Lionel Hampton about the young singing washroom attendant. Hampton, whose band was booked at Chicago's Regal Theatre came to listened to the young

At a Glance . . .

Born Ruth Jones, August 29, 1924, in Tuscaloosa, Alabama; died of an accidental dose of sleeping pills December 14, 1963; daughter of Ollie Jones and Alice Williams; married John Young 1942-43, George Jenkins circa. 1949, Walter Buchanan 1950, Eddie Chamblee 1957, Raphael Campos 1957, Horatio Maillard 1959-60, Jackie Hayes 1960, Richard Lane 1963 (all marriages not confirmed); children, two.

Career: Won talent contest as Chicago's Regal Theater 1938; sang in gospel circuit; 1943 left religious field to perform in Chicago area nightclubs; joined Lionel Hampton's orchestra 1943, and recorded on Keynote label; recorded on Apollo label in Los Angeles 1945; embarked on solo career 1946; signed contract with Mercury Records in 1948, and over the next decade recorded over three hundred sides; 1958 appeared at the Newport Jazz Festival; in 1959 toured Europe signed with the Roulette label in 1962 and owned a Detroit restaurant; performed with Count Basie and Duke Ellington 1963.

Awards: National Academy of Recording Arts and Sciences Grammy Award for Best R&B recording of 1959 (What a Diff'rence a Day Makes). In 1960 voted as one of top ten vocalists of jazz in Leonard Feather's *Encyclopedia of Jazz*; In 1993 the US Postal Service posthumously dedicated a stamp in Washington's honor as part of a tribute to rhythm and blues artists.

singer. Immediately impressed, he invited her to sit-in with his orchestra. Following Jones' impressive Regal guest-performance Hampton hired the young vocalist and gave her the stage name Dinah Washington (other sources credit the name change to Glaser or the Garrick's owner, Joe Sherman). Because of the American Federation of Musician's recording ban (August 1942 to October 1943), and the fact that Hampton's contract with Decca solely required instrumental music, Washington recorded only one side during her three-year stint with the orchestra. Though not a featured recording artist, Washington's live performances with Hampton's orchestra became legendary. As Hampton recalled, in his memoir *Hamp*, "Dinah alone could stop the show....I had to put her down next to closing, because nobody could follow her. She had a background in gospel, and she put something new into the

popular songs I had her sing."

Washington's recording break came in 1943 when pianist and songwriter Leonard Feather organized a session for Eric Bernay's independent company, Keynote. For the session Feather recruited the Lionel Hampton Sextet which included Hampton on drums and pianist Milt Buckner. The Keynote recordings featured Feather's numbers "Evil Gal Blues" and "Salty Papa Blues," which became hits within the African American record market. Despite the success of her blues recordings, Washington did not return to the studio until May of 1945 when she cut Leonard Feather's "Blow Top Blues" with the Lionel Hampton Sextet (a single that later became a 1947 hit). While in Los Angeles in December of 1945, Washington made several blues recordings for the Apollo label. Backed by saxophonist Lucky Thompson's eight piece band, the Apollo dates featured several guest musicians such as Charles Mingus and vibraphonist Milt Jackson. Washington's voice on the Apollo sides, noted Arnold Shaw in *Honkers and Shouters*, "had a velvet sheen, and, in its bluer moments, it tore like silk, not satin."

Embarked On Solo Career

In late 1946 Washington left Hampton's band for a solo career. During the same year, she recorded her anthem "Slick Chick on the Mellow Side" for Verve Records. Around this time, Washington received the billing "The Queen of the Blues"—a title she vehemently rejected (originally the title belonged to Bessie Smith). Yet she could sing blues with authority, as evidenced on her 1947 number "Long John Blues." Written by Washington "Long John Blues" told, in double entendre and bawdy lyricism, the tale of a dentist lover and his sexually satisfying ways.

In 1948 Washington signed a contract with the recently founded Mercury label and cut the single "West Side Baby." In 1949 she scored number one on the *Billboard Charts* with "Baby Get Lost." A year later, she recorded with the saxophonist Dave Young's orchestra, and by 1952 scored a number four hit with the blues classic "Trouble in Mind." By 1953 Washington made numerous sides with strings. As Mercury records producer Bobby Shad recalled, in *Honkers and Shouters*, "I recorded Dinah with strings and probably cost the company hundreds of thousands of dollars ... She was a fantastic singer, unbelievable artist. But you had to catch her on the right night. She thought nothing of being up all night to eight a.m. and then record at ten a.m."

Recorded Jazz Material

During the mid to late 1950s Washington recorded in the company of many of the finest jazz musicians of the period from drummer Jimmy Cobb to saxophonist Julian "Cannonball" Adderly. Washington's 1954 album, *Dinah Jams,* caught her in a live Mercury studio date. The LP's Los Angeles-based sessions included a nucleus group made up of the newly formed Clifford-Brown Max Roach Quintet, and guest trumpeters Clark Terry and Maynard Ferguson, as well as Washington's sideman, pianist Junior Mance and bassist Keeter Betts. During March of 1955, Washington returned to the studio. Rejoined by Cobb, Terry, and other guests including saxophonist Paul Quinchette and pianist Wynton Kelly, she recorded the LP *Dinah Washington: For Those in Love.* Arranged by Quincy Jones, this jazz-based collection of standards included "This Can't Be Love," "I Could Write a Book," and "You Don't Know What Love Is." The latter number, noted Barry Kernfield in *The Blackwell Record Guide,* "is a song of love leading to agony," and "[Washington] convinces us that she knows fully, direct from experience." Among the album's plaintive torch songs, "Blue Gardenia," noted Jazz scholar Dan Morgenstern, in the liner notes to *Dinah Washington, The Jazz Sides,* emerged "one of Dinah's greatest ballads. The tune and lyric are first-rate, and she creates and sustains a rare mood....Dinah does the bridge ad lib and then the band follows her out as she reaches the lofty plateau inhabited by Billie Holiday."

Despite her expanding artistic talent, Washington possessed a difficult and demanding personality. In 1957 she worked an extended engagement at Chicago's Roberts Show Club. In *The Autobiography of Black Jazz,* the club's owner, Herman Roberts, recalled, "Dinah was a very complex person ... If I made a comment about her show and she knew it wasn't her idea, she would automatically reject it. She wanted to be the creator of everything she did." As Roberts added, "She was both vain and insecure," and would "cuss out" customers "without really knowing whether they were saying something derogatory or whether they were complimenting her." In the following years, Washington would often make headlines regarding foul-mouthed comments and abrupt behavior. She often appeared in multi-colored wigs, full length and tight fitting-dresses, and was known to openly criticize performers whom she considered distastefully dressed.

Broke Into Pop Market

By 1957 Washington married her fifth husband, tenor saxophonist Eddie Chamblee, and would, over the next few years, marry four more times (though not all of these nine marriages were legally confirmed). Though she suffered through several successive short-lived marriages and battled personal problems, Washington continued on a promising music career. She performed two sets at 1958 Newport Jazz Festival—one of which appeared in part for the documentary film *Jazz On a Summer's Day.* After years of being featured as a blues and jazz-style singer she broke into the pop music market with the 1959 Mercury single "What a Difference a Day Makes" (written and listed on the original recording as "What a Diff'rence a Day Made"). The single made the top ten, appeared on *Billboard's* 1959 honor roll of hits, and won a Grammy for best R&B record. During the following year, Washington topped the Billboard charts with two pop duets sung with Brook Benton, "Baby (you've Got What it Takes)" and "A Rockin' Good Day." 1960 also saw the release Washington's hit single "This Bitter Earth." A ballad set in an orchestral accompaniment, "This Bitter Earth" opens in bleak lyrical mood and, by its closing lines, is transformed by Washington into a ballad of love found within an otherwise cold and uncaring world.

Voted as one of the "Giants of Jazz" (in the vocalist category) in Leonard Feather's 1960 work, *The Encyclopedia of Jazz,* Washington began the decade in anticipation of reaching new artistic and commercial heights. During 1962 she recorded for the Roulette label. Though most of Washington's Roulette material proved weak pop material, she did cut *Back to the Blues,* an album that, as John Koetzner noted in *Jazz: The Essential Record Guide,* "captures the moment when Washington made an effort to return to her roots, and while it might not quite get there, she handles the material in such a way that it recalls her best singing on those early records." Six of the tracks were co-written by Washington, and, as Koetzner added, "she closes with 'Me and My Gin,' and there's an ominous sense that's she's long been living the song."

Around the time of her Roulette recordings, Washington established a small restaurant in Detroit. In 1963 she worked with Count Basie in Chicago and Duke Ellington in Detroit. That same year, at age 39, she married her ninth husband, Detroit Lions defensive back, Dick "Nightrane" Lane. Recently married and not planning to perform until after the New Year, Washington, who persistently fought to keep her weight down, went on a crash diet. On December 14, 1963, she died from an accidental overdose of sleeping pills. Singer Ruth Brown recalled, in her memoir *Miss Rhythm,* "I know Dinah's death was accidental, for that lady had too much in life to ever put an end to it. I believe she got those pills mixed up because she was desperately trying to lose weight with the aid of mercury injections pumped into her by her 'weight doctor'....We know today that mercury builds up in the system and can cause liver failure....[Her] final deadly cocktail of brandy and sleeping pills" may have quickly ended her life. Washington's funeral services were held by prominent Detroit church leader, Reverend C.L. Franklin (the father of Aretha Franklin) at his New Bethel Church, where the Queen's body laid in a bronze coffin.

Washington left behind a vast body of work containing powerfully moving performances and accompaniment by some the finest jazz and studio musicians of the period. Often backed by modernist jazzmen, she nevertheless remained uninfluenced by the scat stylings of bebop. A powerful exponent of blues, Washington's role in the idiom has, nevertheless, been overemphasized by journalistic music writers (despite her stereotyped billing as "blues singer" she is rarely listed in books on the subject). By emphasizing Washington's early blues period many writers have overlooked her gospel training--the integral influence responsible for a projecting delivery and vibrant soulfulness. Proud of her claim that she could sing any kind of music, Washington possessed, as Linda Dahl asserted in *Stormy Weather: The Music and Lives of a Century of Jazz Women*, "a riveting personality" which "came through all her material." Testament to her musical diversity, Washington is often mentioned in works dealing with jazz, blues, and rhythm and blues.

> "Dinah alone could stop the show....I had to put her down next to closing, because nobody could follow her. She had a background in gospel, and she put something new into the popular songs I had her sing."

Today Washington's voice accompanies commercials and film soundtracks such as *Bridges of Madison Country*, which included the numbers "Blue Gardenia" and "Soft Winds." Among the large number of her rerelease are *The Complete Dinah Washington on Mercury Vol. I-7*, a seven volume CD set as well as reissues of her earlier blues material. In 1993 the US Postal Service issued, as part of a tribute to rhythm and blues singers series, a stamp in the Queen's honor, reminding Americans of a great vocalist and a woman of unique character and uncompromising integrity.

Selected discography

Dinah Washington, Mellow Mama, (1945 Apollo recordings), Delmark, 1992.
Dinah Washington, The Queen of the Blues 1943-1947, EPM (French CD import), 1998.
Dinah Washington, The Complete on Mercury, Vol I (1946-49), Vol. 2 (1950-52), Vol. 3 (1952-54), Vol. 4 (1954-56), Vol. 5 (1956-59), Vol. 6 (1958-60), Vol. 7 (1962-65), EmArcy, 1989.
Dinah Washington, The Jazz Sides, EmArcy, 1976.
Dinah Jams, (recorded 1954), EmArcy, CD reissue 1990.
Dinah Washington, In the Land of Hifi, EmArcy, 1956.
What a Diff'rence a Day Makes, EmArcy.
September in the Rain, EmArcy.
Unforgettable, EmArcy.
I Concentrate on You, EmArcy.
For Lonely Lovers, EmArcy.
The Fats Waller Songbook, EmArcy.
Dinah '62, Roulette.
Back to the Blues, Roulette.
Dinah Washington, Jazz Masters 15, Verve, 1994.
Dinah Washington Sings Standards, Jazz Masters 40, Verve, 1994.
Ultimate Dinah Washington, Verve, 1997.
Slick Chick (On the Mellow Side), Indigo Records, 1997.
The Ultimate Dinah Washington (as selected by Abbey Lincoln), Verve, 1997.
The Singin' Miss D, Verve, 1998.

Sources

Books

Brown Ruth, *Miss Rhythm: The Autobiography of Ruth Brown, Rhythm and Blues Legend*, Donald Fine Books, 1996, pp. 247-249.

Dahl, Linda, *Stormy Weather: The Music and the Lives of a Century of Jazz Women*, Limelight, 1984, p. 53.

Dempsey, Travis J, *An Autobiography of Black Jazz*, Urban Research Institute, 1983, pp. 192-194.

Feather, Leonard, *The Encyclopedia of Jazz*, Da Capo, 1960, p. 90.

Hampton, Lionel, with James Haskins, *Hamp: An Autobiography*, Warner Books, 1989, pp. 85-88.

Koetzner, John, *Music Hound; Jazz, The Essential record Guide*, Invisible Ink Press.

Shaw, Arnold, *Black Popular Music in America: From the Spirituals, Minstrels, and Ragtime, to Soul, Disco, and Hip-Hop*, Schirmer, 1986, pp. 181-182.

Shaw, Arnold, *Honkers and Shouters: The Golden Years of Rhythm and Blues*, MacMillan, 1978, pp. 143-147.

The Blackwell Guide to Recorded Jazz, second edition, edited by Barry Kernfield, pp. 335-336.

liner notes: Dan Morgenstern, *Dinah Washington, The Jazz Sides*, EmArcy, 1976.

—John Cohassey

Jesse White

1934—

Secretary of State for Illinois

On November 3, 1998, Jesse White became the first African-American to be elected secretary of state for the state of Illinois. White had begun his political career by serving for 16 years in the Illinois General Assembly, representing the most culturally, economically, and racially diverse district in the state. In 1992, he was elected Cook County recorder of deeds, a position previously held by Carol Moseley Braun, who went on to become a US Senator for Illinois. White won reelection as recorder in 1996, resigning two years later to become secretary of state.

While White has had a long and distinguished career in state politics, outside Illinois he is better known as the founder and coach of the Jesse White Tumbling Team. The team, which White established in 1959, was designed to provide a positive alternative for children growing up in tough inner-city neighborhoods. According to John Blades, writing in the *Chicago Tribune,* "White's aggressive efforts to provide his boys and girls with a way of escape from the crippling, often fatal effects of ghetto life have brought him...national attention."

"The youngsters who live in housing projects are some of the most talented and nicest kids you'll find anywhere," White was quoted as saying in the *Tribune*. "But they're right on the cutting edge—they could go either way. You have to work with them, guide them, and mold them like a piece of clay."

White was born in on June 23, 1934, in Alton, Illinois. When he was four years old, his family moved to Chicago, settling on the near north side—a neighborhood where he lived most of his life, and where he still lives today. At the time, the area was called Little Italy, and, as White recalled, it had none of the problems typically associated with urban neighborhoods. "There was a large number of Italians living here," White told Norma Libman of the *Chicago Tribune*. "There were also some blacks, some Irish, some Germans. We got along well. We never had problems with gangs, drugs, or alcohol."

White's family was poor, and had to rely on public assistance for about ten years. "I've never looked down on anyone who uses the system, but I believe that it's a temporary station in life and that we should all work toward getting off it. And once we get off it, we should pay back to that system," he told Libman of the *Chicago*

Tribune. White sees his 33 years as a teacher and administrator in Chicago public schools, as well as his 40 years as coach of the tumbling team, as an attempt to repay this early investment. "What I'm doing right now, particularly through the Tumblers, where I have never taken a salary, is giving back to Chicago all that it gave to me when I was growing up."

As a young man, White excelled at several sports. "I was not a good student; I was an average student," White told Libman of the *Tribune.* "In order to play basketball and baseball, I had to go to school every day. And so I was pretty good in terms of attending school." As a basketball star at Waller High School (now Lincoln Park Academy), he once scored 69 points in a single game—an accomplishment that earned him a headline in the sports section of the *Tribune.* White was offered a basketball and baseball scholarship to Alabama State College (now Alabama State University), where his record as all-time basketball scoring leader has stood since the mid-1950s.

Founded Jesse White Tumblers

In 1956, White signed a contract to play with the Chicago Cubs, but he was drafted into the army before he could report to spring training. From 1957 to 1959 he served with the 101st Airborne as a paratrooper. He then returned to Chicago, taking a job as a physical education teacher at Jenner Elementary; four years later, he transferred to Schiller Elementary, where as a child he had attended school. "After being away at college and in the Army, I never considered living anywhere else. I loved Chicago then, and I love Chicago now," White told Norma Libman of the *Chicago Tribune.*

In 1959, while working with the Chicago Park District, White was asked to stage a gymnastics show. He recruited some talented youngsters, and drained his own savings account to buy uniforms. Eventually, "the word spread and we started getting requests from parks, YMCAs, block clubs, art festivals, schools, the Cubs" to put on performances, White was quoted as saying in the *Chicago Tribune.*

In the forty years since then, more than 3500 children have performed with the Jesse White Tumblers, most of them residents of public housing projects in Chicago. To remain on the team, tumblers must stay in school and maintain average grades; stay away from drugs, alcohol, and gangs; and stay out of trouble with the law. Fewer than 100 have been kicked off the team for violating the rules, White told the *Chicago Tribune.*

The Jesse White Tumblers perform more than 500 shows a year, in Chicago and around the world. The team has been featured on "Good Morning America" and "The David Letterman Show," and made an appearance in the film *Ferris Bueller's Day Off.* White's team even inspired a children's book, "I am a Jesse White Tumbler," written from the perspective of Kenyon Conner, a young team member.

"What Jesse White has done is to use his athletic skills and help teach children to do extraordinary things," the Rev. Jesse Jackson was quoted as saying in the *Sun-Times.* "Jesse has gone into a side of town that is often stereotyped and has taken the rejected stones and made them into cornerstones....He has turned pain into power." Members of his team have gone on to attend major colleges and universities. Some of them became lawyers, teachers, police officers, or electricians; one became a fashion designer.

Elected to State Legislature

After more than ten years as a coach and educator, White decided to expand his activism to the state legislature. In 1974, he was elected to the Illinois House of Representatives for the 8th district, a diverse area that includes some of Chicago's richest and poorest residents. White became only the second African-American in Illinois history to be elected from a majority-white district.

He served in the state legislature from 1975 to 1977, then again from 1979 to 1993. During his 16 years as a legislator, White developed a solid record for anti-crime and education initiatives. He chaired the Human Services Committee, which oversees all state social programs; he was also an active member of the Elementary Education Committee and the Select Committee on Aging.

After the 1990 census, when the boundaries of White's district were changed to reflect population changes, he decided to run for Cook County recorder of deeds, winning election in 1992. One of his major accomplishments, according to an editorial in the *Chicago Sun-Times,* was to "transform an outmoded paper-and-pen operation" into an up-to-date computerized office. "White earned the gratitude of real estate agents, lawyers and homeowners for reducing from six to two weeks the time it takes to record a document and return it to the customer," the *Sun-Times* editorial continued. As a result, White saved county taxpayers $4 million annually and generated record levels of revenue for the county.

During his campaign, White had promised to transform the recorder's position from an elected to an appointed office. After a few years in the job, however, he changed his mind: "Once you get in there involved with administering a large budget, hundreds of employees and major projects, you have to be accountable to the taxpayers and voters," he told the *Chicago Tribune.* In 1996, White was elected for a second term.

Elected Secretary of State

In 1998, White declared himself a candidate for Illinois secretary of state, a high-profile position often seen as a stepping-stone to a run for governor. The responsibilities of the secretary of state's office include a wide range of activities: issuing vehicle license plates and titles, maintaining driver records, registering corporations, enforcing the Illinois Securities Act, overseeing state library and literacy programs, and keeping archival records of legal or historic value. The office provides direct service to more Illinois citizens than any other public agency.

On March 17, 1998, White defeated his opponent, Tim McCarthy, to win the Democratic nomination for secretary of state; he then went on to challenge Republican nominee Al Salvi. In his campaign, White promised to make the office more accessible to working people by

opening earlier on weekdays, and by adding express lines for senior citizens and the disabled. He also proposed "a workable plan," according to a *Sun-Times* editorial, to provide new license plates at no additional cost to Illinois motorists. "White has the know-how to lobby the legislature to approve these changes," the editorial noted.

While the functions of the secretary of state's office are fairly routine, the circumstances as the election approached were not: the office was under federal investigation for accepting bribes to issue commercial driver's licenses. "It needs a tough administrator who can quickly reassure the public that there will be zero tolerance for corruption," the *Sun-Times* editorial stated. "Our endorsement goes to Jesse White." Even the Republican candidate for governor, George Ryan, endorsed White rather than fellow Republican Salvi: "(White) has probably spent a little more time in state government...and has, I think, a better idea of how the secretary of state's office functions."

"A genial, competent Cook County recorder of deeds, White reshaped his office after the chaos left by Carol Moseley-Braun...," Tom Roeser wrote in the *Chicago Sun-Times.* (Moseley-Braun later became the first African American woman to be a US senator.) "The likely defeat of Moseley-Braun (in her bid for re-election as senator) would make him the most influential African American in state politics."

While many former secretaries of state have gone on to run for Illinois governor, White stated many times during his campaign that he does not have that in mind. "I'm not going to seek an office any higher than this or lower than this...," White was quoted as saying in the *Sun-Times.* "I don't care what it is—I will not seek another office."

On November 4, 1998, White was elected secretary of state. While opponent Salvi carried many downstate counties, White was the overwhelming winner in Chicago and its suburbs. He became the first Democrat since 1981, as well as the first African American in Illinois history, to win that powerful office.

One of White's responsibilities as secretary of state is to maintain driver records, and to revoke drivers' licenses if necessary. White's office made headlines in March of 1999, after an Illinois commercial truck driver collided with an Amtrak train, killing 11 passengers and injuring more than 100. Later, it was discovered that, over the last 30 years, the driver had racked up 13 driving-related convictions and had been involved in nine accidents—but had managed to keep his commercial driver's license.

In response to the tragedy, White formed a task force to examine the Illinois Motor Vehicle Code, in order to eliminate loopholes such as the one that allowed the driver on the road. "My intent is to toughen the standards for commercial driver's licenses and for all drivers as well, especially being concerned about drivers who have had problems in the past," White wrote in a letter to the *Chicago Sun-Times.* "My goal is for Illinois to have the safest roads and strongest traffic safety laws in the country. I believe that our task force, which will include nationally known experts in the field of road safety, is an important step in that direction."

> "The youngsters who live in housing projects are some of the most talented nicest kids you'll find anywhere ... you have to work with them, guide them, and mold them like a piece of clay."

Despite the demands of his position as secretary of state, White continues to work closely with the tumbling team that bears his name. In his dual roles as politician and coach, White "likes to flavor his speech with locker- and classroom proverbs," according to John Blades of the *Chicago Tribune,* "such as 'A quitter never wins, and a winner never quits.'" It is an adage that White also demonstrates by example.

Sources

Books

African-American Biographies, by Walter J. Hawkins, Mc Farland & Co., 1992.
I Am a Jesse White Tumbler, by Diane Schmidt, Albert Whitman and Company, 1990.

Periodicals

Chicago Sun-Times, Nov. 4, 1998, p. 4; Oct. 16, 1998, p. 39; Oct. 16, 1998, p. 37; Oct. 14, 1998, p. 9; Oct. 6, 1998, p. 9; Sept. 26, 1998, p. 3; March 18, 1998, p. 5.
Chicago Tribune, June 15, 1994, p. 5; March 21, 1993, p. 8; February 1, 1990, p. 1.

Other

"The Honorable Jesse White," short biography supplied by Illinois Secretary of State's Office, 1999.

—Carrie Golus

Doug Williams

1955—

College football coach

Doug Williams, the first African American quarterback to win the Most Valuable Player Award in a Super Bowl, was born on August 9, 1955 in Zachary, Louisiana. He was the sixth of eight children born to Robert and Laura Williams. His father, who was wounded in the Japanese attack on Pearl Harbor, was a construction worker and a nightclub manager. His mother worked at a local school as a cook. Although they were poor, the Williams were a very close-knit family.

Williams began playing football at the age of seven. He also played baseball and basketball, but it soon became evident that he was destined to become a football quarterback. As a senior at Chaneyville High School, Williams threw for 1,180 yards and twenty-two touchdowns. Despite these impressive statistics, Southern University and Grambling State University were the only schools that recruited him. Because he was so impressed with Grambling coaching legend Eddie Robinson, Williams chose to attend Grambling. In the summer of 1973, Williams reported to Grambling for his freshman year. He was red-shirted during his first season at Grambling. Williams was so disappointed that he thought seriously about quitting school and his grades began to suffer. After his first semester, he carried a lowly 1.5 grade point average.

When Williams's dad saw his report card, he threatened to take his son out of school and make him find a job.

During his sophomore year, Williams was listed as Grambling's third-string quarterback. Dissatisfied with his lack of playing time, he tried to quit the team. Williams got his big break when the team's first-string quarterback was injured and eventually worked his way into a starting role. He started every game for the remainder of the 1974 season and during the next three years of his college career. He won 35 of 40 games he played as quarterback and led Grambling to four straight Southwestern Athletic Conference championships. In 1977, Williams was named first-team All-American by the Associated Press and finished fourth in voting for the Heisman Trophy. He finished his collegiate career with 93 touchdown passes and 8,411 yards passing. He also completed a bachelor of science degree in health and physical education.

Played in the NFL

In the 1978 National Football League (NFL) Draft, Williams was the first quarterback taken with the 17th overall

At a Glance . . .

Born Douglas Williams on August 9, 1955 in Zachary, LA; son of Robert (a construction worker) and Laura (a cook) Williams; married to La Taunya Williams; children: Ashley, Adrian, Douglas Jr., and Jasmine. *Education:* Grambling State University, BS in health and physical education, 1977.

Career: Played quarterback for the Tampa Bay Buccaneers, 1978-82; played in the United States Football League for the Oklahoma/Arizona Outlaws, 1983-85; played with the Washington Redskins, 1986-89; founded the Doug Williams Foundation, 1988; head coach at Zachary Northeast High School, 1993; assistant coach at the U.S. Naval Academy, 1994; offensive coordinator for the Scottish Claymores of the World Football League, 1995; scout for the Jacksonville Jaguars, 1995-96; head coach at Morehouse College, 1997; head coach at Grambling State University, 1998-.

Awards: Named first team All-American by the Associated Press and finished fourth in Heisman Trophy voting, 1977; NFL All-Rookie Team, 1978; Most Valuable Player of Super Bowl XXII, 1988.

Addresses: *Residence*—Zachary, LA; *Business*—Athletic Office, Grambling State University, Grambling, LA 71245.

pick by the Tampa Bay Buccaneers. Williams's arrival in training camp was delayed because of a contract dispute, but he eventually signed a five-year contract worth $565,000. Despite coming to camp late, he won the starting quarterback job and led the hapless Buccaneers to a 4-4 record through the first eight games. In the tenth game of the season, Williams suffered a broken jaw and did not return until the season's final game. Although his rookie season was abbreviated, he was named to the NFL's All-Rookie team.

In 1979, Williams led the Buccaneers to a 10-6 record and a berth in the playoffs. Although the Buccaneers lost in the NFC Championship game, they made tremendous strides with Williams as their quarterback. He had his best year statistically in 1980, but the Buccaneers stumbled to a 5-11 record. The following year, the Buccaneers earned another spot in the playoffs, but were soundly defeated 38-0 by the Dallas Cowboys.

In 1982, Williams married Janice Goss. That year, the NFL season was delayed by a players strike. Once the strike was settled, he led the Buccaneers to a 5-4 record and another berth in the playoffs. The Buccaneers again lost to the Cowboys by a score of 30-17. With his initial contract with the Buccaneers about to expire, Williams was confident that the team would give him a substantial raise. However, the Buccaneers offered him a contract that would only pay $400,000 per season. In the midst of these contract negotiations, Williams's wife began to experience severe headaches. In April of 1983, a CAT scan revealed that she had a brain tumor. Surgery to remove the tumor was scheduled immediately, but she died in the hospital one week later. Williams was shattered by the death of his wife and moved back to Zachary. During this time, Williams's father began to experience health problems and eventually had his legs amputated. Williams was also unable to agree to a contract with the Buccaneers and ended his association with the team.

Signed with the USFL

During Williams's negotiations with the Buccaneers, the United States Football League (USFL) was formed. Bill Tatham, the owner of the Oklahoma Outlaws, called Williams and offered him a substantial contract. He signed the contract and began his USFL career. Although Williams played well for the Outlaws, the league was experiencing financial difficulties and was in danger of going bankrupt. After spending the 1985 season with the Outlaws, Williams was ready to return to the NFL. However, he was uncertain whether an NFL team would sign him to a contract and took a coaching job at Southern University.

In 1986, the USFL officially folded and many of its players returned to the NFL. Williams eventually received a phone call from Washington Redskins coach Joe Gibbs, who had coached him in Tampa Bay. Williams quickly signed a contract and joined the Redskins as their backup quarterback. Gibbs told Norb Garrett and Cam Benty of *Sport* about Williams's first day of practice with the Redskins: "(Receivers) Ricky Sanders and Clarence Verdin came in with him from the USFL. In the first practice, we put them in to turn the other team's plays and it was a passing clinic. Doug tore our defense to pieces, throwing balls like darts, and I couldn't believe it... I remember (former Redskins owner) Jack Kent Cooke said to me, 'I'm not going to pay him $500,000 to be a backup,' and I said, 'He might not be a backup. He may win a Super Bowl for us one day.'"

Following the 1986 season, Williams married Lisa Robinson in June of 1987. The marriage quickly soured and Robinson moved out of Williams's house after only five months. Despite his personal difficulties, the 1987 season would prove to be a pivotal one for Williams. In the first game of the season the Redskins starting quarterback, Jay Schroeder, hurt his shoulder and Williams came off the bench to lead the team to victory. Although Schroeder maintained his starting position throughout the season, Williams received increasingly more playing time. During the final game of the season, Williams led the Redskins to an overtime victory over the Vikings and was named the starting quarterback for the playoffs. He led the Redskins to two playoff victories and a berth in the Super Bowl against the Denver Broncos.

Super Bowl Glory

The night before the Super Bowl, Williams experienced a severe toothache. He consulted the team dentist, who informed him that he needed a root canal immediately. Williams underwent the procedure and spent the night taking the pain-killing drug Perkadan. When he awoke the next morning, he felt fine. In the first quarter of the game, Williams twisted his knee. Despite the pain, he remained in the game and led the Redskins to a 35-10 halftime lead. During the second half, Williams threw the ball only eight times because the Redskins running attack was so dominant. The Redskins went on to trounce the Broncos 42-10 and Williams was named the Super Bowl MVP. Williams set Super Bowl records for yards passing (340), yards passing in a quarter (228), touchdown passes (4), and the longest completion (80 yards).

During the off-season, Williams and other Grambling alumni created the Doug Williams Foundation. The foundation raised money to encourage kids to stay in school and away from drugs. Williams also took time to visit two or three schools a day to speak to students about the importance of education. The Redskins also signed Williams to a new contract worth $3.3 million over three years and named him the starter for the 1988 season. However, he was knocked out of the starting lineup almost immediately due to a bout with appendicitis. Williams had an appendectomy and spent four weeks of the season on injured reserve. For the remainder of the season, he was in and out of the starting lineup and the Redskins finished with a disappointing 7-9 record.

As the 1989 season approached, Williams faced stiff competition from Mark Rypien for the Redskins starting quarterback position. During training camp, Williams found that he had difficulty throwing the football. A medical examination showed that a disc in his back was pressing against his sciatic nerve. Williams underwent surgery and struggled to regain his strength. At the same time, the health of Williams's father took a turn for the

worse. In October of 1989, he entered the hospital with pneumonia and died one week later. Williams returned to the Redskins lineup, but experienced back pain after only two games. Midway through the 1989 season, he was benched and did not play for the rest of the season. At the end of the 1989 season, the Redskins released Williams. In an interview with Donald Hunt of *Sport*, Williams related how he felt cheated that the Redskins had given up on him. "It's funny, they give Joe Montana a whole year off to get his elbow together…(Montana) didn't have to worry about a thing. As for me, my team never gave me a chance to rehabilitate my back."

Williams retired from professional football and, although he became involved with other business opportunities, discovered that he still loved the game. In 1993, Williams coached football and taught physical education at his old high school. He then landed an assistant coaching position at the Naval Academy. Williams later served as the offensive coordinator for the Scottish Claymores of the World League and scouted for the NFL's Jacksonville Jaguars. He also spent one year as the head football coach at Morehouse College.

In 1998, Williams was named the head football coach at Grambling State University, replacing legendary coach Eddie Robinson. He assessed the state of Grambling's football program for Donald Hunt of the *Milwaukee Journal Sentinel*: "We have a lot of work to do. We're not reloading. We're rebuilding. There's a big difference. We pretty much have to start from scratch." Williams changed everything about the program from the assistant coaches to the style of play, updating Robinson's Wing-T to a more modern offense. In his first season as head coach, he led the Tigers to a 5-6 record (4-4 in the Southwestern Conference.) Williams summed up Grambling's season for the Associated Press after the team lost to Southern University at the Bayou Classic: "I'm not ashamed of this game or any game we played this year…No one blew us out early. We never gave up. We got better every game. I told my kids to hit the weight room on Monday and next year we'll make the next step." As he has done in college and in the NFL, Williams appears ready to drive a team to success.

Sources

Books

Williams, Doug and Hunter, Bruce. *Quarterblack: Shattering the NFL Myth*. Bonus Books, Inc.: Chicago, Il, 1990.

Periodicals

Sport, February 1995; September 1998.

Milwaukee Journal Sentinel, September 14, 1998.

Other

Additional material was found on the Worldwide web at

http://www.cnnsi.com/football/college/news/1998/11/29/grambling_williams.

—Michael J. Watkins

Mykelti Williamson

1957—

Actor

A busy character actor with an impressive list of film and television credits, Mykelti Williamson is best known for his portrayal of Benjamin Bufford "Bubba" Blue, Tom Hanks's shrimp obsessed army buddy in the 1994 box office smash *Forrest Gump*. Williamson has also appeared in such varied films as *Con Air*, a 1997 action thriller, and the glossy 1995 "chick flick" *Waiting to Exhale*. "He doesn't like to lounge around and watch the grass grow between his toes. He's always juggling things; he's almost hyperactive," *Con Air's* director Simon West said of Williamson to Steve Dougherty of *People*.

Mykelti Williamson was born in St. Louis, Missouri in 1957. His unusual first name (pronounced Michael T.) means "spirit" in the language of the Blackfeet, a Native American tribe from which Williamson is partially descended. When Williamson was an infant, his father abandoned the family. Growing up without a father, Williamson looked to the media for father figures. One of his father substitutes was boxing champ Muhammad Ali. "He was my hero from the time I was a little bitty potato," Williamson told Dougherty. His mother's remarriage and subsequent divorce brought Williamson and his family, which includes an older brother, Jerry, and a younger sister, Jacqueline, to Los Angeles. At age ten, Williamson began appearing in local stage productions. As a teenager, Williamson danced on *Soul Train* and with a disco dance troupe, the Lockers. In 1973, he made is first movie appearance in *Enter the Dragon*, martial arts expert Bruce Lee's last completed film.

After graduating from Crenshaw High School in 1975, Williamson supported himself an as auto mechanic while searching for acting jobs. Using the name Mykel T. Williamson, he appeared on episodes of the television shows *Starsky and Hutch, Kojak, Baretta, Hill Street Blues*, and *Miami Vice*, and in such films as *Penitentiary* (1979), with Leon Issac Kennedy, and *Wildcats* (1986), with Goldie Hawn. Beginning with *The Righteous Apples* in 1980, Williamson was a regular cast member in a string of failed television series, including *The Bay City Blues*, about a minor league baseball team; *Cover-Up*, a foreign intrigue drama starring Jennifer O'Neill; *The Bronx Zoo*, in which he played a teacher at a tough urban high school; and *Midnight Caller*, a drama about a radio talk show host who gets involved in the lives of his listeners. From 1991 to 1993, Williamson played program director Donovan Aderhold on the *New WKRP in Cincinnati*, a syndicated continuation of the late 1970s CBS comedy hit.

Williamson's luck improved when he was cast in the popular film *Forrest Gump*. Directed by Robert Zemeckis and starring Tom Hanks, *Forrest Gump* followed the adventures of a simple-minded and pure- hearted Alabama country boy through post-World War II America. While serving in Vietnam, Gump fights alongside Williamson's character, Bubba Blue, a Louisiana shrimper. Bubba and Forrest later go into the shrimp business and become millionaires. "It is a smart, affecting, easygoing fable with plenty of talent on both sides of the camera...The movie is not only a greatest-hits rendering of twenty-five

At a Glance . . .

Born in 1957 St. Louis, MO, the son of Elaine (an accountant); married to Olivia Brown, c.1983 (divorced 1985); Cheryl Chisholm, 1989 (divorced 1991); Sondra Spriggs, 1997; children: Phoenix. *Education:* Crenshaw High School, Los Angeles, CA, 1975.

Career: Actor in films and television since the early 1970s. Performed with The Lockers, a dance troupe, c.1970s. Film appearances include *Enter the Dragon,* 1973; *Sunnyside,* 1979; *Penitentiary,* 1980; *Desperate Lives,* TV, 1982; *Wildcats,* 1986; *You Talkin' to Me?,* 1987; *Number One with a Bullet,* 1987; *Monster Manor,* 1988; *Miracle Mile,* 1989; *The First Power,* 1990; *A Killer Among Us,* TV, 1990; *Free Willy,* 1993; *Other Women's Children,* TV, 1993; *Forrest Gump,* 1994; *How to Make an American Quilt,* 1995; *Waiting to Exhale,* 1995; *Free Willy 2,* 1995; *Soul of the Game,* TV, 1996; *Heat,* 1996; Con Air, 1997; *Truth or Consequences, N.M.,* 1997; *Double Tap,* TV, 1997; *Twelve Angry Men, TV,* 1997; *Buffalo Soldiers,* TV, 1997; *Species 2,* 1997; *Primary Colors,* 1998; *Having Our Say,* TV, 1999. Television appearances include regular roles on the series *The Righteous Apples,* PBS, 1980; *The Bay City Blues,* NBC, 1983; *Cover Up,* CBS, 1984-85; *The Bronx Zoo,* NBC, 1987-88; *Midnight Caller,* NBC, 1989-91; *New WKRP in Cincinnati,* syndication, 1991-93. Stage appearances include *Distant Fires* and *Vigil,* Pasadena Community Arts Theatre.

Addresses: *Home*—Ladera Heights, CA. *Agent*—William Morris Agency, 151 El Camino Drive, Beverly Hills, CA 90212.

character's on-screen appearance, Williamson did not find *Forrest Gump* as helpful to his career as it might have been. "People thought I really looked like Bubba," he told Dougherty.

Though *Forrest Gump* did not bring Williamson stardom, he has encountered no shortage of work in supporting roles. In 1995's *How to Make an American Quilt,* starring Wynona Rider as a troubled young woman who seeks comfort at her grandmother's rural home, Williamson romanced Alfre Woodard. Also in 1995, Williamson was part of a large cast of rogue males in *Waiting to Exhale,* a screen version of Terry McMillan's best-selling novel about a group of African American women friends who turn to each other when their relationships with men falter. "I'd seen so many guys like that type of guy. I wanted to put a twist on it. I thought the guy should be funny and very real — but nobody would ever want to go out with this guy," Williamson said of his *Waiting to Exhale* character to Tom Green of *USA Today.*

In 1996, Williamson teamed with Al Pacino as cop partners in the thriller *Heat,* directed by *Miami Vice* creator Michael Mann. While auditioning for the role, Williamson discovered that Pacino was a fan of his work. "Michael Mann called saying, 'Al wants to meet you.' I didn't believe it, but I went, and in walks Pacino! I kept telling myself , 'Be cool, brother, be cool,'...Al had a Bubba Gump hat, but it was a second run, not an original. So I gave him one that I signed and he wears it every day," he told Cunningham. *Heat* also featured Robert DeNiro, Jon Voight, and Val Kilmer. In *Con Air*, a 1997 action blockbuster about a hijacked prison transport plane brought to safety by a paroled prisoner, Williamson played a criminal saved from a diabetic coma by star Nicolas Cage. He worked for famed director Mike Nichols in 1998's *Primary Colors,* a thinly-disguised parody of Bill Clinton's 1992 presidential campaign. In the film, which starred John Travolta and Emma Thompson, Williamson was a graduate of an adult literacy program who tells a moving tale of getting shuffled through the educational system.

Many of Williamson's most interesting roles have come in television films. *Soul of the Game,* a 1996 HBO production, examined the politics behind the selection of the first African American player to break the color line in professional baseball. Williamson portrayed Josh Gibson, the Negro leagues superstar slugger whose earthy personality resulted in his being overshadowed by the suave, college-educated Jackie Robinson, played in the film by Blair Underwood. The film also featured Delroy Lindo as famed pitcher Satchel Paige, and Edward Hermann as Brooklyn Dodgers owner Branch Rickey. Williamson's portrayal of Gibson was especially challenging because no film footage of Gibson exists, which might have helped

years of Americana, it's a distillation of humanist culture in commercial movies," said *Time* of *Forrest Gump,* which won the Academy Award for Best Picture of 1994 and was a box office smash. "Everywhere I go, I get free shrimp," joked Williamson to Kim Cunningham of *People* about his association with Bubba Blue. Director Zemeckis told Robert Levine of the *Los Angeles Times* that Williamson "brought the right tone to the character. He can do comedy, he can do drama, he can convey emotion. He's got a real leading man quality." To play Bubba, Williamson, who normally carries about 210 pounds on his 6 foot, 3 inch frame, gained considerable weight and wore a prosthetic device to deform his lips. Because of his

Williamson study Gibson's style and mannerisms. To compensate for the lack of film, Williamson consulted with former Negro leagues players "Prince" Joe Henry of the Indianapolis Clowns and Gene Smith of the Chicago American Giants. "This will be the first time an audience will see an authentic portrayal of Josh," he told *Jet.*

In Showtime's 1997 remake of the legal drama *12 Angry Men*, Williamson was part of a stellar cast including Jack Lemmon, George C. Scott, Hume Cronyn, Ossie Davis, Dorian Harewood, Edward James Olmos, Courtney B. Vance, and Tony Danza. Originally a 1954 television play, and then a highly-regarded 1957 film starring Henry Fonda, *12 Angry Men* follows the deliberation of a jury in a murder case (the trial itself is not seen). In the 1997 version, directed by William Friedkin, four of the jurors were African American. Williamson came up with the idea of giving the story more complexity by making his character an anti-white, anti-Latino bigot. The character was someone whose views are very different from his own. "I hate this character. I hate everything he stands for...To some extent, I felt ashamed that I had created this ugly character. I'm concerned about what I did," Williamson explained to James Sterngold of the *New York Times.* Director Friedkin told Sterngold that, during the shooting of the film, Williamson "had a headache everyday. He was deeply disturbed by the experience, but he was brilliant. This is a character you just don't see in movies." The film gave Williamson the opportunity to work with Ossie Davis, an actor whom he had long admired. Davis played an African American juror at odds with the racist opinions of Williamson's character. "Here's one of my heroes and it's the first time I had a chance to work with him, and I'm insulting him," Williamson told Sterngold. Matt Roush of *USA Today* called *12 Angry Men* "as fresh, relevant and suspenseful an entertainment as ever" adding that Williamson "scores in the reconceived role of a atrident bigot." Mike Lipton of *People* wrote that the racist character in *12 Angry Men* was "rivetingly portrayed" by Williamson.

Williamson helped bring to life a little-known chapter of American history with *Buffalo Soldiers*, a 1997 Turner Network film about the U.S. Army's African American cavalry corps of the late nineteenth and early twentieth centuries. Produced by and starring Danny Glover, the film told the fictional story of an African American cavalry sergeant obsessed with the idea of catching a renowned Native American warrior. *Buffalo Soldiers* gave Williamson, who organizes a monthly horseback ride for fellow actors in the Los Angeles area, the opportunity to display his equestrian skills. "Riding and fellowship with the brothers take me away from the everyday pressures of Hollywood life," he explained to Deborah Gregory of *Essence.* In a 1999 CBS television version of *Having Our*

Say: The Delany Sisters' First 100 Years, the best-selling memoir of African American centenarians Bessie and Sadie Delany, Williamson played the Delanys' father, the first elected African American Episcopal bishop in the United States.

In January of 1998, Williamson's private life took a downward turn when he was charged with attempted manslaughter. Williamson was accused of attacking his ex-wife's boyfriend outside her home in the Baldwin Hills section of Los Angeles. He spent one night in jail and was released on $180,000 bail. According to the *Los Angeles Sentinel*, Williamson told reporters "this has all been a really big misunderstanding, and I will be vindicated." The incident surprised Williamson's friends and colleagues who knew him as a gentle, if sometimes highly emotional, person. "He always comes across as warm and lovable," *Con Air* director Simon West told Carol Day of *People.* Williamson's friend, actor Stoney Jackson, told Day "It's my assumption from what I've heard from him that it was in self-defense." A September 1998 trial resulted in Williamson's acquittal.

Williamson lives in the Ladera Heights section of Los Angeles with his wife, Sondra Spriggs, who works for the Discovery Channel. During his free time, he enjoys scuba diving, restoring classic cars, and collecting African art. He has worked with actor/director Bill Duke on developing a television anthology series based on stories told to him by his grandmother. Williamson told Dougherty — "I don't consider myself a pretty boy. But I'm happy with the way I am."

Sources

Periodicals

Boston Globe, August 16, 1997, p. C1.
Essence, July 1997, p. 50.
Films in Review, March 1996, p. 60.
Jet, April 29, 1996, p. 32; September 15, 1997, p. 62; January 26, 1998, p. 25; September 28, 1998, p. 37.
Los Angeles Sentinel, September 9, 1998, p. A1.
Los Angeles Times, July 30, 1994, p. F1.
National Review, August 29, 1994, p. 62.
Newsweek, June 9, 1997, p. 74.
New York, July 18, 1994, p. 50-51.
New York Beacon, December 11, 1997, p. 30.
New York Times, May 2, 1997, p. C33; August 17, 1997, sect. 2, p. 27.
People, September 19, 1994, p. 218; January 15, 1996, p. 106; June 16, 1997, p. 87-88; August 18, 1997, p. 17; January 26, 1998, p. 64.
Time, August 1, 1994, p. 52.
USA Today, January 16, 1996, p. D8; August 15, 1997,

p D3.
Village Voice, April 30,1996, p. 47.
Washington Post, April 17, 1999, p. C1.

—Mary Kalfatovic

William Julius WIlson

1935—

Sociologist, educator

William Julius Wilson, a professor at Harvard University's John F. Kennedy School of Government, is one of the top authorities on race and poverty in the United States. Wilson has built his reputation on three controversial and widely-read books: *The Declining Significance of Race* (1978), *The Truly Disadvantaged* (1987) and *When Work Disappears* (1996). According to David Whitman of the *Washington Monthly,* Wilson's academic research has been able to "change almost singlehandedly the national debate over why the urban underclass exists and what can be done about it." Before accepting the position at Harvard in 1996, Wilson taught in the sociology department at the University of Chicago for 25 years. Much of Wilson's groundbreaking academic work was based on research conducted in the poor African American neighborhoods of Chicago—some of them within blocks of the university.

Unlike many scholars, Wilson has been able to make his opinions known outside the world of academia. Politicians across the country, from Chicago mayor Richard M. Daley to President Bill Clinton, have consulted Wilson on issues of race and poverty. While his advice has not always been accepted, Wilson's influence is undeniable. Presi-

dent Clinton, for example, told *Time* magazine that Wilson's books "made me see race and poverty and the problems of the inner city in a different light."

Wilson is also well-known to the general public, having appeared on television news programs many times over the years. In 1996, Wilson was named as one of *Time* magazine's 25 most influential Americans. He was described as "a giant" in *The New York Times,* which published excerpts from *When Work Disappears* in its Sunday magazine. While his political beliefs tend to be left-of-center, Wilson also earns respect from conservatives. John J. Dilulio Jr., writing in *National Review,* described him as "America's most thoughtful and morally forthright liberal social-policy scholar."

Taught at University of Chicago

Wilson was born on December 20, 1935 in Derry Township, Pennsylvania, and raised in Blairsville, Pennsylvania, a working-class community east of Pittsburgh. His father, Esco Wilson, a coal miner, and his mother, Pauline Wilson, had to struggle to support the family. The Wilson

At a Glance . . .

Born William Julius Wilson, Dec. 20, 1935, Derry Township, PA; son of Esco Wilson, a coal miner, and Pauline (Bracy) Wilson; married Mildred Mary Hood, Aug. 31, 1957 (divorced); married Beverly Ann Huebner, Aug. 30, 1970; children: Colleen, Lisa, Carter, Paula. *Education:* Wilberforce University, BA in sociology, 1958; Bowling Green State University, MA in sociology, 1961; Washington State University, PhD in sociology, 1966. *Politics:* Democrat.

Career: University of Massachusetts, assistant professor, 1965-69, associate professor, 1969-71; University of Chicago, visiting associate professor, 1971-72, associate professor, department of sociology, 1972-75, professor, 1975-96, chair, department of sociology, 1978-96, university professor, 1990-96. Harvard University, professor of social policy, (joint appointment with Afro-American studies department), 1996-.

Member: Fellow, American Academy of Arts and Sciences, National Academy of Sciences, Sociological Research Association, International Sociological Association.

Addresses: *Home*—75 Cambridge Parkway, Unit E406, Cambridge, MA 02142. *Office*—John F. Kennedy School of Government, Harvard University, 79 John F. Kennedy St., Cambridge, MA 02138-5801.

home was so small that all six children shared one bedroom. When Wilson was twelve, his father died of lung disease. Much to his mother's chagrin, the family was forced to accept public assistance until she managed to find a job as a housekeeper. "The vegetables in our garden literally kept us from starving," Wilson recalled in an interview with the magazine *Chicago*. "We were desperately poor. But I don't remember being unhappy....We simply had no idea how bad off we were."

As a child, Wilson spent summers with his aunt, Janice Wardlaw, a psychiatric social worker in New York City. Wardlaw had a profound influence on Wilson's early life, taking him to cultural attractions in New York and encouraging him to read. Later, when Wilson won a church scholarship to attend Wilberforce University, a predominantly black school in Wilberforce, Ohio, Wardlaw helped to support him financially. "Aunt Janice made

it clear to me that the only impediments to my doing whatever I wished to do would be of my own making," Wilson was quoted as saying in *Chicago*. Wilson's five brothers and sisters also went on to attend college.

Later in life, some conservatives tried to use Wilson's background to argue that government assistance for the poor was unnecessary. "I become angry when people use my life as some kind of example of how black people should 'make it on their own,'" Wilson was quoted as saying in *Chicago*. "That's absurd. You cannot generalize from my experience. The obstacles those in the inner cities now face are nearly insurmountable."

As a sociology major at Wilberforce, Wilson became interested in urban sociology and the politics of race. He earned a BA in 1958, then spent several years in the army. In 1961, he earned a master's degree in sociology from Bowling Green State University in Bowling Green, Ohio. In 1966, Wilson earned a PhD from Washington State University.

From 1965 until 1971, Wilson taught at the University of Massachusetts at Amherst. In 1970, he was honored with a "Teacher of the Year" distinction from the university. Wilson was offered a position in the sociology department at the University of Chicago in 1971. In an interview with *Chicago* magazine, he recalled that while no one at the University of Massachusetts had ever insinuated that he was hired merely because he was African American, "that was less true when I arrived at the University of Chicago," Wilson remarked. "But the idea that some people were suspicious of black professionals' abilities simply drove me to work even harder. I was determined to prove that I was not only capable, but that I was better than the other scholars there."

Wilson's achievements at the University of Chicago were remarkable. He won tenure in his first year, and was appointed as a full professor in 1975. Three years later, at the age of 42, he became chair of the sociology department. In 1984, he was given the title of distinguished service professor and became a university professor in 1990. The following year, Wilson was elected to the National Academy of Sciences. In the words of Gretchen Reynolds, writing in *Chicago*, the appointment is "perhaps the highest honor available to a U.S. scientist, apart from a Nobel Prize."

Wrote Controversial Books on Race, Poverty

Early in his academic career, Wilson had become disillusioned by the urban sociology that was being produced in the 1960s and 1970s, which he considered to be too partisan. In response, he developed a fact-based approach, relying heavily on statistical analysis to back his claims. His first book, *Power, Racism, and Privilege: Race Relations in Theoretical and Sociohistorical Perspectives,* a comparative study of race relations in the United States and South Africa which appeared in 1973, was based on such methods.

In his next book, Wilson decided to focus on class distinctions within the African American community. *The Declining Significance of Race: Blacks and Changing American Institutions,* published in 1978, would become a landmark work of scholarship. In the book, Wilson argued that social class was becoming more important than race in determining the prospects of African-Americans. For middle-class blacks, Wilson wrote, there were fewer and fewer impediments to success, whereas for very poor black Americans, options were increasingly limited.

Wilson's book infuriated many leaders of civil-rights and liberal policy organizations, who thought it provided ammunition to conservatives who wanted to blame the poor for their own misery. When the American Sociological Association honored the book with a top award, the Association of Black Sociologists protested, claiming that the book misrepresented the African American experience. Although Wilson has described himself in *Time* magazine as "an unashamed liberal," he was labeled a neo-conservative following the book's publication. "Inevitably, he was invited to meet President Reagan," Joe Klein wrote in the *New Republic.* "Horrified, Wilson called the White House and told them that a terrible mistake had been made." "One of the things Wilson identified in *The Declining Significance of Race* was the increasing divergence between the two large groups of blacks, the middle class and the impoverished," sociology professor Elijah Anderson of the University of Pennsylvania recalled in *Chicago.* "That idea is accepted wisdom now. But it was controversial at the time....That insight was threatening to many blacks."

Hurt by the angry, and often personal, criticism of *The Declining Significance of Race,* Wilson took pains in his next book to distance himself from conservative scholars. *The Truly Disadvantaged: The Inner City, The Underclass, and Public Policy* appeared in 1987. In this book, Wilson argued that many middle-class and working-class African Americans had moved out of ghetto neighborhoods, taking with them traditional values. The only solution to this problem, in Wilson's view, would be for the government to implement a major, race-neutral project of social and economic reconstruction for American cities. While *The Truly Disadvantaged* was also controversial, it was well-received by many liberals and moderates, and Wilson

was no longer labeled as a neo-conservative.

During this period, Wilson organized a project called the Urban Poverty and Family Life Study, which would grow into one of the most extensive ethnographic surveys of the urban poor in history. Assisted by a large number of graduate students, Wilson organized interviews with 2,500 poor Chicago residents and 190 area employers. The 21 papers that emerged from the project were presented at a symposium held at the University of Chicago in 1991. On the basis of this extensive study, Wilson secured grant money to establish a permanent organization for poverty research at the University of Chicago. This organization, The Center for the Study of Urban Inequality, was inaugurated in 1993.

Criticized Welfare Reform

Over the years, Wilson has been consulted by Mayor Richard M. Daley of Chicago, Senator Bill Bradley of New Jersey, Senator Paul Simon of Illinois, and Mario Cuomo, governor of New York. In 1992, Wilson was recruited to be an adviser during Bill Clinton's presidential campaign. After winning the election, President Clinton continued to ask for Wilson's advice on public policy decisions—though he has not always followed it. In 1996, Wilson professed to be deeply disappointed when Clinton signed the welfare-reform bill. According to the new rules, virtually all welfare recipients, including children, are entitled to receive only five years of welfare assistance throughout their lifetime. After receiving aid for two years, recipients must find work or lose their benefits.

"Most of the welfare mothers who reach the five-year time limit will be left to sink or swim, and for those in the inner city the situation will be catastrophic," Wilson was quoted as saying in *Time* magazine. "The supply of low-skilled workers compared to the number of jobs that are available is so large that it would take 10 to 15 continuous years of economic expansion to absorb them. We've never had a period of sustained economic growth that has lasted that long." The only way to avert this disaster, in Wilson's view, would be for the government to create jobs, just as it did during the Great Depression in the 1930s.

Wilson's most recent book, *When Work Disappears: The World of the New Urban Poor,* was published in 1996. In the book, Wilson argued that it is chronic, community-wide unemployment that produces deviant behavior in the American ghetto. According to Don Wycliff, writing in *Commonweal,* "in Wilson's telling, the central reality has come to be not just poverty, but mind-numbing, spirit-killing, community-destroying joblessness." The result, according to Wilson, is a set of "cultural traits and behaviors" that trap ghetto residents in poverty. As in hisearlier books, Wilson advocated an extensive, race-neutral program of social reforms, including universal health insurance, and a system of low-wage public jobs to replace welfare.

In 1996, Wilson left the University of Chicago to join Harvard University's prestigious John F. Kennedy School of Government. Wilson's move was newsworthy within the academic community, which viewed it as a coup for Harvard and a profound loss for the University of Chicago. According to David R. Gergen, writing in *U.S. News and World Report,* Wilson became a notable addition to Harvard's "dream team" of African American intellectuals, which also includes Henry Louis Gates and Cornel West. "Never before has so much intellectual firepower been gathered in one place to focus on our most intractable problem: racial inequality," Gergen wrote.

In 1997, Wilson and a team of researchers began a study to track the impact of welfare reform on 4,500 low-income workers and welfare recipients in Boston, Chicago, and Baltimore. The five-year study will determine whether Wilson's predictions of disaster are borne out by the actual experience of the poor, who, in his view, are trying to survive without the advantages he had growing up. "Those of us who have succeeded, those of us in the black middle class, should have, and I believe largely do have, a special sensitivity to the problems and overwhelming difficulties of the black poor today," he was quoted as saying in *Chicago.* "...We cannot simply say, do what we did. They don't have thatoption. So we, as a nation, and those of us who are black, in particular, have a responsibility to help those left behind."

Sources

Periodicals

Chicago, December. 1992, p. 80.
Commentary, November, 1996, p. 58.
Commonweal, November 8, 1996, p. 21.
Essence, February 1997, p. 58.
Journal of the American Planning Association, Spring 1997, p. 285.
National Review, January 27, 1997, p. 53.
New Republic, October 28, 1996, p. 32.
Newsweek, February 19, 1996, p. 64.
Time, September 2, 1996, p. 45; June 17, 1996, p. 56; February 26, 1996, p. 58.
US News and World Report, March 18, 1996, p. 116.
Washington Monthly, November 1996, p. 43.

—Carrie Golus

Cumulative Indexes

Cumulative Nationality Index

Volume numbers appear in **bold.**

Farrakhan, Louis **2, 15**
Fats Domino **20**
Fattah, Chaka **11**
Fauntroy, Walter E. **11**
Fauset, Jessie **7**
Feelings, Tom **11**
Fielder, Cecil **2**
Fields, Cleo **13**
Fishburne, Larry **4, 22**
Fitzgerald, Ella **1, 18**
Flack, Roberta **19**
Frazier, Joe **19**
Frazier, E. Franklin **10**
Freeman, Al, Jr. **11**
Freeman, Charles **19**
Freeman, Morgan **2, 20**
French, Albert **18**
Fudge, Ann **11**
Fulani, Lenora **11**
Fuller, Charles **8**
Fuller, S. B. **13**
Fuller, Solomon Carter, Jr. **15**
Gaines, Ernest J. **7**
Gaither, Alonzo Smith (Jake) **14**
Gantt, Harvey **1**
Garnett, Kevin **14**
Garrison, Zina **2**
Gary, Willie E. **12**
Gaston, Arthur G. **4**
Gates, Henry Louis, Jr. **3**
Gates, Sylvester James, Jr. **15**
Gaye, Marvin **2**
Gayle, Helene D. **3**
George, Nelson **12**
Gibson, Althea **8**
Gibson, Josh **22**
Gibson, Kenneth Allen **6**
Gibson, William F. **6**
Giddings, Paula **11**
Gillespie, Dizzy **1**
Gilliam, Sam **16**
Giovanni, Nikki **9**
Gist, Carole **1**
Givens, Robin **4**
Glover, Danny **1**
Glover, Nathaniel, Jr. **12**
Glover, Savion **14**
Goines, Donald **19**
Goldberg, Whoopi **4**
Golden, Marita **19**
Golden, Thelma **10**
Goldsberry, Ronald **18**
Gomes, Peter J. **15**
Gomez-Preston, Cheryl **9**
Goode, Mal **13**
Goode, W. Wilson **4**
Gooden, Dwight **20**
Gooding, Jr., Cuba **16**
Gordon, Ed **10**
Gordone, Charles **15**
Gordy, Berry, Jr. **1**
Gossett, Louis, Jr. **7**
Gourdine, Simon **11**
Graham, Lawrence Otis **12**
Graham, Stedman **13**
Gravely, Samuel L., Jr. **5**
Graves, Denyce **19**
Graves, Earl G. **1**

Gray, F. Gary **14**
Gray, William H. III **3**
Green, Al **13**
Green, Dennis **5**
Greene, Joe **10**
Greenfield, Eloise **9**
Gregory, Dick **1**
Gregory, Frederick D. **8**
Grier, Pam **9**
Grier, Roosevelt **13**
Griffey, Ken, Jr. **12**
Griffith, Mark Winston **8**
Grimké, Archibald H. **9**
Guillaume, Robert **3**
Guinier, Lani **7**
Gumbel, Bryant **14**
Gumbel, Greg **8**
Gunn, Moses **10**
Guy, Jasmine **2**
Guy, Rosa **5**
Guy-Sheftall, Beverly **13**
Guyton, Tyree **9**
Gwynn, Tony **18**
Hailey, JoJo **22**
Hailey, K-Ci **22**
Hale, Clara **16**
Hale, Lorraine **8**
Haley, Alex **4**
Haley, George Williford Boyce **21**
Hall, Lloyd A. **8**
Hamblin, Ken **10**
Hamer, Fannie Lou **6**
Hamilton, Virginia **10**
Hammer, M. C. **20**
Hampton, Fred **18**
Hampton, Henry **6**
Hampton, Lionel **17**
Hancock, Herbie **20**
Handy, W. C. **8**
Hannah, Marc **10**
Hansberry, Lorraine **6**
Hansberry, William Leo **11**
Hardaway, Anfernee (Penny) **13**
Hardison, Bethann **12**
Hardison, Kadeem **22**
Harkless, Necia Desiree **19**
Harper, Frances Ellen Watkins **11**
Harrell, Andre **9**
Harrington, Oliver W. **9**
Harris, Alice **7**
Harris, Barbara **12**
Harris, E. Lynn **12**
Harris, Eddy L. **18**
Harris, Jay T. **19**
Harris, Leslie **6**
Harris, Marcelite Jordan **16**
Harris, Monica **18**
Harris, Patricia Roberts **2**
Harris, Robin **7**
Harsh, Vivian Gordon **14**
Harvard, Beverly **11**
Harvey, Steve **18**
Hastie, William H. **8**
Hastings, Alcee L. **16**
Hathaway, Donny **18**
Hawkins, Coleman **9**
Hawkins, Erskine **14**
Hawkins, La-Van **17**

Hawkins, Steven **14**
Hawkins, Tramaine **16**
Hayden, Palmer **13**
Hayden, Robert **12**
Hayes, Isaac 20
Hayes, James C. **10**
Hayes, Roland **4**
Haynes, George Edmund **8**
Haynes, Marques **22**
Hedgeman, Anna Arnold **22**
Height, Dorothy I. **2**
Hemsley, Sherman **19**
Hemphill, Essex **10**
Henderson, Gordon **5**
Henderson, Wade J. **14**
Hendricks, Barbara **3**
Hendrix, Jimi **10**
Henson, Matthew **2**
Henry, Aaron **19**
Henson, Matthew **2**
Herman, Alexis M. **15**
Hernandez, Aileen Clarke **13**
Hickman, Fred **11**
Higginbotham, A. Leon, Jr. **13**
Hightower, Dennis F. **13**
Hill, Anita **5**
Hill, Bonnie Guiton **20**
Hill, Calvin **19**
Hill, Grant **13**
Hill, Janet **19**
Hill, Jessie, Jr. **13**
Hill, Lauryn **20**
Hilliard, David **7**
Himes, Chester **8**
Hinderas, Natalie **5**
Hines, Gregory **1**
Hinton, William Augustus **8**
Holder, Eric H., Jr. **9**
Holiday, Billie **1**
Holland, Endesha Ida Mae **3**
Holland, Robert, Jr. **11**
Holmes, Larry **20**
Holyfield, Evander **6**
hooks, bell **5**
Hooks, Benjamin L. **2**
Hope, John **8**
Horne, Lena **5**
House, Son **8**
Houston, Charles Hamilton **4**
Houston, Cissy **20**
Houston, Whitney **7**
Howard, Desmond **16**
Howard, Juwan **15**
Howlin' Wolf **9**
Hrabowski, Freeman A., III **22**
Hudlin, Reginald **9**
Hudlin, Warrington **9**
Hudson, Cheryl **15**
Hudson, Wade **15**
Huggins, Larry **21**
Hughes, Albert **7**
Hughes, Allen **7**
Hughes, Langston **4**
Humphrey, Bobbi **20**
Humphries, Frederick **20**
Hunt, Richard **6**
Hunter, Billy **22**
Hunter-Gault, Charlayne **6**

Cumulative Occupation Index

Volume numbers appear in **bold**.

Art and design

Allen, Tina **22**
Andrews, Benny **22**
Andrews, Bert **13**
Armstrong, Robb **15**
Bailey, Radcliffe **19**
Bailey, Xenobia **11**
Barboza, Anthony **10**
Barnes, Ernie **16**
Barthe, Richmond **15**
Basquiat, Jean-Michel **5**
Bearden, Romare **2**
Biggers, John **20**
Brandon, Barbara **3**
Brown, Donald **19**
Burke, Selma **16**
Burroughs, Margaret Taylor **9**
Camp, Kimberly **19**
Campbell, E. Simms **13**
Catlett, Elizabeth **2**
Chase-Riboud, Barbara **20**
Cowans, Adger W. **20**
Delaney, Beauford **19**
Douglas, Aaron **7**
Driskell, David C. **7**
Edwards, Melvin **22**
Ewing, Patrick A.**17**
Feelings, Tom **11**
Gantt, Harvey **1**
Gilliam, Sam **16**
Golden, Thelma **10**
Guyton, Tyree **9**
Harkless, Necia Desiree **19**
Harrington, Oliver W. **9**
Hayden, Palmer **13**
Hope, John **8**
Hudson, Cheryl **15**
Hudson, Wade **15**
Hunt, Richard **6**
Hutson, Jean Blackwell **16**
Johnson, William Henry **3**
Jones, Lois Mailou **13**
Lawrence, Jacob **4**
Lee, Annie Francis **22**
Lee-Smith, Hughie **5, 22**
Lewis, Edmonia **10**
McGee, Charles **10**
Mitchell, Corinne **8**
Morrison, Keith **13**
Moutoussamy-Ashe, Jeanne **7**
N'Namdi, George R. **17**

Pierre, Andre **17**
Pinkney, Jerry **15**
Pippin, Horace **9**
Porter, James A. **11**
Ringgold, Faith **4**
Saar, Alison **16**
Saint James, Synthia **12**
Sanders, Joseph R., Jr. **11**
Savage, Augusta **12**
Serrano, Andres **3**
Shabazz, Attallah **6**
Simpson, Lorna **4**
Sleet, Moneta, Jr. **5**
Tanner, Henry Ossawa **1**
Thomas, Alma **14**
Tolliver, William **9**
VanDerZee, James **6**
Walker, A'lelia **14**
Walker, Kara **16**
Wells, James Lesesne **10**
Williams, Billy Dee **8**
Williams, O. S. **13**
Williams, Paul R. **9**
Williams, William T. **11**
Woodruff, Hale **9**

Business

Abdul-Jabbar, Kareem **8**
Ailey, Alvin **8**
Al-Amin, Jamil Abdullah **6**
Alexander, Archie Alphonso **14**
Amos, Wally **9**
Avant, Clarence **19**
Baker, Dusty **8**
Baker, Ella **5**
Baker, Gwendolyn Calvert **9**
Banks, Jeffrey **17**
Banks, William **11**
Barden, Don H. **9, 20**
Barrett, Andrew C. **12**
Bennett, Lerone, Jr. **5**
Bing, Dave **3**
Borders, James **9**
Boyd, John W., Jr. **20**
Boyd, T. B., III **6**
Brimmer, Andrew F. **2**
Brown, Les **5**
Brown, Marie Dutton **12**
Brunson, Dorothy **1**
Burrell, Thomas J. **21**
Burroughs, Margaret Taylor **9**

Busby, Jheryl **3**
Cain, Herman **15**
CasSelle, Malcolm **11**
Chamberlain, Wilt **18**
Chapman, Jr., Nathan A. **21**
Chappell, Emma **18**
Chenault, Kenneth I. **4**
Clark, Celeste **15**
Clark, Patrick **14**
Clay, William Lacy **8**
Clayton, Xernona **3**
Cobbs, Price M. **9**
Colbert, Virgis William **17**
Connerly, Ward **14**
Cornelius, Don **4**
Cosby, Bill **7**
Cottrell, Comer **11**
Delany, Bessie **12**
Delany, Sadie **12**
Divine, Father **7**
Dre, Dr. **14**
Driver, David E. **11**
Ducksworth, Marilyn **12**
Edelin, Ramona Hoage **19**
Edmonds, Tracey **16**
Elder, Lee **6**
Ellington, E. David **11**
Evans, Darryl **22**
Evers, Myrlie **8**
Farmer, Forest J. **1**
Farrakhan, Louis **15**
Fauntroy, Walter E. **11**
Fletcher, Alphonse, Jr. **16**
Franklin, Hardy R. **9**
Fudge, Ann **11**
Fuller, S. B. **13**
Gaston, Arthur G. **4**
Gibson, Kenneth Allen **6**
Goldsberry, Ronald **18**
Gordon, Pamela **17**
Gordy, Berry, Jr. **1**
Graham, Stedman **13**
Graves, Earl G. **1**
Griffith, Mark Winston **8**
Hale, Lorraine **8**
Hamer, Fannie Lou **6**
Hammer, M. C. **20**
Handy, W. C. **8**
Hannah, Marc **10**
Hardison, Bethann **12**
Harrell, Andre **9**

Townsend, Robert 4
Tucker, Chris 13
Turner, Tina 6
Tyson, Cicely 7
Underwood, Blair 7
Van Peebles, Mario 2
Van Peebles, Melvin 7
Vance, Courtney B. 15
Vereen, Ben 4
Warfield, Marsha 2
Warner, Malcolm-Jamal 22
Warwick, Dionne 18
Washington, Denzel 1, 16
Washington, Fredi 10
Waters, Ethel 7
Wayans, Damon 8
Wayans, Keenen Ivory 18
Weathers, Carl 10
Webb, Veronica 10
Whitaker, Forest 2
Whitfield, Lynn 18
Williams, Billy Dee 8
Williams, Samm-Art 21
Williams, Vanessa L. 4, 17
Williamson, Mykelti 22
Winfield, Paul 2
Winfrey, Oprah 2, 15
Woodard, Alfre 9
Yoba, Malik 11

**Government and politics—
    international**
Abacha, Sani 11
Abbott, Diane 9
Achebe, Chinua 6
Ali Mahdi Mohamed 5
Annan, Kofi Atta 15
Aristide, Jean-Bertrand 6
Azikiwe, Nnamdi 13
Babangida, Ibrahim 4
Baker, Gwendolyn Calvert 9
Banda, Hastings Kamuzu 6
Bedie, Henri Konan 21
Berry, Mary Frances 7
Biko, Steven 4
Bizimungu, Pasteur 19
Bongo, Omar 1
Bunche, Ralph J. 5
Buthelezi, Mangosuthu Gatsha 9
Charlemagne, Manno 11
Charles, Mary Eugenia 10
Chissano, Joaquim 7
Christophe, Henri 9
Conté, Lansana 7
da Silva, Benedita 5
Diop, Cheikh Anta 4
Diouf, Abdou 3
Eyadéma, Gnassingbé 7
Fela 1
Gordon, Pamela 17
Habré, Hissène 6
Habyarimana, Juvenal 8
Haile Selassie 7
Haley, George Williford Boyce 21
Hani, Chris 6
Houphouët-Boigny, Félix 4
Ingraham, Hubert A. 19
Jagan, Cheddi 16

Jawara, Sir Dawda Kairaba 11
Kabila, Laurent 20
Kabunda, Kenneth 2
Kenyatta, Jomo 5
Kerekou, Ahmed (Mathieu) 1
Liberia-Peters, Maria Philomena
    12
Luthuli, Albert 13
Mabuza, Lindiwe 18
Machel, Samora Moises 8
Mandela, Nelson 1, 14
Mandela, Winnie 2
Masekela, Barbara 18
Masire, Quett 5
Mbeki, Thabo Mvuyelwa 14
Mbuende, Kaire 12
Meles Zenawi 3
Mkapa, Benjamin 16
Mobutu Sese Seko 1
Mogae, Festus Gontebanye 19
Moi, Daniel 1
Mongella, Gertrude 11
Mugabe, Robert Gabriel 10
Muluzi, Bakili 14
Museveni, Yoweri 4
Mwinyi, Ali Hassan 1
Ndadaye, Melchior 7
Nkomo, Joshua 4
Nkrumah, Kwame 3
Ntaryamira, Cyprien 8
Nujoma, Samuel 10
Nyanda, Siphiwe 21
Nyerere, Julius 5
Nzo, Alfred 15
Obasanjo, Olusegun 5, 22
Pascal-Trouillot, Ertha 3
Patterson, P. J. 6, 20
Perkins, Edward 5
Perry, Ruth 15
Pitt, David Thomas 10
Pitta, Celso 17
Ramaphosa, Cyril 3
Rawlings, Jerry 9
Rawlings, Nana Konadu Agyeman
    13
Rice, Condoleezza 3
Robinson, Randall 7
Sampson, Edith S. 4
Sankara, Thomas 17
Savimbi, Jonas 2
Sawyer, Amos 2
Senghor, Léopold Sédar 12
Smith, Jennifer 21
Soglo, Nicephore 15
Soyinka, Wole 4
Taylor, Charles 20
Taylor, John (David Beckett) 16
Toure, Amadou Toumani 18
Touré, Sekou 6
Tutu, Desmond 6
Vieira, Joao 14
Wharton, Clifton R., Jr. 7

Government and politics—U.S.
Adams, Floyd, Jr. 12
Alexander, Archie Alphonso 14
Ali, Muhammad 2, 16
Allen, Ethel D. 13

Archer, Dennis 7
Avant, Clarence 19
Baker, Thurbert 22
Barden, Don H. 9, 20
Barrett, Andrew C. 12
Barry, Marion S. 7
Belton, Sharon Sayles 9, 16
Berry, Mary Frances 7
Bethune, Mary McLeod 4
Blackwell, Unita 17
Bond, Julian 2
Bosley, Freeman, Jr. 7
Boykin, Keith 14
Bradley, Thomas 2
Braun, Carol Moseley 4
Brimmer, Andrew F. 2
Brooke, Edward 8
Brown, Elaine 8
Brown, Jesse 6
Brown, Les 5
Brown, Ron 5
Brown, Willie L., Jr. 7
Bryant, Wayne R. 6
Bunche, Ralph J. 5
Burris, Chuck 21
Caesar, Shirley 19
Campbell, Bill 9
Chavis, Benjamin 6
Chisholm, Shirley 2
Christian-Green, Donna M. 17
Clay, William Lacy 8
Clayton, Eva M. 20
Cleaver, Eldridge 5
Cleaver, Emanuel 4
Clyburn, James 21
Collins, Barbara-Rose 7
Collins, Cardiss 10
Connerly, Ward 14
Conyers, John, Jr. 4
Cose, Ellis 5
Crockett, George, Jr. 10
Currie, Betty 21
Davis, Angela 5
Davis, Benjamin O., Jr. 2
Davis, Benjamin O., Sr. 4
Days, Drew S., III 10
Dellums, Ronald 2
Diggs, Charles R. 21
Dinkins, David 4
Dixon, Sharon Pratt 1
Du Bois, W. E. B. 3
Edmonds, Terry 17
Elders, Joycelyn 6
Espy, Mike 6
Farmer, James 2
Farrakhan, Louis 2
Fattah, Chaka 11
Fauntroy, Walter E. 11
Fields, Cleo 13
Flake, Floyd H. 18
Flipper, Henry O. 3
Fortune, T. Thomas 6
Franks, Gary 2
Fulani, Lenora 11
Gantt, Harvey 1
Garvey, Marcus 1
Gibson, Kenneth Allen 6
Gibson, William F. 6

Ramsey, Charles H. **21**
Richie, Leroy C. **18**
Robinson, Randall **7**
Russell-McCloud, Patricia **17**
Sampson, Edith S. **4**
Schmoke, Kurt **1**
Sears-Collins, Leah J. **5**
Stokes, Carl B. **10**
Stokes, Louis **3**
Taylor, John (David Beckett) **16**
Thomas, Clarence **2**
Thomas, Franklin A. **5**
Vanzant, Iyanla **17**
Wagner, Annice **22**
Washington, Harold **6**
Wilder, L. Douglas **3**
Wilkins, Roger **2**
Williams, Evelyn **10**
Williams, Gregory **11**
Williams, Patricia J. **11**
Williams, Willie L. **4**
Wright, Bruce McMarion **3**

Military
Abacha, Sani **11**
Adams Early, Charity **13**
Alexander, Margaret Walker **22**
Babangida, Ibrahim **4**
Bolden, Charles F., Jr. **7**
Brown, Jesse **6**
Bullard, Eugene **12**
Cadoria, Sherian Grace **14**
Chissano, Joaquim **7**
Christophe, Henri **9**
Conté, Lansana **7**
Davis, Benjamin O., Sr. **4**
Davis, Benjamin O., Jr. **2**
Europe, James Reese **10**
Eyadéma, Gnassingbé **7**
Flipper, Henry O. **3**
Gravely, Samuel L., Jr. **5**
Gregory, Frederick D. **8**
Habré, Hissène **6**
Habyarimana, Juvenal **8**
Harris, Marcelite Jordan **16**
James, Daniel, Jr. **16**
Johnson, Hazel **22**
Kerekou, Ahmed (Mathieu) **1**
Lawrence, Robert H., Jr. **16**
Nyanda, Siphiwe **21**
Obasanjo, Olusegun **5, 22**
Powell, Colin **1**
Pratt, Geronimo **18**
Rawlings, Jerry **9**
Reason, J. Paul **19**
Stanford, John **20**
Staupers, Mabel K. **7**
Stokes, Louis **3**
Touré, Amadou Toumani **18**
Vieira, Joao **14**
Von Lipsey, Roderick K. **11**
Watkins, Perry **12**
West, Togo, D., Jr. **16**

Music
Adams, Oleta **18**
Adams, Yolanda **17**
Anderson, Marian **2**

Armstrong, Louis **2**
Ashford, Nickolas **21**
Avant, Clarence **19**
Ayers, Roy **16**
Badu, Erykah **22**
Baker, Anita **21**
Baker, Josephine **3**
Bechet, Sidney **18**
Belafonte, Harry **4**
Belle, Regina **1**
Blige, Mary J. **20**
Bonga, Kuenda **13**
Brandy **14**
Braxton, Toni **15**
Brooks, Avery **9**
Bumbry, Grace **5**
Busby, Jheryl **3**
Caesar, Shirley **19**
Calloway, Cab **1**
Campbell, Tisha **8**
Carroll, Diahann **9**
Carter, Betty **19**
Charlemagne, Manno **11**
Charles, Ray **16**
Cheatham, Doc **17**
Chuck D **9**
Clark-Sheard, Karen **22**
Cleveland, James **19**
Clinton, George **9**
Cole, Nat King **17**
Cole, Natalie Maria **17**
Collins, Albert **12**
Coltrane, John **19**
Combs, Sean "Puffy" **17**
Cooke, Sam **17**
Crawford, Randy **19**
Crothers, Scatman **19**
Crouch, Stanley **11**
Crowder, Henry **16**
Davis, Anthony **11**
Davis, Miles **4**
Davis, Sammy, Jr. **18**
Dixon, Willie **4**
Donegan, Dorothy **19**
Dorsey, Thomas **15**
Downing, Will **19**
Dr. Dre **10**
Dre, Dr. **14**
Duke, George **21**
Dupri, Jermaine **13**
Edmonds, Kenneth "Babyface" **10**
Edmonds, Tracey **16**
Ellington, Duke **5**
Eubanks, Kevin **15**
Europe, James Reese **10**
Evans, Faith **22**
Evora, Cesaria **12**
Fats Domino **20**
Fela **1**
Fitzgerald, Ella **8, 18**
Flack, Roberta **19**
Foxx, Jamie **15**
Franklin, Aretha **11**
Franklin, Kirk **15**
Gaye, Marvin **2**
Gibson, Althea **8**
Gillespie, Dizzy **1**
Gordy, Berry, Jr. **1**

Graves, Denyce **19**
Gray, F. Gary **14**
Green, Al **13**
Hailey, JoJo **22**
Hailey, K-Ci **22**
Hammer, M. C. **20**
Hampton, Lionel **17**
Hancock, Herbie **20**
Handy, W. C. **8**
Harrell, Andre **9**
Hathaway, Donny **18**
Hawkins, Coleman **9**
Hawkins, Erskine **14**
Hawkins, Tramaine **16**
Hayes, Isaac **20**
Hayes, Roland **4**
Hendricks, Barbara **3**
Hendrix, Jimi **10**
Hill, Lauryn **20**
Hinderas, Natalie **5**
Holiday, Billie **1**
Horne, Lena **5**
House, Son **8**
Houston, Whitney **7**
Houston, Cissy **20**
Howlin' Wolf **9**
Humphrey, Bobbi **20**
Hyman, Phyllis **19**
Ice Cube **8**
Ice-T **6**
Jackson, George **19**
Jackson, Isaiah **3**
Jackson, Janet **6**
Jackson, Mahalia **5**
Jackson, Michael **19**
James, Etta **13**
James, Rick **17**
Jean, Wyclef
Jean-Baptiste, Marianne **17**
Jarreau, Al **21**
Jenkins, Ella **15**
Jimmy Jam **13**
Johnson, Beverly **2**
Johnson, James Weldon **5**
Johnson, Robert **2**
Jones, Bobby **20**
Jones, Elvin **14**
Jones, Quincy **8**
Joplin, Scott **6**
Joyner, Matilda Sissieretta **15**
Joyner, Tom **19**
Kelly, R. **18**
Kendricks, Eddie **22**
Khan, Chaka **12**
King, B. B. **7**
King, Coretta Scott **3**
Kitt, Eartha **16**
Knight, Gladys **16**
Knight, Suge **11**
Kravitz, Lenny **10**
L.L. Cool J **16**
LaBelle, Patti **13**
León, Tania **13**
Lester, Julius **9**
Levert, Gerald **22**
Lewis, Terry **13**
Lincoln, Abbey **3**
Little Richard **15**

Miller, Cheryl 10
Moon, Warren 8
Moorer, Michael 19
Morgan, Joe Leonard 9
Moses, Edwin 8
Mourning, Alonzo 17
Murray, Eddie 12
Murray, Lenda 10
Mutola, Maria 12
Mutombo, Dikembe 7
Noah, Yannick 4
Olajuwon, Hakeem 2
O'Neal, Shaquille 8
O'Neil, Buck 19
O'Ree, Willie 5
Owens, Jesse 2
Pace, Orlando 21
Page, Alan 7
Paige, Satchel 7
Patterson, Floyd 19
Payton, Walter 11
Peete, Calvin 11
Pelé 7
Pickett, Bill 11
Pippen, Scottie 15
Powell, Mike 7
Puckett, Kirby 4
Quirot, Ana 13
Rashad, Ahmad 18
Rhodes, Ray 14
Ribbs, Willy T. 2
Rice, Jerry 5
Richardson, Nolan 9
Richmond, Mitch 19
Robinson, Eddie G. 10
Robinson, Frank 9
Robinson, Jackie 6
Robinson, Sugar Ray 18
Rodman, Dennis 12
Rudolph, Wilma 4
Russell, Bill 8
Sampson, Charles 13
Sanders, Barry 1
Sanders, Deion 4
Scott, Wendell Oliver, Sr. 19
Sheffield, Gary 16
Shell, Art 1
Sifford, Charlie 4
Simpson, O. J. 15
Singletary, Mike 4
Smith, Emmitt 7
Smith, Tubby 18
Sosa, Sammy 21
Steward, Emanuel 18
Stewart, Kordell 21
Stone, Toni 15
Strawberry, Darryl 22
Stringer, C. Vivian 13
Swoopes, Sheryl 12
Thomas, Frank 12
Thomas, Isiah 7
Thugwane, Josia 21
Upshaw, Gene 18
Walker, Herschel 1
Washington, MaliVai 8
Watts, J. C., Jr. 14
Weathers, Carl 10
Webber, Chris 15

Westbrook, Peter 20
Whitaker, Pernell 10
White, Bill 1
White, Jesse 22
White, Reggie 6
Wilkens, Lenny 11
Williams, Doug 22
Williams, Serena 20
Williams, Venus Ebone 17
Wilson, Sunnie 7
Winfield, Dave 5
Woods, Tiger 14

Television
Allen, Byron 3
Allen, Debbie 13
Allen, Marcus 20
Amos, John 8
Arkadie, Kevin 17
Banks, William 11
Barden, Don H. 9
Bassett, Angela 6
Beaton, Norman 14
Belafonte, Harry 4
Bellamy, Bill 12
Berry, Bertice 8
Berry, Halle 4, 19
Bowser, Yvette Lee 17
Bradley, Ed 2
Brandy 14
Braugher, Andre 13
Brooks, Avery 9
Brown, James 22
Brown, Les 5
Brown, Tony 3
Burnett, Charles 16
Burton, LeVar 8
Byrd, Robert 11
Campbell, Tisha 8
Carroll, Diahann 9
Carson, Lisa Nicole 21
Cheadle, Don 19
Chideya, Farai 14
Christian, Spencer 15
Clash, Kevin 14
Clayton, Xernona 3
Cole, Nat King 17
Cole, Natalie Maria 17
Cornelius, Don 4
Cosby, Bill 7
Crothers, Scatman 19
Curry, Mark 17
Curtis-Hall, Vondie 17
Davidson, Tommy 21
Davis, Ossie 5
Dee, Ruby 8
Dickerson, Ernest 6
Dr. Dre 10
Duke, Bill 3
Dutton, Charles S. 4, 22
Erving, Julius 18
Esposito, Giancarlo 9
Eubanks, Kevin 15
Fishburne, Larry 4
Foxx, Jamie 15
Foxx, Redd 2
Freeman, Al, Jr. 11
Freeman, Morgan 2

Gaines, Ernest J. 7
Givens, Robin 4
Glover, Savion 14
Goldberg, Whoopi 4
Goode, Mal 13
Gooding, Cuba, Jr. 16
Gordon, Ed 10
Gossett, Louis, Jr. 7
Grier, Pam 9
Guillaume, Robert 3
Gumbel, Bryant 14
Gumbel, Greg 8
Gunn, Moses 10
Guy, Jasmine 2
Haley, Alex 4
Hampton, Henry 6
Hardison, Kadeem 22
Harrell, Andre 9
Harris, Robin 7
Harvey, Steve 18
Hayes, Isaac 20
Hemsley, Sherman 19
Henry, Lenny 9
Hickman, Fred 11
Hill, Lauryn 20
Hinderas, Natalie 5
Horne, Lena 5
Hounsou, Djimon 19
Hunter-Gault, Charlayne 6
Iman 4
Ingram, Rex 5
Jackson, George 19
Jackson, Janet 6
Jackson, Jesse 1
Joe, Yolanda 21
Johnson, Beverly 2
Johnson, Robert L. 3
Jones, Bobby 20
Jones, James Earl 3
Jones, Quincy 8
Jones, Star 10
King, Gayle 19
King, Regina 22
Kirby, George 14
Kitt, Eartha 16
Knight, Gladys 16
Kotto, Yaphet 7
L.L. Cool J 16
LaBelle, Patti 13
La Salle, Eriq 12
Langhart, Janet 19
Lawrence, Martin 6
Lawson, Jennifer 1
Lemmons, Kasi 20
Lewis, Byron E. 13
Lindo, Delroy 18
Long, Nia 17
Lover, Ed 10
McDaniel, Hattie 5
McEwen, Mark 5
McQueen, Butterfly 6
McKee, Lonette 12
Miller, Cheryl 10
Mitchell, Brian Stokes 21
Mitchell, Russ 21
Moore, Melba 21
Moore, Shemar 21
Morgan, Joe Leonard 9

Cumulative Subject Index

Volume numbers appear in **bold.**

Briscoe, Connie **15**
Brooks, Gwendolyn **1**
Burroughs, Margaret Taylor **9**
Campbell, Bebe Moore **6**
Cary, Lorene **3**
Childress, Alice **15**
Cleage, Pearl **17**
Cullen, Countee **8**
Dickey, Eric Jerome **21**
Dove, Rita **6**
Du Bois, W. E. B. **3**
Dunbar, Paul Laurence **8**
Ellison, Ralph **7**
Fauset, Jessie **7**
Feelings, Tom **11**
Fisher, Rudolph **17**
Fuller, Charles **8**
Gaines, Ernest J. **7**
Gates, Henry Louis, Jr. **3**
Giddings, Paula **11**
Giovanni, Nikki **9**
Goines, Donald **19**
Joe, Yolanda **21**
Little, Benilde **21**
Golden, Marita **19**
Guy, Rosa **5**
Haley, Alex **4**
Hansberry, Lorraine **6**
Harper, Frances Ellen Watkins **11**
Himes, Chester **8**
Holland, Endesha Ida Mae **3**
Hughes, Langston **4**
Hurston, Zora Neale **3**
Iceberg Slim **11**
Johnson, Charles **1**
Johnson, James Weldon **5**
Jordan, June **7**
Larsen, Nella **10**
Lester, Julius **9**
Lorde, Audre **6**
Madhubuti, Haki R. **7**
Major, Clarence **9**
Marshall, Paule **7**
McKay, Claude **6**
McKay, Nellie Yvonne **17**
McMillan, Terry **4, 17**
Morrison, Toni **2, 15**
Mowry, Jess **7**
Naylor, Gloria **10**
Petry, Ann **19**
Pinkney, Jerry **15**
Randall, Dudley **8**
Reed, Ishmael **8**
Ringgold, Faith **4**
Sanchez, Sonia **17**
Schomburg, Arthur Alfonso **9**
Shange, Ntozake **8**
Thurman, Wallace **16**
Toomer, Jean **6**
Tyree, Omar Rashad **21**
Van Peebles, Melvin **7**
Walker, Alice **1**
Wesley, Valerie Wilson **18**
Wideman, John Edgar **5**
Wilson, August **7**
Wolfe, George C. **6**
Wright, Richard **5**

African dance
Ailey, Alvin **8**
Fagan, Garth **18**
Primus, Pearl **6**

African folk music
Makeba, Miriam **2**
Nascimento, Milton **2**

African history
Chase-Riboud, Barbara **20**
Clarke, John Henrik **20**
Diop, Cheikh Anta **4**
Dodson, Howard, Jr. **7**
DuBois, Shirley Graham **21**
Hansberry, William Leo **11**
Harkless, Necia Desiree **19**
Jawara, Sir Dawda Kairaba **11**
Madhubuti, Haki R. **7**
Marshall, Paule **7**

**African Methodist Episcopal
Church (AME)**
Flake, Floyd H. **18**
Murray, Cecil **12**
Turner, Henry McNeal **5**
Youngblood, Johnny Ray **8**

**African National Congress
(ANC)**
Baker, Ella **5**
Hani, Chris **6**
Kaunda, Kenneth **2**
Luthuli, Albert **13**
Mandela, Nelson **1, 14**
Mandela, Winnie **2**
Masekela, Barbara **18**
Mbeki, Thabo Mvuyelwa **14**
Nkomo, Joshua **4**
Nyanda, Siphiwe **21**
Nzo, Alfred **15**
Ramaphosa, Cyril **3**
Tutu, Desmond **6**

**African Women on Tour
conference**
Taylor, Susan L. **10**

Afro-American League
Fortune, T. Thomas **6**

Afrocentricity
Asante, Molefi Kete **3**
Biggers, John **20**
Diop, Cheikh Anta **4**
Hansberry, Lorraine **6**
Hansberry, William Leo **11**
Sanchez, Sonia **17**
Turner, Henry McNeal **5**

**Agency for International
Development (AID)**
Gayle, Helene D. **3**
Perkins, Edward **5**
Wilkins, Roger **2**

**A. G. Gaston Boys and Girls
Club**
Gaston, Arthur G. **4**

A. G. Gaston Motel
Gaston, Arthur G. **4**

**Agricultural Development
Council (ADC)**
Wharton, Clifton R., Jr. **7**

Agriculture
Boyd, John W., Jr. **20**
Carver, George Washington **4**
Espy, Mike **6**
Hall, Lloyd A. **8**
Masire, Quett **5**
Obasanjo, Olusegun **5**
Sanders, Dori **8**

AHA
See American Heart Association

AID
See Agency for International
Development

AIDS
See Acquired Immune Deficiency
Syndrome

**AIDS Coalition to Unleash
Power (ACT UP)**
Norman, Pat **10**

AIDS Health Care Foundation
Wilson, Phill **9**

AIDS Prevention Team
Wilson, Phill **9**

AIDS research
Mboup, Souleymane **10**

AIM
See Adventures in Movement

ALA
See American Library Association

Alcoholics Anonymous (AA)
Hilliard, David **7**
Lucas, John **7**

**All Afrikan People's Revolu
tionary   Party**
Carmichael, Stokely **5**
Moses, Robert Parris **11**

Alliance Theatre
Leon, Kenny **10**

Alpha & Omega Ministry
White, Reggie **6**

**Alvin Ailey American Dance
Theater**
Ailey, Alvin **8**

McKissick, Floyd B. **3**
Stone, Chuck **9**

Blackside, Inc.
Hampton, Henry **6**

Black theology
Cone, James H. **3**

"Blood for Britain"
Drew, Charles Richard **7**

Blessed Martin House
Riley, Helen Caldwell Day **13**

**Blood plasma research/preserva
tion**
Drew, Charles Richard **7**

Blues
Collins, Albert **12**
Dixon, Willie **4**
Dorsey, Thomas **15**
Evora, Cesaria **12**
Handy, W. C. **8**
Holiday, Billie **1**
House, Son **8**
Howlin' Wolf **9**
Jean-Baptiste, Marianne **17**
King, B. B. **7**
Muse, Clarence Edouard **21**
Parker, Charlie **20**
Reese, Della **6, 20**
Smith, Bessie **3**
Sykes, Roosevelt **20**
Wallace, Sippie **1**
Washington, Dinah **22**
Waters, Ethel **7**
Watson, Johnny "Guitar" **18**
Williams, Joe **5**
Wilson, August **7**

Blues Heaven Foundation
Dixon, Willie **4**

Blues vernacular
Baker, Houston A., Jr. **6**

Bobsledding
Moses, Edwin **8**

Bodybuilding
Murray, Lenda **10**

**Booker T. Washington Business
College**
Gaston, Arthur G. **4**

**Booker T. Washington Insur
ance Company**
Gaston, Arthur G. **4**

Boston Bruins hockey team
O'Ree, Willie **5**

Boston Celtics basketball team
Russell, Bill **8**

Boston Red Sox baseball team
Baylor, Don **6**
Vaughn, Mo **16**

Botany
Carver, George Washington **4**

**Botswana Democratic Party
(BDP)**
Masire, Quett **5**
Mogae, Festus Gontebanye **19**

Boxing
Ali, Muhammad **2, 16**
Bowe, Riddick **6**
Foreman, George **1, 15**
Frazier, Joe **19**
Holmes, Larry **20**
Holyfield, Evander **6**
Johnson, Jack **8**
Jones, Roy Jr. **22**
King, Don **14**
Lee, Canada **8**
Leonard, Sugar Ray **15**
Louis, Joe **5**
Moorer, Michael **19**
Patterson, Floyd **19**
Robinson, Sugar Ray **18**
Steward, Emanuel **18**
Whitaker, Pernell **10**

Boys Choir of Harlem
Turnbull, Walter **13**

BPP
See Black Panther Party

Brazilian Congress
da Silva, Benedita **5**

**Breast Cancer Resource
Committee**
Brown, Zora Kramer **12**

British House of Commons
Abbott, Diane **9**
Pitt, David Thomas **10**

British House of Lords
Pitt, David Thomas **10**

British Parliament
See British House of Commons

Broadcasting
Allen, Byron **3**
Ashley, Maurice **15**
Banks, William **11**
Barden, Don H. **9, 20**
Bradley, Ed **2**
Brown, Les **5**
Brown, Tony **3**
Brunson, Dorothy **1**
Clayton, Xernona **3**
Cornelius, Don **4**
Davis, Ossie **5**
Goode, Mal **13**
Gumbel, Bryant **14**

Gumbel, Greg **8**
Hamblin, Ken **10**
Hickman, Fred **11**
Hunter-Gault, Charlayne **6**
Johnson, Robert L. **3**
Jones, Bobby **20**
Jones, Star **10**
Joyner, Tom **19**
Langhart, Janet **19**
Lawson, Jennifer **1**
Lewis, Delano **7**
Madison, Joseph E. **17**
McEwen, Mark **5**
Miller, Cheryl **10**
Mitchell, Russ **21**
Morgan, Joe Leonard **9**
Roberts, Robin **16**
Robinson, Max **3**
Rodgers, Johnathan **6**
Russell, Bill **8**
Shaw, Bernard **2**
Simpson, Carole **6**
Simpson, O. J. **15**
Smiley, Tavis **20**
Stewart, Alison **13**
Stokes, Carl B. **10**
Watts, Rolonda **9**
White, Bill **1**
Williams, Montel **4**
Winfrey, Oprah **2, 15**

Broadside Press
Randall, Dudley **8**

Brooklyn Academy of Music
Miller, Bebe **3**

Brooklyn Dodgers baseball team
Robinson, Jackie **6**

**Brotherhood of Sleeping Car
Porters**
Randolph, A. Philip **3**
Tucker, Rosina **14**

***Brown v. Board of Education of
Topeka***
Bell, Derrick **6**
Clark, Kenneth B. **5**
Franklin, John Hope **5**
Houston, Charles Hamilton **4**
Marshall, Thurgood **1**
Motley, Constance Baker **10**
Robinson, Spottswood W., III **22**

Buffalo Bills football team
Simpson, O. J. **15**

Bull-riding
Sampson, Charles **13**

Busing (anti-busing legislation)
Bosley, Freeman, Jr. **7**

Cabinet
See U.S. Cabinet

Commission for Racial Justice
Chavis, Benjamin **6**

Committee on Appeal for
    Human Rights (COHAR)
Bond, Julian **2**

Communist party
Davis, Angela **5**
Du Bois, W. E. B. **3**
Jagan, Cheddi **16**
Wright, Richard **5**

Computer graphics
Hannah, Marc **10**

Computer science
Hannah, Marc **10**

Conceptual art
Allen, Tina **22**
Bailey, Xenobia **11**
Simpson, Lorna **4**

Concerned Black Men
Holder, Eric H., Jr. **9**

Conductors
Jackson, Isaiah **3**
Calloway, Cab **14**
León, Tania **13**

Congressional Black Caucus
    (CBC)
Christian-Green, Donna M. **17**
Clay, William Lacy **8**
Clyburn, James **21**
Collins, Cardiss **10**
Conyers, John, Jr. **4**
Dellums, Ronald **2**
Diggs, Charles C. **21**
Fauntroy, Walter E. **11**
Gray, William H. III **3**
Hastings, Alcee L. **16**
Johnson, Eddie Bernice **8**
Mfume, Kweisi **6**
Owens, Major **6**
Rangel, Charles **3**
Stokes, Louis **3**
Towns, Edolphus **19**

Congressional Black Caucus
    Higher Education Braintrust
Owens, Major **6**

Congress of Racial Equality
    (CORE)
Dee, Ruby **8**
Farmer, James **2**
Innis, Roy **5**
Jackson, Jesse **1**
McKissick, Floyd B. **3**
Rustin, Bayard **4**

Connerly & Associates, Inc.
Connerly, Ward **14**

Convention People's Party
    (Ghana; CPP)
Nkrumah, Kwame **3**

Cook County Circuit Court
Sampson, Edith S. **4**

Cooking
Clark, Patrick **14**
Evans, Darryl **22**

CORE
See Congress of Racial Equality

Corporation for Public Broad
    casting (CPB)
Brown, Tony **3**

Cosmetology
Cottrell, Comer **11**
Fuller, S. B. **13**
Morgan, Rose **11**
Powell, Maxine **8**
Roche, Joyce M. **17**
Walker, A'lelia **14**
Walker, Madame C. J. **7**

Council for a Black Economic
    Agenda (CBEA)
Woodson, Robert L. **10**

Council for Social Action of the
    Congregational Christian
    Churches
Julian, Percy Lavon **6**

Council for the Economic
    Development of Black
    Americans (CEDBA)
Brown, Tony **3**

Council on Legal Education
    Opportunities (CLEO)
Henderson, Wade J. **14**
Henry, Aaron **19**

Count Basie Orchestra
Williams, Joe **5**

Cow hand
Love, Nat **9**
Pickett, Bill **11**

CPB
See Corporation for Public
    Broadcasting

CPP
See Convention People's Party

Cress Theory of Color-Confron
    tation and Racism
Welsing, Frances Cress **5**

Crisis
Du Bois, W. E. B. **3**
Fauset, Jessie **7**
Wilkins, Roy **4**

Cross Colours
Jones, Carl **7**
Kani, Karl **10**
Walker, T. J. **7**

Crucial Films
Henry, Lenny **9**

Crusader
Williams, Robert F. **11**

CTRN
See Transitional Committee for
    National Recovery (Guinea)

Cubism
Bearden, Romare **2**

Culinary arts
Clark, Patrick **14**

Cultural pluralism
Locke, Alain **10**

Cumulative voting
Guinier, Lani **7**

Curator/exhibition designer
Camp, Kimberly **19**
Golden, Thelma **10**
Hutson, Jean Blackwell **16**
Sanders, Joseph R., Jr. **11**
Stewart, Paul Wilbur **12**

Cytogenetics
Satcher, David **7**

Dallas city government
Johnson, Eddie Bernice **8**
Kirk, Ron **11**

Dallas Cowboys football team
Hill, Calvin **19**
Smith, Emmitt **7**

Dance Theatre of Harlem
Johnson, Virginia **9**
Mitchell, Arthur **2**
Nicholas, Fayard **20**
Nicholas, Harold **20**
Tyson, Cicely **7**

DAV
See Disabled American Veterans

David M. Winfield Foundation
Winfield, Dave **5**

Daytona Institute
See Bethune-Cookman College

Dayton Philharmonic Orchestra
Jackson, Isaiah **3**

D.C. Black Repertory Theater
Reagon, Bernice Johnson **7**

Nobel Prize for literature
Soyinka, Wole **4**
Morrison, Toni **2, 15**
Walcott, Derek **5**

Nonviolent Action Group (NAG)
Al-Amin, Jamil Abdullah **6**

North Carolina Mutual Life Insurance
Spaulding, Charles Clinton **9**

North Pole
Henson, Matthew **2**

NOW
See National Organization for Women

NPR
See National Public Radio

NRA
See National Resistance Army (Uganda)

NRA
See National Rifle Association

NSF
See National Science Foundation

Nuclear energy
O'Leary, Hazel **6**
Quarterman, Lloyd Albert **4**

Nuclear Regulatory Commission
Jackson, Shirley Ann **12**

Nucleus
King, Yolanda **6**
Shabazz, Attallah **6**

NUM
See National Union of Mineworkers (South Africa)

Nursing
Auguste, Rose-Anne **13**
Johnson, Eddie Bernice **8**
Johnson, Hazel **22**
Larsen, Nella **10**
Lyttle, Hulda Margaret **14**
Riley, Helen Caldwell Day **13**
Robinson, Rachel **16**
Robinson, Sharon **22**
Shabazz, Betty **7**
Staupers, Mabel K. **7**
Taylor, Susie King **13**

Nutrition
Clark, Celeste **15**
Gregory, Dick **1**
Watkins, Shirley R. **17**

NYA
See National Youth Administration

Nyasaland African Congress (NAC)
Banda, Hastings Kamuzu **6**

Oakland Athletics baseball team
Baker, Dusty **8**
Baylor, Don **6**
Jackson, Reggie **15**
Morgan, Joe Leonard **9**

Oakland Raiders football team
Howard, Desmond **16**
Upshaw, Gene **18**

Oakland Tribune
Maynard, Robert C. **7**

OAU
See Organization of African Unity

OECS
See Organization of Eastern Caribbean States

Office of Civil Rights
See U.S. Department of Education

Office of Management and Budget
Raines, Franklin Delano **14**

Office of Public Liaison
Herman, Alexis M. **15**

Ohio House of Representatives
Stokes, Carl B. **10**

Ohio state government
Brown, Les **5**
Stokes, Carl B. **10**
Williams, George Washington **18**

Ohio State Senate
White, Michael R. **5**

OIC
See Opportunities Industrialization Centers of America, Inc.

Olympics
Ali, Muhammad **2, 16**
Bonaly, Surya **7**
Bowe, Riddick **6**
Christie, Linford **8**
Coachman, Alice **18**
Dawes, Dominique **11**
Devers, Gail **7**
Edwards, Harry **2**
Edwards, Teresa **14**
Ewing, Patrick A. **17**
Garrison, Zina **2**
Hardaway, Anfernee (Penny) **13**
Hill, Grant **13**
Holyfield, Evander **6**
Johnson, Ben **1**
Johnson, Michael **13**
Joyner-Kersee, Jackie **5**

Leslie, Lisa **16**
Lewis, Carl **4**
Malone, Karl A. **18**
Miller, Cheryl **10**
Moses, Edwin **8**
Mutola, Maria **12**
Owens, Jesse **2**
Pippen, Scottie **15**
Powell, Mike **7**
Quirot, Ana **13**
Rudolph, Wilma **4**
Russell, Bill **8**
Swoopes, Sheryl **12**
Thugwane, Josia **21**
Westbrook, Peter **20**
Whitaker, Pernell **10**
Wilkens, Lenny **11**

Oncology
Leffall, LaSalle, Jr. **3**

One Church, One Child
Clements, George **2**

OPC
See Ovambo People's Congress

Opera
Anderson, Marian **2**
Brooks, Avery **9**
Bumbry, Grace **5**
Davis, Anthony **11**
Graves, Denyce **19**
Hendricks, Barbara **3**
Joplin, Scott **6**
Joyner, Matilda Sissieretta **15**
Maynor, Dorothy **19**
McDonald, Audra **20**
Norman, Jessye **5**
Price, Leontyne **1**

Operation Desert Shield
Powell, Colin **1**

Operation Desert Storm
Powell, Colin **1**

OPO
See Ovamboland People's Organization

Opportunities Industrialization Centers of America, Inc. (OIC)
Sullivan, Leon H. **3**

Organization of African States
Museveni, Yoweri **4**

Organization of African Unity (OAU)
Diouf, Abdou **3**
Haile Selassie **7**
Kaunda, Kenneth **2**
Kenyatta, Jomo **5**
Nkrumah, Kwame **3**
Nujoma, Samuel **10**
Nyerere, Julius **5**

Campbell, Bebe Moore **6**
Cannon, Katie **10**
Charles, Mary Eugenia **10**
Christian-Green, Donna M. **17**
Clark, Septima **7**
Cole, Johnnetta B. **5**
Cooper, Anna Julia **20**
Dash, Julie **4**
Davis, Angela **5**
Edelman, Marian Wright **5**
Elders, Joycelyn **6**
Fauset, Jessie **7**
Giddings, Paula **11**
Goldberg, Whoopi **4**
Grimké, Archibald H. **9**
Guy-Sheftall, Beverly **13**
Hale, Clara **16**
Hale, Lorraine **8**
Hamer, Fannie Lou **6**
Harper, Frances Ellen Watkins **11**
Harris, Alice **7**
Harris, Leslie **6**
Harris, Patricia Roberts **2**
Height, Dorothy I. **2**
Hernandez, Aileen Clarke **13**
Hill, Anita **5**
Holland, Endesha Ida Mae **3**
hooks, bell **5**
Jackson, Alexine Clement **22**
Jordan, Barbara **4**
Joe, Yolanda **21**
Jordan, June **7**
Lampkin, Daisy **19**
Larsen, Nella **10**
Lorde, Audre **6**
Marshall, Paule **7**
McCabe, Jewell Jackson **10**
McMillan, Terry **4, 17**
Meek, Carrie **6**
Millender-McDonald, Juanita **21**
Mongella, Gertrude **11**
Morrison, Toni **2, 15**
Naylor, Gloria **10**
Nelson, Jill **6**
Nichols, Nichelle **11**
Norman, Pat **10**
Norton, Eleanor Holmes **7**
Parker, Pat **19**
Rawlings, Nana Konadu Agyeman **13**
Ringgold, Faith **4**
Shange, Ntozake **8**
Simpson, Carole **6**
Terrell, Mary Church **9**
Tubman, Harriet **9**
Vanzant, Iyanla **17**
Walker, Alice **1**
Walker, Maggie Lena **17**
Wallace, Michele Faith **13**
Waters, Maxine **3**
Wattleton, Faye **9**
Winfrey, Oprah **2, 15**

Women's National Basketball Association (WNBA)
Cooper, Cynthia **17**
Edwards, Teresa **14**
Leslie, Lisa **16**

McCray, Nikki **18**
Swoopes, Sheryl **12**

Women's Strike for Peace
King, Coretta Scott **3**

Worker's Party (Brazil)
da Silva, Benedita **5**

Workplace equity
Hill, Anita **5**
Clark, Septima **7**
Nelson, Jill **6**
Simpson, Carole **6**

Works Progress Administration (WPA)
Alexander, Margaret Walker **22**
Baker, Ella **5**
Douglas, Aaron **7**
Dunham, Katherine **4**
Lawrence, Jacob **4**
Lee-Smith, Hughie **5, 22**
Wright, Richard **5**

World African Hebrew Israelite Community
Ben-Israel, Ben Ami **11**

World beat
Belafonte, Harry **4**
Fela **1**
N'Dour, Youssou **1**
Ongala, Remmy **9**

World Bank
Soglo, Nicéphore **15**

World Boxing Association (WBA)
Whitaker, Pernell **10**

World Boxing Council (WBF)
Whitaker, Pernell **10**

World Council of Churches (WCC)
Mays, Benjamin E. **7**
Tutu, Desmond **6**

World Cup
Milla, Roger **2**
Pelé **7**

World hunger
Belafonte, Harry **4**
Iman **4**
Jones, Quincy **8**
Leland, Mickey **2**
Masire, Quett **5**
Obasanjo, Olusegun **5**

World of Music, Arts, and Dance (WOMAD)
Ongala, Remmy **9**

WPA
See Works Progress Administration

WRL
See War Resister's League

Xerox Corp.
Rand, A. Barry **6**

Yab Yum Entertainment
Edmonds, Tracey **16**

Yale Child Study Center
Comer, James P. **6**

Yale Repertory Theater
Dutton, Charles S. **4, 22**
Richards, Lloyd **2**
Wilson, August **7**

Yale School of Drama
Dutton, Charles S. **4, 22**
Richards, Lloyd **2**

YMCA
See Young Men's Christian Associations

Yoruban folklore
Soyinka, Wole **4**
Vanzant, Iyanla **17**

Young Men's Christian Association (YMCA)
Butts, Calvin O., III **9**
Goode, Mal **13**
Hope, John **8**
Mays, Benjamin E. **7**

Young Negroes' Cooperative League
Baker, Ella **5**

Young Women's Christian Association (YWCA)
Baker, Ella **5**
Baker, Gwendolyn Calvert **9**
Clark, Septima **7**
Hedgeman, Anna Arnold **22**
Height, Dorothy I. **2**
Jackson, Alexine Clement **22**
Jenkins, Ella **15**
Sampson, Edith S. **4**

Youth Pride Inc.
Barry, Marion S. **7**

Youth Services Administration
Little, Robert L. **2**

YWCA
See Young Women's Christian Association

ZANLA
See Zimbabwe African National Liberation Army

ZAPU
See Zimbabwe African People's Union

Cumulative Name Index

Volume numbers appear in **bold.**